The Jesus Movement and the World of the Early Church is a solid, simple, straightforward introduction for the undergraduate or general reader to the Jesus movement in its complex cultural and historical world. The people, places, and objects of that world are clearly explained in text and glossaries. This is an excellent resource for the beginning reader.

—Carolyn Osiek, RSCJ, Archivist, Society of the Sacred Heart
United States-Canada Province

Sheila McGinn's book [*The Jesus Movement and the World of the Early Church*] is a masterful example of an important and difficult genre: the scholar's presentation, for an intelligent and educated but non-specialist audience, of . . . the development of Christianity from Jesus to the period of the apostolic fathers. . . . [She treats] all the New Testament writings and some of the early noncanonical writings in their sociopolitical, economic, and religious contexts. In the process she educates her readers in how to handle ancient historical writings. . . . This will be a valuable text for beginning theology students, parish education programs, and independent lay readers.

—Sandra M. Schneiders
Jesuit School of Theology, Santa Clara University

The Jesus Movement and the World of the Early Church is a fascinating, decade-by-decade synopsis of earliest Christianity from Caesar Augustus through Emperor Trajan. Using visual and material culture alongside biblical, Greek, and Latin writings, McGinn has written a condensed version of the history from Jesus through Bishop Ignatius that summarizes most New Testament writings, the *Didache,* and *1 Clement.* An especially notable aspect of her book is extensive use of information from the writings of Eusebius, as well as from Josephus and those Roman historians who wrote about this period of time.

—Vernon K. Robbins, Emory University

The Jesus Movement
and the World of the Early Church

Sheila E. McGinn

ANSELM
ACADEMIC

Author Acknowledgments

This book has been a long time coming and has benefited from the input and advice of so many people, it is impossible to thank them all. First of all, I'd like to thank mentor, friend, and colleague, Joseph Kelly, who has been encouraging from the earliest days of my career; he also helped get this book off the ground and provided editorial feedback on early drafts of it. Richard I. Pervo taught the graduate seminar that unfolded for me the fascinating interfaces between Greco-Roman literature and the New Testament materials and helped hone my skills in social history. Robert Jewett and Rosemary Radford Ruether, advisors during my graduate studies and, since then, respected colleagues, provided both the methods and the angle of vision that opened a new way of reading the ancient texts. Without them, I could never have imagined—to say nothing of written—a book like this.

Thanks also to my students, several of whom read and commented on various chapters as the book was developing, including Jerome Andrews, Carson Bay, Gillian Halusker, Jackie Krejik, Vincent Mudd, and Kristen Slattery. My son, Dónal, deserves special mention for the hours he devoted to talking through issues, offering suggestions, and just generally offering moral support during the times when I was ready to give up the project.

Maura Hagarty, Paul Peterson, and Jerry Ruff of Anselm Academic, have been a marvelous editorial team for this project. I thank them for their persistence, advice, and constancy through the long process of writing and editing this volume.

This book is the better for the input of all these people; any remaining shortcomings, of course, are attributable to me alone. One hopes that Cicero was correct in asserting that *assiduus usus uni rei deditus et ingenium et artem saepe vincit.*[1]

Finally, I'd like to thank Mrs. Kathryn Merhar, administrative assistant extraordinaire, who has kept our office organized (and me with it), has run interference to protect my writing time, and been a great source of encouragement on the days when it seemed hopeless to finish this project while chairing our department. If readers like

---

1. "Constant practice devoted to one subject often outdoes both intelligence and skill."

Kathy find this book of interest, and even of benefit, it will have been well worth the effort.

A.M.D.G.

Feast of St. Theresa of Ávila, Doctor of the Church, 2013.

Publisher Acknowledgments

Thank you to the following individuals who reviewed this work in progress:

Donald C. Polaski
College of William and Mary, Williamsburg, Virginia

Robert Sheard
St. Joseph's College, University of Alberta, Edmonton, Alberta

David Watson
United Theological Seminary, Dayton, Ohio

Created by the publishing team of Anselm Academic.

Cover images: Itinerant vendors on the forum. Mural from Pompeii, Italy, 1 CE. (Erich Lessing / Art Resource, NY). Background image royalty free from www.iStockphoto.com.

The scriptural quotations contained herein are from the New Revised Standard Version of the Bible, Catholic Edition. Copyright © 1993 and 1989 by the Division of Christian Education of the National Council of the Churches of Christ in the United States of America. All rights reserved.

Printed in the United States of America

7049

ISBN 978-1-59982-156-6

To my students

Scientia potestas est.

Contents

Preface

A refrain that I often hear when I do introductory presentations on the New Testament period is "Why didn't anyone ever tell us this before?" A number of fine histories of the New Testament books and the communities that produced them can be found in college libraries, but they tend not to be found on the shelves of public or church libraries. Such works typically are intended for graduate students who are studying the New Testament or early church history, or they are addressed to specialists in the field. The average reader, new to the study of scripture, tends to be overlooked.

As a result, most Americans today, including introductory students in college-level scripture classes, tend to have a very limited understanding of the realities of Jesus' own ministry and the dynamics of the earliest communities of disciples. Whatever knowledge they have of these issues has been gleaned from Hollywood films or, if they are church-goers, side remarks from preachers or church educators. Those who want to know more about Jesus' own theology and practice or the dynamics of Paul's ministry must resort either to texts written primarily for scholars or to the ubiquitous literalistic treatments of the Bible, which do not address the details of historical scholarship and therefore tend to reinforce readers' misunderstandings rather than present a cohesive, intellectually defensible alternative.

This volume is designed to present the findings of contemporary historical scholarship in a narrative format accessible to non-specialist readers. I will take a chronological approach to the New Testament period (the years 20–120 CE), focusing on the wider context of these books and the communities that were producing them. Theological issues raised within the books themselves will come to the fore from time to time, but they will not be the primary focus of this volume.[1] The early churches had to make many

---

1. Those questions are better addressed by taking a topical approach to the material. Several works that do just this are listed in the select bibliography at the end of this book.

theological decisions, so these doctrinal issues are used to illuminate the various ways in which these communities were developing and the challenges they were facing.

This book is intended as a narrative history of Christianity's first hundred years as it arose in and interacted with the wider world of the Roman Empire. Beginning with background on the world into which Jesus was born, the story will move to the life and ministry of Jesus himself and then, decade-by-decade, will present "what was going on" in and around the first Christian communities in terms of political, social, and economic developments. In the final analysis, I hope to help the reader begin to understand the relationships between these external influences and the various structural changes and theological choices made by the early churches over time.

The New Testament as Historical Source

While not the only resource for this period, clearly the New Testament is the most extensive collection of literary material on Jesus and the early churches. A chronological approach to the period then raises the problem of dating the New Testament materials. Should a book whose date is debated be used to highlight community life in the 80s or in the 90s? Should the Gospel materials be used to illuminate only the period in which the texts came to their final form, or might they also shed light on events of an earlier time, when the stories were being transmitted orally? Wherever a scholarly consensus exists on the dating of individual New Testament books and of independent units (*pericopae*; sing. *pericope*) within those books, that consensus has been accepted as the starting point for our discussion. Where there is no clear consensus, I will acknowledge the uncertainty, present my view of the most likely date for the material, and refrain from relying too heavily on it for drawing specific conclusions.

A second problem for dealing with this first Christian century is the paucity of evidence for some periods. Individual *pericopae* in longer texts can help to fill in the gaps. In addition, viewing the New Testament material against the backdrop of Jewish and Roman history and within the context of Jewish and Greco-Roman culture helps to fill in the picture. Recent archaeological finds and social-historical studies provide a firmer footing for such inferences.

Finally, but not the least of our concerns, the historian must face the question of the historical reliability of the New Testament sources. Since the nineteenth century, scholars have recognized that no work in the New Testament is a "history" in the modern sense of the word. Even the book of Acts, Luke's sequel to the Third Gospel, is not the type of detached and "unbiased" report of events that modern historians purport to create, a fact that has made some contemporary scholars disdainful of Luke's work. Yet the same scholars who shun biblical materials as ahistorical routinely turn to Herodotus, Josephus, Livy, and other ancient historians who likewise fall short of the modern ideal.

If one insists on restricting the evidence to only those sources that pass a "litmus test" of modernity, this enterprise is doomed from the start. However, such a radical step is far from necessary. Ancient historians were not simply creating fiction. Historians even then had particular standards for writing their accounts and commonly-accepted methods of handling their data, including the use of multiple sources for corroborating evidence. Perhaps the best contemporary corollary to ancient historiography would be the docudrama. Actual events form the basic framework for the narrative and historical personages provide the focus, but events are presented to convey more than factual information. The narrative also is meant to entertain, challenge, and educate the audience, and to inspire them to debate and perhaps emulate the actions of the protagonists (the "good guys") and to shame the antagonists (the "bad guys"). Interpretation of historical events is embedded within the reportage. Edification and inculcation of common values is at least as important as conveying information.

Some years ago, Richard Pervo published a discussion of the Acts of the Apostles called *Profit with Delight*,[2] and this title aptly encapsulates the key feature of ancient historical writing versus modern works. To entertain their audiences while educating them about the past, ancient historians embellished their narratives, for example, with speeches that focus the audience's attention on the heroes to be honored, virtues to be fostered, and vices to be avoided. In short, ancient history was not merely a matter of conveying information

---

2. Richard I. Pervo, *Profit with Delight: The Literary Genre of the Acts of the Apostles* (Philadelphia: Fortress, 1987).

about persons and events of the past but also—and perhaps more importantly—teaching how one should live as a result of this knowledge. This means that the evidence of ancient histories can be used in contemporary reconstructions of the first two centuries CE, but not all passages in those texts should be given equal weight.

Whether reading Livy's historical writings or Luke's Gospel, the historicity of each section of text must be evaluated on its own terms. For example, speeches convey the basic importance of the event being presented, but they are not exact transcripts of the purported speaker's words on that occasion. Passages that "go against the grain" of the author's basic line of interpretation are more likely to be historical than those that neatly fit with that agenda. To include each of these evaluations in the following discussion would complicate this book unnecessarily, so most of the time the reader will see only the results of this process of critical appraisal. On occasion, however, there is enough debate about a given passage that it is worthwhile to take the reader through the process, step-by-step, to clarify why a particular judgment is being made rather than another.

The Writings of Paul and the Acts of the Apostles

The Acts of the Apostles tends to receive its most critical appraisal in terms of its treatment of Paul, particularly when one compares its account of Paul with what Paul himself states in his undisputed letters.[3] True, the discrepancies between Luke and Paul are noticeable and significant. Yet one must recognize that when Paul gives an account of "what happened," he is following the same kinds of conventions as did the author of Acts. In addition, Paul was a controversial figure, writing in a polemical context. He was criticized by other leaders of the Jesus movement, sometimes including members of his own communities. In his letters, Paul is not making unquestioned statements of fact; he is arguing in favor of his theological and ethical views over against those of his opponents. Hence, one must allow for some justification and even exaggeration on his part. A

---

3. The New Testament includes thirteen letters that bear Paul's name, but scholars long have thought that several of them were written by Paul's disciples rather than Paul himself. Scholars agree that at least seven (i.e., Romans, 1–2 Corinthians, Galatians, Philippians, 1 Thessalonians, and Philemon) derive directly from Paul. These seven are called the "undisputed" letters.

standard practice in historiography is to distinguish between a "primary source" (a person who was an eyewitness or otherwise immediately involved in an event or situation, or a document produced by such a person) and a "secondary source" (a document that discusses the contents of primary source documents or conveys information learned second-hand). Since Paul's epistles constitute primary historical sources, whereas the Acts of the Apostles largely (perhaps entirely) constitutes a secondary-source document, the epistles will be given preference when they and Acts disagree. However, Paul's letters ought not to be used uncritically or dogmatically, as if his every opinion were universally adopted by his contemporaries. If it were, we would have considerably fewer surviving letters from him.

An understanding of Paul as virtually infallible has become an icon for many Christian scholars, but this view is simply untenable. The late Raymond Brown aptly addressed this issue in his book, *Antioch and Rome.*

> Here I am proposing what is virtual heresy in the eyes of many Pauline scholars: namely, that Paul was not always consistent in his major epistles; that Paul even changed his mind; that the defiant Paul of Galatians was exaggerated; and that something is to be said for the position of Peter and James over against Paul on observance of some Jewish customs (so long as the observances were not looked upon as necessary for salvation). It is curious that sometimes a radical scholarship that has been insistent upon the humanity of Jesus balks at any real indication of the fallible humanity of Paul.[4]

Nor are Pauline scholars the only ones who have held this view. The presumption of the priority of Pauline theology and near infallibility of the person of Paul is at least as influential among average Christians today as among scholars. The following discussion will challenge this idealized portrait of Paul, not for the purpose of somehow ridiculing Paul or "debunking" his theology, but simply to make clear his own context as *one* of the evangelists for the message about Jesus. Paul was not a "Lone Ranger" in the early gospel mission field.

---

4. Raymond E. Brown and John P. Meier, *Antioch and Rome: New Testament Cradles of Catholic Christianity* (New York: Paulist, 1983), 114.

The Gospels

It is a truism of biblical studies that the Gospels tell us as much about the communities that produced them as they do about Jesus, since the Gospels were written decades after his life, and their authors, the evangelists, were responding to the perceived needs of their communities. Certainly the Gospels reflect the lives of the early communities that produced them, but this does not mean that they say nothing historically reliable about Jesus himself. The same basic standards for evaluating the historicity of a text as a whole can fruitfully be applied to smaller units within a text such as the Gospels.

Non-Canonical Sources

The traditional assumption that the New Testament books preceded all other Christian writings and literature has now fallen by the scholarly wayside. So, too, have the notions that gnostic and other works now judged as heterodox were invented to corrupt the true faith or that apocryphal works like non-canonical gospels and acts are silly fictions or clumsy forgeries. On the contrary, many non-canonical texts provide important historical witnesses about Christianity in its first century. From the historical point of view, they have much the same value as do the canonical documents and should be evaluated according to the same rules as the New Testament books. As with the Roman historians Suetonius and Tacitus, works outside the canon may very well preserve historical material unknown to or unrecorded by the canonical writers. All our sources—Jewish, Christian, or Roman, canonical or extra-canonical—must be used critically, with great care to test which portions are likely to be historically reliable and which are not.

Women in the New Testament Era

There was a time when one could write a history of the New Testament period without mentioning any women at all—except perhaps Jesus' mother Mary, or Mary Magdalene. Thankfully, this is no longer the case. In recent decades, the role of women in the earliest communities has emerged as a central question among scholars and the wider public—and the center is precisely where this question needs to be if we are to correct the rather skewed understanding of the significance of women in the early Jesus movement. Integrated with the rest of this historical narrative will be a picture of the women disciples of Jesus and the later Jesus movement. Women's roles changed dramatically over this period, so questions will recur about their origins and developments. As this discussion draws to a close, we will face the various forces that prompted some church fathers to attempt to limit or even eliminate women's leadership roles in the burgeoning communities of Jesus' disciples.

Theology

All the New Testament authors had theological concerns. The theology of each text expresses the views of the authors and communities that produced these texts, and possibly also those of the communities to which they were writing. Although theological questions will not take center stage in this book, some will be highlighted in order to demonstrate that the question under debate was of concern to the author (and presumably the recipients) of a particular text. The fact that such questions change over time points to changes and developments within these early Jesus-communities.

This book is intended for students and other non-specialists who are interested in learning more about the authors and original audiences of the New Testament texts by looking at the Greco-Roman world in which they lived and breathed. Keeping a New Testament[5] handy while reading this book, and using it frequently, will help fill in the other half of the historical puzzle that this study is designed to explore.

---

5. Unless otherwise noted, Biblical quotations in this volume are taken from the New Revised Standard Version. Occasionally, when I think it makes a clearer reading, I provide my own translation, which is noted by my initials (SEM).

Introduction

Many people have limited knowledge about Jesus of Nazareth, his early disciples, the people who produced the New Testament books, and the period in general. The following list of facts makes stark claims that run contrary to some of the common preconceptions in the popular imagination about the movement that we (anachronistically) call early Christianity.

1. Jesus was never a Christian.[1]
2. Jesus' disciples were not Christians.[2]
3. Peter, Paul, and other well-known Jesus-movement leaders of that first-generation period were not Christians.
4. The people commonly called "Christians" today did not identify themselves that way until at least the end of the first century CE. Outsiders could not distinguish them from Jews until at least the 60s. In some places (like Antioch in Syria), followers of Jesus continued to identify with and participate in Jewish synagogues well into the fourth century CE.
5. Hence, Jesus did not start a new religion, although eventually his followers did.
6. Jesus did not "found the church" in the sense of establishing a bureaucratic structure remotely resembling any of the various Christian churches that exist today.
7. Saint Paul did not "found the church" either.

---

1. "Christian" means "follower of the Christ (Messiah)." Jesus was raised Jewish and remained a Jew his entire life. His original followers, who also were Jews, believed him to be the Christ. Because of this belief, outsiders eventually began to call them "Christians." However, believers did not identify themselves that way until long after Jesus' death and Resurrection (see #4).

2. The term "disciple" means "student" (in the sense of a protégé to a mentor) and is the most common New Testament term for the followers of Jesus. Jesus' immediate disciples all were Jews, as were the authors of virtually all of the New Testament books. At some point after Jesus' lifetime, non-Jews began to join the Jesus movement.

8. Jesus himself did not "ordain" anyone, if this means assigning someone the permanent status of leadership of a community of believers.

9. Paul and some of the other disciples might have ordained people, although not to the kinds of priestly ministries that some Christian communities have today.

10. Jesus began as a disciple of John the Baptist, only gradually coming to understand that he had his own unique calling from God to a ministry distinct from the Baptist's.

11. Jesus was neither the first nor the last first-century Jewish man to be hailed by some of his peers as God's "Messiah." Nor was he the only one to be killed because of this claim.

12. Jesus was not the only miracle-worker in the first century, in the Jewish homeland or elsewhere.

13. Taken alone, Jesus' miracles did not "prove" anything; certainly not that he was divine. Some of Jesus' contemporaries thought his miracles showed that he was demonic, or that he was in league with or possessed by Satan.

14. "The Twelve" comprised a distinct group among the disciples of Jesus, however . . .

   a. If one combines the various New Testament lists of those belonging to "the Twelve," the names actually number fourteen. Hence, the *idea* of "Twelve" is more important than the reality.

   b. The number of Jesus' disciples far exceeded twelve—by dozens, if not hundreds. Some of them were missionaries who took the gospel message to peoples and places beyond Jesus' immediate circle (i.e., they were "apostles").

   c. Likewise, the group of "apostles"—those who were sent out to preach the gospel message—included substantially more than twelve persons.

   d. Moreover, the Jesus tradition states that the function of "the Twelve" is not to be "apostles" but to serve as judges in the coming kingdom (see Matt. 19:28//Luke 22:30).

   e. To summarize these points mathematically, "the disciples" ≠ "the apostles" ≠ "the Twelve."

15. Jesus gave the "office" of the Twelve permanently to a few specific Jewish men. He did not envision it as a role that could be "handed down" any more than the patriarch Jacob could hand over his parentage of the twelve tribes of Israel.

16. The disciples of Jesus included many women.

17. The early churches, including the ones Paul founded, also included many women disciples.

18. The early churches had women missionaries, teachers, preachers, prophets, deacons, patrons, and apostles. This was not an insignificant or sporadic phenomenon. Rather, in the first century, women served as leaders in various capacities in communities of disciples across a wide geographic area, from the Holy Land to Asia Minor, from Macedonia to Rome.

Christians reading this might be feeling a bit uncomfortable about now. These assertions may strike some readers as intriguing, and others as preposterous. All I can do is ask that you make no snap judgments. Keep in mind that "sound bites" never explain anything; they simply assert. Those who hang in there through the remainder of this book should have a better idea of what these assertions mean—and what they do *not* mean.

As a history of the period in which Jesus and the early disciples lived and in which the New Testament books were being written, this volume certainly will address many more issues than those briefly listed above. However, since the misinformation people "know" when they begin to study a subject shapes their ability to gain new knowledge of it, often there is much "unlearning" to do before new learning can take place. The purpose of listing the "sound bites" is to address head-on some of the misconceptions people may have when they come to the study of the New Testament. Explicitly naming them as misconceptions is intended to help readers consciously set aside their assumptions, thereby making the learning process much more efficient.

A few brief remarks concerning terminology are in order. This text avoids using the terms "Christian," "Christianity," and "church" when referring to the disciples of Jesus, during or after his earthly ministry. The phrases "Christ-believers," "community of disciples," "messianic Jews," and "Jesus-Jews" are somewhat awkward, but they have the virtue of not reinforcing the misunderstandings that are highlighted by some of the points in the foregoing list. "Followers of the Way" is Luke's term for the movement, and it has the virtue of being clear as to its referent and yet relatively unknown. The term "disciples" in itself is fine, but it becomes somewhat problematic because of the way Christian tradition has equated it with "the apostles" and "the Twelve," so I have tried to use it sparingly. Instead of "Christianity," typically I use the expression "Jesus movement," "messianic Judaism," or (following Luke) the "Jesus-Way." When referring to an individual community of disciples, I often use the term "*ecclesia*" rather than "church"; although the former is simply the Greek term, its relative unfamiliarity should help mark the distance between the churches of today and those of the first century. The term "house-church," on the other hand, is retained herein; this technical variation on the term is infrequent enough in popular discussions that it is not likely to tempt readers to merge contemporary experiences of church with those of the earliest believers.

CHAPTER 1

The World Jesus Inherited

Writing probably about 53 CE, Paul of Tarsus asserted, "When the fullness of time had come, God sent his Son, born of a woman, born under the law" (Gal. 4:4). Paul was not unique among the early followers of Jesus when he claimed that the Christ was born at precisely the time that God had prepared for that purpose, when the world had "come of age" and human history had ripened to the perfect moment for this radical divine intervention. Oddly enough, this was not a point in time when the Jews held political power or influence in the surrounding world. They did not even have the power of self-determination, much less the "clout" to influence peoples beyond their borders. Instead, they were aliens in their own land, a conquered nation, vassals to a pagan ruler. Jews lived in a Roman world, occupied by a foreign army devoted to deities the Jews viewed as false or non-existent. The world around them thought like Rome and spoke mainly Greek. How could this be the "ripe time" for a Jewish savior?

The Jewish element is an obvious one. Jesus, the foundation of the religious renewal movement that became Christianity, was himself never a "Christian"—that is, he was never a *follower* of the messiah, nor did he attempt to inaugurate a new religion involving worship of himself as Messiah. He was born into a Jewish family, raised as a Jew, and lived and died a Jew.[1] Regardless of what one may think about Jesus' self-understanding, he never broke from his ancestral traditions. From his baptism by John to the last meal with his disciples, Jesus' words and deeds express a desire for the internal renewal of the Jewish people and their faithfulness to the God of Israel. In fact, the Synoptic Gospels tell a story of Jesus initially refusing to help a Gentile woman who asked him to cure her daughter because he "was sent only to the lost sheep of the house of Israel" (Matt. 15:24 and parallels). All of the earliest disciples, the women and men who traveled with Jesus during his public ministry, were Jews.

After his death and Resurrection, Jesus' followers had to deal with the question of what should be their relationship with those Jews who were not disciples of Jesus. If all of the post-Resurrection converts to the Jesus movement had been born and raised as Jews, this problem is not likely to have arisen. The disciples of Jesus continued to worship at the Temple and participate in the synagogues with other Jews, and there is no particular reason why this should have posed a problem—as long as the converts to the Jesus movement continued to come primarily from among the Jews. However, soon many Gentiles (non-Jews) also were attracted to the gospel of Jesus and the proclamation of his Resurrection. The intermingling of Gentile believers with Jewish disciples is what caused the stir. Disagreement arose as to the relationship of these Gentile proselytes to the Jewish disciples of Jesus and to the wider Jewish community. To understand why this mixing of the "races" raised some hackles,

---

1. While modern Judaism began to be formulated in the period after the Babylonian Exile (586–538 BCE), the entire Second Temple Period (538 BCE–70 CE) was a ferment of developing ideas, codifying the scriptural canon, and navigating the relationship between religious observance and the demands of political leaders who were not necessarily very devout and sometimes openly hostile toward the traditions passed down from Moses. What we, in retrospect, call "Judaism" included a spectrum of beliefs and practices that differed across various geographical locations. The Judaism of Galilee, in which Jesus was formed, seems to have differed somewhat from that of Judea, home base of the authorities who objected to Jesus' preaching. Contemporary Judaism, while not identical to any of them, shares an organic connection with these earlier forms of "Judaism." For the purposes of our discussion, "Judaism" will refer to any religious movement that treasures a connection with ancient Israel and shares a respect for the "Law of Moses" as divinely revealed and, in some sense, normative for faith and life.

one must understand more about the culture of the Greeks and Romans and their historical impact on Judaism. So before looking at the Judaism of Jesus' day, it is important to consider how prior events in the wider world affected and shaped it.

Empires and Ideologies: From Cyrus to Caesar

From the early sixth century BCE,[2] the Persian Empire—which, at its height, extended from Iran to Egypt—included Jews among its subject peoples. Because the Persian King Cyrus liberated the Judean exiles from their captivity in Babylon, paid for the rebuilding of the Jerusalem Temple, and allowed them freely to worship the God of their forebears and follow their other ancestral customs and religious traditions, a sixth-century successor to the prophet Isaiah of Jerusalem acclaimed Cyrus as God's "Messiah" ("Anointed One"; Isa. 44:28–45:6, 13). Still the Jews were not independent, and especially those from noble and priestly families were not likely to forget this fact. Rather, Judea was a vassal state of the Persian Empire, ruled by a governor appointed by the Persian monarch, who might or might not maintain the permissive and conciliatory stance of Cyrus the Great.

After two centuries of Persian dominance in the Middle East, an ambitious young pupil of Aristotle (384–322 BCE) arose to challenge the Achaemenian Empire.[3] Alexander III, son of King Philip of Macedon (356–323 BCE), succeeded his father as ruler of Macedonia and the city-states of Greece. Believing himself called to fulfill a divine mission to bring true civilization to the world, Alexander "the Great" led a combined Greco-Macedonian army against the Persian Empire, the largest state ever created in the Ancient Near East. Against formidable odds, Alexander succeeded in wresting control from Darius III, conquering the Persian Empire—and the Jews with

---

2. "BCE" stands for "Before the Common Era," and refers to the same period of time that Christians traditionally have denoted "BC" ("Before Christ"); "CE" or "Common Era" denotes the period Christian tradition denominates "AD" (*anno domini*, "The Year of Our Lord"). As a gesture of inter-religious hospitality, many scholars use the abbreviations BCE and CE instead of BC and AD.

3. Historians refer to the Persian Empire under Cyrus and his successors as the Achaemenian or Achaemenid Empire.

it. Alexander thereby became the ruler of most of the western world, although an early death from a fever kept him from ruling his new territory. The historical development of the Christ movement was largely determined by this shift of empires in the fourth century BCE.

After his death, Alexander's generals spent two decades fighting for control of the empire. The twenty-one-year civil war ended in 301 BCE with their agreement to divide it into four parts. Lysimachus (ca. 360–281 BCE) took Thrace and Asia Minor; Cassander (ca. 350–297 BCE) received Macedonia and Greece; Seleucus (ca. 358–281 BCE) controlled Syria, Mesopotamia, and Persia; and Ptolemy (ca. 367–283 BCE) ruled Egypt and the Levant (the area encompassed by the modern State of Israel.

It took another decade, however, to resolve how to divide the half of Alexander's empire that girded the Mediterranean basin, in the crescent from Egypt clockwise through Syria and into Persia (modern-day Iraq and Iran). Finally Ptolemy I "Soter" ("Savior") and Seleucus I "Nicator" ("Conqueror") agreed to create two new Near Eastern states: the Ptolemaic Kingdom included Egypt, and the Seleucid Kingdom spanned the regions of Syria, Persia (present-day Iraq and Iran), and eventually Asia Minor (modern Turkey). Of course, this left the Israelite homeland right on the boundary between the two kingdoms, which meant that its control continued to be contested long after this agreement was made. The heirs of Ptolemy and Seleucus engaged in a continual tug-of-war over this region. At first, Israelite territory belonged to the Ptolemaic Kingdom. Later it became part of the Seleucid Kingdom. But never did it belong to those who actually lived there.

The Ptolemies and Seleucids, foreign kings ruling their subjects by force, recognized that they could not control vast populations without some unifying power. Following the plans of Alexander, they introduced Greek culture into the Near East, a process called *Hellenization*, that is, "to make Greek." Part of the process was the founding of new cities on the Mediterranean coastlands, cities that would keep Egypt and Syria in contact with the Greek homeland. The best known of these cities were Alexandria in Egypt and Antioch in Syria, both destined to play key roles in Christian history.

Greek became the lingua franca, the language of commerce and government. Among the aristocracy, any aspiring young man or cultivated young woman had to learn it. Among the lower classes, merchants and shippers would know enough Greek to read an inventory or bill of sale; even tradespersons would likely know the few terms or phrases pertinent to their line of business. More than that, Greek became the language people could use when they traveled, not just in the Middle East but throughout most of the known world. The eastern fringes of the Seleucid Kingdom bordered on India, which Alexander had entered but not conquered. On the western side of the empire, and even before the time of Alexander the Great, some Greeks had settled near Marseilles in southern Gaul (modern France) and in southern Italy. Whether or not they could read and write Greek, knowledge of the spoken language could take travelers from Gaul to the borders of India. This made it indispensable for traders, sailors, soldiers, artisans, and all sorts of people who needed to travel to sustain their occupations—including Jewish merchants and tradespersons traveling from their Israelite homeland to the great Gentile cities of the Mediterranean.

Alexander's conquest of the Persians brought the Jews into the Greek world and, for the first time in their history, into a world that looked west. When Alexander's generals fought for their shares of the empire, much of the fighting took place in Israelite territory. By around 300 BCE, some Jews had been taken to Egypt as captives of war. Others were relocated by Seleucus I when he founded Antioch-on-the-Orontes (contemporary Antakya). In addition, because the continual fighting during the period of civil war impoverished the land of Israel, some Jews left their homeland to seek prosperity elsewhere. This emigration of Jews from their ancient homeland is called the *Diaspora*, Greek for "dispersion." The Diaspora started before the Hellenistic period. By the end of the third century BCE, Jews had become a significant presence in cities throughout the eastern Mediterranean and even in Italy. From that point on, Jews would carry their message of the one true God to receptive Gentiles in these areas.[4] Three centuries later, missionaries of the Jesus movement again followed the path of the Diaspora.

---

4. That Jews proselytized among their Gentile neighbors is attested by several sources of the first century BCE including, Philo Judaeus (*On the Special Laws* 1.320–23), the Jewish historian Flavius Josephus (*Jewish Antiquities* 18.81–84; 20.17–96), the Gospel of Matthew (23:15), and Roman authors Cornelius Tacitus

As residents of the Seleucid and Ptolemaic kingdoms and other Greek-speaking states, Jews were caught up in the process of Hellenization. Typical aspects of Hellenistic city life included the public baths, the theater, the gymnasium (a combination health club, educational complex, and social hall), and the town council or *synedrion*. (In the New Testament, it is spelled "sanhedrin.") The introduction of the Greek language also brought with it new ways of thinking that had originated with pagan philosophers. Many Jews accommodated themselves to the Hellenistic practices of their Gentile neighbors, especially in the Diaspora where they lived in overwhelmingly Gentile circles, but they drew the line when Hellenization threatened their religious beliefs and practices. This was not always an easy boundary to find, however, and Jews continued to debate among themselves what constituted accommodation versus capitulation.

© dtopal / www.shutterstock.com

The classical gymnasium was a center for physical training and for competitions, such as the footrace depicted on this ancient Greek cup. Unlike the modern gymnasium, however, it also hosted discussions about philosophy and the arts. Gymnasia constituted key elements in the promotion of Hellenization.

(*Annals* 2.85), Gaius Suetonius (*Tiberius* 36), and Valerius Maximus (*Memorable Doings and Sayings* 1.3.3); cf. Dio Cassius 57.18.5a and several rabbinic texts, including M. *Nazir* 3.6; T. *Sukkah* 1.1; *Bereshith (Genesis) Rabbah* 46.11. For a recent survey of the evidence, see John P. Dickson, "Winning the Gentiles: Mission and Missionaries in Ancient Judaism?" in *Mission-Commitment in Ancient Judaism and in the Pauline Communities: The Shape, Extent and Background of Early Christian Mission* (Tübingen: Mohr-Seibeck, 2003), 11–50.

Americans tend to assume that religion and politics are inherently distinct from or even opposed to one another, but no one in the ancient world would have agreed. Every kingdom had patron deities whom the people venerated to guarantee the well-being of the nation. Many pagan nations deified their rulers. The Egyptian Pharaoh is perhaps the most well-known example of this "ruler cult," but it was by no means unique. Some upstart rulers even deified themselves— Gaius "Caligula," the third Emperor of Rome, is a case in point. Venerating the ruler was an act of patriotism; refusing to do so could be construed as an act of treason. The precise dynamics of the ruler cult (for example, its centrality and persuasiveness) varied from one nation to the next, but nearly every nation had some form of it. In an earlier period, even Jews asserted that their king was God's "Son" (Pss. 2; 89). However, this notion of "divine kingship"—that the king rules by divine right, being chosen by God rather than mere mortals— should be distinguished from worship of the ruler as a God.

The Torah, from the earliest law code (Exod. 20:23–25, ca. 1250 BCE) to the last (Deut. 6:4–15, ca. 450 BCE), clearly prohibits idolatry (that is, worship of some other person or object in place of the one true God). The Hebrew Prophets concur with a constant refrain abhorring idolatry (e.g., Isa. 44:8–20). The sheer weight of repetition suggests that Jews experienced a chronic temptation to succumb to the influence of their Gentile neighbors and participate in such pagan practices. It also affirms, however, that faithful Jews were convinced they could neither venerate their rulers nor participate in worship of foreign deities. Any Israelite monarch who tried to establish a ruler cult like those of the other nations would have been vigorously resisted.

How ancient pagans understood ruler worship is not clearly understood, but it certainly formed the backbone of ancient patriotism. One could not attend any civic function without witnessing, and thereby tacitly approving, some sort of sacrifice and prayer to the patron deities of the town and the ruling monarch. Hence, devout Jews living outside the land of Israel had to exclude themselves from much of civic life, which meant that they often were suspected of harboring anti-social or subversive tendencies. Once the land of Israel was subject to a Gentile ruler, the same problems arose at home as previously had applied only to Diaspora Jews. However,

Jews could—and routinely did—pray to their one and only God for the health of the ruler and welfare of the state. From the time of King Cyrus the Great, most of their foreign rulers accepted this compromise and the Jews' modification of the divine kingship model, at least until the second century BCE.

This changed dramatically circa 180 BCE with the ascension of a Seleucid ruler, King Antiochus IV, who claimed the title *Epiphanes* ("God manifest"). Antiochus tried to eradicate Judaism by suppressing the Jews' ability to practice their ancestral traditions. He outlawed the teaching of Torah, and even the practice of circumcision, the traditional sign of the covenant between God and the Chosen People (Gen. 17). Some Jews went along with the king, but many were so horrified that they nicknamed the king *Epimanes* ("madman").

Because of the adamant and intolerable persecution by Antiochus IV, five brothers known as the Maccabees organized a revolution. In 167 BCE, the Jews succeeded in driving the Seleucids out of Judea and winning independence. The Maccabean family reestablished the Israelite monarchy under the Hasmonean dynasty, thus founding an independent Jewish state that endured for a century, until the Roman conquest in 63 BCE. However, Jewish independence could not stem the tide of Hellenization. Rather ironically, the history of the Hasmonean revolt, contained in the two Books of Maccabees, was written in Greek rather than Hebrew or Aramaic. Some of the most famous tales about the revolt, included in 2 Maccabees, are based upon the work of a Diaspora Jew (from Cyrene, in North Africa) with the Greek name of Jason. Moreover, in spite of opposition from

© Zev Radovan / biblelandpictures.com

A coin depicting Antiochus IV Epiphanes

traditionalist Jews, at least a few Greek institutions, including the gymnasium and *synedrion*, had been transplanted to Judea to stay. The surest proof that Diaspora Jews had made their peace with a religiously tolerant form of Hellenization is the translation of the Hebrew Bible into Greek. A popular legend from Alexandria in Egypt claimed that, miraculously, seventy scribes independently produced the identical translation, and so the Greek version of the Jewish Bible is called the *Septuagint*, the Work of the Seventy (abbreviated LXX). Exactly when the Septuagint was produced is not known, but a date no later than the third century BCE is probable. Diaspora Jews had a version of the Bible in the language they used for everyday public life. Significantly, virtually all the New Testament citations of the Jewish Bible are from the Septuagint, including Jesus' scripture quotes in the Gospels. Since Jesus spoke largely to Galilean peasants and townspeople, very likely he quoted the Bible in Hebrew. Nevertheless, the Gospel writers (or "evangelists"), with a view toward a wider audience, cited the Septuagint text instead.

Diaspora Jews borrowed other elements from Greek culture. (Some even went so far as to write tragedies in the Greek style.) The most famous of these Jewish writers was Philo of Alexandria (ca. 10 BCE–ca. 45 CE), who made use of Greek philosophy in interpreting the Bible. Yet Philo and other Diaspora Jews maintained their allegiance to Judaism and did not want Hellenistic culture to compromise their religious commitments.

Following the Maccabean War, the Ptolemies (in Egypt) and Seleucids (in Syria) continued to feud with one another over who would control the Holy Land, wasting their political energies and financial resources. Furthermore, many proved to be ineffective or overly ambitious rulers, ill qualified to meet a threat arising in the West: the Roman Republic.

Roman *Imperium* and Religion

From its founding until the middle of the third century BCE, Rome had expanded at the expense of its Italian neighbors. Two third-century BCE wars with the North African state of Carthage made the Roman Republic an international power that could not avoid getting involved in the affairs of the eastern Mediterranean. The Romans wanted land

and they wanted order. In the second century BCE, the Roman Senate, the Republic's ruling body, began a halting but steady conquest of the Seleucid lands. Part of this conquest involved a treaty made in 161 BCE with the Maccabees, a move that furthered destabilized the Seleucid Empire. By the first century BCE, the Seleucid Kingdom had become a petty dynastic state, virtually incapable of governing. The Romans saw their opportunity and decided to take over what was left of the Seleucid lands. The Roman General Pompey conquered Syria in 64 BCE. While he was there, he decided to annex the smaller Jewish state to the south, where there also had been some dynastic disputes. Pompey entered Jerusalem in 63 BCE and put an end to the Hasmonean Kingdom (as the Maccabean state had become known). The Romans reorganized the area as the Province of Judea.

Egypt remained the only country in the eastern Mediterranean not under Roman rule, but in little more than thirty years, after the infamous exploits of the Roman dictator Julius Caesar, the Roman general Mark Antony, and the Egyptian pharaoh-queen Cleopatra VII, Rome annexed that ancient kingdom as well. The Mediterranean had become a Roman lake, what the Romans called *mare nostrum*, "our sea."

At this time, Rome itself changed forever. All the land and riches acquired by the Republic during its conquests had spawned a series of dictators who used money and force to overawe the senators and get their way. One dictator, Julius Caesar, reached too far too soon and was assassinated by several senators, but the Republic itself could not be saved. After his defeat of Cleopatra and Mark Antony in 31 BCE, Gaius Octavian Caesar was acclaimed *Imperator* ("commander"; in English, "Emperor") and became sole ruler of Rome. The calendar inscription raised in about 9 BCE at Priene (in contemporary Turkey) eulogizes the coming of Octavian as a divine intervention:

> It seemed good to the Greeks of Asia, in the opinion of the high priest Apollonius of Menophilus Azanitus: "Since Providence, which has ordered all things and is deeply interested in our life, has set in most perfect order by giving us Augustus, whom she filled with virtue that he might benefit humankind, sending him as a savior [*soter*], both for us and for our descendants, that he might end war and arrange all things, and since he, Caesar, by his appearance [*epiphanein*] (excelled even our anticipations), surpassing all previous benefactors,

and not even leaving to posterity any hope of surpassing what he has done, and since the birthday of the god Augustus was the beginning of the good tidings [*evangelion*] for the world that came by reason of him," which Asia resolved in Smyrna.[5]

While these words are tendentious and exaggerate Octavian's importance, it is true that Augustus ended the strife among Romans, stabilized the economy, and established important legal reforms. Official documents continued to carry the notation *SPQR* (*Senatus Populusque Romanus*, "the Senate and the people of Rome"), implying that the legislation was the result of a democratic process, but the Senate essentially became the Emperor's advisory body at best or rubber stamp at worst. Yet this change in governmental structure had very little impact on the vast majority of the population. In the Republican era, only aristocratic men (that is, wealthy landowners) could vote, and they comprised a very small minority of Rome's inhabitants. What the average person noticed was not that the Senate had been disenfranchised but that the fighting was over, prices had stabilized, and they could afford to pay for their basic needs. Whether the ruler was an *imperator* chosen by the army or a *princeps* elected by a small group of wealthy men, neither arrangement constituted a "democracy" in the modern sense of the word. The only ones who objected to the changes were the other contenders for the throne. Four years later, the cowed Senate gave Octavian the title *Augustus* ("worthy of worship"), the name by which he is known to history (e.g., Luke 2:1, "A decree went out from Emperor Augustus"). Jesus was born during the Augustan era. Jesus himself, his family, friends, and disciples, everyone connected to the New Testament, lived in the Roman Empire established by Octavian.

Movies often have portrayed the Romans as heartless, brutal, and fond of persecuting Christ-believers, but this is a gross exaggeration. Most Roman rulers were interested in two things: peace and taxes. Because he definitively ended decades of civil war, Octavian was celebrated for bringing peace to Rome and acclaimed "Savior of

---

5. The English translation used here is taken from Craig A. Evans, "Mark's Incipit and the Priene Calendar Inscription: From Jewish Gospel to Greco-Roman Gospel," (n.p.); *http://craigaevans.com/ Priene%20art.pdf*. For the Greek text of the inscription, see W. Dittenberger, ed., *Orientis Graecae Inscriptiones Selectae*, 2 vols. (Leipzig: Hirzel, 1903–1905; repr. Hildesheim: Olms, 1960), 2.48–60 [= OGIS 458].

the world." Most people accepted monarchy not only as a legitimate form of government but, in fact, as divinely ordained. They expected the ruler to be just and concerned about the people. Revolts against Roman rule were few, and those that did occur were not intended to establish democracies but to redress social or nationalistic grievances. Presumably nations would have preferred to be ruled by one of their own people, but an impoverished rural peasantry would have worked long, arduous days no matter who the ruler was—Greek, Seleucid, Jewish, or Roman.

The Roman persecution of Christ-believers conveys an image of religious intolerance, but that also is exaggerated. In general, the Romans tolerated any religion as long as it did not promote social unrest. In one of the few instances of official intolerance, the Romans persecuted the Druids in Britain because they feared the Druids would stir up British nationalism and thus cause a revolt. The occasional Roman persecutions of followers of Jesus in the first two centuries resulted not from religious concerns but from fears that the movement was anti-social or a threat to the state.

Official Roman tolerance of Jews is extensively documented. The Romans exempted Jewish men from military service because it would have forced them to violate Torah—for example, they would have had to be a party to pagan sacrifices—and the Roman authorities saw the Jews' desire to maintain their ancestral traditions as a legitimate expression of filial piety. The Romans financially supported the priests at the Jewish Temple in Jerusalem, collecting a Temple tax from Jews all over the Empire earmarked precisely for that purpose.

Anti-Judaism existed at Rome, sometimes at high levels, but it never became official policy, even when the Judeans revolted against the Empire in 66–73 CE. True, the Romans mercilessly suppressed the revolt. When the Legions regained control of Jerusalem (in 70 CE), they indiscriminately slaughtered hundreds of Jews, torched their homes, and burned the Temple to the ground; surviving captives were sold into slavery and the Temple treasures taken in triumph to Rome. Yet even during the war, Diaspora Jews maintained their rights, and Roman officials are remembered for defending those rights against anti-Jewish mobs in places like Alexandria and Antioch. Like Cyrus of Persia, the Romans realized that religious tolerance was good social policy because it gave the occupied peoples one less reason to revolt

Titus assumed command of the Roman troops in Judea when his father, General Vespasian, left for Rome to become emperor. The Arch of Titus celebrates Titus' triumph in the First Jewish War. This panel shows the victorious Romans parading with spoils from the Jerusalem Temple.

against their overlords. As long as the native religions served to pacify their subject peoples, the Romans were satisfied.

In addition to this stratagem of religious tolerance, the Romans had a parallel political practice of co-opting the indigenous elite, especially pre-existing ruling houses, and appointing them to govern on the local level on behalf of Rome. In Judea, the local rulers came from the dynasty of Herod the Great (37–4 BCE). There were many advantages to this policy of using indigenous rulers.

1. It gave the powerful, elite families a strong incentive to cooperate with Rome, since they might get other favors or official appointments.

2. For the peasant class, it made the transition to Roman rule relatively seamless, sometimes even invisible. Often they found themselves obeying laws from and paying taxes to the same monarch as they had before the Roman conquest. Whatever revenues the monarch passed along to Roman coffers, the peasants neither saw nor cared.

3. The indigenous ruler could be expected to have a thorough understanding of the occupied people's attitudes, traditions, alliances, and so forth, which would make the official better able to anticipate—and defuse—potential problems.

4. Other leading families provided a built-in form of "checks and balances" of official abuses. The possibility of being replaced by a member of another influential local family provided the appointee with an incentive to perform well in office. In the case of any misbehavior or mismanagement in office, if the other local leaders were unsuccessful in persuading the Roman appointee to change, they could appeal to Rome to intervene to correct the abuses, even to the extent of removing the person from power and appointing someone else. The Province of Judea is a case in point. When Jesus began his public career (ca. 28 CE), during the reign of the Emperor Tiberius (14–37 CE), Judea was governed by a Roman procurator named Pontius Pilate, while Herod Antipas, son of Herod the Great, ruled Jesus' home territory of Galilee, and Antipas' brother Herod Philip ruled an area called Trachonitis. Yet less than ten years later, by 38 CE, Herod Antipas, Herod Philip, and Pontius Pilate all had been removed from office due to mismanagement of various types. Instead, the Jewish King Herod Agrippa I (10 BCE–44 CE), grandson of Herod the Great and former classmate of Prince Claudius, had become sole ruler over the entire territory.

The local rulers could do nothing that threatened Rome, but otherwise they had considerable latitude. Roman authorities used whatever means and whatever persons were effective, as long as they could maintain peace and collect taxes.

The Way of Jesus versus the Ways of Rome

By the first century CE, the Romans had abandoned attempts at Hellenization, but the Jesus movement could not help but be influenced strongly by the dominant Greco-Roman culture. Less than a decade after Jesus' death, the gospel message had moved beyond Judea and taken root in Gentile territory, most prominently at Antioch in Syria, but also in Asia Minor (modern Turkey), Greece, and Italy.

Greco-Roman culture permeated the social world of Jesus and his followers. One sees its most obvious impact in the fact that all the New Testament authors wrote their works in Greek rather than in Hebrew or Aramaic. Many also had more than a passing familiarity with prominent pagan writers. For example, Mark's Gospel is very like the romance novels of the time; the book of Acts includes scenes reminiscent of Homer's *Odyssey* (e.g., Acts 27); and Luke portrays Paul quoting a Greek poet (Acts 17:28).[6]

Still, where these early members of the Jesus movement recognized a conflict between the Jewish Law and Greco-Roman culture, Torah won out. For example, Torah forbids the making of images of people or animals (Lev. 19:4). Jesus' followers seem to have continued to observe this prohibition, for there are no images of Jesus until at

© Zev Radovan / biblelandpictures.com

The earliest artistic representation of Christ's crucifixion may be this mocking portrayal made by an opponent. The so-called "Alexamenos Graffito" (ca. 210 CE), from the Palatine Hill in Rome, presents an image of a Christ-believer named Alexamenos, one hand raised in the *orans* gesture of worship, standing before a cross on which hangs the corpus of a man with the head of an ass. The accompanying inscription reads ΑΛΕΞΑΜΕΝΟC CEBETE ΘΕΟΝ, "Alexamenos worships [his] God."

---

6. See, e.g., Michael E. Vines, *The Problem of Markan Genre: The Gospel of Mark and the Jewish Novel* (Boston: Brill, 2002); Mary Ann Tolbert, *Sowing the Gospel: Mark's World in Literary-Historical Perspective* (Minneapolis: Fortress Press, 1989); Gilbert G. Bilezikian, *The Liberated Gospel: A Comparison of the Gospel of Mark and Greek Tragedy* (Grand Rapids: Baker Book House, 1977); Benoît Standaert, *Évangile selon Marc: Composition et Genre Littéraire* (Brugge: Zevenkerken, 1998); and Dennis R. MacDonald, *The Homeric Epics and the Gospel of Mark* (New Haven: Yale University Press, 2000).

least the third century CE, and that earliest image (of the crucifixion) was made by an opponent.

Even more than other Jews of this era, it was inevitable that the followers of Jesus would have to negotiate conflicts between Torah requirements or the teaching of Jesus and Greco-Roman mores or Roman law. Their very stance as followers and imitators of Jesus put them in an existential position of opposition to the Roman *imperium* that had slain their innocent Lord. Jesus had lived as an obedient subject of the Roman Empire, preaching a message of return to the God of Israel, the God of Justice. In response, that empire executed him as a threat to the stability of the Roman state.

Jesus' crucifixion, in the eyes of his followers, was the blasphemous result of world structures irreparably opposed to God. God had created this world and did not want to condemn it (John 3:17), but radical surgery was going to be necessary to save it from the evil powers that held it enthralled. Disciples like Paul of Tarsus expressed this belief in their doctrine of the *Parousia* (literally, "coming" or "appearance"), which contemporary Christians usually call the "second coming." Even Jesus seems to have thought that the *Parousia* would occur very soon (see Matt. 16:28), and Paul was convinced he personally would be alive to see it (e.g., 1 Cor. 7:29; cf. 1 Thess. 4:15–5:11). Then all pagan authorities and other enticements to disobey God would be overthrown. Instead, Messiah Jesus would rule on God's behalf, establishing whatever structures would be necessary to ensure that humans would live as God intended, in harmony with God, each other, and the rest of God's creation. For most of the first century, the followers of Jesus did not anticipate having to wait long for God to effect this radical renewal on the face of the earth.

As the end of the century drew near, Jesus' disciples began to realize that they would be in the pagan world for an indefinite period of time. With more pagans converting to the movement, Christ-believers became more receptive to Greco-Roman culture and more transparent in their use of it. For example, Clement of Rome, writing about 95 CE, expressed his admiration for the organization of the Roman army and used the myth of the phoenix (the mystical bird that yearly died in flames and then came back to life) to illustrate a point about Jesus' Resurrection. By the middle of the second century, writers such as Justin Martyr (*fl.* ca. 155–165) openly relied upon Greek philosophical notions to convey the significance of the gospel to their audience of predominantly Gentile converts. However, Greek philosophy had little explicit impact on the New Testament. Luke rather fancifully portrays Paul debating with some Greek philosophers in Athens (while others dismiss him as a babbler), but Colossians 2:8 links philosophy with "empty deceit," and in 1 Corinthians 1–2 Paul warns his Greek converts not to be puffed up with human knowledge. Several New Testament books show that their authors knew at least basic elements of such common philosophies as Stoicism and Platonism. Gnosticism and Docetism, two movements later rejected by the church as heretical, were grounded at least partially in Greek philosophical notions. However, none of the New Testament authors used Greco-Roman philosophy as the foundation for their presentations.

Varieties of "Judaism" in the First Century CE

Neither Greek nor Roman religion had much impact upon Jewish religious practice, but since religion, society, and politics were interwoven, religious developments among the Jews often had social or political ramifications, especially in a land ruled by Gentiles. At least five parties or sects existed within Judaism in the first century CE, and each of them had different ways of making the connections among their religious beliefs, political affiliations, and social policies. The two best-known groups are the Sadducees and Pharisees, both mentioned in the New Testament as disputing with Jesus over religious topics. The other three parties were the Essenes, a variety of armed resistance movements that Josephus calls "Zealots," and the Jesus movement or "Followers of the Way" (as Luke names it in the book of Acts).[7] One could be a Jew and belong to any of these groups or none of them. All of them influenced first-century Judaism. Since the Jesus movement will be discussed throughout the book, this section will focus on the other four parties.

---

7. Mark 3:6; 12:13 (= Matthew 22:16) refers to "the Herodians," presumably supporters of the Roman puppet-king Herod Antipas, but they are mentioned nowhere else. Scholars are not sure what kind of group this actually was or what significance it had.

The Sadducees

The Sadducee party was composed of Temple functionaries and members of the priestly caste, both of whom received their ranks by blood inheritance. They were an established, elite class who ministered in the Jerusalem Temple and performed the sacrifices there. The group probably dates back to the era of Ezra and Nehemiah (ca. 444 BCE), reformers who established the framework for modern Judaism in the midst of the Persian Empire after the Judeans' liberation from the Babylonian exile. As members of the Jewish aristocracy, the Sadducees had tremendous wealth and influence in political and economic life. They seem to have emphasized the importance of religious ritual and the prerogatives of the priestly class. They both accepted and benefitted from Roman rule since the priests functioned as part of the Roman system of authority in the imperial Province of Judea.

Sadducees believed in the Torah (or "Pentateuch," the first five books of the Bible) as the only divinely inspired scriptures, focusing on the letter of the written Torah. They did not accept the Pharisees' oral tradition of interpretation (see below). Since the Torah never mentions a messiah—a divinely sent savior-king—they did not expect one. They believed in neither a resurrection of the dead nor a spiritual afterlife; like the human body, the human soul was mortal. They accepted the divine election of Israel (the idea that Israel was God's own people, chosen for a particular role in human history), but they did not emphasize divine providence. The God of Israel, the only transcendent deity, demanded exclusive worship, yet God did not intervene in daily human affairs. Like most ancient people, the Sadducees had an ethnocentric worldview. Marriage was the accepted way of life for these Jews because it fulfilled the divine command in Torah to "be fruitful and multiply" (Gen. 1:28).

The Pharisees

Somewhere around the second century BCE, the Pharisee movement (from the Hebrew *perushim*, "the pure") arose from a group who called themselves *Hasidim* ("pious ones"), possibly an offshoot of the Sadducees. Over time, the Pharisees seem to have become the majority party in Judaism, and they probably gave rise to the rabbinic movement (the model for what would become Jewish orthodoxy) by about 100 CE. Their movement was a force for "democratization" in the sense that it was a shift from the exclusive influence of the priests and scribes to a primarily lay brotherhood. The Pharisees became influential at the time that local synagogues were established outside of Jerusalem, and they often are credited with their origin. They valued piety and knowledge of the Torah more than sacrificial rites. They did not reject Temple worship, but thought it alone was not enough for a living faith. God should always be worshiped through daily prayer and study of the Torah, even away from the Temple and outside of Jerusalem (cf. 1 Thess. 5:16–18).

The Pharisees promoted the Jewish rituals and scrupulous observance of the Mosaic Law. In their focus on teaching and understanding God's law, they accepted not only the Torah but also the oral tradition of its interpretation. In addition, they held the Prophets and the Writings to be inspired scripture. Synagogues played an important role in Pharisaic Judaism because such gatherings provided a venue not only for daily prayer but also for teaching the scriptures and thereby counteracting the pagan influences that surrounded Jews on a daily basis. The Torah was not a static revelation; rather one should read it with reason according to its spirit. This permitted an evolution in decisions concerning how to understand the Torah. It also required a greater fluency in the legal decisions of various rabbis (teachers and scholars of the Jewish scriptures).

While the Sadducee form of Judaism looked very much like other Greco-Roman religions of the day, with its emphasis on cultic observance administered by a priestly caste located in one cult center, Pharisaic Judaism looked to outsiders more like a philosophical school. The synagogues were gatherings for prayer but not sacrifice. The Pharisees made them places where participants could discuss how the scriptures could be applied to the pertinent issues of the day—religious, political, social, and economic.

For Pharisees, the divine election of Israel meant that Jews had a predestined role in the world, but this was coupled with individual free choice and responsibility. The one true God loves all humanity since he is their Creator; all are equal in God's sight, but Israel is set apart for a special role in the world. Of particular importance is the role that Israel plays in giving birth to God's Anointed, the Messiah who will gather all Jews and, indeed, all nations under divine rule. Marriage not only fulfills the divine command in Genesis 1:28 but also makes it possible to share in God's salvation of the world by bringing forth the Messiah. Ritual purity is one means of witnessing to this special role of Israel, the nation God chose to teach justice to the whole world.

Like many non-Jews, Pharisaic Jews believed in an afterlife of the immortal soul. Unlike non-Jews, they believed this afterlife was based upon a resurrection of the body on the "last day" or "Day of the Lord" (Dan. 12:2–3; Hos. 6:2), when divine judgment would be meted out to all people and they would receive their just rewards or retribution. God is transcendent and beyond human understanding. Yet the law of God has been revealed to his people; it can be understood—and must be obeyed. The purpose of human freedom is to make it possible to choose willingly to follow God's law. For the most part, the Pharisees accepted the ruling authority of Rome, but it could never be absolute; the ruling authority of God manifest in the divinely revealed Law and the Prophets trumped all. The classical Judaism that began to emerge in the late-first and early-second centuries shared more in common with the Pharisee movement than with any other first-century Jewish group.

The "Followers of the Way" also shared the most similarities with the Pharisee movement, which may be one reason why the evangelists depict more debates between Jesus and the Pharisees than with any other Jewish sect. Both groups believed in miracles and angelic messengers sent by God to communicate with human beings; Jesus' disciples claimed that he himself did miracles by the power of God. Both accepted the Torah and Prophets as divinely inspired scriptures, and believed in the efficacy (even necessity) of ongoing interpretation of those scriptures in light of the contemporary situation; Jesus' disciples privileged his interpretation over any others. Both groups believed in the resurrection of the just in the "final days"; Jesus' disciples affirmed that those final days had already begun when God raised Jesus from the dead.

The Essenes

Like the Pharisees, the Essene party also arose out of the *Hasidim* in about the middle of the second century BCE. The Essenes' primary goals were to study the Jewish law, uproot pagan influences from the midst of Israel, and promote Jewish rites, including scrupulous observance of the Mosaic Law. The Essenes accepted both the Torah and the Prophets as inspired by God. They also included other written traditions in their study of religious texts. The library of scrolls found in 1948 at Kîrbet Qumran on the Dead Sea usually is attributed to the Essenes. It includes several biblical texts as well as such non-biblical works as *The Community Rule* (a sort of "constitution" for the community), *The War Scroll* (an exposition of how believers should behave in the coming messianic war), a psalter (a hymn book), and commentaries on writings from the Bible.

The Dead Sea Scrolls tell us several things about the Essenes. The very existence of the library shows that this was a scribal community. This in turn puts the group among the aristocracy of their day. The *Copper Scroll*, which lists their treasures, shows that the community had considerable wealth. The *Community Rule* indicates that this was a communalist sect that was mostly celibate, although they did not forbid marriage. The Essenes emphasized ritual purity, including various ritual ablutions and a water baptism, along with study of the Torah, which was interpreted in light of their sect and its ideals. The Essenes believed they were a people set apart by the one God to become a "saving remnant" in Israel, a people of the "new covenant." The Jerusalem Temple was God's proper house of worship, but it had been profaned by those currently exercising priestly authority in Jerusalem. Those priests had sold out to the pagan rulers and had thus profaned Temple worship and the sacrifices. God would intervene at the proper hour and restore both the kingship and Temple to Israel through the agency of two messiahs, a general-king of the line of David and a priestly one descended from Aaron, Moses' brother and Israel's first priest. Meanwhile one must wait and pray.

The Essenes held a dualistic worldview in which God loves the "sons of light" and hates the "sons of darkness." Not only are non-Jews excluded from the children of light but even some Jews as well. Only the "true Israel" is the elect of God. One becomes a member of the elect by divine predestination. This election brings Israel responsibility but entails no human free choice. The primary responsibilities in the present involve study, prayer, worship, and preparation for the coming messianic war against the "sons of darkness." God is the world ruler whose providence determines the future, for good or for ill. Those who are obedient to this divinely ordained plan will be rewarded with immortal life for their souls, while the disobedient will be punished.

Resistance Movements and the "Zealots"

The armed resistance movements are the most difficult of these four Jewish groups to describe. Some may have begun as smaller groups of brigands and then coalesced and developed a tighter organization. Although often viewed as purely political, in fact they had religious motivation for their militancy. These groups seem to have shared a belief that God had chosen Israel to be a people directly ruled by him, worshiping only him. It was an affront to the chosen people to be ruled by idolatrous foreigners. Consequently, the militants had little or no use for the Temple priests, who were appointed and paid by Rome. According to them, only when Israel (the promised land) had been liberated would true worship of God be possible.

Styling themselves defenders of Mosaic Law and Jewish national life, the resistance movements gradually began to coalesce so that by the sixties, with the onset of the first Jewish Revolutionary War against Rome, the Jewish historian Flavius Josephus can call them a Zealot party. While different armies gave their allegiance to at least three different Generals, overall the Zealots engaged in relentless political activity, refusing to pay taxes and harassing both Romans and the Jews they thought to be in league with Rome—including the Sadducees who controlled the Temple priesthood. Some of the revolutionaries even used coercion and violence against other Jews in an attempt to intimidate them into supporting the revolution. They did not shy from punishing those who would not cooperate, and earned the nickname *sicarii* ("dagger-carriers") from their guerilla tactics and assassinations.

The dominant religious beliefs among the revolutionaries included a fierce nationalism and the messianic expectation that God would redeem Israel from Gentile rule and restore a Davidic-type monarchy. This suggests that they accepted both the Torah and the Prophets, since only the prophetic writings proclaim the coming of a messiah. They shared this messianic expectation with many other first-century Jews, including those of the Pharisee and Essene parties, although the Zealots' militant nationalism seems rather a distinguishing feature.

Exactly when the Zealots became a formally organized military movement is not known, but it was no later than 66 CE, when the Jews began their war of independence from Rome. Josephus depicts the Zealots as mere outlaws, but one must remember that his *Jewish War* is a tendentious production created at the behest of a Roman master whose patronage was so important to Josephus that he had taken the name "Flavius" in his honor. Josephus' imperial patron did not want to hear that the Jews had a legitimate claim for independence, nor that they were coordinated and competent strategists. Josephus remarks about the internecine strife among the revolutionaries but, whatever internal squabbles they may have had, the revolutionaries agreed on the objective of ousting Rome from the land of Israel. In addition, they obviously had sufficient strength and coordination in prosecuting the hostilities against Rome, for they sustained a protracted seven-year war against the world's strongest military power. That achievement is not the result of mere bandits. The fact that they had sufficient money for weapons suggests that at least some of their supporters came from the aristocratic class; in fact, Josephus mentions that some of the younger priests initiated the revolt.

The fall of Jerusalem to the Romans in 70 CE largely put an end to the revolution, but a group of *sicarii* under the leadership of one Eliezer held out at Herod the Great's fortress at Masada until 73 CE, when Josephus tells us that the besieged Jews committed mass suicide rather than fall into Roman captivity (*Jewish Wars* 7.8–9). If their suicide was fueled in part by a belief in some kind of resurrection and an afterlife, then they shared somehow the beliefs of the Pharisees and Essenes. In any case, the Jews who made the "last stand" at Masada took their place with the heroes of the Maccabean era as iconic figures, faithful martyrs in the cause of divine justice.

Historical Sources and Their Uses

Having considered the historical setting of the earliest communities of Christ-believers, it is well to look at the sources of information about them.

Sources come in all forms. Archaeology can provide information about the physical lives of people and can support written evidence. History and geography can explain such things as why the communities of disciples expanded to the West rather than to the East (they lived in the Roman Empire and followed the Diaspora) or what road the Apostle Paul probably took on his travels (the only usable road in a particular area). However, the bulk of the evidence is literary.

The most obvious sources are the books of the New Testament. Some have clear historical value, such as the Pauline Epistles. For example, Paul's First Epistle to the Corinthians not only tells us what the apostle thought the Corinthians should do, but also provides evidence for what was occurring in the Corinthian community that prompted Paul's response. Anonymous or pseudonymous (falsely named) epistles present problems and must be used more cautiously; examples of these would be Hebrews (attributed to no one in the text itself) and Colossians (attributed to Paul but probably not written by him).

Under the general "Pauline" heading would be seven undisputed letters (Romans, 1 and 2 Corinthians, Galatians, Philippians, 1 Thessalonians, and Philemon), and then six more letters that are attributed to Paul in the New Testament but that scholars doubt were written by Paul himself (Colossians, Ephesians, 2 Thessalonians, 1 and 2 Timothy, and Titus). The letter to the Hebrews was attributed to Paul by some early church fathers, although the letter itself is anonymous. Some of these letters clearly are linked to one another (1 and 2 Timothy); others legitimately may be linked to the Pauline tradition (Colossians), while still others stand on their own (Hebrews). The genuine Pauline Epistles trace the thought and activities of the most well-known apostle, while the others reflect the situations in the post-Pauline communities.

Since the eighteenth century, the seven New Testament letters not written by or traditionally attributed to Paul (that is, James; Jude; 1 and 2 Peter; and 1, 2, and 3 John) have been called the "Catholic Epistles." Unlike the Pauline letters, they were thought to have been addressed to all the followers of Christ rather than to particular ecclesial communities; thus, "catholic" (meaning "universal").[8] Grouping

---

8. Scholars now know this assumption to be mistaken; each of these writings seems to have a particular community in mind.

these letters together under the title "Catholic Epistles" might seem to imply that all seven letters have something in common, but that is not the case. The two letters attributed to Peter are related to each other, as are the three letters attributed to John, but nothing links all seven letters except their inclusion in the New Testament.

The Book of Revelation is a complex vision of the imminent transformation of the world to one where God is totally in charge and directly present to the faithful. The vision provides no direct historical content, but the existence of the book demonstrates that revelatory thinking was known among Christ-believers at the end of the century. In addition, the book reflects the views of some late first-century disciples (e.g., the very anti-Roman stance), and the letters included in the first three chapters convey some information about their communities in Asia Minor at the turn of the century.

The four Gospels—Matthew, Mark, Luke, and John—focus on Jesus, but they too can provide some information about the early communities of disciples. To use a brief example, the earliest Gospel (ca. 70 CE), that of Mark, contains no infancy narrative. The next two Gospels (ca. 80–90 CE), Matthew and Luke, do contain accounts of Jesus' birth. These later two Gospels convey information about Jesus that Mark did not: the tradition that he was born in Bethlehem. In the process, they also demonstrate that sometime between the publication of Mark and the composition of the next two Gospels, Jesus' disciples had acquired an interest in his birth. The last Gospel, John (ca. 100 CE), speaks not of Jesus' birth but of his divine generation. This study will attempt to discover what elements in the history of the Jesus movement in general or of specific local communities prompted these particular theological interests.

Only one book says anything about the earliest, post-Resurrection communities, and that is the Acts of the Apostles, a product of the same person who wrote the Third Gospel, traditionally called the Gospel according to Luke. Who was this "Luke"? Has this author reported reliable information about the early "followers of the way"?

Starting in the second century, ecclesial tradition identified the author of the Third Gospel as Luke, a fellow-worker of Paul who appears in the letter to Philemon (v. 24) and two post-Pauline works (Col. 4:14; 2 Tim. 4:11). Second Timothy repeats what Philemon says, that Luke was a fellow-worker of Paul, and thus adds no new information. Colossians, on the other hand, identifies Luke as a physician. Gallons of ink have been spilled trying to validate or invalidate this identification. For example, for generations scholars noted that Luke used medical terminology in his writings. Yet modern scholars have demonstrated that the medical terminology one finds in the Third Gospel and Acts was common knowledge, rather than terms that only physicians would know because of their technical training; thus the use of such terms does not prove Luke was a physician. On the other hand, the evangelist was not writing the Gospel for physicians but for a general audience. Hence, even if he were a physician, it would be logical for him to use non-technical language. Whether or not the New Testament author was a physician or a colleague of Paul must remain an open question, but this does not mean one can know nothing of the author.

Luke was probably a Gentile by birth, since he confuses the ritual requirements of Torah concerning purification of a mother after childbirth and circumcision of a son (Luke 2:21–24). He does show some familiarity with Torah, however, and has a pattern of showing Jesus and his parents as observant of Jewish law (e.g., Luke 1:59; 2:21–24). This suggests that he either was a convert to Judaism or a "God-fearer" (a Gentile who studied Torah and observed its prohibitions, but had not yet accepted circumcision and the other positive requirements of the law).

Luke wrote no earlier than the 80s, a half-century after Jesus' death, when his disciples were beginning to realize that they would be in the world for some time—a significant change from their earlier views that the world would end soon (see, e.g., 1 Cor. 15:51–52; 1 Thess. 4:13–17). Luke wrote the Acts of the Apostles partly to legitimate the community of disciples as the continuation of Jesus' work. He did not want believers to think that the *ecclesia* was a sort of last resort—if the world is not going to end, one might as well form some kind of lasting community—but that community-in-discipleship was part of Jesus' plan. Of all the evangelists, only Luke includes an account of Jesus' ascension into heaven. In fact, he tells the story twice, once at the end of his Gospel and again at the beginning of Acts, thus linking the two works. This scene serves as a transition point between the earthly life of Jesus and that of the apostolic community. The risen Christ has returned to his Father in heaven. (In the first century, this was believed to be above the sky, which is why Jesus had to "ascend.") From heaven, Jesus sends the Holy Spirit to continue his work on earth. Luke emphasizes this by having some disciples, in the power of the Spirit, perform miracles similar to those performed by Jesus. This earthly work of the Spirit-filled disciples in imitation of Jesus cannot be confined just to Jews; Luke's hero, Paul, under divine guidance, spreads the gospel message to the larger Roman world while the other apostolic leaders acknowledge the rightness of Paul's cause (e.g., Acts 15:1–33).

This may sound as if Luke did not write an entirely objective history of the earliest community. That is true; he did not. However, no historian writes a totally objective history. No matter how objective one tries to be, every historian brings personal background and attitudes to any topic, however unconsciously; this is true even today when it is expected that histories will be written objectively. (The author is bringing her outlook and background to the writing of this book, and readers are bringing their outlook and backgrounds to the reading of it.) In the ancient world, on the other hand, historians were not expected to write objective histories. On the contrary, they were expected to glorify rulers, to further a cause, or to instill patriotism in their readers. More than that, in order to be convincing, historians had the freedom to put speeches in the mouths of their characters, as long as they believed that the speech reflected what the character would have or should have said. This was not the practice of hacks but of truly great historians, like the Greek Thucydides (ca. 455–ca. 400 BCE) and the Roman Tacitus (ca. 56–ca. 118 CE). Luke follows their example. In his Gospel, everyone from peasants to aristocrats speaks the same educated style of Greek, and the characters in Acts give impressive speeches.

To say that modern people cannot rely on Luke would be an overreaction. If one is willing to read only writers who took a modern approach, one would never be able to read any ancient history at all—whether Roman, Jewish, Egyptian, Greek, or any other. Although ancient writers imposed their own views on the materials, they are not likely to have created events that never happened. One can use their works but must do so with care, considering how the author's background and outlook may affect the presentation of the material.

For example, Luke may have elevated the role of Paul in spreading the message of Jesus throughout the Roman Empire, but no scholar doubts that Paul did bring the gospel message to the Gentiles of the eastern Mediterranean.

Non-biblical works contemporaneous with the New Testament typically resemble the epistles in being occasional documents written to address particular situations. All reflect the views of the diverse groups that produced them. One source, much later than the New Testament, is uniquely significant because of its scope. In the fourth century, Bishop Eusebius of Caesarea (ca. 260–339 CE) compiled his *Ecclesiastical History*, the first history of the Jesus movement. This work traces the period from the earliest communities of disciples to the reign of Constantine the Great (314–337 CE), the first Roman Emperor to take the name of "Christian." Eusebius often saw history as a form of apologetics, so one must use his work carefully, but he has preserved a large number of traditions, some very ancient, which modern scholars accept as historical. Frequently he is the only source of information about some of the great figures and events of this nascent period.

One of Eusebius' main sources was a second-century believer named Hegesippus (*fl.* ca. 150–180 CE), whose work is known solely from quotations by Eusebius. Hegesippus apparently journeyed by sea from Corinth (in Greece) to Rome, collecting information about episcopal succession from various bishops along the way. Hegesippus was well informed about events in Judea, leading scholars to think he had roots there and perhaps was from a Jewish family. Scholars vigorously debate how much of what Eusebius quotes is actually from Hegesippus and how much from Eusebius himself. Still, the traditions Eusebius reports are worth examination.[9]

In general, Jewish and pagan sources say little about the Jesus movement, but the little they say is often of great value. These sources will be discussed later on.

---

9. Since the extant (surviving) source is Eusebius, not Hegesippus, quotations and references to the traditions from Hegesippus will cite Eusebius.

Why Bother with History?

To people accustomed to contemporary historiography, when everything is dated and authors' names are known, studying ancient history can seem daunting, but it can be done. One cannot do it in the way that one can with modern history, but one can follow the general outline of early ecclesial developments, focus on many of the specifics, and get a good idea of how the early followers of Jesus understood themselves and their communities.

This history also may help one to understand the church of the present day by helping to explain how it came to take the particular forms that it did in those early times. For example, because Jesus and his disciples were Jewish and lived in the Roman Empire, the Jesus movement expanded along the routes of the Jewish Diaspora within the empire. Consequently, it gradually became a primarily Western religion in culture and outlook. Awareness of this phenomenon should raise important questions for contemporary Christians. For example, as Christianity today becomes a universal religion in a way that the New Testament authors could never have imagined, and as the numbers of Christians in Africa and Asia continue to grow, should the church continue to express itself exclusively in Western ways or should it incorporate the images and practices of these other cultures as well?

Summary

Half a millennium of strife in the Mediterranean world preceded the birth of Jesus of Nazareth. Augustus Caesar had brought an end to a century of Roman civil war, which led the Romans to acclaim him "Savior of the World." Prices stabilized, roads were built, and the local aristocracy was coopted into the Roman power structure. Once the actual fighting had ended, the average peasant noticed little difference from the previous period under Jewish (Maccabean) rule. They continued to pay onerous taxes, as they had in the past, little aware that the funds now flowed along those Roman roads to Italy. Soon the gospel would follow the same routes to Rome.

Several groups within the Jewish people took different stances toward the political shifts in the period leading up to and following the Roman conquest. Jews were torn on the one hand between an aristocratic priesthood, beholden to the Roman regime for their control of the Jewish Temple, and the abhorrent prospect of syncretism with powerful Gentiles ("pagans") on the other hand. Two of the Jewish responses to this dilemma, those of the Pharisees and Sadducees, figure in the biblical materials; those of the Essenes and "Zealots" are known from the Jewish historian, Flavius Josephus. Jesus himself, always and only a Jew, became the foundation of the "fifth philosophy" when his disciples acclaimed him "Messiah."

Social and political pressures in the centuries before Jesus, during which time the Jewish people had suffered as political pawns of shifting world powers, inspired them to dream for a time and realm in which the peace and bounty of God would prevail. Apocalyptic hopes and moves toward political liberation during the centuries preceding Jesus made the people ripe for his message of the "kingdom of God." Several of the intertestamental and New Testament books reflect this apocalyptic attitude. Meanwhile, however, what determined power was where one stood in relation to Rome.

Jesus and his message represented an explicit challenge to Roman power and the supremacy of Caesar. The evangelists present Jesus, not Caesar, as the divinely born savior of the world, advancing God's kingdom. Religious, economic, and political spheres all were one in the ancient mind: religious claims had simultaneous political, social, and economic implications; all of life was spiritual, social, and political-economic at the same time.

This last point in particular holds the key for a responsible reading of the historical sources. Knowledge of Jesus' contemporaries, predecessors, and successors, derives from documents written at a time and place dramatically different than the present. These histories and letters refer to people and events fresh in common memory, so their contents would have been much more easily understood by the original audience. The best strategy for reconstructing the history is, whenever possible, to use multiple sources that talk about the same events.

Christianity always has been a religion that functioned in history, preserving the heart of Jesus' message while constantly interacting with the world in which it found itself. It still does. The next chapter will turn to the earliest disciples as they began this balancing act.

Questions for Review

1. What factors contributed to make the early first century CE the "right time" for the successful spread of the Jesus movement?
2. What does "Hellenization" mean, and how were the people of Judea affected by it?
3. What is the "Diaspora" and how did it come about?
4. What was the Hasmonean Dynasty? How did it begin, and how did it end? How was Judea governed thereafter?
5. Who was Caesar Augustus and what was his significance?
6. What was the attitude of the Roman Empire toward Jews?
7. What was the First Jewish War? Why did it begin and what was its outcome?
8. What sources are available for a historian wishing to reconstruct the early history of the Jesus movement?

Questions for Discussion

1. The spread of Greek culture and language was appealing to many of the inhabitants of Judea, especially members of the upper class. Why do you think some Jews accepted Hellenization? Why did some reject it?
2. Why do you think ancient peoples accepted the intermingling of religion and state (as in ruler cults) as natural and appropriate? What are the advantages of such an approach? What are the disadvantages?
3. Most of the Greek rulers who succeeded Alexander the Great saw it as their duty to "improve" the lives of subject peoples by forcing them to accept Greek culture, even when that meant coercing people to abandon their traditional beliefs and practices. Even today the state is sometimes called upon to override citizens' religious beliefs so as to serve their best interests—for example, in cases when parents refuse, on religious grounds, necessary medical treatment for a child. Is this sort of state intervention essentially different from Antiochus Epiphanes'

program of suppressing Jewish beliefs and practices? Why or why not?

4. Each of the four major Jewish "groups" within first-century Judea managed to attract a certain following; what was the appeal of each group for the people of that time and place? Which group do you think you would have joined, had you lived at that time, and why?

CHAPTER **2**

The World of Jesus
(21–30 CE)

The Gospels tell many stories about events of Jesus' life, particularly those that occurred during his public ministry, traditionally dated to 28–30 CE. Incidental to those stories there are off-hand remarks about political events, religious disputes, and important Jewish and Roman leaders. What the Gospels do not describe is the context for these events, disputes, and figures. There are at least two reasons for this. First, the evangelists could assume that their audiences already would know much of this background information: some of the older members would have lived through the events, while others would have heard of them from relatives and friends. Such "oral history" reinforced important social relationships and encouraged respect for elders as guardians of communal knowledge and wisdom. Second, the evangelists tended not to view this background information as important to their story of Jesus. Contextual details, which provide the "thick description" essential to contemporary historiography, typically played little to no role in ancient treatments of history.[1]

---

1. The phrase "thick description," drawn in part from the work of philosopher Gilbert Ryle, was used by cultural anthropologist Clifford Geertz (*The Interpretation of Cultures* [New York: Basic Books, 1973], 5–6, 9–10) to describe his method of ethnography. Geertz insisted that ethnographers must provide detailed enough descriptive data concerning not only the behavior being observed but its context as well. This "thick description" would render the meaning of the behavior recognizable not only to insiders, but outsiders as well.

Ancient historians did not concern themselves with helping their audiences to understand events from the vantage point of an insider; in fact, the whole question of differentiating between an "insider" versus "outsider" view probably would make no sense to them. The "meaning" of events derived from their significance, in retrospect, to the author of the history and, derivatively, the author's projected audience. This approach to history certainly kept the project less complex, and suited the historian's purpose of conveying cultural mores and evaluating certain behaviors and attitudes as virtuous (and so to be cultivated) or vicious (and therefore to be avoided). If a political figure made a decision that turned out to have ill effects on the public welfare, that was sufficient evidence of it being a bad decision—and it would be fair to impute vicious motives behind it. If someone made a decision that ended up bringing great benefits to the public, that was a good decision and evidence of the virtue of the decision-maker. It would not matter if the decision actually was driven by self-serving motives; this question would never even be raised. The end result could speak for itself.

One of the reasons why each of the Gospel narratives is overshadowed by the event of Jesus' death and Resurrection is because the evangelists agree with ancient historians that the end result of one's life determines its value. The crucifixion of Jesus, taken in isolation, would provide a pretty abysmal commentary on the value of his life. Combined with the Resurrection proclamation, however, Jesus' life is transfigured. His figure is transformed into one that stands alone in human history, and alongside the divine realm. For the evangelists, the Resurrection provides the only "context" necessary for understanding the meaning of Jesus' life and message.

Contemporary readers may find this idea theologically compelling, but they tend not to find it very satisfying as historiography. Most want to know about contexts and motivations, and they do differentiate between what may be self-evident in retrospect versus what was likely noticeable at the time. The entire "quest for the historical Jesus" is based upon this distinction between "then" and "now."

The main point of this chapter is to provide the wider context for the life and mission of Jesus. Precisely because the evangelists were able to assume such knowledge on the part of their audiences and thus omitted it from their narratives, such details are tremendously important if contemporary readers are to understand the stories themselves and the significance of Jesus in his own time and place. The modern reader now recognizes—as ancient historians did not—that lack of knowledge of the historical contexts can badly skew one's understanding of events and people of the past. If readers want to understand Jesus and his message, and not simply reinforce their preconceived notions of Jesus and his message, they have to go beyond and behind the Gospel narratives to reconstruct where those narratives fit in the overall context of early-first-century life in the Roman Province of Judea.

Herod the Great

Jesus was born during the reign of Herod the Great (ca. 74–4 BCE), client king to the Roman state from 37–4 BCE. This means Jesus came into the world more or less as Herod was passing out of it (Matthew 2). What else is important about Herod?

Herod came to power during the chaos of the Roman civil war after the assassination of Julius Caesar. Herod's father, Antipater, was executed for supporting the wrong side (Cassius, who helped slay Caesar), and one of Herod's first challenges (in 42 BCE) was to persuade Marc Antony and Octavian (later Emperor Caesar Augustus) that his father's true loyalties—and by extension, Herod's own—lay elsewhere.[2] About two years later, the Roman Senate conferred upon Herod the title of "King of the Jews."[3] Herod eventually ruled a territory roughly equivalent to that of the ancient kingdom of David.

While opportunistic in seeking the throne, King Herod was a savvy politician and competent ruler. He carried out an exceptionally ambitious building program, including impressive fortresses, aqueducts, temples, and ports. Much of the cost of these building projects was borne by Herod's subjects, either in the form of taxes or forced labor.

---

2. About ten years later (in 31 BCE), Herod would have to make a similar argument, this time to persuade Octavian that he really would be as faithful to him as he had been to Octavian's former ally, Marc Antony, who had been vanquished with Pharaoh Queen Cleopatra at the Battle of Actium.

3. Matthew in particular uses Herod as a foil to Jesus, the only other person in the Gospels to be given this regal title.

One might suppose that a "Jewish" official like Herod would be more conscientious in respecting the traditions and laws of Torah, but this does not seem to be the case. Certainly Herod engaged in practices that supported Rome in contradiction to Jewish beliefs and interests. These actions did not go entirely unchallenged. Sporadically during his reign, and then on a fairly regular basis throughout the first century CE, at least some religious leaders were ready to object. An important case in point occurred shortly before Herod died. Apparently, Herod had installed a golden eagle above the Temple gate. This symbol of Roman power would have been offensive anywhere in the Holy City, but it was the height of insult to violate the commandment against images by installing this idol on the very entrance to the Temple Mount. Two eminent (Pharisaic?) teachers from Jerusalem, Judas ben Sariphaeus and Matthias ben Margolathus, incited their students to tear down the eagle. When the gravely ill Herod had the scholars arrested and brought before him for trial, they lectured their captor in words reminiscent of those found in the martyr stories of 1–2 Maccabees: "We esteem those laws which were given Moses by God [as] more worthy of obedience than your laws" (cf. 2 Macc. 7:30). Herod responded by burning the scholars alive.[4]

Unfortunately, this shocking holocaust was no isolated incident. Paranoid and cruel, Herod brooked no challengers. When over 6,000 Pharisees refused to swear allegiance to Herod, he fined them heavily and executed the ring-leaders.[5] Herod was infamous for having executed his wife and many other family members whom he suspected of conspiring to supplant him. The Gospel of Matthew portrays Herod's brutality as so extreme that he would not balk at the mass-murder of infants and children (Matt. 2:16–18)—that Herod might have done such a thing doubtless appeared plausible based on his past practices.

---

4. Josephus, *Jewish Antiquities* 17.149–67 (English translation taken from *http://data.perseus.org/citations/urn:cts:greekLit:tlg0526.tlg001.perseus-eng1:17.278*; *Jewish War* 1.647–55.

5. Josephus, *Jewish Antiquities* 17.2.4. It is not clear how many Pharisees died in this incident.

Pontius Pilate

Pontius Pilate, the Roman prefect who ruled Judea a generation after Herod's death (26–36 CE), shares a level of notoriety with Herod for having ordered Jesus' execution. The evangelists present Jesus' trial in isolation, which conveys the impression that this event was unique. Additionally, because the Gospels mention only those events that are directly related to Jesus, they tell us nothing about other resistance movements or "messiah" figures in Jesus' day, or how Pilate or other regional authorities treated them. If Herod the Great could be brutal, Pontius Pilate is remembered for an almost casual savagery. By framing Jesus' birth and death with two political officials most remembered for their cruelty, the evangelists create a tragic context for the crucifixion that links the death of their Messiah with the deaths of hundreds of Jews who had gone before him.

Flavius Josephus reports that Pilate's first major act was to order the Roman legionary "standards" brought into Jerusalem and displayed near the Temple and adjacent Antonia Fortress.[6] Sacred objects to the legionaries, the standards were kept in a shrine when not in use;[7] perhaps Pilate viewed the Jewish Temple as the appropriate place for them. The standards carried bird or animal images—a clear violation of the Biblical prohibition. The Jews staged a sit-in to protest and, when threatened with death, they "laid their necks bare, and said they would take their death very willingly, rather than the wisdom of their laws should be transgressed."[8] Pilate

© Zev Radovan / biblelandpictures.com

This Roman coin depicts standards carried by the Roman Legions. Such standards were objects of veneration to the soldiers; the Jews considered them idolatrous.

---

6. See Josephus, *Jewish War* 2.169–74; *Jewish Antiquities* 18.55–59.

7. In addition to their religious function, the standards also had a practical use. Each legion had its own distinctive symbols, so its standard could be used to signal the troops in battle and to mark the location of their encampment.

8. Josephus, *Jewish Antiquities* 18.59.

did agree to remove the standards, but a course of mutual animosity had been set.

Sometime later, Pilate commandeered money from the Temple treasury to build an aqueduct. Again the Jews protested, but this time Pilate did not yield. Ordering some of his soldiers to dress like civilians and infiltrate the crowd, he then signaled them to draw daggers hidden beneath their clothes and attack the peaceful protesters. Of the "tens of thousands" of protesters, Josephus says "a great number" of them were killed and wounded.[9]

These two incidents suggest that either Pilate was totally ignorant of Jewish traditions and sensibilities—a characterization difficult to credit of a Roman official at this level of government—or that he cultivated a cavalier disregard of those customs and beliefs. The calmly philosophical Pilate depicted in John's Gospel and popularized by Hollywood Jesus-films simply cannot be accurate. Disdain for the Jewish people under his authority and heavy-handed enforcement of his will must be included in any historical picture of Pilate. Public execution of a "rabble-rouser" like Jesus would be a relatively unremarkable event in the life of Pontius Pilate.

Between Herod and Pilate: Supporting Roles on the Roman Stage

Herod the Great's kingdom was divided upon his death, and Archelaus, his eldest surviving son, was named "ethnarch" of Judea, Idumea, and Samaria.[10] Archelaus' ten-year reign (4 BCE–6 CE) was rife with "bandit" rebellions, the first beginning at Passover of 4 BCE, soon after his father's death. Dissidents took control of the Jerusalem Temple, supported by loyalists in the city, and managed to repulse the first cohort their new king sent to evict them. Finally, Archelaus "sent out [his] whole army" against them and succeeded in recapturing the Temple. Josephus says that 3,000 resisters were killed and the rest put to flight.[11]

---

9. See Josephus, *Jewish War* 2.175–77; *Jewish Antiquities* 18.60–62.

10. *Ethnarch* refers to a ruler of an *ethnos* or national group (in this case, the Jews).

11. Josephus, *Jewish Antiquities* 17.213–18; *Jewish War* 2.5–13.

Thinking that the rebellion was suppressed for good, Archelaus went to Rome to plead with the Emperor Augustus for his share of Herod's kingdom, against the claims of his youngest brother, Herod Antipas. In the absence of both claimants for the throne, there arose a massive, spontaneous rebellion. According to Josephus, "this sedition . . . was a great one" wherein "the whole nation was in tumult."[12] The newly appointed governor of Syria, Publius Quinctilius Varus (46 BCE–9 CE), brought his three legions to Judea to "pacify" the Jews. Varus must not have trusted this imposed silence, however: when he returned to his capital city of Antioch, he left his assistant, Sabinus, and an entire legion stationed in Jerusalem.[13]

This measure may have quieted the city, but it did not quell the rebellion. By Pentecost, fifty days after the initial uprising, tens of thousands of Jews had flocked to Jerusalem and formed three armed camps, laying siege to the Roman legion. Even when the Romans sacked the Temple and slaughtered thousands, some of the Jews persisted in their revolt.[14] Indeed, Josephus speaks of "countless other disorders" throughout the land: "And so Judea was full of brigandage and, as soon as any of the companies of rebels lighted upon anyone to head them, he was created a king immediately."

The "Bandit Kings" Judas the Galilean, Simon, and Athronges

Josephus singles out three bandit-kings for special attention.[15] Judas the Galilean,[16] he says, attacked the palace armory and treasury of Sepphoris[17] "out of an ambition to attain the royal dignity." Simon,

---

12. Josephus, *Jewish Antiquities* 17.250–51.

13. Ibid., 17.251.

14. Ibid., 17.254–68; *Jewish War* 2.41–54.

15. Josephus, *Jewish Antiquities* 17.271–84.

16. Apparently revolution was somewhat of a family tradition for Judas. Josephus (*Jewish Antiquities* 14.159) identifies him as the son of that Ezekias (sometimes spelled "Hezekias") who was leader of a "great troop" of bandits that had operated in the northern reaches of Herod's kingdom when he first came to the throne. The young Herod captured and killed Ezekias, thereby suppressing that movement.

17. Sepphoris was the recently established capital of Galilee, located about five miles from Jesus' home of Nazareth.

one of Herod's freedmen, was crowned and "declared to be a king"; he and his army captured and burned the Herodian palace complex at Jericho before Simon was captured and beheaded. The most successful of the three regal pretenders was a shepherd named Athronges. With the support of his own troops and those of his four brothers, who were his subordinate commanders, Athronges "set himself up as king" and led a number of successful actions against Roman forces as well as those of King Archelaus before they finally were suppressed by the joint action of their opponents.

> [Those who joined Athronges and his brothers] were very numerous. . . . [Athronges] put a diadem about his head, and assembled a council to debate about what things should be done, and all things were done according to his pleasure. And this man retained his power a great while; he was also called king, and had nothing to hinder him from doing what he pleased. He also, as well as his brethren, slew a great many both of the Romans and of the king's forces, [and] managed matters with the like hatred to each of them. *The king's forces they fell upon, because of the licentious conduct they had been allowed under Herod's government; and they fell upon the Romans, because of the injuries they had so lately received from them.* [Josephus here gives three examples of major engagements against the forces of Rome and of Archelaus.] Now these four brethren continued the war a long while by such sort of expeditions, and much grieved the Romans; but did their own nation also a great deal of mischief.[18]

Although Josephus attempts to "balance" his account by suggesting that the Jews also suffered at the hands of the self-styled "King" Athronges and his troops, he includes the telling admission that these revolutionaries sought to redress grievances against the Roman and Herodian forces.

Bearing with him the "peace of Rome," Quinctilius Varus returned from Syria with his additional two legions, burning and

---

18. Josephus, *Jewish Antiquities* 17.278; emphasis added. The English text is taken from Flavius Josephus, *The Works of Flavius Josephus*, trans. William Whiston (Auburn and Buffalo: John E. Beardsley, 1895); *http://www.perseus.tufts.edu/hopper/text?doc=Perseus:text:1999.01.0146:book=17:section=278.*

The remains of a crucified man, probably dating to the first century, were discovered in a tomb in East Jerusalem in 1968. The photograph shows the man's heel bone; still embedded in the bone is one of the nails that had fastened him to his cross.

© Zev Radovan / biblelandpictures.com

looting cities and villages as the army progressed south toward Jerusalem. Varus closed the book on this revolt by capturing and crucifying 2000 rebels.[19] For miles and miles, the roadways were lined with crosses and their tortured victims.[20] Rome required "peace" and taxes, and Varus intended to ensure that Rome would get what was required. The Gospel of Luke hymns the birth of Jesus of Nazareth amid the divine proclamation of "good news of great joy for all the people: [the birth of the Savior-Lord, the Davidic Messiah], and on earth peace among those whom [God] favors" (Luke 2:10b, 14). For those members of the audience who

---

19. Josephus, *Jewish Antiquities* 17.10.10.

20. The Roman rhetorician Quintilian explained the retributive and deterrent agenda behind these cruel, but not unusual, public executions: "Whenever we crucify the guilty, the most crowded roads are chosen, where most people can see and be moved by this fear. For penalties relate not so much to retribution as to their exemplary effect" (Quintilian, *Declamations* 274).

remembered the year of Jesus' birth, the angelic voices in Luke's foreground overlay a background rife with similar examples of the implementation of the *Pax Romana.*

Seeds of Unrest before "Messiah" Jesus

Israel may have been a hotbed of revolution in the first century CE, but this phenomenon should have come as no surprise to the over-lords (Roman and Herodian) who had perpetrated crimes against the Jewish people. The "bandit-kings" and other revolutionaries, who tried to rectify injustices perpetrated by Roman imperial appointees in the Holy Land, provided a key context during Jesus' lifetime for the Jewish understanding of the "messiah" promised by God to Israel. Jesus shared many of the concerns of these earlier messiah-kings, although his methods for addressing those concerns differed substantially.

Economic and social unrest marked the Roman Province of Judea for much of the remainder of the first century CE. In addition to the harsh economic realities endemic to empire, there were chronic insults to Jewish sensibilities. The most fundamental outrage was the Roman claim to ownership of the land of promise, which often meant the eviction of Jews from their ancestral properties in favor of the conquering elites. The imperial take-over of the Holy Land led to wealthy Romans gaining ownership of cultivable land that had belonged to the locals. Profits from agricultural enterprises stopped being channeled back into the local economy and began to be sent to absentee landlords in places like Caesarea and Rome. Peasant farmers paid one-third to one-half of their produce in taxes to Rome and the Jerusalem Temple.[21]

Urbanization under Herod Antipas during Jesus' formative years fostered tensions between city-dwellers—largely wealthy and

---

21. William R. Herzog, II, *Prophet and Teacher: An Introduction to the Historical Jesus* (Louisville: Westminster John Knox, 2005), 54; citing Douglas Oakman, *Jesus and the Economic Questions of His Day* (Lewiston, NY: Edwin Mellen, 1986), 65; and Richard Horsley, *Galilee: History, Politics, People* (Valley Forge, PA: Trinity Press International, 1995), 59. See also Magen Broshi, "The Role of the Temple in the Herodian Economy," *http://isites.harvard.edu/fs/docs/icb.topic1202633.files/Lesson%208 /8c%20Broshi.pdf.*

powerful landowners—and those in the countryside who gradually were being stripped of both income and livelihood through a spiral of taxes, loans, and indebtedness.[22] The canonical Gospels may hint at this antipathy through their portrayal of Jesus avoiding major cities during his public ministry.[23]

Unlikely "Historical" Traditions

When dealing with ancient sources, the modern scholar must distinguish between those that provide an accurate picture of events versus those that are tendentious, exaggerated, legendary, or even mythical, divorced from actual events. To illustrate this problem, here are two accounts from Eusebius that purport to present events in the time of Jesus, but which most scholars believe have little or no basis in fact.

Eusebius of Caesarea says that, when reporting to the Emperor Tiberius about Jesus' execution, Pontius Pilate also mentioned a widespread belief in the Resurrection.[24] Several versions of this "report" survive, but all of them date to centuries after the event. While it is possible that Pilate might have used a routine report to mention that some locals believed a crucified criminal had risen from the dead, it is highly unlikely that he would risk committing such potentially dangerous information to writing. In addition, the legend portrays Pilate in the (equally unlikely) role of a Christ-believer. While legends of the "conversion of Pilate" became very popular in late antiquity, they are late in origin and have no historical foundation.

Eusebius also records an exchange of letters between Jesus himself and King Abgar of Edessa, a small territory in what today is southeastern Turkey.[25] Abgar asked Jesus to cure him of an illness

---

22. Herod Antipas, youngest son of Herod the Great, was born before 20 BCE and died sometime after his exile in 39 CE. By the grace of Rome (in the persons of the Emperors Augustus and Tiberius), Antipas ruled the territories of Galilee and Perea for over forty years, from 4 BCE–39 CE.

23. Remarkably, the Gospels never once mention the city of Sepphoris (*Tzippori*), the capital of Galilee situated barely five miles from Nazareth, which Antipas rebuilt during Jesus' boyhood.

24. Eusebius, *Ecclesiastical History* 2.2.

25. Ibid., 1.13.

and to preach to his people. Jesus responded that he could not come in person, but would send a disciple instead. Faithful to this promise, Thaddaeus (Mark 3:18) was sent to Edessa, where he cured the king and preached the faith. Thaddaeus became known as "Addai" in Syriac, the language of the region. These letters are purely apocryphal, and again are quite late in date.

However, might there have been an early apostolic mission to Edessa? The city is only 180 miles from Antioch, the home church for missionaries like Paul and Barnabas. Certainly the gospel message quickly traveled to places much farther afield. There is evidence of Christ-believing communities in Edessa by about 200 CE. An early or mid-first-century mission to Edessa is possible, but unlikely. Regardless of when the gospel spread to Edessa, the legendary Addai should be seen as a composite figure that gives an identity and an apostolic pedigree to now anonymous missionaries.

Summary

No true biography of Jesus exists; the Gospels and other sources for his life and the events of his time are not concerned with telling the entire story of Jesus. Historically conditioned, like all sources, most of the details of Jesus' life and times are omitted simply because they were common knowledge to persons of that time. Powerful and important figures of the time are known to us, however, including Herod the Great, King of Judea (i.e., "King of the Jews") at the time of Jesus' birth, and Pontius Pilate, the Roman procurator of Judea at the time of Jesus' death.

Neither Herod nor Pilate were ideal rulers. Both Roman and non-Roman sources portray Herod as a paranoid, violent puppet-king whose architectural genius was matched only by his cold oppression of his own people. Jesus was born into a society living under the heavy hand of this ruthless dictator. Pontius Pilate, the Roman prefect who ordered Jesus' crucifixion, combined a similar autocratic style with a disdain for the Jewish people that bordered on hatred. Whether apathetic or ignorant, Pilate consistently offended Jewish sensibilities while attempting to maintain order in Palestine and impress his Roman superiors—tasks at which he did not always succeed. All of Jesus' life was spent under the political oppression of the world's great power.

Numerous rebellions and martial tumults occurred during Jesus' early years. Bandit kings like Judas the Galilean, Simon, and Athronges led tax revolts and other uprisings. Although these rebellions were squelched definitively, lack of success did not prevent other rebels arising in their place. The first-century Jewish peasantry had the opportunity to become accustomed to such claims to kingship long before any were made on behalf of Jesus.

While one cannot be certain of precisely what type of messianic expectations were held by Jews of Jesus' day, it seems clear that at least the lower-class Jews wished for freedom from the powers (foreign/Gentile and domestic/Jewish) that exploited and threatened them. One could expect—from them, at least—a warm welcome for Jesus' message of God's sovereignty and defeat of all such unjust human powers.

Historical sources have to be handled carefully and critically in light of their origins and agendas. Eusebius includes some traditions that are doubtful and cannot be corroborated by other sources. Legends such as he reports may have some underlying validity, but one cannot tell without additional evidence.

Questions for Review

1. How does the writing of history in ancient times differ from historical writing today?
2. Who was Herod the Great, and what was his significance?
3. What happened to Herod the Great's kingdom after his death?
4. Describe Pontius Pilate's rule over Judea. How does his crucifixion of Jesus compare to his governing style in general?
5. Describe one of the popular uprisings mentioned in Josephus' *Jewish Antiquities*.
6. How did the lot of peasants in Judea differ from that of city-dwellers? What was the general relationship of either group toward the Roman authorities?

Questions for Discussion

1. The Romans tended to be tolerant and accepting of the traditional religious beliefs and practices of the peoples subject to them—and yet they often clashed with their Judean subjects over religious issues. What caused such clashes?

2. Consider what is known about the Roman management of first-century Judea, and the occasional Jewish attempts to throw off the imperial yoke. How would a member of the Roman administration have reacted to news that certain Jews believed they had found the "Messiah"? How would a Jewish peasant probably have reacted to the same news? Would someone belonging to one of the elite ruling families of Judea have reacted differently?

3. The author mentions two "unlikely" historical traditions involving Pontius Pilate and Jesus' disciple Thaddeus. Why would most historians regard these accounts as unreliable, but would take seriously Josephus' account of the peasant uprising under Athronges? What factors affect the reliability or unreliability of an ancient source?

CHAPTER 3

Life after Jesus

(31–40 CE)

No one can be sure when Jesus died. Pontius Pilate, the Roman procurator who sentenced him to death, was recalled to Rome in 36 CE, ten years after his initial appointment to Judea, so Jesus must have been executed sometime between 26–36 CE. The traditional dates, between 30–33 CE, are probably reliable. Jesus left behind a frightened and confused collection of disciples who were in shock over the death of their beloved leader. However, events soon transpired to keep the Jesus movement alive. The letters of Paul and the Acts of the Apostles speak of some of Jesus' followers having visions of him, and the four canonical Gospels tell of postmortem appearances by Jesus to various disciples, the women first and then the men. These were different ways of expressing their conviction that Jesus had transcended the bonds of death. Without this, Jesus' movement would have died with him. Because of this faith in his Resurrection, Jesus' followers had the courage and determination to persevere in his footsteps.

In worldly terms, Jesus' execution by the Roman regime marked the failure of his mission and seemed to demonstrate the falsity of any claims that he was the long-awaited Messiah of Israel. However, Jesus' disciples rejected the validity of the Roman sentence, instead insisting that he was truly a just man, an innocent victim of capital punishment. Furthermore, they insisted, God had confirmed this by raising Jesus, the Anointed One, from the dead. This vindicated

This first-century tomb near Nazareth is similar to the tomb of Jesus as described in the Gospels, with a stone that can be rolled across the entrance. The claim that Jesus' tomb was found empty and that he had risen from the dead was central to the proclamation of the early Christ-believers.

Jesus before the entire world and proved that his message concerning God and God's kingdom was indeed the truth. The proclamation of Jesus' Resurrection, therefore, was a message not about God resuscitating a corpse, but about God's final proof of the divine authority behind Jesus' words and deeds.

This first decade, then, marks the birth of the gospel: the proclamation of Jesus, the Christ, crucified and raised from the dead. It is not known how soon after the crucifixion Jesus' followers began to make this proclamation; the Gospels portray a three-day time frame between Jesus' death and Resurrection, thereby aligning this event with the final implementation of the justice and judgment of God, which the Hebrew Bible connects with "the third day" or "Day of the Lord" (e.g., Hos. 6:2). The latter prophets announced that, on that day, God would raise up the just from their graves to a new life (e.g., Ezek. 37). In Jesus, the disciples claimed, God had begun to do precisely that.

The Gospels of Matthew, Mark, and John show the male disciples returning to Galilee after Jesus' crucifixion, and this is where they experience the resurrected Jesus. It is safe to assume that they shared this marvelous news with their kinfolk and acquaintances in the region. It is also possible that a mission to the neighboring regions of Samaria and the Decapolis began at this early date. In fact, the Gospels of Mark and John portray this mission beginning already during Jesus' lifetime (Mark 5; John 4). Luke depicts the gospel of the Resurrection first being preached in Jerusalem, where he says the disciples were gathered in a prayer vigil, but this is at least in part because Luke has a literary motif that emphasizes Jerusalem as the geographical point of origin of the Jesus movement. In his Gospel, he shows Jesus moving from Galilee to Jerusalem, the center of the Jewish world. His sequel, the Acts of the Apostles, depicts Jesus' disciples picking up from where their master left off, beginning in Jerusalem and taking the gospel message all the way to Rome, the center of the empire—indeed, the center of the world.

Acts highlights only a handful of the people who spread the word about Jesus. Peter, Stephen, and Paul certainly became preachers, but so did Mary Magdalene (John 20:18) and other women whom Luke omits from his story. Still, in Acts 2, Luke portrays the inauguration of the gospel mission as deriving from all of the disciples—including the women—who were gathered in Jerusalem for the Jewish Feast of Pentecost, the annual commemoration of God's gift of the law to Moses and all Israel. Luke chooses this setting to highlight Jesus' message as comparable to the first covenant, and to show that it is in Jesus that all Israel will be gathered into one people once again. Luke's impulse to portray the gospel originating from the entire group of disciples is not simply a contrivance, however. All of these believers were "missionaries" in the sense that they brought their faith with them and spoke of Jesus to other people—initially other Jews. Most do not fit the later model, however, of moving from town to town and preaching full-time. Some did become itinerant preachers, but most simply took their new faith with them when they went home, to work, on business trips, or whatever they did as part of daily life.

The Jerusalem Community in the Book of Acts

The one source for the history of the *ecclesia* in this period is the Acts of the Apostles. In the preface to the book of Acts, Luke tells someone named Theophilus that this volume would continue the story he told in his Gospel. Theophilus also appears at the opening of the Gospel according to Luke, where the author dedicates the book to him and addresses him as "most excellent Theophilus." The phrase "most excellent" implies that he was a nobleman and most likely the author's patron. However, the name Theophilus in Greek means "beloved by God," so it may be an honorific title rather than a personal name. Other than the fact that this "Theophilus" was a person of sufficient means to sponsor lengthy research for a two-volume work about Jesus and his followers, nothing is known about him, although a later ecclesiastical tradition made him a bishop of Antioch.

Luke opens the Acts of the Apostles with the risen Jesus promising to send his disciples the Holy Spirit and then ascending into the heavens. This repeat of the ascension scene, with which Luke had concluded the Gospel story, is a literary device to make sure the two volumes would be read together rather than as independent works. The story about Jesus should ground the readers' understanding of this sequel about Jesus' followers. The parallels Luke draws between the life of Jesus and the lives of his followers also convey Luke's key catechetical point in this two-volume work: a true disciple of Jesus is one who follows his "Way," imitating Jesus' life and treasuring his word.

The book of Acts opens in Jerusalem, where "the eleven and their companions" were residing at the end of Luke's Gospel (Luke 24:33, 52–53). Other data suggest, however, that most of the eleven—and, in fact, probably most of the wider group of disciples—returned to Galilee soon after the death of Jesus (Matt. 28:10, 16; John 21:1–2). Acts 15 finds James, Cephas (Peter), and John gathered in Jerusalem for a council—a point confirmed by Paul's discussion of the meeting, which he and Barnabas also attended (Gal. 2:1–10)—but this takes place some years later. Writing this book at least fifty years after the death of Jesus, Luke knows that the Jerusalem community of disciples became the "mother church" for all of Christianity, so one way to convey this significance is to identify its origins with the Twelve.

Luke depicts Jesus' inner circle of disciples residing in Jerusalem, worshipping in the Temple and engaging in constant prayer while awaiting the promised gift of the Holy Spirit. This group includes "certain women, including Mary the mother of Jesus, as well as his brothers [and sisters]" and the eleven, who are mentioned by name (Acts 1:13–14).[1] Unlike the Qumran Jews who rejected the Temple in Jerusalem and founded a new sanctuary in the wilderness, Luke insists that the Way of Jesus is in continuity with Second-Temple Judaism. The movement is inaugurated in the capital city of the Jewish homeland, and Luke envisions it as destined to become a transforming influence for the world at large: "You will be my witnesses in Jerusalem, in all Judea and Samaria, and to the ends of the earth" (Acts 1:8).

Luke's portrayal of the selection of a "replacement" for Judas, to fill out the number of the Twelve, is another literary strategy for showing that the Jesus-Way stands in continuity with Judaism and God's promises to Israel. Sometime after the split of the Davidic Monarchy into two rival kingdoms (961 BCE), "Israel" in the north and "Judah" in the south, there arose a tradition about the "lost" members of "the House of Israel."[2] By Jesus' day, this appears to have been a widespread Jewish belief. Corollary to this belief was the insistence, based upon the prophets, that "all Israel" would be restored in the final age of God's redemption. Jesus' followers believed that his words and deeds had inaugurated this new age and that God indeed was gathering the lost and restoring all of the chosen people to the fold. Among Jesus' disciples, the Twelve symbolized all Israel, and Jesus was remembered as affirming that they would judge the twelve tribes at the end of the age (Matt. 19:28; Luke 22:30). Jesus'

---

1. This passage in Acts uses the general term *adelphoi* ("brothers" or "brothers and sisters"; singular *adelphos*, "brother"). The Synoptic Gospels also mention Jesus' siblings (Matt. 12:46; Mark 3:32; Luke 8:19). James "the Just" sometimes is called James *bar Joseph* (James, son of Joseph), and sometimes is identified as "the Lord's brother" (Gal. 1:19).

From the second century onwards, at least some sectors of developing Christianity affirmed the perpetual virginity of Mary, the mother of Jesus. Those who accept this belief usually construe the term *adelphos* as referring to some other close relative like a first cousin rather than a full-blood sibling. A second-century non-canonical work entitled the *Protoevangelion [Proto-Gospel] of James* "explains" how Jesus could have brothers and sisters if Mary was always a virgin by depicting Joseph as a widower when he took Mary as his wife, with children from the first marriage. Hence, Jesus' *adelphoi* were half-brothers and half-sisters, Joseph's children but not Mary's.

2. "The House of Israel" here refers to all the descendants of the twelve sons of Jacob, not just those who lived in the northern kingdom.

followers knew that one of the Twelve (Judas Iscariot) had been lost. Luke "replaced" the "lost" disciple to signify the universality of divine mercy in gathering Israel back to God in the form of this new community of Jesus' disciples.

In narrating this scene, Luke specifies that this substitute member of the Twelve must be "one of the *men* who have accompanied us during all the time that the Lord Jesus went in and out among us, beginning with the baptism of John until the day when [Jesus] was taken up from us" (Acts 1:21–22, emphasis added). Luke insists the replacement be one of the *male* disciples in order to maintain this parallel with the Israelite patriarchs. In doing so, however, he sets an impossible standard. Luke well knows that, among Jesus' disciples, only the *women* stood by him throughout his entire career. The three Synoptic Gospels (Matthew, Mark, and even Luke's own) depict Jesus' male disciples fleeing at his arrest, while women disciples are present at the crucifixion and hold vigil at the tomb. The Fourth Gospel breaks the mold a bit by portraying the Beloved Disciple as the one *man* who was faithful to Jesus to the last. Luke is not concerned with history here, but theology: the restoration of "all Israel" and consequent salvation of the entire world even now is coming to pass through Messiah Jesus and the followers of his Way.

The ensuing scene in Acts 2, set on the Day of Pentecost (the annual Jewish festival commemorating God's gift of the Torah at Sinai), combines creation imagery and features of ecstatic prophecy to depict the fulfillment of Jesus' prediction that the disciples will be Jesus' "witnesses . . . to the ends of the earth" (Acts 1:8). Like the Spirit hovering over the waters of primordial chaos at the beginning of God's creative act (Gen. 1:1–2), the Holy Spirit descends upon Jesus' followers as they are gathered for prayer. The "tongues of fire" image highlights the divinely given speech that ensues as the disciples preach to Jews from all over the known world, while the listeners understand in their own native languages (Acts 2:8–11). The Holy Spirit at work in and among the followers of Jesus empowers the previously frightened disciples to preach fearlessly and openly, and the gospel proclamation reunites all of humanity into one people, overcoming the barriers of language and culture and thereby reversing the effects of the Tower of Babel (Gen. 11).

Developments among the Early Disciples

In an account so thoroughly theological, does Luke tell us anything about what "really happened" from a historical point of view? If one means dates and times, and even names of those involved in the events, then the historian would have to admit "probably not." If one takes the category of "event" in the broader sense of the term, however, there are at least a few solid facts that can be derived from Luke's grand "nativity story" of the church.

1. Immediately after the death of Jesus, many of his followers were inclined to view their hopes as dashed, their faith in him as misplaced. The Messiah should be victorious, Israel's liberator. Instead, Jesus was dead at the hands of the Gentile powers that controlled the land and people of Israel.

2. Some of Jesus' early disciples went into hiding for fear they would share a death like his; others fled Jerusalem or simply returned home to Galilee and business as usual.

3. Fairly soon after Jesus' death, some of the disciples began to have experiences that dramatically transformed their attitudes and restored their confidence that indeed he was the Messiah sent by God to Israel. They knew he had been put to death—some had witnessed this with their own eyes—yet they experienced Jesus as alive again. Some spoke of dreams and visions; some heard his voice; some spoke of sight or even touch. Whatever the medium or image, they became convinced that Jesus had been raised by God to a new fullness of life and justice beyond the grave: Resurrection. History cannot tell us what these events involved, which is why Luke and the other evangelists use symbol and story to convey the idea. History shows that *something* happened. Luke's story interprets for the audience the significance of that historical something. This act of God—this "Resurrection" foretold by the prophets—was the harbinger of God's final salvation of all of creation, and all of humanity with it.

4. The realization of Jesus' Resurrection was such a transforming experience to the believers that it was tantamount to entering into a new creation. No longer afraid, they began to share the message of Jesus and the saving activity of God through him. Believing that the entire world should hear this good news, some

of them "hit the road" as traveling missionaries, while others stayed in one location and preached to those around them. In either case, voices that had been silent began to be "on fire" with this new message that they believed to be inspired by the Spirit of God.

Illustrating this powerful influence of the divine Spirit in the earliest gospel proclamation, Luke has Peter give a speech that encapsulates the historic role of Jesus: he fulfilled the promises of the Hebrew Bible, but his own people rejected him and turned him over to Gentiles for execution. God raised Jesus from the dead, vindicating him and his message before "all Israel" and, indeed, the whole world. Now Peter's fellow "Israelites" must turn to Jesus, the Messiah. Luke's speech is certainly no verbatim account of what Peter (or any other disciple) first preached. Rather, Acts presents a distillation of what Luke views as the essence of those proclamations. The Hebrew Bible repeatedly shows the God of Israel working in and through

This reconstruction shows the Temple of Jerusalem as it would have appeared in the time of Jesus. According to the Acts of the Apostles, members of the Jerusalem *ecclesia* continued to worship in the Temple, demonstrating that the early Christ-believers saw no contradiction between their faith in Christ and their Judaism.

historical events. So, if their fellow Jews were to be able to accept the claim that Jesus was sent by God as Messiah of Israel, the disciples had to show where Jesus fit into that historical picture.

Their message certainly enjoyed some success, among both Jews and non-Jews. In keeping with the biblical style of exaggerating numbers, Luke magnifies the success the disciples had in winning adherents: on the first day three thousand new believers in a city of twenty thousand inhabitants! Significantly, he mentions that the Christ-followers continued to worship in the Temple, clearly indicating that they formed a movement *within Judaism*, not a new religion. In fact, Luke claims that as "the word of God continued to spread . . . a great many of the priests became obedient to the faith" (Acts 6:7). He also mentions disciples "who belonged to the sect of the Pharisees" (15:5).

The "Followers of the Way"

Jesus' disciples did not identify themselves as "Christians," although their opponents began to do so by sometime in the 40s or 50s. Luke's name for the group is the "followers of the Way," which may very well be an early group self-identification within the broader stream of Judaism. The moniker alludes to a traditional Jewish ethical framework that scholars call the Two Ways doctrine. Every human being has conflicting inclinations toward goodness (*yetzer ha tov*) and toward evil (*yetzer ha ra'*). The way of goodness brings life, while the way of evil brings death. Each individual must choose one of these two ways. For Luke and the early disciples, the Jesus-Way becomes identified with the path of goodness and life. One follows the Jesus-Way by imitating Jesus' life and living his word.

Since following Jesus' Way means continuing Jesus' work, Luke illustrates parallels between the disciples' initial experiences and those of Jesus, including miracles, arrests, and trials. While Luke's style of storytelling no doubt has influenced the details somewhat, the basic facts are credible. Paul reports the same kinds of occurrences when giving biographical details in his letters to various communities of disciples. Luke claims that the same Temple officials who had opposed Jesus were upset when Jesus' followers began preaching about him and working miracles in his name

(Acts 3–4). In particular, several members of the high-priestly family are named as opposing the movement (Acts 4:6). Again, details of speeches and conversations are not historically verifiable, but the basic account is a quite plausible reconstruction of the wary and watchful attitude that the Judean elite necessarily adopted in order to survive as underlings in the Roman political structure. Paul's few remarks about the environment in Jerusalem bear out this same kind of suspicious but not overtly antagonistic attitude among the Jewish leaders there.

Although external relations with other Jewish groups dominate the early chapters of Acts, Luke mentions some distinctive practices of the new community, which again are corroborated by remarks in the letters of Paul. Believers shared in daily prayer at the Temple—or, beyond the city of Jerusalem, in synagogues—and also met for a common meal "at home" (*kat' oikon*, an early reference to the "house-churches"; 2:46), where they "devoted themselves to the apostles' teaching and fellowship, to the breaking of bread and the prayers" (2:42). This historical reference to "house-church" meetings, as they later came to be called, provides an important demographic detail: at least some believers were wealthy, aristocratic householders with formal dining spaces in their homes large enough to accommodate such meetings.

Luke suggests that these early believers supported one another by holding property "in common"; those with possessions sold them and distributed the proceeds to all those who had need (Acts 2:44–45; 4:34–35). Sometimes this remark is read as implying that *all* disciples who owned property divested themselves of *all* their possessions at once and gave the proceeds to the common fund. Then the story of Ananias and Sapphira (Acts 5:1–11; cf. 2 Sam. 6:6–7) is used to illustrate the radical nature of this early practice. However, this must be a misunderstanding, since it would contradict what Luke previously said about the house-church meals. What Luke appears to be saying is that wealthy members of the community viewed their possessions as communal property and supported the poorer members out of their own funds, even selling possessions when necessary to meet existing needs. Once again, this scenario fits quite well with Paul's remarks about how communal life should work. Luke seems to think the funds were handed over to the ecclesial leaders

to distribute when needed, although Paul's letters suggest that sometimes the householders provided funds for particular needs as they
arose. Other Jewish groups like the Essenes, the community of the
Dead Sea Scrolls, and the Therapeutae practiced a similar form of
community property.[3]

However the funds were distributed, this practice is not quite
the "common purse" that Jesus and his itinerant disciples are said to
have had (e.g., John 13:29), but one other aspect of this "community
property" ideal does seem to have functioned in the same way among
Jesus' first-generation disciples as it did for Jesus himself: support
for itinerant preachers and prophets. When traveling from town to
town, missionaries like Paul relied on the hospitality of believers in
whatever place they were visiting. A non-canonical work called the
Didache implies that this continued to be standard practice through
the end of the first century.[4]

The community of disciples continued to grow apace—although
Luke's claim (Acts 4:4) that their number reached "about five thousand" within the first few weeks is clearly hyperbolic. One reason
Luke gives for such popularity with the people is that the disciples—
again paralleling the work of Jesus—did healing miracles in Jesus'
name; this claim also is corroborated by Paul (e.g., Rom. 15:19; 2
Cor. 12:12). Neither Luke nor Paul suggests that the community
property ideal drew people to the Jesus-Way—they simply view it as
an inherent feature of communal life among the disciples—but social
historians certainly would highlight this as a key attraction for persons in the lower echelons of Roman society. With no social welfare
programs to provide a "safety net" for those who were unemployed,
disabled, ill, or otherwise disadvantaged, a community that made a
point of ensuring that every member was taken care of would have
great appeal.

The Temple authorities are said to have had several disciples arrested and flogged for preaching about Jesus (Acts 5). Those
arrested considered it a mark of honor to have suffered "for the sake
of the name" (Acts 5:41).

---

3. Josephus, *Jewish Antiquities* 18.1.5.

4. Although that author, in order to prevent the community being duped by charlatans, establishes a three-day term limit for visitor support.

The "Hellenists" and the "Gentile Question"

Luke next recounts a very controversial passage. "Now during those days, when the disciples were increasing in number, the Hellenists complained against the Hebrews because their widows were being neglected in the daily distribution of food" (Acts 6:1). So the Twelve met, decided that they could not "neglect the word of God in order to wait on tables" (6:2), and told the "friends" (the Hellenists) to choose seven of their number to deal with the task. The number seven here is probably figurative since it was thought to signify perfection. Luke says that the community chose seven men, all with Greek names, to service. The Greek word for "one who serves," *diakonos*, would eventually refer to one who held a specific ecclesial office, that of deacon. Given that the central celebration of Jesus' disciples was a memorial meal, this means that the "deacons" are thought to have been the ones who distributed the food at these banquets.

Luke's account does not work well. Luke says that the Twelve did not want to neglect the word of God to wait on tables, implying that they were already overworked. But if that were the case, why was not the entire community affected rather than only the Hellenist widows? Is it possible that these widows were separated as a group? Luke does not say. Moreover, if the Seven were to serve at tables so the Twelve could serve the word of God, why does Luke not show them engaged in table service? In fact, the very next passage shows Stephen, one of the Seven, preaching. This suggests that Luke is making an artificial distinction here and that the Hellenist leaders both preached and served at table.

Scholars have advanced literally dozens of explanations for the Hellenists. The consensus is that they were Greek-speaking Diaspora Jews and proselytes who had accepted the gospel of Jesus. The "Hebrews" were Jews living in the land of Israel who spoke Aramaic, a Semitic vernacular close to Hebrew. At the time, most Jews in the land of Israel spoke Aramaic, although Hebrew survived in religious services. While it is unlikely that there was a formal or structural separation, both groups were recognizably distinct. Did the two groups remain aloof from one another, or did the leaders in Jerusalem introduce division into the community, although Luke stridently insists it was unified? And was the difference between the two groups simply a practical issue that was easy to solve, as Luke seems to suggest (i.e., taking care of the widows), or were there deeper differences? But could there be such deep differences in the community only weeks after Jesus' death? Given that Luke wrote a half century later, he may be reading later controversies back into this early period.

Even so, Luke may not be that far off the mark. It is known that already in the 40s there was a significant point of contention between the Judean Christians (the "Hebrews") and those outside of the Holy Land, and it did pertain to eating practices. Both Acts 15 and Galatians 2 mention a significant disagreement over whether or not disciples who were kosher Jews could eat with Gentile converts who did not keep kosher. Paul says that he and Peter had a public dispute about this in front of the *ecclesia* in Syrian Antioch, during which Paul accused Peter of hypocrisy for refusing to eat the same food and at the same table as the Gentile disciples (Gal. 2:11–14). This was an issue of paramount importance precisely because the central act of community gatherings was to share a meal in memory of Jesus. It may seem far-fetched that Luke could portray such a deep difference appearing within weeks of Jesus' execution, but in fact this issue about Jewish-Gentile relations, especially in regard to eating practices pre-existed the Jesus movement. A long-standing problem of such magnitude was bound to surface sooner rather than later among the followers of the Way.

According to Luke, one of the Hellenists, Stephen, antagonized the religious authorities in Jerusalem and was arrested. Stephen then gave a very offensive speech to the Jewish leaders, repudiating the validity of the Temple and accusing them and their ancestors of opposing the Holy Spirit, killing the prophets, and murdering the Righteous One whom the prophets foretold (Acts 7).[5]

Abandoning both politics and law (only the Roman officials could authorize a legal execution), the Jewish leaders dragged Stephen outside the city and stoned him to death, making him the first martyr of the Jesus movement (ca. 33 CE). To hint at what will come in the second half of Acts, Luke adds a small detail: those who stoned Stephen laid their coats at the feet of a young man named Saul, who approved of the killing.

---

5. This is a good example of ancient historiography. Luke was not at the speech—if Stephen even gave one—yet it is perfectly acceptable for Luke to create a speech vividly portraying Stephen saying what Luke thinks he should, would, or could have said.

Luke clearly has paralleled Stephen's trial and execution with that of Jesus. Most strikingly, Stephen's prayer for forgiveness for those who are putting him to death echoes Jesus' last words on the cross (Luke 23:34).[6] The parallel between Stephen and Jesus emphasizes Luke's view that the community of disciples continued the work of their Lord. Still, allowing for that literary device, why was one of the Hellenists the first of Jesus' followers to be executed? Was Stephen's message more offensive than that of the "Hebrews"? Luke seems to think so, if you compare this speech with those attributed to Peter.

Was the content of Stephen's message also a point of separation between the Hellenists and "Hebrews" within the community of disciples? Did the Hellenists hold the view so strongly defended later by Paul, that Gentiles who accepted the gospel did not have to become circumcised and follow all of the Jewish laws? Is that what enraged both the "Hebrews" and the Jewish authorities? Luke hints that this was the case when he depicts Stephen preaching against the Temple itself.

Luke claims that, after Stephen's death, "a severe persecution began against the church in Jerusalem, and all except the apostles were scattered throughout the countryside of Judea and Samaria" (Acts 8:1). This is undoubtedly overstated and anachronistic. How could the Jewish leaders have started a persecution, when the Romans would have objected to such a disruption of the peace? And why not persecute "the apostles," the recognized leaders of the community? Even though Luke says that "all except the apostles were scattered throughout the countryside," in fact he only mentions one person who was driven out, and that was Philip, a Hellenist who was one of the Seven.

It is difficult to decipher exactly what happened. Luke must have known that disciples of Jesus lived "throughout the countryside" of Judea and beyond. The earlier evangelists (Mark and Matthew) portray Jesus' death as the impetus for this dispersion. Luke, however, recognizes the formal origins of the *ecclesia* as rooted in Jewish tradition, and reinforces this point by showing the first community of disciples arising and planting roots in Jerusalem after the death-Resurrection of Jesus. Luke then must find another event significant enough to spur many of those disciples to leave the

---

6. The passage appears only in Luke's Gospel. Some have questioned its authenticity (i.e., whether it originally belonged to Luke's Gospel).

Holy City. Stephen's lynching, viewed as part of a wider reaction against Jesus' followers, serves the purpose.

Developing Evangelism of Non-Jews

Philip is then said to have evangelized in Samaria, home of a people who were hated by the Judeans as apostate Jews, heretics who opposed the true (i.e., Judean) interpretation of Torah and rejected Judean claims regarding the uniqueness of the Jerusalem Temple. Given this antipathy between the Judeans and Samaritans, the clear rejection of the Jerusalem Temple mentioned in Stephen's speech would make the Hellenists' version of the gospel more easily accepted there. In Samaria Philip is said to have met a magician named Simon, who was impressed by the miracles Philip performed.[7] Luke says that several Samaritans, including Simon, received baptism, but does not mention what they were expected to do next (Acts 8:12–13). Were they supposed to follow the Jewish laws in the same way as the believers in Jerusalem who met in the Temple? Were they following a Samaritan interpretation of the law instead? Or were they not expected to be law-observant? If Luke knew, he did not feel compelled to mention it.

Emphasizing the unity of these early believers, Luke says the Jerusalem community dispatched Peter and John to Samaria. (While Luke seems to want the reader to believe this had to do with fellowship between the mother-church in Jerusalem and the new community, it could be construed as a means of making sure this Hellenist in Samaria was doing everything right.) Philip had baptized the Samaritans "in the Name of the Lord Jesus," but "as yet the Spirit had not come upon any of them" (Acts 8:16).[8] Luke says that "Peter and John laid their hands on them, and they received the Holy Spirit" (Acts 8:17). Is he implying that the Judean understanding of the Jesus-tradition is more complete than that of the Hellenists? That remains unclear, but there is no mention that they asked the converts to conform to the Judean interpretation of Torah. Nothing specific is known about the faith in Samaria after these events.

---

7. In fact, Simon was so impressed that he wanted to buy Philip's "magical" secret, hence the origins of the term "simony" for the selling of church offices.

8. This distinction between baptism in the name of Jesus and baptism in the Holy Spirit has not previously appeared in Acts and is not explained here.

Later Luke makes it clear that the Apostle Paul had to struggle (not very successfully) for years to convince the Jerusalem community that the gospel message should be readily available to Gentiles without requiring them to conform to Jewish law. Paul's letters confirm this—and demonstrate that he himself struggled deeply with the question. It is inconceivable that, almost immediately after the death of Jesus, the Hellenists had arrived at the solution that Jesus' followers did not have to follow the regulations of Jewish law, when Paul and others had to struggle with this issue for years. Nor is it likely that the leaders of the Jerusalem community accepted the Hellenists' view so readily. Luke's account may reflect one aspect of the historical situation, but it cannot be the entire story.

Since many Diaspora Jews went to Jerusalem at some point in their lives, there not only were converts to the Jesus movement who were not Jews by birth but also Jews who had frequent contacts with Gentiles and believed that the gospel should reach out to them. Probably there were even Gentiles in Jerusalem who heard the first preaching by the disciples. It is not impossible that even at this early date sympathy existed for a mission to the Gentiles that would not require acceptance of the kinds of Jewish practices that might deter converts (e.g., circumcision and kosher dietary laws).

Another, more likely possibility is that the fact preceded the theory. Luke shows that, beyond a certain point, the message about Jesus as Messiah was not well received by the people of Jerusalem, and some of Jesus' followers, perhaps especially Hellenists like Philip, found Gentile areas more amenable. When such exiles encountered a certain curiosity about the events in Jerusalem there is no reason to think that they declined to preach to Samaritans and to Gentiles. If they did not know it beforehand, these preachers would soon have realized that requiring certain Jewish practices would pose obstacles to converting Gentiles. Given that there had been Jewish missionaries before this time, it is likely that the disciples were aware of such obstacles before they even began this mission. However, only after they recognized the extent of Gentile interest in the gospel did the earliest believers begin to give systematic consideration to the nature of a Gentile mission.

After mentioning the spread of the disciples beyond the Holy City, Luke moves his account out of Jerusalem and into heavily Gentile areas such as Lydda, Joppa, Caesarea, Damascus and, most importantly, Antioch of Syria. Thereafter, Jerusalem reappears in Acts only when prominent apostles go there (e.g., Peter and especially Paul).

James "the Just" and the Jerusalem Community

The church historian Eusebius of Caesarea (*fl.* ca. 310) records one further detail about the Jerusalem community. He says that after Jesus' ascension, Peter, James, and John humbly declined to assert the honor Jesus had shown them (e.g., choosing them to be with him at the Transfiguration and at Gethsemane) and instead chose James the Righteous to be bishop of Jerusalem—that is, James bar Joseph, the brother of Jesus (Mark 6:3; Gal. 1:19). The choice of James as "bishop" of Jerusalem cannot be accurate. It presumes a structured community in existence within weeks of Jesus' ascension. It also contradicts Acts, which shows a variety of leadership models: sometimes the Twelve take charge (Acts 6), sometimes the whole community is involved in making choices (Acts 2), and sometimes it is the trio of James, John, and Peter (Acts 15). Clearly, Eusebius is reading the situation of his day—that is, an "episcopal" (bishop-centered) church structure—backwards to the first century.

Nevertheless, Eusebius may be correct in placing the choice of James the Righteous as leader of the Jerusalem community in this decade. One cannot be certain when James acquired this role, but it could have been in the late 30s, especially if the Twelve already had left the city. None of them appears in Jerusalem again except Peter and John, but by then James the Righteous already heads the community. This second James makes his first actual appearance in Acts (12:17) only after Peter has returned from Caesarea and after James ben Zebedee (of the Twelve) has been martyred (12:1–2). That event occurred in 41 CE, but James bar Joseph already is accepted by Peter as the leader of the Jerusalem community and as one to whom he felt obliged to report. Peter's show of respect suggests James the Righteous had been leading the Jerusalem community for some time.

Scholars have wondered if James bar Joseph used his blood relationship as a claim to office. To be sure, the primacy of blood relationship repeatedly is rejected in the New Testament, and Mark phrases it bluntly: "And . . . [Jesus] said, 'Here are my mother and my brothers! Whoever does the will of God is my brother and sister and mother'" (3:34–35). However, all the Gospels were written decades after James assumed leadership. Furthermore, Eusebius says that when James died (in the 60s), "Symeon, the son of [James'] uncle Clopas, was appointed bishop."[9] Possibly a blood relationship did count in the Jerusalem community, especially since the Jewish priests were supposed to be descendants of Aaron, the brother of Moses and first of the Israelite priests.[10]

On the other hand, James also had personal qualities to recommend him. Eusebius preserves a tradition that James "was holy from his birth; he drank no wine or intoxicating liquor and ate no animal food; no razor came near his head; he did not smear himself with oil, and took no baths. . . . He was often found on his knees (in the sanctuary of the Temple) beseeching forgiveness for the people, so that his knees grew hard like a camel's from his continually bending them in worship of God and beseeching forgiveness for the people."[11] The description suggests that James was a Nazirite, that is, a Jewish man specially committed to God and manifesting that commitment by abstention from certain foods and drink and from cutting his hair. This is why James bar Joseph was given the nickname "the Righteous."

Whether or not the details of this description are accurate, Eusebius still witnesses to James' reputation for sanctity. The Jewish historian Josephus also acknowledged the esteem James bar Joseph enjoyed among the people of Jerusalem.

James the Righteous may have been chosen because of his personal qualities, and possibly in these early days of uncertainty when the community was groping for a structure, blood ties carried more weight than they would later. Most likely James could combine personal qualities with family ties.

The Growing Mission to Non-Jews

Luke next turns to events outside Jerusalem. With the infallibility of hindsight, one can see the historical importance of the Gentile

---

9. *Ecclesiastical History* 4.22.

10. Josephus, *Jewish Antiquities* 20.1.

11. *Ecclesiastical History* 2.23.

mission in terms of the growth of the Jesus movement, both in numbers and geographically, but it also had an enormous effect upon Christology, the community of disciples' understanding of Jesus as God's Messiah (Christ, Anointed One). In Acts 2, Luke has Peter give an address to the people of Jerusalem about "Jesus of Nazareth, a man attested to you by God with deeds of power, wonders, and signs that God did through him among you, as you yourselves know" (2:22). The people of Jerusalem and of Galilee knew the historical Jesus, but the Gentiles did not. Missionaries to the Gentiles would preach a different Christ; in future, "Christ is proclaimed as raised from the dead" (1 Cor. 15:12). The post-Resurrection Christ became so central to the message that modern scholars believe that the historical Jesus was virtually lost in the image of the risen one. Paul would be the great preacher of Christ crucified and raised from the dead (1 Cor 1:23), with hardly a quote of Jesus' teachings nor reference to events in Jesus' earthly ministry. Although one cannot know what other missionaries to the Gentiles of this first decade preached, the risen Christ seems a more likely choice than the historical one. In addition, it is very likely that, when the disciples preached about Jesus' miracles and Resurrection, the Gentiles in their audience heard a different message than the preachers intended. The "superman" idea familiar to them from the Greco-Roman mystery cults would have led Gentiles to view Jesus as a "divine man" and wonder-worker. The historical Jesus could easily get lost in the shuffle.

The Evangelist Philip

Luke claims that the evangelist Philip did not stop with the Samaritans. Along the road, he met and converted the treasurer to the royal court of Queen Candace of Ethiopia. It seems that the man already was a Jew or a proselyte (a Gentile in the process of converting to Judaism); Luke even claims that he was studying the book of the prophet Isaiah as he traveled (Acts 8:26–39). While the account is probably somewhat exaggerated, it does suggest that evangelists outside Judea initially targeted other Jews. But at Azotus, Caesarea Maritima, and other coastal towns (8:40), Philip—or the missionaries he personifies—evangelized in heavily Gentile areas.

The fourth chapter of John describes a dialogue between Jesus and a local woman at Jacob's Well in Sychar in Samaria. Some scholars believe this passage preserves echoes of an early mission to the Samaritans. A church was subsequently constructed around the supposed site. The above photo shows Jacob's Well as it appears today.

The Samaritan Woman

The Gospel of John may preserve some other evidence of a mission to the Samaritans. In John 4:1–42, Jesus encounters a Samaritan woman at Jacob's well. This account reflects John's theological and literary concerns, and scholars question whether it is historical. But verse 39 says, "Many Samaritans from [the woman's] city believed in him because of the woman's testimony." Hence it is likely that John's Gospel witnesses to the role of women in the conversion of the Samaritans, with the unnamed Samaritan woman, like Philip, symbolizing the work of several missionaries.

Tabitha and the "Widows"

Early in Acts, Luke stresses the continuity of the work of the apostles with the work of Jesus, and he transfers this theme to the budding Gentile mission. Peter has moved from Jerusalem to the coastal cities of Joppa and then Lydda, where Christian communities already existed (Acts 9:32–43). He performed miracles among them, including raising a woman named Tabitha (Dorcas in Greek) from the dead, again continuing the work of Jesus (cf. Luke 8:40–42, 49–56). Luke says Tabitha was a disciple known for personal works of charity such as making garments for "the widows." "Widow" eventually became a technical term among the early Christians, but Luke does not make it clear whether these widows belonged to an already recognizably defined group in the community. Since Acts 6 speaks of the distribution of food to Hebrew and Hellenistic widows, the order of widows may actually go back to the earliest days of the Jesus movement. (The first indisputable mention of the order of widows appears in 1 Timothy 5:3–16, written ca. 100.)

Peter and Cornelius, the Centurion

Luke's real interest now, however, lies with Peter. Having established by the miracles that Peter walked in the footsteps of Jesus, Luke now enlists Peter in support of the mission to Gentiles by reporting that he converted a Roman centurion named Cornelius and baptized him and his family without requiring them to follow Jewish kosher practices. Peter initially did not wish to do so, but a heavenly vision told him, "What God has made clean, you must not call profane" (10:15). The vision involved the non-kosher foods eaten by Gentiles, but the analogy to the Gentiles themselves is unmistakable. This story makes it clear to the reader that God stands behind the Gentile mission; when Peter reported these events to the Jerusalem community (11:1–18), those who had doubts "were silenced."

In this same decade the faith spread rapidly outside Judea, going "as far as Phoenicia, Cyprus, and Antioch" in Syria (11:19), where Luke says the disciples preached only to Jews. However, Gentiles also heard the message, and some approached the preachers about conversion. The question could not be avoided. Luke provides no details about the work in Phoenicia or Cyprus but concentrates instead on Antioch in Syria.

Barnabas of Cyprus

The Jerusalem community (James?) sent a wealthy Cypriot man named Barnabas to evaluate the situation at Antioch, the first place where Jesus' followers were called "Christians" (11:26). Perhaps Gentiles, not knowing the significance of the term *Christos*, thought of Christ as a surname and then used "Christian" to refer to those people who revered Jesus. It probably had a negative connotation at first: note that within the New Testament, followers of Jesus never use the term.

Barnabas of Cyprus appeared earlier in Acts as a wealthy Jewish benefactor who sold a field and donated the proceeds to the Jerusalem community (4:36–37). He may have had relatives in the Holy City. Colossians 4:10 calls Mark a cousin of Barnabas; Acts 12:12–17 speaks of the mother of Mark who owned a house in Jerusalem. If both texts refer to the same Mark—which is likely since the pseudonymous author of Colossians is trying to establish a connection with Paul's missionary companion, John Mark—then Barnabas did have relatives in Jerusalem. Luke tells us that Mark's mother owned a large house and slaves, details consistent with his picture of Barnabas as both wealthy and owning land in Palestine. That both families owned property shows that some aristocratic Jews did accept the message about Jesus, and indirectly illustrates how important it was for the early communities to have wealthy benefactors who offered space for gatherings and financial support for missionary work. (Eusebius identifies Barnabas as one of the seventy disciples sent out by Jesus in Luke 10:1–12—highly unlikely, given that Barnabas' home was on Cyprus.)[12]

Clearly, Barnabas had considerable stature in the Jerusalem community to be the ambassador to Antioch, but he quickly was overshadowed by a figure with whose name he is inseparably linked. Antioch in Syria provided the base of operations for perhaps the most important missionary to the Gentiles and undoubtedly the most controversial figure of the first generation of Christians: Paul of Tarsus.

Paul of Tarsus

Paul was a Jew from the town of Tarsus in Cilicia, a smaller region within the Roman province of Asia. Otherwise known as Asia

---

12. Ibid., 2.1.

Minor, this province encompassed the territory bordered by the Baltic Sea at the north, the Mediterranean to the south, the Aegean Sea to the west, and Armenia and Syria to the east. Cilicia was on the southern border of the province, along the Mediterranean coast, and ran roughly from the center to the eastern border of Asia. Tarsus itself was a coastal city toward the eastern end of the Mediterranean.

Born in Asia Minor, Paul was a Jew of the Diaspora, descended of the tribe of Benjamin, and educated as an interpreter and a strict observer of the Torah as understood by the Pharisaic tradition. Even after his call to be a Christian missionary, Paul viewed his previous lifestyle as "blameless" under the law (Phil. 3:4–6).

Paul first appears in Acts under the name Saul. Luke places him at the martyrdom of Stephen, standing by and watching the cloaks of those who were doing the stoning (7:58–8:1). That Saul approved of this act is clear from his tacit support of the executioners, but his non-participation in the act suggests he was too young to carry out the sentence being imposed by his elders.

Paul was a staunch Jew of the Pharisee tradition, trained in the Jewish scriptures and "zealous for the traditions" of his ancestors (Gal. 1:14). By his own admission, Paul's initial opposition to the Jesus movement was extreme (Gal. 1:13), but he experienced a vision of the risen Lord, which transformed his attitude toward Jesus and his entire life (ca. 35 CE). This revelation from God is sometimes called Paul's "conversion" experience, but this is a misnomer that derives not from Paul but from the vivid accounts in Acts, a secondary source, which should not be given precedence over the letters. Paul himself indicates that he viewed this not as a conversion event and rejection of his previous life, but rather a call experience akin to those of the Hebrew prophets (Gal. 1:12, 15–16). For Paul, it was a continuation of God's action in his life via the commission to preach Christ to the Gentiles. As is true of the other disciples—and of Jesus himself—Paul never abandoned his Judaism. Paul did cease being a Pharisee, but he continued to view himself as a Jew and tried to reconcile his belief in Jesus with the faith of his ancestors. Zealous as ever, Paul became a missionary for Jesus, preaching the message that he was the long-awaited Messiah of Israel who had inaugurated the final age in God's plan, the age of divine judgment upon evil and justice for God's holy ones.

The period of Paul's life right after this visionary experience is shrouded in fog. Luke says that Paul was baptized by Ananias, a Christian leader from Damascus, and that Paul immediately began preaching about Jesus in the synagogues there, "saying, 'He is the Son of God'" (Acts 9:20). After leaving Damascus (ca. 39 CE), Luke says Paul went to join the Jerusalem community—which was none too eager to accept him; they eventually made room for Paul after Barnabas vouched for his sincerity (Acts 9:26–28). Paul, however, contradicts this account at every point. Paul claims that, after his vision, "I did not confer with any human being, nor did I go up to Jerusalem to those who were already apostles before me, but I went away at once into Arabia, and afterwards I returned to Damascus" (Gal. 1:16–17).

Most likely both of our witnesses are exaggerating a bit, Paul to distance himself from the leaders in Jerusalem and validate his message on its own merits, and Luke to demonstrate that Paul was more cooperative with (and submissive to) the Jerusalem community than some—including Paul—would have us believe. For Paul, the divine origins of his message had to be ensured by distinguishing it from the faith as taught at Jerusalem, while his divinely sanctioned authority as an apostle could only be guaranteed by illustrating that he was sent by God directly, not by the leaders there (especially James). For Luke, on the other hand, the divine origins of the gospel were validated by the cooperation and unity of its teachers. The best reconstruction, given these two conflicting reports, is that Paul indeed was baptized in Damascus or Antioch, studied and preached the faith there for two or three years, and then went to Jerusalem for a consultation with Peter and James the Righteous.

In spite of his protests of independence from the Jerusalem leadership (e.g., Gal. 1:1, 12), Paul admits the high stakes of this meeting: "I laid before them . . . the gospel that I proclaim among the Gentiles, in order to make sure that I was not running, or had not run, in vain" (Gal. 2:2). Was his circumcision-free gospel legitimate or not? Paul insists a partnership agreement was reached by which the "pillars" of the Jerusalem *ecclesia* showed their support of Paul's gospel (Gal. 2:9), imposing only one condition—"that we remember the poor, which was actually what I was eager to do" (Gal. 2:10). The story in Acts, however, is more circumspect. There is no explicit mention of a partnership between Jerusalem and Paul, and further conditions are imposed upon the Gentile disciples: "Abstain from what has been sacrificed to idols and from blood and from what is strangled and from fornication" (Acts 15:29a). This implies that the Jerusalem *ecclesia* viewed Paul's gospel—which laid on Gentiles no obligation to follow Jewish law—was not entirely sufficient. Paul returned to Syria, and Antioch became the home base for the missionary trips Paul would take in the next decade.

Summary

Jesus did not have the kind of long, successful career as "Savior" that Augustus Caesar did. In fact, it was not until after his death that the understanding of Jesus as savior really began to "catch on" with a wide group of people. Whereas Caesar left a record of his accomplishments (*res gestae*) prominently displayed for public consumption, Jesus' most public display involved his death on the cross. Rather than leaving the wider world with the joyful memory of an end to civil strife, Jesus left the world with the painful memory of a crucified "messiah." Hopes dashed, Jesus' disciples seem to have disbanded after Jesus' death. When Jesus later "appeared" to a number of his followers, they began proclaiming the Resurrection (that God had raised Jesus from the dead). The disciples' experience of the Resurrection convinced them that Jesus had been raised to fullness of life, thereby giving the impetus for a revival of the "Jesus movement" and proclamation of the gospel among the nations and Jews who lived in the Diaspora (outside the Holy Land).

Data in the Acts of the Apostles cannot be used in an unquestioning manner, but there is ample evidence concerning the growth of the early *ecclesia*. This author emphasizes the disciples sharing communal resources and a common way of life, and appears to underestimate disagreements among the Christ-believers. This understatement is apparent when comparing Acts with the evidence from the letters of Paul.

Whether one follows Paul or Acts, one can see that the disciples pursued some activities common to first-century religions (e.g., a common meal). Nascent "Christianity" also had some relatively distinctive features, including *glossolalia* (speaking in tongues), the Agape meal or Eucharist ("Lord's Supper"), and baptism (a ritual bath marking one's conversion and entrance into the community of believers). Leaders of the group (e.g., James, Phoebe) spread the good news and represented this religious group to the wider world. Although not yet great in numbers, Christ-believers came from all levels of society, with male aristocrats apparently the least well-represented demographic group. At this point, the *ecclesia* continued to escape immediate and widespread notice because it blended well with first-century Judaism. Converts to the movement were adopting a version of Judaism; in fact, many of the early Christ-believers continued to participate in Jewish festivals, synagogue services, and other aspects of Jewish communal life. Surprising growth in the number of Gentile converts provoked the question of the community's relationship to Israel—often called the "circumcision question." The New Testament authors provide different responses to this question, which increased in urgency as the first century progressed.

Thus the growth of Christianity, as it would later be called, after Jesus' death represents a remarkable feat from the perspective of religious history. This religious movement outlived its publicly humiliated leader, whom the rest of the world despised, and spread far beyond Judea into Asia Minor, Italy, Egypt, and elsewhere. This religion was an integral part of the disciples' life, with ramifications for politics, economics, and social relations. Thus began the legacy of Jesus of Nazareth, "Christ crucified and raised from the dead."[13]

Questions for Review

1. Why was the Resurrection of Jesus crucial to the Jesus movement? What did it signify for followers of Jesus?

2. According to Luke's Gospel, the early followers of Jesus were centered in Jerusalem in the years following Jesus' Resurrection. Describe the makeup of this community and its activities.

3. Why, in the book of Acts, are the early followers of Jesus concerned to choose a replacement for Judas? What criteria must the replacement meet and why?

---

13. Cf. Acts 4:10. The expression summarizes a key theme of the Pauline letters.

4. The Acts account indicates that members of the early Jesus movement were called "followers of the Way." What did that expression mean? How does it compare with the contemporary term "Christians"?

5. What can one infer about the demographics of the early "followers of the Way"?

6. Who was James the Just? What was his significance?

7. What was a "divine man"? Why is the concept important within the context of the early Jesus movement?

8. What is the significance of the Acts (chapter 10) account of the conversion of a Roman centurion?

Questions for Discussion

1. The first followers of Jesus were convinced that God had raised him from the dead. What did this claim mean in the context of first-century Judaism? What are the similarities and differences between this claim and the belief that one's soul survives after death?

2. An ongoing question within Christian circles is whether, or to what extent, the beliefs and practices of the first disciples should be considered normative for all Christians throughout time. According to Acts, the early "followers of the Way" shared their goods freely with needy members of their community. What evidence can be used to discern the historical accuracy of this tradition? If the tradition is historical, does this mean that today's Christians are obligated to do likewise?

3. Scholars think that when Jesus' followers began to spread into the Gentile world, their message tended to shift from the message *of* Jesus to a message *about* Jesus, including a claim for his personal divine status. Does this seem plausible? Why or why not?

4. Paul and other early evangelists of the "Hellenist" persuasion argued that Gentiles who wished to join the Jesus movement should not be required to observe the entire Torah. How did this affect the ultimate course of Christianity? What would Christianity look like had this step not been taken?

CHAPTER 4

Early Missionary Expansion
(41–50 CE)

This decade is the least well-known of the first Christian century, although it is crucially important for three reasons. First, it is the time when Jesus' followers begin to make a collection of his sayings (now called "Q"), as well as collections of the stories of Jesus' miraculous deeds and of the events surrounding his arrest and execution. Second, this is when the Apostle Paul began his missionary journeys beyond the Arabian Peninsula. Finally, it is the first time that larger political events began to have a substantive effect upon the nascent movement.

The Roman Empire, through the person of Pontius Pilate, had executed Jesus, but the Romans fade from the picture in the first decade after the death of Jesus. The book of Acts presents the picture of the Jesus movement as a community that could safely go in public and proclaim its message. The only people who take action against Jesus' followers belong to the same group that attacked Jesus, that is, the Jewish leaders in Jerusalem. (As in the Gospel, Luke makes it clear that the citizens of Jerusalem as a whole did not reject Jesus or his disciples, but the ruling parties feared them.) Acts portrays Stephen's martyrdom as a mob action, and does not explain how the persecution mentioned in Acts 8 got started or if anyone controlled it. The only "persecutor" Luke describes in any detail is Saul (Paul of Tarsus), and the historical reliability of that portrait is questionable.

In the next decade, however, things changed, both in Jerusalem and in Rome. They changed in Jerusalem because of the growth of the Jesus movement. One may safely discount Luke's exaggerated numbers (Acts 2:41; 4:4), but these probably reflect a considerable increase in the number of disciples, possibly to the alarm of the authorities.

Rulers in Jerusalem and Rome

In this decade, Jerusalem had a new ruler, the Jewish king Marcus Julius Agrippa, better known as Herod Agrippa I.[1] Agrippa's ancestors included the illustrious Maccabees and the notorious Herod the Great. Agrippa's father Aristobulus (whom Herod murdered in 7 BCE) was Herod's son by the beloved Hasmonean princess Mariamme. At about the age of six, Agrippa was sent to Rome for upbringing—and perhaps for safe-keeping. Agrippa enjoyed life in the capital city, living in the imperial court, making many useful contacts, and becoming friendly with the imperial family. He lived prodigally as a young man and returned in some disgrace to his homeland, earning the anger of his uncle and brother-in-law, Herod Antipas, Rome's Jewish appointee as "tetrarch" of Galilee.[2] Agrippa did not stay long in Jerusalem but returned to Rome and made the friendship of the Prince Gaius, better known to posterity by the nickname given him by his father's soldiers: Caligula ("little boots."). It was an opportune friendship.

© PLRANG / www.shutterstock.com

Emperor Gaius Caligula

---

1. Agrippa I lived 10 BCE–44 CE, and reigned over various territories in the Jewish homeland from 37 CE until his death.

2. Antipas is identified in the canonical Gospels as the ruler who ordered the execution of John the Baptist.

Heir to the throne, Gaius Caligula did not care to wait for the Emperor Tiberius to die, so he murdered him in 37 CE. Caligula named his friend Agrippa as ruler over the territories formerly governed by Lysanias and Agrippa's uncle Philip (regions in modern-day Syria and Lebanon). Agrippa soon accused Herod Antipas of treachery to Rome. Caligula believed the charge, exiled Antipas, and gave that territory to Agrippa as well.

If not mentally deranged at the time of his accession, Caligula had surely become so by the year 40, insisting on his own divinity and engaging in rash and even dangerous acts. Jewish law expressly forbade the making of images as idolatrous, but Caligula insisted that the Jews put up a statue of himself in the Jerusalem Temple. Agrippa knew the trouble this would cause, so he journeyed to Rome to try to pacify the emperor. But Caligula's other outrages had convinced many aristocratic Romans that his continued rule threatened the empire's welfare, and in 41 a band of conspirators assassinated him. By the time Agrippa arrived, the emperor was already dead.

Agrippa's presence in Rome proved fortuitous to another friend of his among the imperial family, a middle-aged prince named Claudius. Agrippa used his contacts with the Roman senate and his diplomatic skills to help Claudius achieve the throne. The grateful emperor, who ruled from 41–54 CE, rewarded Agrippa by significantly increasing his territory, adding Judea and Samaria. As the emperor's favorite, Herod Agrippa I ruled a territory as large as that of his grandfather, Herod the Great.

Like many members of his family, Agrippa did not take his Judaism very seriously. Too much a man of the Hellenistic and Roman worlds, he observed Jewish customs publicly but still led a life many Romans could have enjoyed; he even took part in pagan ceremonies. Nevertheless, he was loyal to his people and worked for their welfare in a way that Roman governors did not.

Yet, as a Roman appointee, he still had to convince the people that he was a legitimate ruler. Unfortunately for the Christ-followers, he chose a tyrant's method to do so: persecution of supposed enemies. Luke says, "About that time King Herod [Agrippa I] laid violent hands upon some who belonged to the church. He had James, the brother of John,[3] killed with the sword. After he saw that it

---

3. James and John were the sons of Zebedee (Mark 3:17).

pleased the Jews, he proceeded to arrest Peter also" (Acts 12:1–3). This event occurred right at the outset of the decade—a rather ominous beginning.

But why was there a persecution at all? Did Agrippa fear what Jesus' followers would do since they believed Jesus was the Messiah? Did Agrippa think they would rise up against him in Jesus' name? Then why not arrest and execute many of them? Luke says that Agrippa arrested Peter only after he saw that the execution of James ben Zebedee pleased the people, suggesting that James' arrest was an isolated event. Indeed, Agrippa seems not to have kept Peter imprisoned for long (cf. Acts 12:6–19), which reinforces the uniqueness of James' death. Was the nickname of James and John—Boanerges ("sons of Thunder"; Mark 3:17)—an indication of a more militant stance against Rome, and therefore against Agrippa? There is no reason to doubt the historicity of the basic information in this passage, but the details remain obscure.

Had King Agrippa lived, he could have caused much trouble for the disciples, but his reign lasted only three years longer. In Luke's story, the ancient Phoenician cities of Tyre and Sidon provoked Agrippa's downfall. Luke says the king was angry with the people of these pagan cities, which depended upon him for much of their food supply. The leaders of Tyre and Sidon prudently bribed the king's chamberlain and gained a public audience with Agrippa. When the king appeared at the audience in his royal robes, the pagan ambassadors hailed him as a god—a common honor ancient Near Eastern pagans bestowed upon their kings. According to Luke, Herod Agrippa did not repudiate the compliment, and the one true God retaliated: "And immediately, because he had not given the glory to God, an angel of the Lord struck him down, and he was eaten by worms and died" (Acts 12:23). The Jewish historian Josephus corroborates the basic outline of the story, but provides different details: he claims that Agrippa was in the pagan city of Caesarea, and the people who called him a god were not pagan supplicants but his own flatterers and sycophants.[4] Like Luke, Josephus sees Agrippa's death as resulting from divine retribution because he did not silence the flatterers or reject their blasphemous compliments. Josephus says that God sent not an angel but an owl—a pagan symbol—to warn

---

4. Josephus, *Antiquities* 19.8.2.343–361.

Agrippa of his impending death, which was caused by a severe stomach ailment.

King Agrippa's death took the pressure off the Jerusalem *ecclesia* for a time. Agrippa's son, Herod Agrippa II, was seventeen and living in Rome in the year 44. The Romans considered him too young to succeed to his father's territories and instead placed a Roman procurator in charge of the region for the rest of the decade. But Herod Agrippa II eventually would get territories to rule and would play a role in the history of the early Jesus movement.

Missionary Expansion among Gentiles

The 40s were a time of great missionary expansion for the fledgling Christian faith. After the stoning of Stephen (Acts 7), many Hellenistic Christians fled north to Antioch in Syria, or east to Pella in the Decapolis region, or west as far as Alexandria in Egypt. These Judean émigrés looked for cities with substantial Jewish populations and already established synagogues. According to the book of Acts, these early missionaries almost always began their evangelistic work in a particular town by preaching to Jews.

Many Jews thus heard of the Messiah Jesus, as did Gentiles who were associated with the synagogues but had not completed their conversion via circumcision. Such proselytes were known as "God-fearers." Whether women were technically included in this group is not clear. Circumcision not being possible for them, there were various ways to handle female converts—including a water-bathing ritual—and the practice varied from place to place. The most common way to become a Jewess was probably still to marry a Jewish man, or to have one's husband convert to Judaism. Women and men both were included in the "audience" at synagogues, and there is some evidence that, at least initially, Jewish women were more likely than Jewish men to accept the message of Jesus as the promised Messiah.[5]

---

5. This is particularly true of the aristocratic class. E.g., the only ministers named in Paul's letter to the Philippians are women; Lydia's conversion brought her whole household into the faith (Acts 16:13–15), which means she functioned as head of the household; Prisca apparently converted before her husband, and even before Paul (Acts 18:26); a great number of the leaders in Romans 16 are women.

The gospel message at this point comprised the claim that Jesus of Nazareth was the long-awaited Messiah of Israel, anointed as God's ambassador to bring about divine rule (the "kingdom of God") on earth. Gentiles who were not associated with the synagogues and knew nothing of the Hebrew Bible—especially the prophets—would not even have understood the message, much less accepted it. Therefore, when the New Testament sources speak of Gentiles converting to the Jesus movement, one must recognize two things:

1. They viewed themselves as converting to a new and unique form of Judaism based on the claim that Jesus fulfilled Israel's messianic hopes.
2. Many of these non-Jews already had been affiliated with Judaism as "God-fearers" or proselytes before they heard the proclamation of Jesus as Messiah.

One of the key advantages to hesitant male proselytes hearing this message was that this strand of Judaism—at least in the Diaspora—did not require circumcision for one to be included as a full participating member of the community. This lenient understanding of inclusion, however, created the anomaly that such converts were considered Jews by their fellow Christ-believers but not by other Jews who had not accepted Jesus as the Messiah. As one can imagine, this gave rise to disagreements within the Jesus-community and also between messianic and non-messianic Jews.

As already mentioned, between 35–40 CE there was a mission to Samaria. Acts 8 identifies Philip with this mission, while John 4 mentions an anonymous woman evangelist as the key figure. The openness of the Jesus movement to those considered apostate by many Judean Jews, including the Jerusalem leaders, no doubt contributed to the disagreement—known to scholars as "the Gentile problem"—over how much of the Jewish law was essential for Jesus' followers to keep. Fundamentally, the issue was whether or not converts to the Jesus movement had to take upon themselves "the yoke of the Torah" as understood by the Judean religious leaders, including the laws of kosher, circumcision, and the religious festivals that were central to this strand of Judaism.

This problem would become a major focus for Christians in the 40s, the first period of missionary expansion. The message of Jesus was taken back to hometowns in Galilee, and probably to relatives and business contacts in Egypt and Syria, and even as far away as Rome. Because of his centrality in the book of Acts, readers often tend to think of Paul as the only missionary of this period. However, that was by no means the case, nor was Paul's method the only way of spreading the Christian message. Some evangelists were merchants bringing the message of the Jewish Messiah to their patrons, clients, and friends, in much the same way that Jewish merchants had interacted with their contacts in the past. Some were itinerant prophets and preachers who traveled from town to town, relying entirely on the support and hospitality of their audiences.[6] Some took the message from one place to another and then more or less settled in that new place, as did Prisca and Aquila when they left Rome for an extended stay in Corinth (Acts 18). Some, like Paul, developed a hybrid model, traveling from place to place, but staying long enough in each one to organize a local *ecclesia*, meanwhile supporting themselves by their own labor as well as donations from their home church. There must have been dozens of unknown missionaries for every name that is known.

The House-Church

The house-church became a standard institution for centuries. Early evidence of a house-church appears in Acts 12. Luke says that an angel appeared to Peter during his escape from prison, and Peter concluded that the Lord had rescued him for a purpose. "As soon as he realized this, he went to the house of Mary, the mother of John whose other name is Mark, where many had gathered and were praying. When he knocked at the outer gate, a maid named Rhoda came to answer. On recognizing Peter's voice, she was so overjoyed that, instead of opening the gate, she ran in and announced that Peter was standing at the gate" (Acts 12:12–14). The assembled worshipers doubted her claim, thinking she had seen a ghost, but Peter kept knocking and eventually was admitted, to the surprise of all there.

The text says that they were gathered together to pray—that is, this was communal worship, often referred to as a liturgy, and it was held in a house. The first believers did not have buildings of their

---

6. Compare, for example, the mission of the seventy in Luke 10.

own specifically devoted to worship; recall that the very earliest disciples in Jerusalem met together in the Temple. Failing that, they met in private homes. Scholars call these gathering places "house-churches," but the title is misleading since it suggests that the building now used for church gatherings had once been a house. The term "house-church"—like the term "church" itself—properly applies to the congregation that meets in someone's house, rather than to the structure in which they meet. It is applied to the structure only by derivation. The earliest house "churches" continued to be houses in which people lived, but also served to host liturgies from time to time.

What did the house-churches look like? No identifiable house-church survives from the first century. A later one survives in the remains of Dura Europos, a town on the Euphrates River that the Romans held until 257 CE. House-churches of this later period have been excavated in Rome and in Britain as well. The building at Dura Europos had "a small courtyard surrounded by a room for the instruction of neophytes [newly baptized converts]; a room with a place for an altar and a bishop's throne, and large enough for fifty to sixty people; a baptistery with a canopy over the baptismal tank; and

© Zev Radovan / biblelandpictures.com

The earliest identifiable house-church is the site shown here, in Dura Europos, in Syria, dating from the first half of the third century. Only the more wealthy Christ-believers could afford houses large enough to accommodate the community gathered for worship.

rooms which were probably sacristies and store-rooms."[7] The baptistery also contained wall paintings. The appointments mentioned in this third-century house-church show a shift toward a structure specifically intended for use as a church. Earlier examples probably had none of these appointments and looked much more like an average Roman villa, but one cannot know for certain without more archaeological data.

Some literary information exists about the earliest house-churches. Luke refers to a second house-church in Acts 20:7–12, when Paul was in Troas in the northwestern corner of Asia Minor (modern Turkey). Luke says only that there were "many lamps in the room upstairs" where the meeting was going on. He also mentions that Paul stayed in the house of a wealthy convert named Lydia (16:11–15). Although he does not say if worship services were held there, that would be a logical deduction. One of Paul's letters is addressed to a husband and wife named Philemon and Apphia, who apparently were aristocratic landowners with a sizeable household, including slaves, and who hosted a house-church (Philem. 1–2).

The Role of Wealthy Believers

This sketchy evidence suggests that wealthy believers hosted the liturgies. Rhoda is a slave, implying that John Mark's mother, like Philemon and Apphia, had both property and wealth. Luke identifies Lydia as a dealer in purple dye, a rare luxury item that brought a fine price and earned great wealth for the seller. The house in Troas has a second floor and is large enough to accommodate "many lamps." Since the lamps provided illumination for more than one person each, the house could hold many people. It is only logical that wealthy believers would host the liturgies since their homes would have the room to accommodate sizeable numbers, unlike the tenement apartments of the poor.

It may at first sound surprising that the Jesus movement attracted wealthy people, for there is a persistent misconception that the early church consisted exclusively of the poor and outcast. Surely some of Jesus' followers were poor, but even in his own day, wealthy people

---

7. Peter and Linda Murray, *The Oxford Companion to Christian Art and Architecture* (Oxford and New York: Oxford University Press, 1996), 145.

attached themselves to him; in the Gospels, he often appears teaching at dinner parties. Some of these wealthy believers were Joanna, the wife of Chuza, steward of King Herod (the Jewish client-king appointed by Rome to govern the region; see Luke 8:3), and Joseph of Arimathea (Matt. 27:57).

What did the houses of the wealthy look like? "The rooms were built around a central garden court with a colonnade around the court."[8] The house would have an atrium or entrance area, rooms for dining and conversation, bedrooms for the family members, and quarters for the slaves as well as functional rooms such as kitchens. Life centered on the open area inside the house; the structure tried to insulate the wealthy from the life of the city around them.

Something else emerges from these earliest accounts of house-churches: some wealthy Christians owned slaves. Christian attitudes toward slavery will be discussed more fully in the next chapter, in conjunction with the epistle to Philemon. Here, suffice it to say that at least some wealthy Christians seem simply to have accepted slavery as a fact of life; they had never encountered a society without slavery, and probably never even asked the question of whether society could exist without it. Perhaps the educated ones followed the great Greek philosopher Aristotle (384–322 BCE), who argued that some people simply have servile natures; that is, they are, in effect, born to be enslaved by others. They also could look to the precedent of revered ancestors (even Biblical ones) who kept slaves.[9] Perhaps more important, most disciples in this period expected the imminent return of Jesus to inaugurate God's direct rule on earth.[10] Therefore, it would not be surprising if some were inclined to leave to God any structural societal changes. (Also not surprisingly, the people who thought this way were not themselves slaves.)

Women Leaders of House-Churches

The texts mentioning the house-churches also suggest that the person in whose house the community met was the one who presided at

8. Everett Ferguson, *Backgrounds of Early Christianity* (Grand Rapids: Eerdmans, 2003), 128.

9. For example, Gen. 24:35 includes slaves among Abraham's God-given possessions.

10. See, for example, Matt. 24:34; Mark 13:30; 1 Thess. 4:15.

the liturgy. The liturgical meal in the Corinthian church (see 1 Cor. 11:20–34), seems to have followed the basic pattern of a Greco-Roman symposium which would mean that the householder was in charge of the event. Luke says that the disciples were worshiping in the home of John Mark's mother, and Paul greets the church that meets in the house of Apphia and Philemon. If indeed liturgies were celebrated in the house of Lydia, that would be a third example that in the earliest communities, women sometimes provided the setting for worship, hosted the liturgies, and even presided at them—an important role which they were to lose before the end of the next century. This suggests a gender equity among the first disciples that was notably different from society at large. In addition, both Paul (1 Cor. 11:21–22, 33–34a) and the letter of James (2:1–9) explicitly call for a remarkably egalitarian attitude and practice among members of different social classes, in contradistinction to prevailing Roman and Jewish customs.

It is not known specifically what the presider at liturgy did. Luke mentions only that the disciples were praying in the house of John Mark's mother; earlier he says that they also devoted themselves "to the breaking of bread and the prayers" (Acts 2:42). It is logical to infer that the presider's role included leading the prayers at the liturgical banquet, just as the host of a symposium would offer prayers and libations to the patron deities of the city and household. The precise content of these early prayers is unknown, but it seems safe to assume that they included hymns, recitation of psalms (cf. Eph. 5:19; Col. 3:16), and blessing prayers like those common among Jews ("Blessed are you, Lord our God, King of the universe . . .").

Other Notable Leaders

Another bit of information can be gleaned from these texts. John Mark is a combination of Jewish and Roman names, which suggests that his family had some Gentile connections and possibly important ones. Clearly, they were prominent in the Christian community, since Peter is said to have gone there after his escape from prison.

John Mark appears again in several New Testament texts, twice in Acts as John (13:5, 13) and once as Mark (15:39), where he is a

companion of Paul and Barnabas on one of their missionary journeys. He is probably the Mark mentioned in Philemon 24 and in
pseudonymous letters such as Colossians 4:10, 2 Timothy 4:11, and
1 Peter 5:13. These later references provide little reliable information
about him, except that he clearly was a major figure in the early community. As will appear subsequently, other ancient traditions gave
him two additional careers.

Luke also says that in this decade "prophets came down from
Jerusalem to Antioch. One of them named Agabus stood up and
predicted by the Spirit that there would be a severe famine over all
the world; and this took place during the reign of Claudius" (Acts
11:27–28). If Luke is correct, this reference reinforces the presence
of charismatic prophecy in the communities and their belief in the
continued presence of the Spirit that was experienced by the earliest
disciples at that first Pentecost (2:1–4).

Agabus is otherwise unknown, but, significantly, he predicts
the future. Modern biblical scholarship has emphasized the contemporaneous social message of the Israelite prophets, but the New
Testament clearly and repeatedly highlights prophets' ability to predict. For example, consider Matthew's Infancy Narrative (Matt. 1–2)
in which the events surrounding the birth of Jesus fulfill no fewer
than five prophecies. The willingness of the community to believe
such charismatic prophecies appears again when Luke says that,
based on Agabus' word, the believers organized relief efforts for
those in need.

In his writings, Luke mentions Roman emperors by name, the
only New Testament author to do so. Jesus is born during the reign
of Augustus (Luke 2:1), and begins his public career in the reign of
Tiberius (Luke 3:1); Agabus prophesies during the reign of Claudius. This last emperor reappears in one of the earliest references to
Christianity outside the Bible itself.[11]

The Jesus Movement in Rome

The Roman author Gaius Suetonius Tranquillus (69–140 CE)
wrote the *Lives of the Caesars*, a collection of history and gossip

---

11. That of Suetonius in his *Life of Claudius*. See below.

(although when gossip ages sufficiently, it becomes history). He reported that in 49 CE Claudius "expelled the Jews from [the city of] Rome because they were rioting at the instigation of Chrestus."[12] (Although Suetonius seems to imply that Claudius expelled *all* the Jews of Rome, it is much more likely that exile was imposed only on those Jews implicated in the riot who were of sufficient status to be figureheads for a popular movement.) Suetonius did not identify this Chrestus, but the scholarly reconstruction is as follows.

The Acts of the Apostles and Paul's letters make it clear that Paul's preaching often offended not only local Jews but also those believers, possibly including James of Jerusalem, who thought that God's Messiah was not merely *from* Israel but exclusively *for* Israel. In this final age, salvation was open to Gentiles as well, but many believers thought this applied only to those who would become "righteous Gentiles," adopting at least a minimal observance of the Jewish law by keeping its prohibitions. Luke reports actual physical violence (Acts 13:50, 14:19) against Paul and others who preached the same kind of "law-free" gospel as Paul did.

The Latin word for Christ is *Christus*, which is pronounced like the common slave name, *Chrestus*. Thus scholars believe that Suetonius simply misunderstood the name. (Suetonius couldn't possibly have meant Jesus, since Jesus obviously was not alive in 49 CE to be stirring up any riots.) Presumably some sort of conflict, similar to those that occurred in the course of Paul's mission, also occurred in Rome; some Jews reacted strongly against the new religion being spread among the city's Jewish community. Suetonius did not have all the facts and did not know (or care) much about Christianity; in a book about the first twelve emperors, besides this passage, he mentions Christianity only one other time in a one-sentence reference to Nero's persecution. He apparently assumed (erroneously) that the founder of the sect started the trouble himself. Echoes of Claudius' expulsion of the Jews from Rome appear in Acts 18:2. Paul meets the Jewish converts Priscilla (the "Prisca" of Rom. 16:3 and 1 Cor. 16:19) and her husband Aquila in Corinth, where they had fled after the expulsion.

---

12. Suetonius, *Life of Claudius* 25.4.

Suetonius provides the first evidence of Christianity in Rome, but it is not known who first brought it there or exactly when. By the end of this decade, there were enough Christians there to cause difficulties within the local Jewish community—enough, in fact, to have provoked the aforementioned Claudian edict. When Paul wrote to the churches in Rome in the late 50s, he addressed an established community with twenty-nine leaders he knew by name and reputation, even though he had never been there nor met most of them. The New Testament provides no evidence that either Peter or Paul played any role in the initial establishment of the Roman church. The only apostles that are known to have been connected with Rome were Andronicus and Junia—probably a married couple—and nothing more is known about them than what Paul says in his brief reference in Romans 16:7. There were other leaders of churches there (like Mary, Julia, Nereus, and Olympas), but again the remaining sources are silent about them. There must have been many other individuals promoting the faith who were not even remembered by name, for within twenty-five years after the death of Jesus the movement had spread widely in the Roman Empire, circumnavigating the eastern Mediterranean world (Egypt, Syria, Italy, Macedonia, and Asia).

Early Missionary Strategies

According to Acts, Barnabas and Paul were commissioned by the church in Antioch of Syria for the first foreign mission—to the island of Cyprus, about 45 CE.[13] They preached in the synagogues and the marketplace to whomever would listen. This seems strange because people think of synagogues (like churches) as closed buildings in a section of town usually away from the shopping centers. In the Roman period, however, the synagogues were relatively open buildings with archways for entrances but no doors, and built with colonnades so passers-by could hear what was going on inside the synagogue without actually entering the building. Alternatively, one

---

13. The following discussion relies heavily on the book of Acts. The reader should be aware, however, that some scholars have raised a number of questions about the historical reliability of the Acts account. See the preface for more on this issue.

could stand unobtrusively inside the synagogue without being in the center of the space—that is, not in the center of attention. In addition, it seems that synagogues were often built right in the marketplace. The Jewish market in Ephesus, for example, had at least one synagogue at its center and shops lining the two main streets on either side of it. One could easily preach on the steps of the synagogue and be heard by the crowds at the market. Also, potential converts could go back and forth between shop and synagogue to hear the preacher with the strange new message. Like Paul and Barnabas' home church of Antioch, the church in Cyprus arose from both Jewish and Gentile converts. Again, this is easier to understand when one bears in mind that Gentiles did not have to pass through closed doors in order to hear someone preaching in the synagogue.

The "Circumcision Question"

Eventually there were enough Gentiles for circumcision to become a concern to those Jewish Christians who wanted to ensure that Jewish law and customs would be honored and Jewish moral teaching adopted as part of accepting the message of Jesus the Messiah. The disagreement over this issue is often termed "the Gentile problem," but that is misleading. It may suggest that somehow the Gentiles were considered deficient as persons, but this was not the case. The issue may better be termed "the circumcision question" because one's stance on whether or not this was required of all of Jesus' male followers became the litmus test for how one understood matters of tremendous significance: God's covenant with Abraham, the gift of the law to Moses, the moral standards set by Torah, and the unique calling of the people of Israel. Some of Jesus' Jewish followers (e.g., Paul) believed one could value all these things and yet not undergo circumcision, and others (e.g., a party of Jerusalem believers, possibly including James) did not.

For the early church, the issue had both practical and theological dimensions, for it determined whether or not Jews could eat with Gentiles without becoming ritually unclean. Separation of Christian Jews and Gentiles at table fellowship—that is, the Eucharist—challenged and undermined the unity of the church, which was supposed to comprise one community of believers in Messiah Jesus. It also gave rise to practical questions of how to resolve the issue. For example, should there be "parallel" meals in the same house where Jewish and Gentile Christians ate from different dishes? Should there be distinct house-churches for Jewish and Gentile Christians? Should there be one shared meal and one church where everyone keeps kosher, including the Gentile converts? Such a central question of Christian fellowship would create a "deep difference" indeed.

The Jerusalem Compromise

When the disagreement began to cause strife, Luke claims that a council was held in Jerusalem to decide the best path to take (Acts 15). Led by James the Righteous, John, and Peter, the assembly eventually reached a compromise: if Gentiles keep three requirements (avoid immorality, and eat nothing that has been strangled or that has blood in it) then they would accept a "two-track" model for acceptance as a follower of Jesus. One track was the Jewish model, which required Torah observance, including circumcision. The other track was the Gentile model, which did not require these practices. In this way, Jewish and Gentile converts could share the same Eucharistic banquet together without violating kosher laws, but otherwise they would have a "separate but equal" status.

If Luke's account of this compromise is based in fact, it would seem that Paul found it unacceptable, not only because "separate but equal" to him meant that Gentile Christians essentially were *not* equal to Jewish Christians, but also because he believed that there must be no divisions in the one body of Christ. In Paul's understanding, because Christ had ushered in the beginning of God's reign on earth, worldly distinctions, such as those between Jews and Gentiles, freedpersons and slaves, men and women, were part of the old age that was contrary to God's plan and was now passing away (cf. Gal. 3:26–28). The church was the vanguard of God's kingdom, and this new reality must be manifest in the church. Hence, there must be one track to salvation, not two.

Given that, according to Luke, Paul left from Antioch of Syria on his third missionary journey (ca. 55 CE) but did not return there, it is likely that his was the minority view and the compromise of Jerusalem won the day.

Missionary Journeys of Barnabas, Paul, and Companions

On the first missionary journey, Barnabas, Paul, and John Mark (Barnabas' nephew) had gone to Cyprus, visiting Barnabas' home of Salamis and then crossing the island to Paphos, the capital city. Luke says they met with the provincial governor, one Sergius Paulus, and this Roman official became a convert to Christianity (Acts 13:7, 12). A man of wealth and power, Sergius Paulus seems to have become a patron for the three missionaries. Whereas Paul is referred to by his Hebrew name prior to this, from this point on Acts refers to Paul by this Roman name, suggesting that Paul adopted it in Sergius' honor.

Some first-century Jews, like Elymas (Acts 13:6–12), practiced magic. Incantation bowls like these have been recovered from some ancient Jewish sites. The bowl was intended to incapacitate demons, who are attracted to the spiral inscription inside the bowl; by the time they finish reading, they are trapped at the bottom.

Luke also records a contest between Paul and a Jewish magician named Elymas in Paphos (13:8–11). The story is problematic, especially since Paul calls upon divine power to strike Elymas blind, but it probably reflects not so much Jewish opposition to the mission as the contests between wonder-workers to attract crowds in urban areas.[14]

According to Luke, the missionaries left Cyprus and sailed for the mainland of Asia Minor, preaching just in the port city of Perga, where John Mark left them. Luke does not say why he did so, but this would later become a point of contention between Paul and Barnabas. Barnabas and Paul went on from Perga to the Roman colony of Antioch in Pisidia, where Sergius Paulus had influential friends and kin as well as sizeable estates. From there the two remaining missionaries went to three other Roman colonies in Pisidia, the cities of Iconium, Lystra, and Derbe. Very likely it was the influence of Sergius Paulus—perhaps through letters of recommendation to other provincial officials—that accounts for the good reception Barnabas and Paul received in these Roman towns. No doubt, they stopped in smaller towns as they passed through them, but Luke only mentions the larger cities in Acts.

In Antioch in Pisidia, Paul and Barnabas encountered a sizeable Jewish community. Acts 13:14–41 portrays them attending a synagogue service, during which the leader of the synagogue asks for a "word of exhortation for the people." This gives Luke an opening to have Paul deliver a speech arguing that the entire history of Israel points to Jesus.[15] Luke portrays the congregation initially giving Paul

---

14. Nor does Paul remove the blindness. Negative miracles—miracles that harm people or objects rather than helping or restoring them—rarely are reported of Jesus or the disciples, but this is not the only example of one. The cursing of the fig tree (Mark 11:13–14 and parallels) is the sole negative miracle of Jesus reported in the canonical Gospels, but an apocryphal work called the *Infancy Gospel of Thomas* portrays the young Jesus killing various people by his curses. One notable victim was a teacher who struck Jesus for impertinence (*Infancy Gospel of Thomas* 12.1–2). At least two victims were other children Jesus' age (2–3). In one case, Jesus is accused of killing a neighbor boy by pushing him off the roof of the house (8). When the dead boy's father complains to Joseph, Jesus comes down from the roof of the house and raises the child back to life. The fig tree in the canonical Gospels is not so lucky.

15. As mentioned earlier, Luke follows the ancient historiographic convention of constructing speeches for his leading characters to deliver at appropriate points in the narrative. In this case, Paul is the putative speaker, but compare the previous speeches attributed to Peter and Stephen in Acts 2 and 7, respectively.

and Barnabas a courteous reception, discussing their ideas and inviting them to return the next Sabbath (Acts 13:42–44). When they do return, Luke depicts some of the Jews as contradicting Paul's message, thereby prompting Paul to turn from them to the Gentiles, which they do with some success (Acts 13:45–49).

No doubt there were disputes with some Diaspora Jews during Paul's missions, but here Luke encapsulates a recurrent theme in the New Testament writings (one also found in Paul's letters and the Gospel according to Matthew), that the People of Israel had the first opportunity to accept Jesus as Messiah. When many of them chose to reject the gospel message, God prompted the disciples to turn to the Gentiles.[16] This approach is a combination of history and apologetics. It reflects actual historical situations while simultaneously conveying the notion that Jesus' own people did not join the movement in larger numbers because God wished to save the whole human race, Jews *and* Gentiles, not just the people of Israel. Luke concludes the account of Pisidian Antioch in dramatic fashion: Barnabas and Paul shake off the very dust from their shoes as they leave the city, having been expelled thanks to pressure from local Jewish leaders.[17]

---

16. Luke often has been read as a supercessionist—that is, that this shift in missionary strategy entailed a permanent realignment of God's plan of salvation to include the Gentiles (non-Jews) *instead of* the Jewish people. The framework of the storyline in Acts undercuts such a reading. Each time the missionaries come to a new town, Luke shows them preaching to the synagogue community first. If the message is rejected by a majority of influential Jews in a town, only then do Paul and Barnabas direct their message to the non-Jews. Paul's own letters confirm the basic perspective that the disinterest (and even hostility) of many Jews toward the gospel message provided the impetus for him to preach to the Gentiles, but he is confident that this "hardness of heart" exhibited by his fellow Israelites would be overcome in due time (e.g., Rom. 11:25–29) and that "all Israel will be saved" (v. 26). While Acts never portrays a change of heart on the part of those Jews who were antagonistic toward the disciples, neither does it demonize the Jewish people or write them out of God's salvific plan. Each scene has *some* Jews accepting the gospel message, even if others object to it. Contemporary readers need to be careful not to read back into the New Testament texts a later (and historically disastrous) theological development whereby "the church" becomes the "new Israel," which supercedes and replaces the "old Israel" (i.e., the Jewish people).

17. Shaking the dust off one's feet when leaving a town was a way of figuratively disowning any connection with it. The Synoptic Gospels quote Jesus telling the disciples, "If any place will not welcome you and they refuse to hear you, as you leave, shake off the dust that is on your feet as a testimony against them" (Mark 6:11; cf. Matt. 10:14; Luke 9:5). The final clause, "as a testimony against them," suggests that the action invokes a curse upon the residents of that place.

In the next city, Iconium, Paul and Barnabas again begin their missionary activity in the synagogue. However, Luke reports the same results as in Pisidian Antioch. The two missionaries are rejected by "the Jews" (the synagogue leaders? Jewish elders?), enjoy success among the Gentiles, and then are driven from the city. Such a formulaic presentation raises doubts about the historicity of the details of this scene.

In Lystra, according to Luke, Paul and Barnabas preached so successfully to the Gentiles that the locals thought they were Gods in human form. Led by a pagan priest, the people brought animals to sacrifice to them (Acts 14:13). Shocked at this, the missionaries scarcely were able to prevent the sacrifice. The scene is almost humorous, but it probably echoes a historical situation. Many ancient pagans put few or no limits on the number of deities they could worship; furthermore, they routinely deified prominent humans. As good Jews, Paul and Barnabas believed people should worship only the one true God, but Gentiles had no such scruples. Perhaps this story echoes a situation where Gentile "converts" gave the gospel only superficial allegiance, adding Jesus to the list of gods they worshiped rather than turning entirely to monotheism.

Luke says that the Jewish leaders in the region, recognizing how dangerous the missionaries were, sent representatives to Lystra to stir up the people against them. This detail illustrates the way in which Roman law functioned at that time. Each city had its own government and laws, and had jurisdiction only over the territory encompassed by the city itself. The accuser had to be present at the trial. If a person accused of a crime left the city, the accuser would have to follow the person to the next town to renew the effort at prosecution or the charge would be dropped. Luke says that the effort to carry over the charges from Iconium was successful; the people actually tried to stone Paul to death, but he survived (Acts 14:19–20). Inexplicably, Luke does not say why Barnabas went unscathed. (In 2 Cor. 11:25, Paul says, "Once I received a stoning." Was this the occasion?) The exhausted disciples continued on to Derbe.

In spite of these apparent disasters, Luke says the missionaries "made many disciples" (Acts 14:21). On leaving Derbe for the long trip back to Antioch in Syria, Paul and Barnabas returned by the longer route through Pisidian Antioch to Attalia. Retracing their steps through Lystra, Iconium, and Antioch, Paul and Barnabas encouraged their fledgling churches along the way and "strengthened the souls of the disciples" (Acts 14:21–22). Contact with many disciples could hardly be kept secret, so why did Paul's accusers not move against him during this return trip? Luke has exaggerated the number of disciples, the extent of the Jewish opposition, or perhaps both. However, he has succeeded in presenting a stirring picture of Paul as the former persecutor who has become the fearless and effective missionary to the Gentiles. Following Luke's account, from Attalia, Paul and Barnabas again took ship, returning to the church in Antioch of Syria in approximately 49 CE.

Meanwhile other Christian leaders also were engaged in missionary work, but no details on this have survived. All that is known is that when Paul and Barnabas returned from their mission, the "Gentile problem" was coming to a head because Paul's missionary strategy was different from the one employed by the other preachers.

Summary

The 40s were thus a period of great expansion for the Christian movement. Many missionaries spread the gospel, the most famous and perhaps the most problematic of whom was Paul of Tarsus. By the end of this decade, Christianity was established in the capital city of many of the Roman provinces of the Mediterranean world: Jerusalem in Judea, Antioch in Syria, Alexandria in Egypt, Antioch in Pisidia, Paphos in Cyprus, Corinth in Greece, Ephesus in Asia, and in the imperial capital itself. Hardly more than fifteen years had passed since the death of Jesus, and the gospel of the Resurrection had traveled 3,000 miles around the Mediterranean world. This growth would continue apace in the next decade.

Questions for Review

1. Why did Herod Agrippa I fear that the inhabitants of Jerusalem would riot if Gaius Caligula set up a statue of himself in the Jerusalem Temple? Why might a Roman fail to grasp that such an act was likely to be offensive to Judeans?

2. Who were "God-fearers"? Why were they important in the early Jesus movement?

3. While the book of Acts concentrates on the missionary journeys of Paul, many other early followers of Jesus also were spreading the "good news." What was the message of the early Jesus-followers in this period, and how did they spread the gospel?

4. What was a "house-church"? What can be inferred about the economic status and social classes of different members of these early communities?

5. What is known (or can be inferred) about worship services in the early Jesus movement? What evidence suggests that women sometimes presided over the "Lord's supper"?

6. What is known about prophecy in the early Jesus movement?

7. The ancient Roman historian Suetonius describes the expulsion of Jews from Rome in 49 CE; what probably lies behind his apparently garbled account of this event?

8. What was the "circumcision question"? What did the "Jerusalem Council" decide with respect to this question, according to Acts 15? What suggests that Paul was not satisfied with the outcome?

Questions for Discussion

1. Luke does not explain why Herod Agrippa I had James executed and Peter imprisoned, but in view of the Jesus-followers' talk about a "Messiah" and the coming "kingdom of God," he probably viewed them as a threat to the stability of the state. Did the followers of Jesus pose such a threat? Why or why not?

2. To most people the word *church* refers to a specialized type of building; but, for the first few centuries of the Jesus movement, meetings often were held in private homes. What are the advantages and disadvantages of homes versus specialized church buildings as places of worship? Does one or the other seem more in keeping with the gospel message?

3. The book of Acts, the primary source of information on the spread of the Jesus movement in this period, often is interpreted as promoting the idea that the church replaces Israel as the people of God. The author believes this misinterprets Acts. Which position is correct? Why does it matter?

CHAPTER 5

Pressing On Toward the Goal

The Developing Gospel Mission (51–60 CE)

The 50s was an era of great expansion for the Jesus movement. No doubt, this was made possible by the efforts of many individual teachers and preachers, both women and men. Some of these influential figures are named in the book of Acts: Simon Peter, Barnabas, Stephen, Paul of Tarsus, John Mark, Silas, Timothy of Lystra, Lydia of Thyatira, Damaris of Alexandria and Dionysius the Aeropagite, Prisca and Aquila (of Rome?), Justus and Crispus of Corinth, Erastus (of Ephesus?), Sopater of Beroea, Aristarchus and Secundus of Thessalonica, Gaius and Timothy of Derbe, Tychichus of Asia, Trophimus of Ephesus, Philip the evangelist of Caesarea Philippi and his "prophetess" daughters, and Mnason of Cyprus. Others are known from the letters of Paul, who mentions them as partners in the gospel—for example, Junia, Mary, and other church leaders from Rome; Euodia and Syntyche of Philippi; Philemon, Apphia, and Archippus from an estate possibly near Colossae; Phoebe of Cenchrea; Aristarchus; and Apollos of Corinth. Others Paul mentions because he objects to some of the things they had been preaching and doing (see, e.g., 1 Cor. 1:10–17). There must have been still others whose names are lost. One such group was the "Q" community, a group of itinerant preachers in the Jewish homeland.

Jesus' circle of disciples is often depicted as consisting of fisherfolk and other illiterate peasants or tradespersons, but this cannot be the whole story. Some of Jesus' followers must have been fairly well educated—both literate and knowledgeable of scribal traditions and methods—because this decade reveals a number of hints that a flurry of scribal activity in the fifteen-to-twenty years after Jesus' death was beginning to bear fruit. One group collected a string of Jesus' sayings to use in evangelism and catechesis. While originally the collection probably was transmitted as a set of oral traditions, eventually the sayings were compiled in a written collection (now lost), which today is known as the "Sayings Source," abbreviated "Q."[1] Scholars believe that other disciples developed a rudimentary outline of the passion narrative—the story of Jesus' last days, his arrest, execution, and burial—dubbed "the Cross Gospel."[2] Still other disciples sorted distinct forms of traditions relating to Jesus' life and work, creating a collection of his parables and a collection of stories about the miracles he performed.

Among all these various collections, the most explicitly "scribal" endeavor included the construction of a list of passages from the Hebrew Bible that were seen as relevant to the life and death of Jesus. In particular, evangelists needed texts that could be used in constructing a convincing theological argument for Jesus truly being the long-awaited Messiah of Israel, even though he did not meet the common messianic expectations of his Jewish contemporaries (who thought the messiah would vanquish the Gentile powers in the land of Israel). Because they were construed to explain "why things had to turn out the way they did," texts such as the "Servant Songs" of Isaiah (in Isa. 42, 49, and 53) could be used to legitimate the claim for Jesus as a suffering (rather than victorious) messiah.

Paul of Tarsus

Certainly the most well-known writer of this period—and perhaps the most prolific, to judge from the surviving material—was Paul of Tarsus. Paul himself acknowledges that he was a zealous beneficiary of

---

1. It may seem counterintuitive that a "sayings source" should be represented by the letter Q rather than S. This is because the Q hypothesis was developed by German scholars, and the German word for "source" is "*Quelle*" (pronounced "kvella"). See Appendix 2 for more details.

2. John Dominic Crossan, *The Cross That Spoke: The Origins of the Passion Narrative* (San Francisco: Harper & Row, 1988).

Pharisaic training (Phil. 3:5–6), which would have involved education in scribal traditions and strategies for interpretation of biblical texts and traditions. The forms and strategies of argumentation that Paul uses in his letters also reveal that he attained at least a secondary-level education in the Greco-Roman system of grammar and rhetoric.

The chronology of Paul's letters is somewhat debated, but most scholars agree that the first of these was 1 Thessalonians (ca. 48) and the last was Romans (ca. 58). Galatians was probably written around 53, and the four "imprisonment letters"—1 Corinthians, 2 Corinthians, Philippians, and Philemon—were composed over the course of the next three years (54–56). At least one of these four letters is likely to be a composite of what originally were shorter missives.[3] In addition, it is thought that Paul wrote at least one letter that is now lost; only a fragment remains in 2 Corinthians 6:14–7:1. There are six other letters in the New Testament with Paul's name on them, but they generally are viewed as coming from some of Paul's successors in the churches he founded.

The seven letters from Paul himself provide an inside view of what kinds of concerns arose in some of the early church communities that he founded in Asia Minor, Macedonia, and Greece. Several themes recur in those seven letters written over the decade of 48–58 CE, including the assertion of the sovereignty of God in Christ, and of Christ as the divinely appointed means of saving the entire world; the demands of discipleship, including the type of transformed mindset and lifestyle that believers should exhibit; the relationship between Jewish and Gentile believers, and between the Jesus-community and the Jewish people as a whole; the attitude one should take toward the world at large, particularly in light of the imminent glorious return of Christ in judgment (i.e., the *Parousia*); and Paul's defense of his authority as a divinely-appointed apostle of Jesus Christ. Certainly there were other questions raised by these early converts, and of course there would have been many things handed down through oral tradition (teaching, preaching, prophecy), but what those might have been is not known.

Most of this chapter will focus on the letters and missionary activities of Paul and other early believers with whom and for whom Paul worked. While the letters of Paul cannot give the entire

---

3. For example, 2 Corinthians 8 and 9 could have been independent "collection" letters.

picture of Pauline Christianity—even less of the Jesus movement in general—they are the best surviving evidence for reconstructing this influential strand of the Jesus movement. The following reconstruction of Paul's journeys is based on the information in Paul's own letters, supplemented by Luke's account in the Acts of the Apostles.[4]

The Jerusalem Council

Acts 15 mentions a meeting in Jerusalem to decide what would be required of Gentiles who wanted to join the Jesus movement. Although this was discussed in the previous chapter, there is value in reviewing it here, specifically from Paul's perspective, derived largely from Galatians 2. The two accounts exhibit significant differences, so much so that some scholars question whether they are both describing the same meeting. In both accounts, the key question was whether Gentile believers would need to convert to Judaism first—including keeping the laws of kosher and, for the men, undergoing circumcision. The Antiochene delegation (Barnabas and Paul) represented the group opposed to such a requirement, and a group of Judean disciples (whom Paul thinks of as the "James-party") represented the group in favor of it. Acts indicates that James presided over the meeting, and Peter and John were present at it. After some deliberation, it was decided that neither circumcision nor keeping kosher was necessary for Gentile converts; instead, they should honor certain taboos to maintain ritual purity so Jews and Gentiles could eat together at the Lord's Supper.[5] Sometimes called the first ecumenical council because of the disparate groups that gathered to resolve such a key doctrinal question, this watershed decision is what made possible the rapid spread of the gospel among the Gentiles and set the stage for the Jesus movement to become a religion distinct from Judaism.

---

4. Historical reconstruction of this period necessarily draws upon the book of Acts, but readers should remember that its historical reliability is disputed at points, particularly where Luke's rhetorical or theological agenda is at play.

5. Paul appears to have left the meeting with quite a different understanding of the agreement. When he presents his view in Gal. 2:2–10, he makes no mention whatsoever of any kosher laws or ritual purity taboos. In fact, he claims that the council "contributed nothing" to his gospel (v. 6) and enjoined only that the Gentile communities "remember the poor, which was actually what I was eager to do" (v. 10). This point will be discussed at greater length later in the chapter.

Barnabas and the Cypriote Mission

According to Luke's account in the book of Acts, Paul and Barnabas returned to Antioch when the meeting with James had concluded. Acts 15:36–41 indicates that, shortly after the meeting in Jerusalem, Paul suggested to Barnabas that they visit the Asian communities they had founded. More likely, the community of believers in Antioch, who had sent them on the first evangelistic mission, decided on a second. Barnabas liked the idea but wanted to bring John Mark. Paul had not forgotten John Mark's desertion of the mission in Pamphylia and opposed Barnabas' suggestion. Paul and Barnabas had a "sharp" disagreement that they could not bridge, so "Barnabas took Mark with him and sailed away to Cyprus" (15:39). Colossians 4:10 says that the two men were cousins, which may explain Barnabas' loyalty to someone who had let him down.

Luke says nothing about Barnabas and John Mark's activities in Cyprus. Since Barnabas initially had accepted Paul's suggestion to revisit places they had gone on their first missionary journey, presumably Paphos was on the itinerary, but nothing more is known about this second Cypriote mission. Since it occurred after the meeting with James of Jerusalem (ca. 48–49), the journey probably began about 50 CE.

There are a few more references to Mark in later decades, but Barnabas disappears from history at this point. No details are known about the missionaries' work in Cyprus; in fact, very little is known about Cypriote Christianity until the fourth century.

Paul, Silas, and the Mission to Asia and Macedonia

According to Acts, to replace Barnabas, Paul chose Silas.[6] Silas was already mentioned as one of the delegates sent to Antioch by the Jerusalem church to report the outcome of the Jerusalem Council. Luke says Silas was a prophet, and implies that he had left Antioch for Jerusalem at some point before Paul began to organize this second mission. Luke does not mention Silas' location when Paul recruited

---

6. Silas sometimes is known by the Latin version of his name, Silvanus (e.g., 2 Cor. 1:19; 1 Thess. 1:1).

him—presumably, he had returned to Antioch. Acts 16:37–38 implies that Paul and Silas both had Roman citizenship, which would surely help the mission in Gentile areas. In addition, Silas was respected enough by the Jerusalem church to be sent as an ambassador to the church in Syria, a point that would help bolster Paul's tenuous reputation among conservative Jewish-Christians. Whatever Paul's reasons for choosing Silas, the two men were to make a great partnership as evangelists and church leaders, sharing the difficulties and successes of this second missionary journey.

Luke says that on this second missionary journey (ca. 50–52 CE), Paul and Silas took the land route through Asia into Macedonia and Thrace. Churches were established at Ephesus (capital of the Roman Province of Asia), as well as in Philippi and Thessalonica (leading cities in Macedonia), and Corinth (in Greece). Luke mentions Paul preaching in Athens, but nothing seems to have come of that. Ephesus was another matter, and Paul spent a considerable time there, first founding a community of disciples and then using it as his home base for further ventures in the region. At some point along the way, he and Silas also preached in Phrygia and Galatia, but Luke does not say exactly which towns were included on this circuit or precisely where they founded new churches.[7]

Paul and Silas began their journey by traveling through Syria and Cilicia, meeting with and "strengthening the churches" there (Acts 15:41). Luke claims that they went on to Derbe, Lystra, Iconium, and probably Pisidian Antioch as well, returning to the communities Paul and Barnabas had founded on the first missionary journey. In Lystra, Paul met a disciple named Timothy who had a Jewish mother and a Greek father. Acts 16:3 claims that Paul had him circumcised "because of the Jews who were in those places, for they all knew that his father was a Greek."[8] Here Luke discreetly

---

7. Given Paul's practice of evangelizing in the major cities and towns, the most logical choices would be Gordion and Ancyra, the leading cities in the region.

8. This detail seems somewhat in tension with Paul's own writings, especially Gal. 2:3, where Paul defiantly reports that the Jerusalem apostles did not insist on the circumcision of Paul's Greek companion, Titus. However, Timothy probably constituted a special case: his mother was Jewish, which would make him a Jew by birth, regardless of his father being a Gentile. Paul thus may have thought Timothy was obligated to be circumcised. Paul does not seem willing to compromise on the question of whether believing *Gentiles* needed to follow the Torah.

suggests that Paul took another step in the direction of his Jewish critics, very likely with at least the tacit support of Silas if not at his suggestion. Timothy's circumcision would have demonstrated Paul's respect for the Law of Moses, and implied that Paul continued to follow it himself. That may explain why Paul apparently had no difficulty with the local Jewish community, although some had opposed him on his earlier visit. Their views may not have been so different from those of James of Jerusalem.

Luke says that "the Spirit of Jesus did not allow" the missionaries to enter Bithynia (Acts 16:7). Instead, a vision convinced Paul to go on to Macedonia (16:9–10). The Roman colony of Philippi, one of the leading cities of the region, would give rise to the church that had the closest relationship to Paul of all those he founded. Luke mentions a new approach here: the missionaries began by preaching to a group of women (16:13). The first convert mentioned, apparently a Gentile proselyte to Judaism, was a woman from Thyatira named Lydia.

Lydia of Thyatira

Luke claims that Lydia's entire household was baptized with her (Acts 16:14–15). This is an interesting detail for at least two reasons. First, it shows that conversion among the earliest disciples was not viewed in the individualistic way in which it is seen today. The household converted when Lydia accepted Paul's gospel simply because Lydia did, and she was head of the household. (Luke said the same of the centurion Cornelius in Acts 10.) Roman custom had it that the religion of the householder should be the religion of all the members of that household, and at least some Gentiles who converted to the Jesus movement became disciples precisely for this reason. Second, it shows that Lydia indeed was an independent woman, the head of her own household. It is often thought that women in the Roman world were not able to be independent of men, controlling their own wealth, managing their own households and businesses. The case of Lydia illustrates that this is a misconception. Wealthy women did have opportunities to do things like this.

Lydia was a successful businesswoman, a dealer in purple cloth. Purple dye was a very valuable commodity in the ancient world, a luxury item available only to the wealthiest persons. According to Roman law, only the highest-ranking aristocrats (Senators) were permitted to wear even a band of purple on their clothing. Wearing a purple garment or cloak was reserved for the Emperor alone. This suggests that Lydia was not only quite wealthy, but that she had connections with extremely influential people. Lydia offered the missionaries the hospitality of her home, presumably a second home in Philippi rather than in Thyatira, which was on the Asian mainland. In this, she provides yet another example of the wealthy women who provided support for Jesus and his followers (e.g., Luke 8:3; Acts 17:12). There was certainly a community of Christ-believers in Thyatira by the end of the century, because it is addressed in one of the letters at the beginning of the Apocalypse of John (Rev. 2:18–29). One of its leaders was a woman who is roundly criticized in that letter. Who founded the church in Thyatira is not known, but quite possibly Lydia brought the message back with her when she returned to her mainland home.

In Philippi, Luke says that Paul had his second run-in with a street magician, this time a slave who was a fortune-teller. When her owners found out that Paul had exorcized the spirit of divination,

© www.holylandphotos.org

This site in ancient Philippi is believed by some to be the jail in which Paul was imprisoned. According to Acts, the Philippian jailor converted and was baptized along with his entire family. Acts records a number of such "household conversions."

they accused the missionaries of inciting the people to break the law and got a crowd to join in condemning them. Luke says that the magistrates ordered that Paul and Silas be flogged and thrown into prison, only later learning that they were Roman citizens (whom it was unlawful to chastise). If they truly were citizens of Rome, one wonders why Paul and Silas did not mention this fact at their trial and so avoid this harsh sentence in the first place.

Paul and Silas made the most of their time in prison. Although he likely exaggerates their success, Luke says that the other prisoners listened to the two missionaries' prayers and hymns, and they even succeeded in converting their jailer, whose whole household was baptized with him.

When they left prison, Paul and Silas went to Lydia's house where they saw all "the brothers and sisters" (Acts 16:40). In addition to emphasizing her financial support of the church, the fact that the church meets in her house implies that Lydia was the head of the Philippian community.

On to Greece

As the Acts account continues, the missionaries head south through Thessalonica and Beroea where they have difficulties with some members of the local Jewish community, presumably similar to those encountered on the first mission. Nevertheless, Luke mentions converts from among both the Jews and "devout Greeks" (Acts 17:4; proselytes to Judaism, perhaps?), again including some influential, wealthy women. Other than that, he says little about Thessalonica, which is unfortunate because Paul sent his oldest extant letter to that community shortly afterwards (in late 50 or early 51). Instead, Acts shows Paul hustling along to two Greek cities that really interest Luke: Athens and Corinth.

The story of Paul's Athens visit consists mostly of a speech, but, significantly, "some Epicurean and Stoic philosophers" mock what Paul had to say and, at the end of his speech, some of them burst out laughing (Acts 17:18, 32); this is an echo of the disdain in which educated pagans originally held Christians. In the Acts account, Paul had become accustomed to opposition but not to mockery, and he had little success in Athens. Luke mentions "some" who became believers, but names only two, a woman and a man, Damaris and Dionysius. From their names, both appear to have been Gentiles.[9]

It appears that at some point while they were in Athens, the missionaries heard about some problems with the fledgling Thessalonian *ecclesia*. Unable to go there together, Paul sent Timothy to Thessalonica to find out what was happening and to encourage the new believers in that city (1 Thess. 2:17–3:5). Paul remained in Athens, continuing to try to spread the gospel there.

Acts claims that from Athens Paul went to Corinth, one of the most important of his foundations. There he met Prisca and Aquila, a Jewish couple who had left Rome because of Claudius' edict of expulsion (49 CE).[10] Prisca and Aquila opened their Corinthian home to Paul, and he initially joined their leather-working shop, preaching in the synagogue on the Sabbath. After Silas and Timothy joined him, Paul "was occupied with proclaiming the word" (Acts 18:5). Paul had limited success with his Jewish audience, but among the converts was the ruler of the synagogue, Crispus, whose "whole household" converted with him, thereby following the pattern for conversions noted above in regard to Lydia and her household. Titius Justus is the one Gentile convert mentioned by name, and he was a proselyte to Judaism.

It seems likely that at some point during his stay in Corinth, Paul wrote his first surviving letter, addressed to the community in Thessalonica, which he had left only a short time before. Apparently, the Christ-believers there were encountering some hostility from their non-believing neighbors (1 Thess. 2:14), but the letter does not give any details as to what this involved. Paul does mention "great opposition" to the gospel when he and his companions first brought the message to Thessalonica (1:6, 2:2), and he seems to imply that this opposition was from Jews who did not accept the gospel message (2:16), but he offers only hints.

By the time of Paul's writing, Timothy had returned from his excursion to Thessalonica and had brought Paul news of the church there. The one key issue in the Thessalonian church seems to have been some believers' misunderstanding of Paul's message about the

---

9. Dionysius is named after a Greek god.

10. Sometimes the diminutive form of her name is used: Priscilla, instead of Prisca.

imminent coming of Christ, that is, "the day of the Lord" (5:1–2), which seems to have prompted some members of the community to quit their jobs and engage in other disruptive activities. The hostility toward the church in Thessalonica was serious enough that it seems some of the believers had been killed (4:13). What provoked such an attack is not known, but Paul does exhort them to avoid sexual immorality, live quietly, and continue at their own labors (4:3–12). The very fact that he mentions such things suggests that at least some members of the Thessalonian community were not following these instructions and needed the reminder. Paul's explicit goal in repeating these injunctions is "that you may behave properly toward outsiders and be dependent on no one" (4:12), which implies that some had been behaving toward outsiders in a way that Paul viewed as "improper"—and which may very well have provoked at least some of the hostilities against the church.

Addressing the "Circumcision Question"— Again

The letter to the communities of Galatia, probably Paul's second (ca. 53 CE), also seems to have been written from Corinth. The central issue of this letter is the extent to which the Gentile followers of Messiah Jesus are required to observe the Jewish law (sometimes known as "the circumcision question"). Paul aims to refute an argument presented by an opposition party, whom he thinks of as outsiders who came to the Galatian churches after him. These opponents in evangelism are unsettling the Pauline communities by preaching that Gentile believers must first convert to Judaism in order to become "real" members of the Jesus movement. The opponents often are called "Judaizers" because of this view.

It may be that, to this group, Paul was not requiring enough of Gentile converts, but it is incontrovertible that this "circumcision party" was demanding more than Luke says that the Council of Jerusalem imposed upon Gentile believers (Acts 15:19–20). Paul responds with a vehement polemic against the enduring validity of the Jewish law. In a rather convoluted *midrash* of Genesis 12–21, Paul argues that God's promise to Abraham takes precedence over the law given to Moses (Gal. 3–4). The divine requirement of circumcision, which binds a Jewish man to keep all the laws of Torah, came after God's promise to Abraham. Hence, while God's promise endures, circumcision was not always a requirement for inheriting that promise; nor is it any longer a requirement in this final, messianic age, for Gentile men who wish to have a share in that divine promise.

For Paul, what was at stake in this argument was more than simply whether or not a particular Jewish custom should continue to be required of male Gentile converts. Paul recognized that using circumcision as the rite of entry into the Jesus movement would continue the kinds of social divisions—for example, between Gentiles and Jews, slaves and freepersons, women and men—that are hallmarks of "the present evil age" (Gal. 1:3) rather than the age of the Messiah. Since Jesus is God's Messiah, and since he inaugurated the "kingdom of God," the new age of God's justice on earth, the *ecclesia* must be the place where this new way of life is most visible. Circumcision as an entry rite both represents and reinforces the social divisions inherent to the age that is "passing away" (cf. 1 Cor. 7:31). Baptism into Christ Jesus, on the other hand, is the rite by which a person dies to all this and rises to the new life of the messianic age, where social divisions like this no longer exist (Gal. 3:26–29).

In this argument, Paul adroitly avoids the "two-track" model of salvation that was inherent in the ruling of the Jerusalem Council as told by Luke (see above), but in so doing he also essentially abrogates any agreement he might have made to abide by such a ruling. (See Galatians 2:6–10, where he explicitly claims that no obligations were laid upon Gentile believers except to "remember the poor.") Except for Sabbath observance, which curiously is omitted, Acts says that the Jerusalem Council required Gentile converts to observe the minimum obligations of the law that were incumbent upon resident aliens in the land of Israel.[11] What this meant was that Gentile converts to the Jesus movement did not really become part of the people of Israel, but remained alongside as "aliens." Thus they had no real claim to be heirs to God's promises to Israel, which Messiah Jesus brought to fruition. Essentially Gentile believers could be "hangers on" and perhaps ride on the coattails of the "true" Israelites;

---

11. See Lev. 17:8–18:29; 20:2; cf. Ezek. 14:7–8. Acts simply presents the requirements without identifying their connection with the Old Testament laws for resident aliens.

they themselves could not be considered part of Israel and heirs in their own right. Paul, on the other hand, believed that the final age had already begun. Thus, even now, Gentiles who recognize Jesus as the Messiah of Israel can become co-heirs with Israel to the divine promises (cf. Isa. 2:2–3; 45:20–23; 60:1–4); and they become heirs precisely *as Gentiles*.

In Luke's account, Paul and his co-workers spent a year and a half in Corinth before any major conflicts arose there. Only after Gallio was appointed proconsul of the Roman province of Achaia did certain Jews complain about Paul to the authorities. Luke's account at this point is a bit ambiguous, so the accusers may have been outsiders rather than Jews from Corinth. Reflecting the attitude of the Athenians, Gallio dismissed the dispute as "questions about words and names and [the Jewish] law" (Acts 18:15) and not worthy of his attention. Gallio's cynicism made it clear to Paul's opponents that they could not use Roman law against him. For some reason, the mob took out their anger on a man named Sosthenes, who is described as a leading official of the synagogue, rather than on Paul and his companions (18:17).[12]

The first-century "Gallio Inscription" from Delphi in Greece[13] shows that Gallio served as proconsul of Achaia[14] from the summer of 51 to the summer of 52, "the one fixed date for an absolute chronology for Paul's life and one of the relatively few certain dates in New Testament history."[15] Since Paul worked in Corinth for eighteen months, that is, longer than Gallio was there, it is difficult to say when Paul first arrived. Luke implies that Paul had been there for some time before Silas and Timothy came, which was earlier than

---

12. Luke's account appears to be a bit confused at this point. Earlier the narrative identifies one "Crispus" as the *archisynagōgos* and goes on to assert that he "became a believer in the Lord" along with his household (Acts 18:8). At the end of the same scene, Luke names a previously unmentioned "Sosthenes" as the *archisynagōgos* who is beaten by the crowd for no apparent reason, in the presence of the Roman proconsul, who does nothing (v. 17). If someone other than Paul and Barnabas were to be chastised, one would think that a known sympathizer like Crispus would have made a more logical candidate.

13. Published by Émile Bourget in his University of Paris thesis, 1905. See Everett Ferguson, *Backgrounds of Early Christianity* (Grand Rapids: Eerdmans, 2003), 549.

14. "Achaia" was the Roman name for the province that included Greece.

15. Ferguson, *Backgrounds*, 550.

© www.holylandphotos.org

The inscription shown here indicates that Gallio served as proconsul of Achaia from 52–53 CE. The Gallio Inscription provides a rare fixed date in the chronology of Paul's travels. The name ΓΑΛΛΙΩΝ is visible in the fourth line.

Gallio's appointment. At the latest, Paul may have come to Corinth in late 50 or early 51, but he probably arrived somewhat earlier than that. Many scholars would date Paul's time in Corinth from winter of 50 to spring of 52 CE.

Sometime after this, according to Luke, Paul sailed for Syria from the Corinthian port of Cenchrea, with Prisca and Aquila accompanying him. He stopped briefly in Ephesus, where the local Jews gave him a favorable reception and elicited from him a promise to return. By a rather circuitous route (Caesarea Philippi to Jerusalem to Antioch), Paul finally returned home.

This second missionary journey marked a new era in evangelization, as Paul encountered Greek and Roman culture in areas that had few Jews. The Jesus movement had met its future as a predominantly Gentile religion. Possibly sensing the importance of this, Luke gives Paul's return to Antioch a meager verse and a half. Then, with no explanation of the Antiochene church's reaction to Paul's second journey, Luke sends him off on another one (ca. November of 52 CE), beginning with Galatia and Phrygia (Acts 18:23).

Christ-Believers in Ephesus

For the third journey, Luke focuses on Ephesus, a Greek city on the west coast of Asia Minor. Luke speaks first of Apollos, an Alexandrian Jew (most likely an adult convert, given his pagan name) who came to Ephesus and preached about Jesus in the local synagogue, even though he personally "knew only the baptism of John [the Baptist]" (Acts 18:25). Luke says that Prisca and Aquila, who had moved to Ephesus, taught Apollos more accurately about "the Way of God" (18:26). The fact that Luke mentions the wife first, contrary to common Roman practice, suggests that Prisca was the leading member of this partnership. The comment also proves that women were teachers in the earliest communities. Apollos moved on to Corinth while Paul was still traversing Galatia and Phrygia. When Paul arrived in Ephesus, again he met about a dozen Christ-believers who had received only the baptism of John. Paul promptly saw to it that "they were baptized in the name of the Lord Jesus . . . [and] the Holy Spirit came upon them" (19:5–7), enabling them to speak in tongues and prophesy.

Incidentally, these two episodes show that the disciples of John the Baptist continued his movement after his death, and apparently engaged in missionary activity. Paul met these believers two decades after John's death and hundreds of miles from Jerusalem. Unfortunately, no writings from the Baptist movement survive.

This scene also suggests that Jesus' followers may have seen John's disciples as rivals, or at least that the message of John posed an alternative to the gospel of Jesus (see Matt. 11:11; Mark 6:14–16). Christ-believers countered this by "adopting" John into the Jesus movement, teaching that John was a forerunner of Jesus and his message (Luke 3:15–16), but this may not have been altogether persuasive to John's disciples.

The Jews of Ephesus were as good as their word, and Luke says that Paul preached for three months in the synagogue until those opposing him forced him to find another venue for his preaching. He rented a hall and opened up his preaching to Gentiles as well as Jews, as usual enjoying more success with the former than the latter. In all, Paul spent at least two years in Ephesus, and Luke portrays Paul's preaching and miracle-working as producing dramatic results among both Jews and Gentiles.

In most of the Roman Empire, Artemis (Diana in Latin) was a virgin goddess of the hunt and wild animals. In Asia Minor, however, she was a fertility goddess, often represented with multiple breasts, as in this statue from ancient Ephesus, where she was the patron deity.

As the number of Christ-believers in Ephesus increased, veneration of the local Goddess Diana diminished to the point where the silversmiths (who made her statues) began to worry about their trade. They rioted against the evangelists, dragging two of Paul's companions into the theater, but a local official convinced them to disperse so that no harm came to anyone.

Here Luke points out a key fact of life to people of this time. Ancient religions were not simply about "spiritual matters"; adherence to a particular religion also had economic and social consequences. Judaism was and is an aniconic religion—no images or statuary are permitted in a worship context[16]—and the Jesus movement upheld this traditional Jewish prohibition. Thus, widespread conversions would harm the silversmiths' trade. (Presumably, if Paul had asked the silversmiths to make statues of Jesus instead of Diana, there would have been no cause for a riot.) The effect of religion on industry was no small issue, and it would come up again in the early second century when a Roman governor named Pliny would decide that economic woes justified a persecution.

Paul's Corinthian Correspondence

While Paul was in Ephesus (53–56 CE), he wrote a series of letters to the *ecclesia* in Corinth. By the end of the first century, Paul's letters were being put into a collection (which later would be included in the New Testament), and it appears that the many letters to Corinth were compiled into two. Scholars have sorted out these letters in different ways, but it is certain that the first letter Paul sent there has been lost—there is only Paul's mention of it in 1 Corinthians 5:9. The letter now known as 1 Corinthians is actually the *second* letter Paul wrote to Corinth (in the spring of 54), after receiving a letter back from the Corinthians as well as a personal embassy from Chloe, who appears to have been a woman of status and a leader in the Corinthian *ecclesia*. Between his second and third letters to Corinth, Paul traversed Macedonia and Achaia, visiting Philippi and Corinth along the way. It seems as if his time in Corinth was rather strife-ridden, for he talks about it as a "painful visit" (2 Cor. 2:1). Most scholars believe that fragments of Paul's third letter (composed late fall or early winter 54) are preserved in 2 Corinthians 10–13, sometimes called "the Tearful Letter" because scholars think it is the letter Paul wrote with "much distress and anguish of heart and with many tears" (2 Cor. 2:4). Paul had returned to Philippi by the time he wrote his fourth letter to Corinth (thought to be preserved in 2 Cor. 1–9), in the winter of 55–56.

---

16. This practice is based on the injunction to worship God alone and the prohibition of "graven images" in the first of the Ten Commandments (see Exod. 20:1–6; Deut. 5:6–10; cf. Deut. 12:1–4).

Paul's series of letters to Corinth reveal several issues that had come to a head in this fledgling *ecclesia* since Paul was there. The first half of his second letter (1 Cor. 1–6) is devoted to Paul's response to the embassy from Chloe, while the second half replies to several concerns raised in the letter Paul received from the community (1 Cor. 7–15), and the final chapter asks for their support of the collection being taken for the believers in Jerusalem. All that remains of Paul's third letter (2 Cor. 10–13) is a defense of his own ministry and of the validity of his gospel over against that of the "super-apostles" (2 Cor. 11:5; 12:11). Elements of this power struggle appeared already in the prior letter, and the third letter contributes nothing to the content of the debate, so the second letter will be discussed next.

Factionalism

The key issue raised by "Chloe's people" is one of factionalism in the *ecclesia*, where the members of the Corinthian community were aligning themselves with different preachers and claiming superiority for their version of the gospel (1 Cor. 1:11–12). Founded as a colony by Julius Caesar in the mid-first century BCE, Corinth was one city in the empire where upward social mobility was a viable possibility, and it was home to a number of entrepreneurs who were interested in becoming successful and climbing that social ladder. It appears that at least some of the believers in Corinth were taking a similar approach to their new religion, claiming superior spiritual wisdom and vying for control of the *ecclesia*. Paul addresses this quest for divine wisdom and tacitly affirms its desirability (2:6–13), but he challenges the factionalism in Corinth as indicative of mere human grasping—which is foolishness to God (3:3–7) rather than a sign of divine wisdom. Human teachers are merely "servants of Christ and stewards of God's mysteries" (4:1). Those who believe that becoming a Christian should bring them glory and honor in this age are misguided; they seek human glory rather than the glory of God. Rather than glory, real disciples—especially real apostles—suffer slander, persecution, and deprivation.

"All Things Are Lawful"

The other two issues raised by Chloe's embassy are sexual immorality and the use of pagan courts. Viewing themselves as having superior wisdom, some members of the Corinthian community had decided that moral laws no longer applied to them. The two specific examples mentioned are the continued frequenting of prostitutes by some of the men in the church (1 Cor. 6:15–20) and an incestuous liaison between a man and his stepmother (5:1–5). Paul quotes with approbation their slogan, "All things are lawful for me" (6:12a), but he argues that there remain some behaviors which are inimical to being a disciple of Jesus, which cause one to be dominated by the flesh rather than led by the Spirit (6:12–13). Baptism does not free one to do whatever one chooses with one's body, but rather frees one to glorify God in the body, which now has become God's very temple. Similarly to excessive behaviors in sex and eating, resorting to pagan courts for litigation against other disciples shows that those who initiate such proceedings have not really imbibed the spiritual wisdom of the gospel.

Paul then turns his attention to the series of topics raised in the Corinthians' letter to him: marriage and other states of life (1 Cor. 7:1–40); eating practices; the "strong" and the "weak" conscience; the Christian use of freedom (8:1–11:2); liturgical dress and practice (11:3–34), including spiritual gifts (12:1–14:40); and the resurrection (15:1–57).

Marriage and Other States in Life

Paul's basic response to questions about a believer's state in life is to "stay as you are," since the *Parousia* (the glorious return) of the Lord is imminent (1 Cor. 7:20, 29–31). It does not matter whether or not a man is circumcised (7:18–19). If one is a slave and cannot get free, then one should use that position to further the gospel (7:21–23). Believers who were married at the time of their conversion should continue in their married state (7:10–17). Those who were not married might consider a celibate lifestyle (7:24–40), but marriage remains a legitimate choice for the Christian—and certainly is preferable to a life of sexual profligacy.

Idols and Eating Practices

The issue of spiritual superiority again arises, now in the context of questions about eating practices, payment of evangelists, and idolatry. While all food is acceptable to God—even what has been sacrificed to pagan deities, because those idols do not really exist—it is more important to be concerned for the conscience of a fellow believer than it is to demonstrate one's freedom to eat whatever one chooses.

Paul and Barnabas preached to the Corinthians free of charge, and this made some members of the community think their gospel was inferior (even "cheap"), but Paul insists that this makes him a better evangelist than those who claim the right to financial support (1 Cor. 9:15–23).

While idols do not exist, pagan worship involves sacrifice to demons; hence, no believer can participate in acts of pagan worship (1 Cor. 10:14–22). For cases when one is invited to a dinner party at the home of a pagan friend, Paul takes basically a "don't ask, don't tell" approach: one is free to eat anything offered—as long as no one spells out that a particular food has been sacrificed to an idol. If someone does reveal that the food comes from a pagan temple, then the Christ-believer must not eat it. At that point, avoiding harm to the conscience of an observer takes precedence over one's right to eat (10:27–29).

Worship Practices and Inversion of Social Norms

From this discussion of worship of idols, Paul shifts to worship practices. First he discusses how women should dress when they prophesy during worship, insisting that they wear a head covering (1 Cor. 11:2–16); this would eliminate the distinction between Corinthian women prophets of divergent social status, while at the same time creating a distinction between the Christ-believing prophetesses and those in the ecstatic pagan cults that flourished in Corinth (e.g., Apollo, Dionysius). Greco-Roman religions viewed bound and braided hair as an obstacle to divine inspiration, so a woman prophet in the cult of Apollo or Dionysius removed her *stola*, the aristocratic woman's mark of her social status, and let her hair down (both literally and figuratively speaking). To make sure that both insiders and outsiders realize the dramatic difference between the Jesus movement and these ecstatic pagan cults, Paul tells the Corinthian community that their women prophets should keep their hair bound and covered.[17]

Continuing somewhat in this vein, Paul then rebukes the Corinthians for displaying a social and economic hierarchy at their common meals, so that some members of the church get drunk while others go hungry (1 Cor. 11:17–34). While this was normative practice for dinner parties in Paul's time, he sees it as inimical to the Eucharist. Paul's solution is to eliminate the two-tiered practice for the Eucharistic meal: "So then, my brothers and sisters, when you come together to eat, wait for one another" (11:33).

Spiritual Gifts

This flattening of the social hierarchy has a counterpoint in Paul's discussion of the hierarchy of *charismata* or spiritual gifts (1 Cor. 12–14). While *glossolalia* ("speaking in tongues") is a "flashy" gift, Paul reminds the Corinthians that every spiritual gift comes from the one God and makes an essential contribution to the life of the *ecclesia*. No one gift is sufficient on its own, nor can any believer do without the others (12:11–27). Mature disciples will recognize that boasting and self-aggrandizement stand in fundamental opposition to the Spirit; on the contrary, the greatest of all the gifts of the Spirit

---

17. In spite of the propensity of translators and commentators, ancient and modern, to insert the word "veil" into this discussion, Paul never uses the term in this context. In fact, it would be contradictory to do so, since a veil is worn to cover one's face as a sign of silent submission, whereas the prophetic women Paul mentions are in fact speaking in the congregational worship setting.

When Paul enjoins the Corinthian women prophets to cover their hair, he seems to be referring to the *palla*, a large rectangular scarf or shawl that was wrapped around the shoulders and could also be used as a head-covering. Respectable women would not go out in public without the *palla* but certain cities, especially in the eastern empire, enacted laws prohibiting slave women and prostitutes wearing a head-covering in public. In that light, having all the women prophets cover their hair would elevate the status of the slave women because they would be dressed like the "respectable" matrons and free women, with the head-covering that showed them worthy of respect and honor.

For a more extensive discussion of this passage, including a careful treatment of Paul's terminology, see Sheila E. McGinn, "'*Exousia echein epi tēs kephalēs*': 1 Cor 11:10 and the Ecclesial Authority of Women," *Listening: Journal of Religion and Culture* 31, no. 2 (Romeoville, IL: Lewis University, 1996): 91–104.

is *agapē*, self-giving love like that illustrated in the voluntary sacrifice of Jesus (chapter 13). The Corinthians should rein in the practice of *glossolalia*, show preference for the more edifying gifts, especially prophecy (14:1), and use all the gifts for the benefit of the entire community, in the spirit of *agapē*. Prophecy is preferable to *glossolalia* because it builds up the believers and persuades unbelievers of the truth of God's message (14:21–25). Prophecy should be done in a decent and orderly manner, however (unlike the common practices in the pagan cults), to show that God is a God of peace rather than of chaos (14:26–33).

The Resurrection

Paul turns from the topic of spiritual realities to an affirmation of the concrete, human reality of the death and Resurrection of Jesus. Jesus was not simply a spiritual being, for he really died and was buried (1 Cor. 15:3–4). Nor was his Resurrection a merely spiritual reality, for he appeared to many disciples afterwards, including Paul (15:5–8). Since Christ was raised, there also will be a resurrection of the dead at the *Parousia* (15:12–23). The earthly, human body will perish, but believers will receive a spiritual body at the resurrection (15:35–54). Thus baptism is the believer's entrance into the spiritual reality of Christ, and the spiritual gifts experienced by the Corinthians are a foretaste of things to come; but baptism is not the same as resurrection, nor does it translate the believer into the final age. Only the *Parousia* of Christ will bring this about.

What Do Laws Indicate?

One should keep in mind a simple fact about Paul's prohibitions and warnings: laws, prohibitions, and injunctions are made to control existing behaviors that are causing some sort of disturbance or encourage more frequent exhibition of ideal behaviors. Paul made these statements, in other words, precisely because some members of the Corinthian *ecclesia* were doing the things he wanted to discourage. For example, some actually were "eating in the temple of an idol" (1 Cor. 8:10), just as they had done before their conversion, else how could another believer of weaker conscience see them doing so? Some were using the Eucharistic meal as an opportunity to display their social rank and humiliate other members of the *ecclesia*. Some men continued to frequent prostitutes.[18] Women were prophesying with bare heads, as was the practice in pagan cults. These details show that the members of the fledgling church in Corinth had accepted the message of the gospel, but were viewing it as they might have viewed a pagan mystery cult—as a spiritual truth disconnected from their daily life. Paul's letters to the Corinthians demonstrate his insistence that accepting the gospel means recognizing that "the present form of this world is passing away" (7:31b). Those who believe in Messiah Jesus must live now as if they already belong to the new era that is unfolding.

Paul concludes this second letter to the Corinthians by telling them that he was planning to come to visit them after he returned to Macedonia, but he would not be leaving Ephesus until after Pentecost (1 Cor. 16:5–8). Unfortunately for Paul, political events intervened and he remained in Ephesus longer than he had hoped.

Paul's Ephesian Imprisonment

Shortly after Paul wrote 1 Corinthians, the proconsul of Asia was murdered (October 54) and Paul was imprisoned in Ephesus. From prison he wrote a letter to the Philippian community (ca. January 55), at least in part to thank them for sending one of their number, Epaphroditus, to help him. Paul also mentions that they sent him a gift, and hints that he expects his imminent release so that he can return to visit them fairly soon. This suggests that at least some of the gift was monetary and was used to bribe officials to effect his release—a very common practice in the ancient world. The letter to Philemon also was written from prison, probably about the same time as this letter to the Philippians.

---

18. Rather than simple prostitution—a widespread and legal business practice in the ancient world—this may have involved continued participation in the cult of Aphrodite, whose temple in Corinth is reputed to have had 1,000 priestesses who served as consorts for men who came there to make the sacred marriage with the Goddess of Love. If so, it makes even more understandable Paul's apparent surprise at the need to levy this objection.

The Letter to Philemon

Although often called a personal letter, Paul actually addressed it to "Philemon our dear friend and fellow worker, to Apphia our sister, to Archippus our fellow soldier, *and to the church in your house*" (vv. 1–2, emphasis added). When Paul refers to the *ecclesia* "in your house," the Greek word "your" is in the plural and thus includes Apphia and perhaps also Archippus. Apphia, possibly Philemon's wife, is another example of a woman leader of a house-church. Because of a later letter that mentions many of these people, tradition has it that this house-church was in or near Colossae, but that association is not certain.

The main body of the letter is addressed to Philemon in the singular, which gives the impression that the topic is a personal one. Onesimus, one of Philemon's slaves, had left his master and come to Paul in prison. Now Onesimus is returning to Philemon, and Paul writes this letter for him to carry back to his master and asks to have it read to the entire house-church. The letter certainly is personal in the sense that Philemon is Onesimus' owner and has the legal power to affect his future; hence Philemon is the most able to respond to Paul's request in this letter. However, the fact that Paul addresses it to the entire house-church shows that Paul views the issue as a matter of concern to the entire *ecclesia* in that district.

The apostle recounts Onesimus' conversion during his stay with Paul—perhaps a subtle critique of Philemon who, as patron of a house-church, certainly could have shared the gospel with Onesimus before he ever left the estate, but apparently did not. Paul boldly claims that, as an apostle, he has the right to command Philemon to do what he wants (v. 8), and that he would have liked to keep Onesimus as his own servant "in your (sing.) place" (v. 13). Nevertheless, Paul instead is returning Onesimus so Philemon can freely decide what to do (v. 14). Paul urges Philemon to take Onesimus back, "no longer as a slave but more than a slave, a beloved brother" (v. 16). Paul urges, "Welcome him as you would welcome me" (v. 17). In case Philemon has missed these less-than-subtle hints and still is wavering about the proper course of action, Paul inserts two additional points of persuasion. First, he offers to pay any debt Philemon thinks Onesimus owes him (v. 18–19a)—which could be taken to include not only personal expenses but also his emancipation price—although

Paul mitigates this offer by pointing out that Philemon owes Paul an even greater debt, that of his own life of freedom in Christ (v. 19b). Second, Paul mentions that he will be released from prison very soon and will then be visiting Philemon (v. 22)—just to make clear that Paul will be checking up on Philemon and that he intends to find out how this issue was resolved.

Paul does not blatantly instruct Philemon to free Onesimus, but rather points out that he is respecting Philemon's own freedom to choose what is right (vv. 9a, 14). In the social context of his time, this is a powerful rhetorical strategy, and clearly conveys that Philemon should imitate Paul in making Onesimus free to do the same. However, this rhetorical context was forgotten over the long history of interpretation of this letter, which eventually led to the letter being read in precisely the opposite way, as proof of Paul's legitimation of slavery. Especially in the American context, this had drastic consequences, with both abolitionists and pro-slavery advocates quoting Paul to support their positions, so it is worthwhile at this point to comment further on Paul's understanding of slavery of Christians.

Slavery in the Ancient World

In the ancient world, slavery was not a racial matter but could result from three different factors: conquest in war, exposure as an infant, or overwhelming debt. In Paul's time, financial ruin was the single most frequent reason why someone would become enslaved.[19] For example, a farmer would borrow seed money from some aristocratic financier (someone like Philemon), and then the harvest would be so poor that he could not repay the debt. Perhaps the lender would give him a second chance, charging extra interest of course, but what if the next year's harvest was no better? The farmer would be forced to sell his wife and children into slavery to repay the debt. If the debt were high enough, he would sell himself into slavery as well. This scenario happened frequently enough that Caesar Augustus enacted new legislation forbidding a man selling his wife into slavery without likewise selling himself.

---

19. One should not underestimate the terrible significance of such a situation.

As in other historical settings, there were different grades of slavery. The lowest was that of slaves on large agricultural plantations, or those who worked in mines or as rowers on ships. Poorly fed, poorly dressed, poorly housed, and devoid of medical care, these slaves had a relatively short life expectancy. Household slaves, on the other hand, often lived with the family and had living conditions similar to those of servants in later generations. They might be tutors, or secretaries, or administrators of their mistresses' or masters' businesses, and might even have their own small businesses to the side where they could earn their own money. However, the fact that those who did have such side ventures saved that money to buy their freedom should help allay any romanticism about how most slaves viewed their state. The frequency of sexual use of slaves is illustrated by the Augustan legislation decreeing that a female slave who had borne four children to her master must be emancipated (although her children remained her master's property). Sexual exploitation was so commonly experienced by both male and female slaves that a typical way of teasing a slave was "to remind him of what his master expects of him, i.e., to get down on all fours."[20]

Torah put additional restrictions on slavery among Jews. Jewish owners were forbidden to work their slaves on the Sabbath (Exod. 20:10; Deut. 5:14), whereas no such holy day was observed by Gentile slaveholders. Jews were permitted to have Gentiles as slaves, but

---

20. Paul Veyne, "Homosexuality in Ancient Rome," in *Sexualities Occidentales*, ed. Philippe Aries and Andre Bejin (Paris: Editions du Seuil/Communications, 1982); ET *Western Sexuality: Practice and Precept in Past and Present* (Oxford: Blackwell, 1985), 26–35, at 29. Slaves always were at risk of sexual use (and abuse) by their masters—and by others as well, with the master's permission. The bodies of freeborn Romans, on the other hand, were to be inviolate. These contradictory perspectives raised serious concerns when freeborn Romans pledged themselves as bond slaves as collateral for a loan (a contractual arrangement called *nexum*). After a notorious case involving the sexual harassment of a freeborn son of a Roman family, the *Lex Poetelia Papiria* abolished this contractual form of debt slavery. Promulgated in 326 BCE by the republican-era dictator, Gaius Poetelius Libo Visolus, this law did not prevent the accumulation of debt, merely *the use of one's person* (or the persons of one's wife and children) *as surety* for that debt. The potential remained that one might get so deeply into debt as to require the outright relinquishment of liberty and sale of one's wife, children, and oneself into a permanent slave state. Modern bankruptcy laws prevent the confiscation of property connected with a person's livelihood, to prevent the bankrupt person entering into a state of utter destitution. The Greco-Roman world evinced no such safeguards for those who fell to the bottom of the socio-economic ladder.

were forbidden to enslave fellow Jews; all Israelites were "slaves" to God, who had ransomed them, so they could not belong to another (Lev. 25:39–55). Jews could keep other Jews as indentured servants to pay off debts, but a man's servitude could not last more than six years (Exod. 21:2–3). On the other hand, a female slave was not to be emancipated—as in Roman law, Torah implicitly recognized that she was likely to be used for sexual purposes. Rather, any man who bought a Jewish woman must make her his wife or give her as wife to his son (Exod. 21:7–11).

Paul must have had these regulations in his mind when composing his letter to Philemon, for it seems he was applying the same principles in the context of the disciples of Jesus. Presumably Paul thought it permissible for Philemon to have Onesimus as slave prior to Onesimus' conversion. Paul had been at Philemon's estate earlier and would have had ample opportunity to persuade him to release his slave, but there is not the remotest hint that Paul had made any such attempt. Rather, it is Onesimus' acceptance of the gospel that prompts Paul's appeal for his freedom (vv. 10–11). Therefore, Paul does not condemn the practice of slavery per se; in this, he clearly was a man of his time. Nevertheless, he does ask Philemon to set a daring precedent by emancipating a slave—or giving him to Paul to do so—simply because that slave became a disciple of Jesus. Paul must have realized that such an act could have drastic consequences, perhaps inciting mass conversions of slaves (which he probably would have thought quite good) or even provoking a slave revolt (which he likely would have viewed as very bad). Perhaps this is why he gave Philemon the option of "laundering" the act through Paul. However, Paul betrays no inclination that such pragmatic considerations could excuse any evasion of one's responsibility toward a fellow Christ-believer. In this, the apostle puts a human face on his claim that baptism radically alters the believer's mode of being in the world: "As many of you as were baptized into Christ have clothed yourselves with Christ. There is no longer . . . slave or free . . . ; for all of you are one in Christ Jesus" (Gal. 3:27–28).

It is not known whether Philemon responded positively to this letter. One might like to think that, if Paul's importuning had failed, the letter would not have been preserved. On the other hand, while many other people named in this letter appear in later

Christian literature—including, most strikingly, the letter "to the Colossians," which names nearly all the same persons as in this letter to Philemon—there is no further mention of Philemon (nor Apphia) in any surviving text.

Lesser-Known Associates of Paul

In this brief "book," one of the shortest in the New Testament, Paul mentions several of his associates, starting with Timothy and Epaphras, who share his imprisonment, but also "Mark, Aristarchus, Demas, and Luke, my fellow workers" (v. 24). The name Mark, mentioned by Paul only here, suggests that he and Mark had become reconciled since the apostle refused to take him on the second journey described in Acts. As for Luke, this is the only place Paul mentions his name, but this association with Paul (mentioned also in Col. 4:14 and 2 Tim. 4:11) and the "we passages" in Acts led to the belief that this Luke had written the Acts of the Apostles—and thus also the Third Gospel, since it is clear that the same author wrote both works. Some early church writers thought that, when Paul spoke of "my" gospel (Rom. 2:16; 16:25), he was referring to the Gospel of Luke. Nothing is known about Aristarchus or Demas, although, like Luke, both are mentioned in Colossians. Demas also is named in 2 Timothy and in the second-century apocryphal *Acts of Paul and Thecla*.

Epaphras likewise reappears in the letter to Colossae, where a disciple taking Paul's name credits him with founding the church there (1:7). In Philemon, Paul distinguishes Epaphras from his other associates, implying that Epaphras was known to his readers. This has led to the belief that Philemon's estate was in or near Colossae. However, the letter to Philippians is the one other place where Epaphras is mentioned (there under his full name, Epaphroditus), and there he is credited with bringing a gift to the imprisoned Paul from the Philippian church (4:18). Given that Paul mentions his imminent release (from the same Ephesian imprisonment) in both these letters, and also declares his intention to visit both the Philippians and Philemon's church, it may be that Philemon's estate was in or near Philippi rather than in Asia.

Turning again to the Acts account, it appears that Paul was released from his Ephesian prison in the spring of 55, and spent the next several months in Ephesus recuperating from a serious illness he contracted while he was incarcerated. By the fall, he was able to travel again and, true to his promise in these two letters, Paul set off for Macedonia. Spending time in Troas along the way, Paul reached Philippi in the winter of 55–56 and spent several months there. It was during this time that Paul wrote his fourth letter to Corinth, now preserved as 2 Corinthians 1–9.

In this fourth letter, Paul briefly mentions the previous "angry" letter he had sent (2 Cor. 10–13) and then offers a rather extensive defense of his ministry and of his gospel. He mixes in remarks about the "new creation" that exists in Christ, alluding to the resurrection, the physical nature of which had been in dispute in the second letter (1 Cor. 15). Paul briefly returns to the issue of "boasting," which also was a concern in that letter, and uses irony to contrast his claims to authority with those who thought of themselves as "superior apostles." The letter concludes with an appeal (2 Cor. 8–9) asking the Corinthian community to contribute generously to the collection Paul was taking to provide relief for the *ecclesia* in Jerusalem. By this time, Paul had determined to go to Jerusalem for Pentecost, and he mentions that he will be paying another visit to the Corinthian community while on his way there. Paul reached Corinth in early 57, and it was from there that he wrote his last letter, the one to the Christ-believers in Rome.

Paul's Final Letter: To the Romans

Romans, the final letter of Paul, is the only one addressed to a community he did not found. Well aware that the audience may have heard about his preaching, and that some of those reports may have been fairly critical, Paul takes time at the start of the letter to present his apostolic credentials. He specifically mentions the apostolic call "to bring about the obedience of faith among all the Gentiles for the sake of [Christ's] name" (Rom. 1:5b), thereby hinting at the two fundamental and intertwined themes of the entire letter: first, obedience to God is "the obedience of faith," that is, it derives from and grounds faith; second, this faith is now open to the Gentiles as well as Jews. Both Gentiles and Jews are under the judgment of God, "for God shows no partiality" (2:11).

Paul then embarks upon the primary topic of Romans, the significance of circumcision and law-observance for salvation. Arguing that true circumcision is a matter of the heart (Rom. 2:29), he opens the door for Gentiles and women to be considered "real" members of the church without undergoing the ritual of circumcision. Jews have precedence over Gentiles, for they were "entrusted with the oracles of God" (3:2), but this law, which was God's gift to humanity, shows not the superior righteousness of Israel but that "both Jews and Greeks [Gentiles] are under the power of sin" (3:9b). Now a new revelation has come, one that is confirmed by the sacred scriptures, and this is the justice of God revealed in the faith of Jesus Christ (3:22). God justifies people not through legal observance but through "the law of faith" (3:27). Both Jews and Gentiles are brought back into harmony with God by the same faith (3:30).

Paul embarks upon a rather convoluted discussion of the relationship between the law and sin, which brings death, whereas the Spirit of faith brings life (Rom. 5–8). All the baptized have died to sin and to the power of sin over the law, being born to a new way of life (6:3–12). The fact that Christ-believers are led by the Spirit of God shows that they have been adopted by God and are co-heirs of God with Christ (8:10–17). The entire cosmos eagerly awaits the time when all God's children will be made known and will receive their promised inheritance (8:19–23). Meanwhile, persecution and hardships exist, but these cannot take away the promise of God's justice and mercy (8:35–39).

The idea of inheritance raises the issue of the status of believing Jews, believing Gentiles, and Jews who do not believe in Jesus as Messiah. This occupies Paul's mind in Romans 9–11, the pivotal section of this letter, and has led some commentators to suggest that it was conflict among these groups in Rome that prompted Paul to write this letter to congregations he had never met. The burden of this extensive *midrash* is to argue that the unbelief of some Jews is what makes it possible for the Gentiles to come to faith (11:25).[21] Paul insists that the belief of the Gentiles, in turn, will make those unbelieving Jews turn back to accept the faith of

---

21. Incidentally, some of Paul's fellow Jewish-Christians believed exactly the opposite: that all Israel must first come to faith before the Messiah could be preached to the Gentiles.

Christ. Therefore, even though some Jews are causing difficulties for the followers of Jesus, believers must not condemn them nor think themselves superior to them. "As regards the gospel they are enemies of God for your sake; but as regards election they are beloved, for the sake of their ancestors; for the gifts and the calling of God are irrevocable" (11:28–29).

The ensuing section of the letter is a series of exhortations to lead lives of hope, love, and perseverance. Paul acknowledges a variety of practices among the disciples in Rome—some are vegetarians, some are not; some keep the Sabbath, while others do not. As long as each one follows these practices for the sake of serving Christ, then that is all that matters. Diversity of practices should be accepted; but no one should do anything that causes scandal, putting another believer's faith at risk (Rom. 14:13–15).

In the last section of the letter, Paul returns to a description of his ministry among the Gentiles and tells the Roman Christians that he is on his way to Jerusalem with the collection from the (predominantly Gentile) communities in Macedonia and Achaia. He mentions plans to come to Rome afterwards, and to go even further west to proclaim the gospel in Spain, all the while dropping subtle hints that he would appreciate financial support from the Roman Christians to pursue that mission (Rom. 15:23–29). He anticipates trouble in Jerusalem, both from unbelievers and from Jewish Christians who disagree with Paul's gospel and who may not accept the validity of his apostolic ministry (15:31). Perhaps these Jewish-Christians believed that the gospel should not be preached to Gentiles until after all Israel had accepted it, or at least that any Gentile converts should become full-fledged members of the Jewish community (including circumcision, for the men). Paul asks the faithful in Rome to pray for his success—and he also may have hoped for a more immediate show of support to help persuade the Jerusalem community to validate his ministry. Paul follows this request with a sort of "list of references" in Romans 16, greeting over twenty-five leaders he knows among the Roman Christ-believers, several of them women, including one Junia, whom he calls a "well-known apostle" (16:7; SEM). If the Roman churches were not sure about whether they ought to support Paul's gospel, they would have had plenty of people to consult.

Paul's Journey to Jerusalem

Departing from Corinth to continue his journey to Jerusalem, Paul is said to have sailed along the coast of Asia, stopping at several mainland and island ports but bypassing Ephesus. Paul asked the elders of the church at Ephesus to meet him at Miletus, where Luke portrays Paul delivering a moving farewell address filled with foreboding and justifying his mission (Acts 20:17–38). While unlikely to be a verbatim reprise, the account probably reflects authentic tradition since, as just mentioned, Paul also hinted in his letter to the Romans that he expected difficulties in Jerusalem. He had justified his mission not only in Romans, but also in several of his previous letters, most notably those to Galatia and Corinth.

When Luke mentions the "elders" (*presbyteroi*) of Ephesus whom Paul asked to meet him in Miletus, he does not describe what their position entailed, nor does he suggest what kinds of structures Paul left behind in his communities. The letter to Philippi mentions elders, deacons, and overseers (*episcopoi*), but it is unique in this respect.[22] Acts and the letters to Corinth mention many prophets (including the four daughters of Phillip in Caesarea), apostles, teachers, and miracle-workers. Respected Jewish leaders were designated elders (Luke 7:3), so it is logical that some early communities of Jesus' disciples were organized along these lines, but not all of

---

22. These terms eventually come to designate the offices of priest, deacon, and bishop, respectively. Even in Philippi, it is not clear that these are formal ecclesial offices and, if so, there certainly is no evidence that they carried with them a life-long status among the community. Nor is it known what were the duties and qualifications of those who held these various offices. Given that Euodia and Syntyche are among the few people named in the letter as leaders of the Philippian ecclesia, it is reasonable to assume that these two women were included among the "elders, deacons, and overseers" addressed at the outset of the letter.

The church historian Eusebius says that Paul's disciples became influential men in the church. He lists several of them as bishops of important cities. Dionysius the Areopagite, whom Luke says Paul converted in Athens (Acts 17:34), became first bishop of Athens; Titus, mentioned in Gal. 2 and 2 Cor. 7, became first bishop of Ephesus; Timothy, mentioned in the Corinthian and Thessalonian correspondence, became first bishop of Crete (*Ecclesiastical History* 3.4). The New Testament provides no support for these claims. Eusebius is the only source and he prefers to portray the history of the true church as the succession of orthodox bishops. These men may well have been "bishops" of those places, but such information must be used very tentatively, and it is not really known what that office would have entailed at this time in the development of the churches.

them were. Different communities seem to have developed their own leadership models. Nor was leadership restricted by gender; several women leaders are mentioned in the Pauline congregations, including apostles, deacons, prophets, and patrons. Paul took charismatic gifts very seriously, so community leaders were probably selected according to some sign of their spiritual endowments.

First stopping at Tyre and Caesarea, Paul arrived at Jerusalem. According to Luke, Paul was in Jerusalem barely a week before he was arrested—at the instigation of some Jews from Asia (Acts 21:27). Paul's accusers incited a lynch mob, which was interrupted by a Roman tribune named Claudius Lysius, who ordered Paul taken into custody. After an attempt to offer a defense before the crowd (basically a reprise of the "call" story in Acts 9, with slight variations), Paul was closeted until the next day, when the tribune called a meeting with the Sanhedrin to discover precisely what charge they were making against Paul. Finding that it concerned Jewish rather than Roman law, Lysius was inclined to release Paul; however, he heard from Paul's nephew of an assassination plot. Instead of releasing the prisoner, Lysius wisely passed the responsibility to his superior, sending Paul under heavy guard to the provincial governor, Felix, in Caesarea Maritima (Acts 23:26–30). This lead to another hearing before the governor—and another opportunity for Paul to make a defense—after which Felix placed Paul under house arrest, where he remained (58–60 CE) until Felix was succeeded as governor by Porcius Festus. Festus offered Paul the opportunity to return to Jerusalem to be tried—a choice that certainly must have looked like a setup given the attempts on Paul's life when he was last there. Paul appealed to Caesar, and so was bundled on to Rome. After a three-month stay on Malta due to a shipwreck, Paul finally arrived in the Eternal City. Luke ends his story of Paul with him again under house arrest (60–62 CE). Tradition says that Paul eventually was executed in Rome.

Origins and Challenges of the Believing Communities in Rome

Apparently, missionaries also had been active in Italy while Paul and his companions were preaching elsewhere. Acts 28:11–16 says that, when Paul arrived in Italy, believers came out to meet him first at

Puteoli (near Naples), then at Three Fountains (another town south of Rome), and finally in the capital itself. Since most scholars place Paul's arrival in Italy about the year 62, clearly the Christian community in Italy had been built up in the 40s and 50's. How did that happen? As seen in the last chapter, historical data do not support the traditional notion of Peter founding the Roman *ecclesia*, so credit for the evangelization of Italy must go to now anonymous missionaries.

Summary

While not a complete picture of the Jesus movement in general, Paul's missionary activities and his surviving letters give important insight into the expansion and development of the Jesus movement during the 50s. In his second and third missionary journeys, Paul traveled to several Asian communities, as well as communities in Macedonia and Greece. Converts to the Jesus movement during these endeavors included women and men, poor and wealthy, slave and free, Gentile and Jew. Oftentimes whole households converted together, following the lead of the head of the house, such as with the conversion of Lydia of Thyatira. While Paul preached Jesus' message to all people, he viewed his particular call as bringing the gospel to the Gentiles.

Paul's letters address specific problems within the communities, which gives an understanding of what life was like for believers in this era, as well as the development of Paul's theology. Descriptions of these communities in Acts and in Paul's letters mention elders, prophets, teachers, apostles, deacons, and patrons, which highlight the diversity of leadership models employed. Early communities were concerned about the relationship between Jewish and Gentile converts, questioning whether Gentiles had to follow the Jewish laws in order to convert. Issues also arose regarding how to live a transformed life in Christ while surrounded by nonbelievers, including proper sexual behavior, avoidance of idolatry, appropriate worship practices, and elimination of divisions within the community. Paul's responses to these specific issues highlight the foundation of his message, which is that through baptism a person dies to the old life and is born anew in Jesus. The baptized are called to live a transformed life here on earth, in preparation for the imminent return of Christ.

The wider picture in the 50s was rather quiet. Rome saw tax riots in the mid-to-late-50s, a hint of which appears in Romans 13:1–7, but they seem to have been rather short-lived and to have had little impact on the daily life of the city.

In 54 the Emperor Claudius died, poisoned by his fourth wife, Agrippina, so that Nero, her son by a previous marriage, could become emperor.[23] Contrary to what one might expect, Claudius' assassination did not cause chaos in Rome. The city was relatively inured to such traumas since both of Claudius' predecessors had also been assassinated, Tiberius in 37 and Caligula in 41. The transition to the new government went smoothly and, no matter how despicable his personal life, Nero governed the empire well throughout the 50s.

One of the immediate effects of Nero's accession was the reversal of the Claudian edict of expulsion, so that Jews who had gone into exile in the 40s (see above) were now able to return home to Rome. Included among those returning Jewish exiles would have been Prisca and Aquila, Paul's tent-making partners in the evangelization of Corinth.

The average Roman could not have anticipated the transformation that would take place in Nero once he was elevated to the throne. He came to engage in progressively more perverse behaviors and "entertainments," some of which he seems to have done just to prove that he could. In the 50s, however, he had not yet shown his true colors. In the 60s, his megalomania began to consume him; Nero then became responsible for the most famous incident—outside those recorded in the New Testament—of the first Christian century (to be discussed in the next chapter).

Questions for Review

1. Although many Jesus-followers were responsible for the spread of the movement in this period, the Acts of the Apostles focuses almost exclusively on Paul. Why do you think the author chose to tell the story this way?
2. Who were Prisca and Lydia, and why are they significant?

---

23. Unfortunately for Agrippina, the new emperor's gratitude had its limits; Nero had his mother murdered in 59 when she tried to influence how he governed.

3. In Galatians, Paul sets out his opposition to Gentile converts receiving circumcision. What was Paul's position on this issue? How does Paul's position differ from the rulings of the council in Jerusalem in Acts 15? Why does Paul insist on a different course?

4. What is the "Gallio Inscription," and why is it important for the chronology of the early Jesus movement?

5. What was Paul's ruling on the question of whether Christ-believers may eat meat that had been offered to an idol? What was Paul's rationale for saying this?

6. What is *glossolalia*? What problems arose in the Corinthian Church around the practice of *glossolalia*? How did Paul address these problems?

7. Describe slavery in the Roman world. How might one become a slave? What did that mean for a person's way of life?

8. What can be inferred about positions of leadership within the churches Paul founded? How similar or dissimilar is this picture to the ordained positions of deacon, priest, and bishop that eventually developed within the church?

Questions for Discussion

1. The book of Acts describes several instances, like that of Lydia, when a head of a household converted to Christianity and, as a result, all members of the household (presumably including the slaves) received baptism. Contemporary Christians tend to emphasize a *personal* commitment of faith in Christ. Why do you think the early Jesus movement accepted and even applauded such conversions of households en masse, and what do you make of this difference between the practice and attitude of the early ecclesia versus the church of today?

2. It appears that the followers of John the Baptist continued to make converts in this period, even in Gentile territory; why do you suppose the John the Baptist movement eventually died out, while the Jesus movement grew to become the dominant religion of the Roman world?

3. Some members of the Corinthian church seem to have concluded that acts performed by their *physical* bodies could not harm them *spiritually*. Describe how they applied this principle. Do they have a point? Why or why not?

4. Although Paul and other leaders of the early Jesus movement insisted that all Christ-believers were brothers and sisters, regardless of social status, they appear not to have objected to the institution of slavery. As a result, many American Christians in the antebellum period cited Paul as proof that slavery is not immoral. Do you think it is fair to cite Paul in support of slavery? Why or why not?

CHAPTER 6

Ferment and Fire

Christ-Believers in (and against) the Roman Empire (61–70 CE)

The 60s proved to be a crucial decade for both the Romans and the Christians. It began for the Romans with a revolt in Britain in 61, led by Queen Boudicca of the Iceni, one of the tribes of Britons, and it ended with a series of internal revolts, which saw four different emperors in the space of one year (68–69). Nero ruled until 68, when his mis-governance fomented a revolt led by a general named Galba. Sensing defeat and fearing execution, Nero committed suicide. Galba became emperor, only to find that other generals shared his ambition. Otho dethroned and killed Galba in 69, only to commit suicide after being dethroned a few months later by Vitellius. Vitellius in turn was dethroned and executed by Vespasian who finally put an end to the chaos and reigned from 69 to 79. Yet, in a tribute to the organization and efficiency of imperial administrators and bureaucrats, the Roman Empire continued to function rather smoothly on a daily basis. Most citizens remained unaffected by the palace coups.

While they had no "palace coups" of their own, the followers of Jesus in this decade witnessed a series of events that were arguably even more earth-shaking: their persecution by the Roman state; the deaths of some of their great leaders, including James of Jerusalem, Simon Peter, and Paul of Tarsus; the Romano-Jewish War, which ended the traditional primacy of the Jerusalem community; and the writing of the first known Gospel.[1] Any one of these events would have been significant. Taken together, they profoundly and irreversibly changed the face of the Jesus movement. Nero's targeting of the group as his scapegoat for the great fire indirectly shows that the *ecclesia* in Rome was becoming big enough to cause concern. The executions of key leaders like James, Peter, and Paul, in Jerusalem and then in Rome, indicate the growing concern with the popularity of the Jesus movement in the Jewish and imperial capitals. Any attempts at containment, however, would prove fruitless, and the war in Judea, ironically enough, actually strengthened the movement in two key ways: it spread many more believers beyond the boundaries of Judea, and sparked the first continuous narrative of the life and teachings of Jesus—the book that later Christians would call the Gospel according to Mark.

Both Peter and Paul preceded those Jewish émigrés, probably arriving in Rome in the early 60s, early enough that Christian tradition claims that both died in the persecution instigated by Nero. While little is known of how or when Peter arrived in Rome, there is substantial information about how it was that Paul came there.

Paul and the Believers in Jerusalem

In the mid-50s, Paul had spent some of his time collecting money from his communities for an offering of support to the churches in Judea, which had come into hard times. It is likely that Paul also viewed the offering as a show of solidarity with the Jewish-Christians who, by accepting the money, would be indicating their acceptance of Paul's Gentile converts as equals with themselves (Rom. 15:25–27). There are several mentions of the collection in various letters Paul wrote (e.g., 1 Cor. 8–9). In his letter to the Romans, Paul's last, he asks the Roman believers to pray that his offering—literally, of money, and figuratively, of his converts—would be accepted by the leaders in Jerusalem (Rom. 15:30–31). He hints that he would not mind if the Roman church would intercede with Jerusalem for him, so that his mission there would be successful.

---

1. The Gospel according to Mark was probably finished ca. 70, which places it right on the dividing line between this chapter and the next. It will be discussed in chapter 7.

However, Paul is not blind to the fact that he has had some serious disagreements with other believers in Jerusalem, and that there have been many times when his message provoked enough public outcry to lead to his arrest (Rom. 15:31). Not long before he wrote this letter, Paul had spent two years in prison in Ephesus for some offense relating to his preaching. So, as he anticipates his journey to Jerusalem and speaks hopefully about an ensuing mission to Spain (Rom. 15:28), Paul also has to recognize that his return to Judea is fraught with peril.

As mentioned in the previous chapter, Luke tells a poignant story of Paul's welcome in Jerusalem and meeting with James "and all the elders" (Acts 21:18). While these church leaders welcomed Paul's news about the many Gentiles who had converted, there also was more than a little consternation about the rumors that Paul taught Diaspora Jews "to forsake Moses" and no longer to observe the laws of Torah—charges which may be a bit exaggerated but still are plausible, depending upon how one interprets some of Paul's comments in his earlier letters, perhaps especially the one to the Galatians (ca. 53). So the leaders of the Jerusalem church suggested an alternate way of handling this monetary gift from the Gentile believers that would show Paul's "orthodoxy" as an observant Jew: Paul joined four of their number who are being released from a vow, and he paid the collection money as the offering for their rite of purification.

Thus the community accepted the money from the Gentile churches while yet refusing to recognize the members of those churches as equal partners in the gospel (Acts 21:20–24). Instead, they reinforced the "foreign" status of the Gentile believers, reiterating that they should follow the three prohibitions incumbent upon foreigners who live in the land of Israel (21:25). If Luke's scenario is accurate—and there certainly is no reason to expect that he would be *over*stating the case—this means that Paul's hope for acceptance of the Gentiles as equal partners with Israelite believers was shattered. Unless they became proselytes to Judaism, Gentile believers were not to have an equal share in the blessings of God bestowed on those who follow the Messiah.

Before the week was out, Paul was forcibly removed from the Temple by a mob intent on stoning him, but they were interrupted in the act by the Roman tribune, who took it upon himself to arrest Paul and find out what he has done (Acts 21:27–33). Luke suggests that those who instigated this lynching attempt were Diaspora Jews who had followed Paul to Jerusalem from Asia Minor (21:27). Regardless of who started the action, both the reasons for and fact of Paul's arrest are certainly plausible. Luke offers a series of scenes of interrogations of Paul by Jewish and Roman officials, and speeches to defend himself and his actions, stylized expositions of Luke's understanding of Paul's fundamental theology and self-understanding. In his letter to the Romans, Paul had intimated his concerns about returning to Jerusalem, not entirely certain of how he would be received there, and Acts suggests that those concerns were well-founded. Apparently Paul indeed was arrested in Jerusalem and then taken in chains for trial by Roman officials, first in Caesarea Maritima (the government center for the Province of Judea) and, if Acts is correct, then finally in Rome, where the community of disciples welcomed him.

Traditions about Peter in Rome

What about Peter in Rome? The New Testament never speaks of Peter going to Rome. The farthest destination of Peter named by either Paul or Acts is the city of Antioch in Syria. Peter apparently became a significant leader in that community of disciples by the late 40s (Gal. 2:11–14). Later traditions about Peter and Paul as "founders" of the Roman community of believers highlight the centrality of these two figures in the development of later church doctrine and structures. However, these second- and third-century traditions say more about the times in which the traditions arose and cannot be relied upon for evidence of the mid-first-century communities.

On the other hand, some small indicators suggest there may be a historical kernel to the claim of Peter having died in Rome. Given his later importance, it is significant that no other ancient Christian bishopric claimed to be the place of Peter's death. Furthermore, in 1 Peter 5:13, "Peter" sends greetings from the church in "Babylon," a Jewish euphemism for Rome (cf. Rev. 17). Paul speaks of a "Cephas" party in Corinth—disciples in this Greek city claiming allegiance to teaching attributed to Peter (1 Cor. 1:12), which shows that Peter's influence extended to Corinth. Although this does not prove that he personally visited that city, such a visit certainly would explain Peter's influence there. Extra-canonical traditions (e.g., *Acts of Peter,*

According to Christian tradition, Saint Peter's Tomb is located beneath St. Peter's Basilica in Rome. No contemporary sources indicate the place of Peter's demise, but the fact that no other Christian community claims that honor adds weight to the assertion that Peter died in Rome.

ca. 200) claim that Peter was crucified near the Roman Circus (the track for chariot racing) during the persecution under Nero (64 CE). Even if true, exactly how or when Peter arrived in the Eternal City is not known.

Emperor Nero's Persecution of the Christ-Believers

Why did Nero persecute the Christians? The oldest and most reliable answer to this question comes from the Roman historian Tacitus (ca. 56–ca. 118 CE). In his *Annals* he gives a long account of the great fire, which destroyed approximately 40 percent of the city of Rome in the year 64, including much of the central city with its public buildings. Tacitus never explicitly claims that Nero planned the fire, but he does say that, whatever Nero said or did afterwards, whatever prayers and gifts were offered to the pagan gods, he could not persuade the people that the fire was not the result of an imperial order. Finding himself unable to avoid suspicion in this way, Nero then adopted a more traditional and effective technique to avoid blame for the fire: he found a scapegoat. He chose the Christ-believers, Tacitus says, because they were despised for their many vices. The Roman historian labels the Christ movement a superstition and, in an argument for guilt by association, claims that its name derives from someone named "*Chrestus*" (pronounced the same as "*Christos*") who had been executed by Pontius Pilate during the reign of Tiberius (14–37 CE).

Nero arrested people who "confessed," but Tacitus does not state precisely what they confessed—being followers of the Christ, or setting the city on fire. Nero made a terrifying example of those who were convicted. Some were dressed in animal skins and torn to pieces by hungry dogs in the arena; others were covered with pitch and burned alive, used as torches to light Nero's gardens at night. Nero's tortures were so severe and the emperor's motives so questionable that Tacitus says many of the Roman people began to pity the victims.

Tacitus does not enumerate the "vices" which made the Christ-believers so distrusted in Rome but, in the second century, when such persecutions were more frequent, Christian writers such as the North Africans Tertullian (ca. 160–ca. 200) and Minucius Felix (*fl.* ca. 200) listed the three main charges then in circulation.

Accusation 1: Cannibalism

At the head of the list stood cannibalism, often referred to as Thyestian feasts (the name coming from the Greek myth of Thyestes, the tragic father who was tricked into eating the flesh of his own sons). The cannibalism charge obviously derives from Christian liturgical terminology about eating the flesh and drinking the blood of Christ.

Accusation 2: Sexual Immorality

The second common charge against the disciples was sexual immorality, in particular, of having orgiastic feasts that included even incest. Christ-believers already were suspect because they held their meetings during and after the evening meal in private homes. If they could not conduct their business in public, then any self-respecting Roman would assume that it must be shameful. Moreover, while staying at these gatherings late into the night might have been a rare occurrence, Luke's comment in Acts 20:7 suggests that it did happen on occasion. Outsiders easily could wonder what might make a private party last so long into the night if not excessive eating, drinking, and raucous entertainment. On top of this, given that the disciples referred to one another as "brother" and "sister," any suspected orgies would sound incestuous to an outsider.

While most scholars dismiss such charges as slander, they may have had some basis in fact. In 1 Corinthians 6:12, Paul quotes some Corinthians as saying, "All things are lawful for me" and again at 10:23, "All things are lawful." Possibly he was hearing a somewhat distorted variation of his own familiar claim about Christians' being free from the obligation to observe the Jewish law. However, particularly in a cosmopolitan and rather racy city like Corinth, where orgiastic cults were quite popular, it is understandable that some would hear Paul's claim as meaning that those living a new life in Christ were no longer bound by traditional mores. It is also significant that one result of this libertine attitude was a relationship that Paul himself viewed as incestuous (5:1–2), although his brief description suggests that it would not have been classified as such according to Roman law. Following Jewish mores, Paul condemns such behavior as scandalous. If the case became known to outsiders, especially Jewish ones—and there is no particular reason to expect that it would not—it certainly would provide grist for the rumor mill.

Accusation 3: Atheism

The third typical charge was "atheism," because converts to the Jesus movement rejected their ancestral gods, replacing them with this new "superstition" about a dead criminal coming back to life as a god. This also led to the charge of "hatred of the human race," because the gods were patrons of the empire; indeed, each city and trade union had its patron deity as well. When they were happy, these divine patrons ensured the well-being and prosperity of their human worshipers. However, it did not bode well for those who angered the gods, especially by snubbing them to worship a mere mortal. As everyone knew, the gods were jealous and would punish any who tolerated such proud and rebellious people.

Did Some Christians Encourage the Fire?

There remains one more possibility that readers often overlook—namely, that some Christians may actually have been guilty of setting or encouraging the fire. Many first-century Christ-believers expected Jesus' imminent return on the clouds of heaven and in power. Like other apocalyptically-minded Jews, they believed that this glorious Coming would involve the violent overthrow of the existing pagan kingdoms. These early believers looked forward to the destruction of the present structures of the world to make way for a new world of justice with God as direct ruler.[2] Such attitudes appear most strongly in the Book of Revelation, which gives a colorful description of the destruction of worldly powers—depicted as stars falling from the sky, the moon turned to blood, plagues and pestilence—to make way for the new and eternal Jerusalem to come down from heaven. But the imagery in Revelation explicitly includes the fall of "Babylon," the city of the seven hills (17:9)—that is, Rome.

The Book of Revelation was composed in the 90s of the first century, well after the fire that destroyed much of Rome in Nero's day, but Paul taught the same kind of apocalyptic views already in his earliest letter (1 Thessalonians, ca. 48–50 CE). Many scholars believe such ideas go back to the very beginnings of the Jesus movement and that Jesus himself held strong apocalyptic views. Certainly such beliefs were not unknown in the Judaism of Jesus' day, and the Gospels say that John the Baptist preached such ideas before Jesus. It is thus possible that, when the great fire of Rome broke out, apocalyptic Christ-believers in the city thought that the destruction of Babylon had begun and rejoiced at Christ's imminent return.

---

2. Note that this is not an expectation that God will destroy the ecosphere—even less of nuclear annihilation—as some contemporary apocalypticists have claimed. The New Testament insists that God created the universe and it is good, not worthy of destruction. The problem lies with the unjust structures that human beings have created, conforming to selfish human desires rather than the gracious will of God.

This is speculation, but it illustrates an important historical point, namely, that one cannot allow current views of Christianity to color one's view of the historical reality nearly 2,000 years ago. Contemporary Christians routinely assume that Nero's accusation against the disciples had to be false, but that is largely because most modern Christians simply cannot understand the apocalyptic mind-set or empathize with its rejection of the present structures of life. Especially in America, there is a tendency to focus on the goodness of the world (consider the prominence of eco-spirituality) and people are in no great rush to see the present social and political structures dismantled. Perhaps they are in need of reform here and there, but their abolition certainly would be going too far. Nevertheless, apocalyptically oriented believers of the first century truly did wish the destruction of such structures in their world, and it is quite possible that at least some of them rejoiced at the Great Fire in 64.[3]

How Widespread Was Nero's Persecution?

Nero did not give a theology quiz to distinguish among the Roman Christ-believers. He simply had a number of them arrested and executed to remove suspicion from himself. Nero limited the persecution to the city of Rome; there is no evidence of similar activity outside the city.[4] How many believers were arrested? No one knows for sure. Medieval traditions and movie spectacles make it look like hundreds were caught up in the frenzy, but the actual numbers could have been just a few dozen. Yet the image of sizeable numbers should not be entirely discounted. As the dispute over "Chrestus" shows, Christ-believers were in Rome before 49 CE.[5] When Paul writes to Rome in about 58 CE, he greets two dozen apostles and evangelists

3. A scenario somewhat like this is depicted in the Hollywood film, *Barabbas*. Arriving in Rome a generation after the crucifixion to find the Eternal City in flames, Barabbas is told that the Christians started the fire. Believing that the end of the world has come, and having heard Christian leaders teaching that the world would end in fire, he promptly begins to add fuel to the fire. Just to make sure that the viewing audience gets the gospel message straight, Peter later disabuses Barabbas of his mistake and teaches him that Jesus wanted his disciples to be peacemakers.

4. The first empire-wide persecution did not occur until 250 CE, under the Emperor Decius.

5. See page 110, chapter 4.

and mentions several different house-churches. Acts says that, on his way to Rome, Paul met believers at Puteoli, near Naples, and then disciples from Rome met him at Three Taverns, south of the capital. The Christ movement clearly had put down roots in Italy and in the imperial capital itself. When the persecution against Christ-believers broke out in 64 CE, there may well have been a sizeable population that was targeted.

Another factor suggesting a major persecution was that the Roman disciples did not hide. Nero's persecution was the first volley from the Roman authorities; before that, the Roman believers had no need to fear for their safety. The Roman historian Tacitus says the Christ-believers were loathed for their vices, but Rome had long been home to foreign cults, especially from the Eastern Mediterranean. As early as 200 BCE, conservative Romans complained about the growing popularity of Eastern cults, but these cults continued to win new devotees, apparently some Romans included. Furthermore, Acts repeatedly shows Paul being saved by Roman officials from angry mobs (19:23–41; 21:27–36); the Romans were at least neutral parties in such situations, if not allies to the Christ-believers. Even allowing for questions about the historicity of individual episodes of Acts, the pattern remains—prior to Nero's persecution, the disciples of Jesus had nothing to fear from the Roman state. This in turn means that, up until that time, they had no reason to mask their religious affiliation. When the persecution broke out, they would have made easy targets.

As Paul's Epistle to the Romans indicates, the community of disciples in the imperial capital had a strong Jewish background, while the continuing use of Greek in all literature emanating from the community down to the early third century suggests a sizeable foreign, or at least non-Latin-speaking, element. However, none of the sources indicates that ethnic resentment or xenophobia played any role in Nero's choice to scapegoat the Christ-believers.

What of Peter and Paul?

Eusebius (*Ecclesiastical History* 2.25) records the tradition that Paul and Peter died in this persecution. This may have been true for Peter, but it almost certainly was not the case for Paul. He had gone to

Rome (in 58–60?) as a prisoner involved in a capital case, a legal situation far different from a persecution involving the random arrest of any Christian. Most scholars agree that Paul died in Rome, but that he lost his appeal and was convicted and legally executed around the year 62—that is, two years before the fire. Eusebius says that Paul was beheaded, the quick death permitted to Roman citizens rather than a grotesquely painful death like crucifixion.

Assuming Peter did make it as far as Rome, he would have been very likely to be caught up in the persecution. As a member of Jesus' inner circle, he would have been a prominent figure among the Roman believers and, as such, a key target of the Romans. Eusebius says that Peter suffered crucifixion, and the *Acts of Peter*, an apocryphal writing of the second century, is the first to report the story that Peter asked to be crucified upside down, a wish the Romans granted. The Vatican was built upon the traditional site of his martyrdom.

Consequences of Nero's Persecution

What consequences did Nero's persecution have? For the Roman community of disciples, it seems to have had few long-lasting effects. The persecution came through like a hurricane, doing great destruction but not lasting long. After Nero had gotten his scapegoats for the fire, he returned to his policy of ignoring the Christ-believers. No record survives of a subsequent persecution by him. Nor is there any record of persecution in Rome for another thirty years. In fact, the communities of believers certainly thrived during that time, for there is definite evidence of literary and liturgical activity. The survival of the community as a whole does not, of course, mitigate the suffering of those caught in the persecution and of their desolate family members. The Roman *ecclesia* had gained the first in its long list of martyrs.

The consequences for the larger Jesus movement, on the other hand, were significant. With the deaths of Peter and Paul, two major figures of the first generation had died. By this time, James of Jerusalem also had been killed by a Jerusalem mob, and no doubt others of the earliest disciples also had died. The passing of these giants meant that the era of great individuals who knew Jesus personally also was ending. The leaders of the next generation are not even known by name—think of the authors of the Gospels and of the pseudony-mous epistles such as the Pastorals—and even when definite names are preserved, such as John the Seer (Rev. 1:4, 9), next to nothing is known about them.

The persecution had another, more ominous significance: it set a legal precedent. The Roman Empire officially had moved against the communities of Christ-believers. After Nero's death, his successors generally avoided following his path and the disciples were safe, but the existing precedent could be used at any time by later emperors. Like African-Americans in the South before the civil rights move-ment, Christ-believers might live a completely safe life, but they could never be sure when the authorities might turn against them.

The First Jewish War of Liberation from Rome

The Roman State also played a decisive role in the second great external event that affected the communities of disciples in the 60s, the Romano-Jewish war of 66–73. This conflict usually is called sim-ply "the Jewish War" from the title of the book (*De Bello Iudaico*) written about it by the Jewish historian Josephus (ca. 37–101 CE), who initially was a general on the Jewish side but was captured and then went over to the Romans.

Poor Local Leadership

Roman rule in the province of Judea often provided a model of mismanagement. Governors typically stayed for only two years, or maybe four at the outside; only Valerius Gratus (15–26 CE) served longer than Pontius Pilate, whom the Emperor Tiberius recalled to Rome for his cruelty and inefficiency. Roman nobles did not con-sider Judea a prime government assignment, especially in contrast to the provinces in Italy or Gaul, and the Roman governors did not always set high standards for other, lesser officials. Rome preferred to rule through local monarchs, which in Judea meant the Herodian family. When Herod Agrippa I died in 44 CE, his son and successor, Herod Agrippa II, did not immediately succeed to the title because he was only seventeen. His uncle, Herod of Chalcis ruled until his death in 50 CE, at which point Rome recognized Herod Agrippa II as King. Acts 25–26 aptly portrays the young king as given to pomp, obsequious to the Roman Governor Festus, maintaining an incestuous relationship with his sister Berenice, and frightened that Paul might be speaking the truth. Herod Agrippa II provided no local leadership for the Jews.

Persecution in Judea and the Martyrdom of James the Righteous

If Herod had been an effective leader, the Jerusalem community might not have produced its most prominent martyr. In the year 62, Governor Festus died in office. Emperor Nero appointed Albinus as Festus' successor, but before Albinus arrived to take the reins of office, the High Priest Annas II (son of the Annas mentioned in the Gospels) seized the opportunity to execute James "the Righteous" (later known as James II), the brother of Jesus and leader of the Jerusalem community. The Jewish historian Josephus criticizes Annas II for being "a bold and audacious man," and goes on to charge that, when Annas brought James and some other Christ-believers before the Sanhedrin and arranged for their death by stoning, "the most moderate of the citizens and strictest in the observance of the laws disliked the deed and secretly sent a message to King Agrippa II beseeching him to bid Annas to refrain from similar actions in the future."[6] Agrippa could have intervened but did not. Annas' opponents then appealed to Albinus, the new Roman governor, who threatened Annas with punishment. Knowing how the governor felt, Agrippa II finally deprived Annas II of the high priesthood.

Eusebius of Caesarea cites Hegesippus' second-century account of James' death. In a much longer account than that of Josephus, Hegesippus claims that the scribes and Pharisees in Jerusalem feared that too many Jews were joining the Jesus movement, so they seized James bar Joseph, brought him to the parapet of the Temple, and ordered him to tell the people not to follow Jesus. According to Hegesippus, these Jewish leaders respected James, addressing him as "righteous one"—a title that implies that they thought he was strictly obedient to the law of Moses. They told the people that they would

---

6. Josephus, *Antiquities* 20.9.1.

vouch for what James said, and waited for his public retraction. Rather than denying his faith, James instead spoke of Jesus' imminent coming on the clouds. Many in the audience believed, and the Jewish leaders realized that they had made a mistake. Acting quickly to save the situation, Hegesippus says they threw James from the parapet. Miraculously, James survived the fall, so his enemies resorted to more crude means, stoning and clubbing him to death. Hegesippus continues with an allusion to the stoning of Stephen in Acts 7, claiming that, before he died, James asked God to forgive his killers because they did not know what they were doing. Hegesippus does not mention that any others were martyred with James. He also goes on to observe that "the more intelligent Jews" recognized presumably in retrospect, that so heinous an act was one of the factors that eventually led to the Roman destruction of Jerusalem.

The unsubtle parallels to the death of Jesus in Luke's Gospel as well as the coarse apologetic about the destruction of Jerusalem make scholars doubt the historicity of the account of Hegesippus and thus to prefer that of Josephus. However, Josephus gives no reason for Annas' attack on James and the other Jerusalem disciples, so Hegesippus may be right about this detail. Clearly, James enjoyed some status in the city, and not just among the followers of Jesus; Josephus says that the more religious among the Jews wanted King Agrippa II to prevent similar occurrences. The New Testament evidence (in both the Letter of James and the Acts of the Apostles) suggests that James the Righteous wanted Jesus' followers to continue living like Jews, observing the regulations of Mosaic law. This would have earned James some respect among Jewish Christ-believers who had reservations about Paul's version of the gospel, and would have made the Jerusalem community of disciples less offensive to those Jews who did not believe in Jesus as Messiah. To outsiders like the Romans, it is likely that this policy made the Jerusalem disciples appear to be members of another Jewish sect rather than a competing religion. If so, Hegesippus probably is correct in saying that the opposition to James the Righteous derived from his success in persuading the people of Jerusalem to accept the message about Jesus.

However, Hegesippus blames *all* the leading Jews for the death of James and, unlike Josephus, makes no mention of any moderate or religious Jews who opposed it. Hegesippus wrote ca. 165 CE when Jews and Christ-believers in many parts of the world had begun to go their own ways. Both sides continued to have ill feelings about that split, and used exaggerated rhetoric in their polemics against the other.

Soon after James' death, the Jews began a messianic revolution to oust the Romans from Judea and restore God's kingship in the Holy Land. The war lasted for seven years, from 66–73, although the Roman capture and destruction of Jerusalem in 70 CE was the decisive turning point in the war. The few surviving Jews fled the city, and the remaining Jewish forces (known as *sicarii*) installed themselves in Herod the Great's impenetrable fortress at Masada, along the Dead Sea. There they held out for three years against a Roman siege, until their famous last stand in 73. Meanwhile there were other pockets of resistance, very likely including the members of the Qumran community, who then hid their sacred texts to prevent their destruction by the Romans in case of capture. But Jerusalem had been the center of operations for the revolutionaries, and the Temple had been their command post. Without those strategic locations, the revolt could not succeed.

Consequences of the War for the Followers of Jesus

The revolt had enormous consequences for Jews, but it also had significant consequences for the followers of Jesus. The Jewish historian Josephus gives a stirring account of the Romano-Jewish War without even mentioning disciples of Jesus. The church historian Eusebius gives an account of what happened to the believers in Jerusalem, but clouds his account with anti-Semitism. Eusebius says that Josephus blamed the Jewish losses in the war on the martyrdom of James the Righteous in 62 CE, but Josephus' work mentions nothing of the kind. Moreover, it is difficult to see why the death of James would instigate a war four years later, in 66 CE. To ecclesiastical writers like Eusebius, the real cause of the Roman destruction of Jerusalem was God's vengeance upon the Jews for the death of Jesus. It fulfilled Jesus' prophecy about the city (Matt. 24:19–21); even the disposition of the Roman army followed exactly Jesus' prophecy in Luke (21:20). In claiming that the destruction of Jerusalem was divine retribution for the killing of Jesus, Eusebius unfortunately reflected the views of many early Christians.

Pella, in modern Jordan, is about two miles east of the Jordan River and about eighteen miles south of the Sea of Galilee. According to Eusebius, Jesus-followers fled to Pella during the Jewish War, in response to a divine oracle warning of the impending destruction of Jerusalem.

We must reject much of what Eusebius says, especially his anti-Semitic justification for the Roman success, but also his interpretations of New Testament prophecies. Eusebius wrote when people thought the Gospels gave an exact historical reporting of Jesus' words. Hence they simply assumed that all the Gospel statements concerning the destruction of the Temple and the Holy City actually were spoken by Jesus, an entire generation before the Jewish War. Scholars now believe that the Gospels of Matthew and Luke should be dated after the war, between 80–90 CE (see chapter 8), and that Jesus' words were reworked by the evangelists after the fact so they would fit the actual description of the Roman siege. But does Eusebius say anything of historical value?

Eusebius claims that, before the war broke out, "an oracle given by revelation to acceptable persons" in the Jerusalem *ecclesia* ordered the community to flee Jerusalem and settle in a pagan town named Pella, east of the Jordan River.[7] The members of the community

7. Eusebius, *Ecclesiastical History* 3.5.3.

obeyed the oracle. Many scholars have been reluctant to accept this tradition, partly because of Eusebius' generally questionable account of the Jewish War, partly because they dismiss the notion of a miraculous message prompting the supposed move, and partly because Eusebius implies that the entire Jerusalem community fled the city. Nevertheless, there may be a historical kernal here.

The grain of historical fact lies in the make-up of the Jerusalem community. Scholars usually speak as if all the members were Jewish converts strongly insistent upon the keeping of Jewish customs and Torah regulations. Yet Paul's letters and the Acts of the Apostles make it clear that James of Jerusalem, no matter how reluctantly, agreed to the Gentile mission. Unless he was a hypocrite, it seems that James would have welcomed visiting or even resident Gentiles into the Jerusalem community. When it had become clear to prescient observers that a revolt was likely, Gentile believers could well have emigrated from Judea, fearful for their lives, and it is logical that they would have headed back to Gentile territory. And they may not have been alone. Josephus recounts how the revolutionaries turned on the rich, robbing and sometimes killing them. Since some wealthy Jews belonged to the Christ-believing communities (e.g., Barnabas and the family of John Mark), they also may have left the city if they feared they would be special targets of the revolutionaries—although they would not necessarily head for Pella.

Sources other than Eusebius throw additional light on the Jesus movement and the Jewish War. The Jewish historian Josephus names the Zealots as leaders of the revolt. Clearly, the Zealots expected all Jews to join them—could they count upon the Christ-believers? Most readers would see no point to asking such a question because of a tendency to think that first-century believers thought just like modern Christians. However, it is highly likely that, at least for some of Jesus' followers, the answer to this query was a resounding "Yes."

As mentioned in the discussion of Nero's persecution, contemporary readers should not let their own views get in the way of possible historical evidence. Modern people may believe that Jesus' kingdom is not of this world, but this was by no means the uniform belief among Christ-believers in the mid-first century. In addition, today people may think of Jesus' followers as "Christians," or even "Jewish-Christians," but Judean believers thought of themselves as

Jewish and continued to practice Jewish customs as well as their new "Christian" ones. They knew the Jewish people's long history and proud heritage, and they deeply resented the idolatrous Romans— who were oppressing their people, had put Jesus to death, and just two years earlier had persecuted their sisters and brothers in the imperial capital. It would not be at all surprising that some, at least, would want to join the revolt, and the Gospels seem to provide some evidence of this desire.

Luke (6:15; cf. Acts 1:13) says one of the Twelve named Simon (not Simon Peter) was a "zealot." In the time of Jesus, the term "zealot" probably meant someone who was zealous to observe the laws of Torah. The Gospel accounts, however, were written after the Jewish War, in which this term was preempted by the Jewish freedom fighters. Luke may use this term (somewhat anachronistically) to indicate that Simon embraced revolutionary ideas against Rome. If so, the term can be read in two non-contradictory ways. One is that during Jesus' ministry some of his followers did indeed expect him to establish a political kingdom (cf. Matt. 20:21 // Mark 10:37). Given Jesus' execution on precisely these grounds, this fact seems indisputable, although it is not clear that Jesus himself shared this expectation. If one recalls that the evangelists wrote not modern biographies of Jesus but works that deal with his life and teachings as they pertained to issues important for the evangelists' own communities, one or two generations later, then this reference to the "zealot" may have a second meaning. It may be less a historical report than a remark aimed toward the evangelists' contemporaries.

The evangelists composed their Gospels when memories of the Jewish War were still fresh in the mind, and some members of these communities may still have anticipated God's imminent establishment of a new and just earthly kingdom. Certainly, the Roman authorities continued to be sensitive about messianic expectations for precisely this reason. If one compares the Gospels in their order of composition (Mark, Matthew, Luke, and John), one sees an increasing tendency to downplay the political and nationalistic elements of Jesus' words and deeds. Including a "zealot" among Jesus' most intimate disciples and then having Jesus teach these disciples about a heavenly rather than earthly kingdom would be a persuasive strategy for dealing with overly zealous members of the evangelists' own congregations.

Whether or not one accepts as historical the characterization of this Simon as a "zealot," it is not only possible but likely that some of Jesus' followers joined in the revolt. Apocalyptic speculation among Jews of this period spoke of an imminent end of this present evil age and the coming of God's Anointed to establish divine justice on earth. Jesus had proclaimed the establishment of a divine kingdom on earth, and his followers concluded that he was the expected Messiah who would return in cloud and power to do just this, overthrowing the established social and political order in the process. If wars and tribulations were to precede this cataclysmic event, as Jesus himself may have predicted (e.g., Mark 13), it would not be a great surprise if some believers viewed the Jewish Revolt as precisely the kind of ordeal that Jesus had said would be a prelude to his glorious return.

Nor was the war a purely nationalist conflict; indeed, for many it was more a religious struggle than a political one. Josephus says that Jewish apocalyptic speculations fueled the Judaean revolt, and made many Jews view it as a "holy war." Jesus' disciples held similar apocalyptic expectations. Like the fire in Rome, the war in Judea easily could have garnered support from the more zealous of Jesus' disciples, hoping thereby to hasten the day of his return. The only ecclesial document that comes from the period during the war is the Gospel according to Mark, and it indicates that the community that produced it was indeed debating the question of whether or not to support the war effort. In fact, probably the war itself was a key provocation for producing this first surviving narrative of Jesus' life and teachings. While our immediate reaction might be to dismiss the possibility that Jesus' disciples would become involved in this kind of political struggle, this simply shows how effective were the evangelists' efforts at spiritualizing Jesus' message.

An example from Mark's Gospel may better illustrate this point. Mark 5 opens with a story about a Gentile man, possessed by an uncontrollable and destructive spirit, who lived among the tombs. Jesus happened to be traveling through his town and, when he came within view, the man rushed toward him and bowed down before Jesus, while the demon within begged Jesus to go away and leave him alone. Intent upon exorcizing the demon, Jesus asks its name; it is "Legion," the term used for a main unit of the Roman army.[8] Mark writes that "Legion" begged Jesus "not to send them out of the country" (5:10)—which, of course, implies that Jesus has the power to do precisely that. Instead, Jesus heeds the demon's plea and sends it into a herd of swine about 2,000 strong, which promptly plunges over a cliff in a frenzy of self-destruction (v. 13). The story ends with the townsfolk, struck with fear, pleading with Jesus to leave their region.

While a modern audience could hear this story as simply an exorcism, Mark's audience would not miss the remarkable allusions to the Roman *imperium* and the display of Jesus' power over it. If Jesus can cast out the Legion with a word of command, why would his followers need to take up arms to effect Rome's removal? Even more, Jesus heeds the townspeople's request not to cast them from the region, which suggests that God has some reason for permitting the Roman presence to continue. Finally, the Legion ends by destroying itself while Jesus and his disciples simply look on; this is what Mark's audience can expect to happen in their time and, as Jesus' followers, their role is to stand by and wait. In Exodus 14:14 the Israelites are told, "The Lord will fight for you, and you have only to keep still." This exorcism is one way in which Mark's Gospel argues that the same will be true for Jesus' disciples who want to gain freedom from the Romans.

Early Christ-believers did not all think alike any more than modern ones do. Mark's Gospel argues against Jesus' disciples participating in the revolt, but this shows that some in his audience were inclined to do just that. No doubt, Judaean Christians in particular had diverse reactions to the revolt. Some may indeed have fled to Pella before the war or shortly after its outbreak. Some may have

---

8. The Roman legions, the core of the Imperial Army, were instrumental in the conquest and subsequent control of new territories. By the time of Jesus, each legion comprised about 5,000 infantry soldiers, Roman citizens recruited from Italy and the provinces. Commanded by a professional administrator called a *legatus legionis*, each legion was organized into ten Cohorts, which in turn were subdivided into six "centuries" of eighty men, each commanded by a "centurion," who trained the corps and led them into battle. Legionary soldiers wore helmets and protective body armor and were equipped with two javelins, a broad-bladed sword called a *gladius*, and a dagger. They served in the army for twenty-five years. On retirement, they were granted a pension of land or money, typically on the fringes of the empire, where they served as natural reinforcements to the frontier armies. See "Legion," in *Ancient Origins* (Tempe, AZ: Piranha Interactive Publishing; London, UK: Maris Multimedia, 1997), CD-ROM.

joined the revolutionaries, either to fight for Jesus or as turncoats supporting one of the Jewish generals who were aspirants to the title of messiah (e.g., Simon bar Giora, John of Gischala). No doubt some, perhaps most, stayed where they were, laying low and hoping to survive.

One fact about the impact of the war on Jesus' followers is indisputable: after the war, the Jerusalem community lost its traditional influence over the other *ecclesiai*, and this had dramatic and far-reaching effects for the future of the movement. The center of gravity for the disciples turned from the Judaean capital to the imperial one, and the focus of preaching shifted from the "Jewish world" to the dominant Gentile culture. Many factors played a role.

The first was the Roman destruction of much of the city. The Temple was razed, homes were burned, and many of the inhabitants were slaughtered—not only rebel soldiers but also women and children. Between the fire from the burning Temple, the dead bodies of the slain, and the blood of the dead and injured flowing through the streets, the ground was nowhere visible (*Jewish War* 6.5.1), an image remembered and heightened in the Apocalypse (Rev. 14:20). Josephus also reports that the Romans expelled any surviving Jews from the city and forbade them re-entry except for one day of the year, the ninth of Av, the day on which the city had been re-conquered by the Roman forces. While the Jerusalem *ecclesia* probably had some members who were not of Jewish birth, it is unlikely that the Romans would distinguish between them and Christ-believing Jews, especially given that members of the Jerusalem community apparently worshiped in the Temple alongside other Jews (e.g., Acts 2:46; 22:17; 24:18, referring to events in the 30s, 40s, and 50s, respectively). Any followers of Jesus who survived the siege of Jerusalem likely were expelled from the city with the rest of the Jewish population.

In addition, Jewish factions during the revolt were known to attack those who did not support the war effort. Jewish members of the Jerusalem *ecclesia*, and perhaps the Gentile converts as well, would have been subject to this same kind of pressure. Eusebius may be right when he says that some of them fled the Holy City while the war was yet raging.

A third factor is the change in the religious status of Jerusalem. What is Jerusalem without the Temple? With the Temple, Jerusalem

This part of the retaining wall for the Temple Mount is all that remains of the Temple complex in Jerusalem. Due to the destruction of the Temple and much of the city in 70 CE, the *ecclesia* in Jerusalem lost its prominence in the Jesus movement. Thereafter, the movement's center of gravity shifted to the major Gentile cities.

had been a center of pilgrimage; without it, why would Jews have any reason to journey there? Where would they worship since the Temple had been razed? No longer a seat of religious authority, and long after the city had ceased to be a center of kingly authority, bereft of the Temple and dominated by pagan images, Jerusalem could no longer be the center of gravity for any Jews, whether they followed Moses or Jesus.[9]

Fourth, the war caused the Romans to see Palestinian (but not Diaspora) Jews as subversive and disloyal. Gentile and Diaspora converts to the Jesus movement may not have been eager to stress an association with Jerusalem for fear they would be subject to the same suspicion. Without the persecution under Nero, this may not have posed a very serious threat but, with the stories of that police action still fresh in their minds, it is unlikely that they

---

9. The Romans exacerbated this problem in 130 CE by renaming the city Aeolia Capitolina and dedicating it to the chief Roman God, Jupiter. Jerusalem's changed religious status meant that it would be blasphemous for devout Jews (including Christ-believers) to try to worship there, since it would imply their belief in this pagan deity.

would see any advantage to associating themselves with a messianic revolution. Certainly the emerging Judaism under the rabbis did not, as can be seen a decade later in the embassy of Gamaliel II to Emperor Domitian.

Fifth, as more and more converts came from the ranks of the Gentiles, cultural differences would have made a Torah-observant form of the Jesus movement (like that of the Jerusalem community) more difficult to maintain. This had an impact not just on Christ-believers' practices, but even on their ways of thinking and the images they used. They could not expect their Gentile listeners to understand Biblical images nor to know the important stories from the Hebrew Bible; instead, preachers had to find other images to convey their beliefs. For example, around 95 CE Clement, a Jewish Christ-believer living in Rome, praised the organization of the imperial army and used pagan analogies to convey Christian teachings (see chapter 9).

Whatever the reasons, after the Romano-Jewish war, Jesus' disciples outside Judea no longer looked to Jerusalem for leadership. Instead, they looked to Alexandria, Antioch, Ephesus, and Rome, the leading cities in the Roman Empire. There are no more records of missionaries reporting to the leaders of a Jerusalem *ecclesia*, nor of a collection for its needs. From Jerusalem, there is only silence.

Developments in the Wider Empire

Outside of Rome and Judea, Eusebius reports that, in the eighth year of Nero's reign (62), Annianus became the first person after Mark to take charge of the bishopric of Alexandria in Egypt. Eusebius was generally knowledgeable about Alexandrian affairs, and historians accept this as a reliable statement, which is "clearly derived from a bishop list of the church of Alexandria."[10] One appealing element of this tradition is that Annianus' accession does not occur after Mark's death, that is, scholars do not have to accept the theory of Mark being the first Bishop of Alexandria to accept the episcopacy of Annianus.

---

10. Birger A. Pearson, "Earliest Christianity in Egypt: Some Observations," in *The Roots of Egyptian Christianity*, ed. Birger A. Pearson and James E. Goehring, Studies in Antiquity and Christianity (Philadelphia: Fortress, 1986), 132–59, at 140.

Summary

The fourth decade of their history proved to be traumatic for the disciples of Messiah Jesus. The great leaders of the first generation— James, Paul, and Peter—all died violent deaths. The Roman Empire had persecuted the movement, and the mother church that had been their source of unity for three decades was now dispersed. The future must have looked bleak to the disciples and, ironically, one of the problems was that there would be a future for this world. Contrary to what Jesus, Paul, and others had promised, God's Kingdom had not come before the passing of this generation.

Yet here history merged with theology. The Hebrew Bible taught that God was with all Israel, all the chosen people, not just their leaders.[11] While such great figures as James, Peter, and Paul had done important and notable deeds, other disciples, many whose names are now unknown, had been working as well, building local communities and carrying the message of Jesus the Christ through- out the empire. In the next decade, these "unsung heroes" would rebuild a church shattered by adversity.

Questions for Review

1. How did the first state-sponsored persecution of Christians come about?

2. What were the three common accusations that were leveled against Christians, as the Roman state developed its policy of persecution?

3. What were the long-term effects of Nero's persecution of Christians?

4. How did the death of James of Jerusalem come about?

5. What is the evidence that Jesus predicted the destruction of Jerusalem? Why do some scholars doubt that he made such a prediction?

6. What became of the followers of Jesus in Jerusalem at the time of the Jewish War?

---

11. Similarly, Christian theology today teaches that the Spirit of God resides in the whole church, not just its leaders.

7. Explain how the Mark 5 exorcism story may have conveyed a subtle message to the followers of Jesus not to take up arms against Rome.

8. What were the major centers of the Jesus movement after much of Jerusalem was destroyed in the First Jewish War?

Questions for Discussion

1. The question of whether the Apostle Peter actually became Bishop of Rome is a matter of great significance to many contemporary Christians, while others consider it to be of little or no importance; explain why such diversity of opinion exists on this topic. How have strong convictions one way or the other influenced the kind of data that have been preserved, and the way those traditions have been interpreted?

2. Roman persecution of Christ-believers appears to have stemmed in part from misunderstanding of their practices. Do you think the Roman state could have tolerated the Jesus movement if it had been better informed about what Jesus' followers actually believed and did? Why or why not?

3. If the Jerusalem *ecclesia* had not been scattered by the First Jewish War, would the Jesus movement have developed along different lines? Why or why not?

CHAPTER 7

Life from the Ashes
(71–80 CE)

The seventies was a period of great change in both the Jewish and Jesus-movement worlds. The First Jewish War against Rome ended with the destruction of the Temple, the burning of the city, the routing of the Jewish army, and the expulsion of the Jews from the city. Some remaining leaders re-grouped in Yavneh (Jamnia), near the Mediterranean coast, and set about re-inventing a Judaism now bereft of the Temple—no small feat when Temple and Torah had been the two hallmarks of Judaism for the preceding five centuries.

Meanwhile the followers of Jesus also were re-grouping, now deprived of their center of gravity, the *ecclesia* in Jerusalem. The communities of disciples in Alexandria, Antioch, Ephesus, and Rome became very influential in this re-organization, and the members of the Jesus movement increasingly looked toward the West.

The disciples faced a unique situation in this decade. For the first time in the movement's existence, there were no longer any leaders who knew Jesus personally. Key leaders of "the first generation" were now dead. Peter, Paul, and James had been killed even before the war began. No extant source reports anyone else from that generation being active at this time, so presumably they had all passed away.

Contemporary Christians take it for granted that there would come a time when all the eyewitnesses to Jesus would have died, but many of the early disciples, perhaps even most of them, did not.

Belief in the imminent return of the Lord was widespread, as noted previously. This was not the belief of merely a few credulous people but of most of Jesus' followers, including well-educated ones like Paul, and seems to have been taught by Jesus himself (Matt. 16:28). Nor did this expectation die out with the first generation; the pseudonymous author of II Peter, writing about 125 CE, still defended the notion (2 Pet. 3:8–10).

One of the key issues for Jesus' followers in this decade was to rethink this idea of the imminent return of Jesus—as scholars would put it, they had to explain to themselves "the delay of the *Parousia*." The Gospels of Matthew, Luke, and John clearly show how different communities tried to work through this problem. One of the strategies they chose was to establish more stable ecclesial structures for the "interim" between the present era and the return of the Lord. In the process, they also recognized new leaders and new kinds of "offices" in the communities of disciples.

Renewal of the *Pax Romana*

The transition to this "second generation" of Jesus-movement leaders was eased by a growing peace in the world around them. Especially in contrast to the previous decade, the Roman Empire enjoyed a relatively quiet period. After the fall of Jerusalem in 70 CE, the Jewish revolt continued in the Palestinian countryside, ending only in 73 CE when the Romans took Masada after a heroic Jewish last stand. At the other end of the empire, on its northwestern frontier, turmoil continued: the Legions successfully pressed the Roman war against the Celts into the northern part of the isle of Britain. However, in the heart of the empire, the central Mediterranean where the Jesus movement was spreading, there was peace.

General Vespasian, returning to Rome from a campaign in the Romano-Jewish War, rose to imperial power in 69 CE, thus putting an end to the year of turmoil and repeated palace coups that followed Nero's suicide. Vespasian brought a return to stability in Rome; he ruled until 79 CE. A tolerant, unpretentious man, he had no interest in persecuting Christ-believers. Nero was widely reviled after his death (68 CE), and Vespasian was not keen to continue Nero's policies. The new emperor's own attitude toward the imperial cult was

The Arch of Titus, in the Roman Forum, celebrates Titus' victory in the Jewish War. The arch was constructed by Domitian, Titus' brother, who succeeded him as emperor. See page 37 for a close-up of a panel from the Arch of Titus, showing spoils taken from the Temple after the fall of Jerusalem.

quite skeptical. By this time, it had become a tradition that, when the Roman emperor died, the Senate voted him divine honors, legally making him a deity. Vespasian took this with the proverbial grain of salt. When lying on his deathbed, he wisecracked to his family, "Alas, I think I am becoming a god."[1]

The emperor's older son Titus succeeded him. When Vespasian left the Jewish War to fight for the imperial throne, he put his son in charge of the war, and it was Titus who captured Jerusalem. After Titus' death in 81 CE, his brother and successor, Domitian (81–96 CE), erected an arch to commemorate Titus' triumph; the arch still stands

---

1. Suetonius, *The Lives of the Twelve Caesars: Vespasian* 33.722.

in the Roman Forum. While in Judea, Titus began a love affair with Berenice, sister of the Jewish King Herod Agrippa II (ca. 50–ca. 92 CE) and even thought of marrying her, but Roman aristocratic opinion would not tolerate the marriage of a future emperor to one who was, in Roman eyes, a petty Asiatic princess. Titus chose the Empire over Berenice, who was sent home. Titus was a conscientious emperor, providing considerable relief to the citizens of Pompeii when the city was destroyed by the eruption of Mount Vesuvius in 79 CE.

Second-Generation Christ-Believers

Paul's letters and, later, the Acts of the Apostles both make it clear that the Jesus movement could be an occasion of trouble for outsiders. The movement's literature from this decade (e.g., Mark 13:9–10, 12), illustrates that there continued to be points of contention with other Jewish groups. However, the disciples of Jesus more and more were residents of the Mediterranean provinces outside of Judea. They generally lived securely in the Empire, and the second generation progressed largely without external threats.

The leaders of this new generation are unknown. Either only their names are recorded, with virtually no other identifying information (such as John the Seer, the author of the Book of Revelation), or they are totally anonymous. Technically, many of the writings are not anonymous in the sense of being nameless but rather are pseudonymous, that is, they were written under false names—or erroneous names were ascribed to them.

This chapter will cover three key writings of this period, one of which was anonymous (the Gospel according to Mark) and two of which are pseudonymous (Colossians and Ephesians). The two epistles of Colossians and Ephesians each claim in their opening verses (1:1) to have been written by Paul. The Gospel now identified as "according to Mark" originally did not name an author, but since the early second century it has been attributed to someone named Mark. Eusebius preserves an attribution from a Bishop Papias (d. ca. 120 CE) of Hierapolis (modern Pamukkale, Turkey), who passed along a tradition he got from a "presbyter" or elder named John.[2] This

---

2. Eusebius, *Ecclesiastical History* 3.39.

otherwise unknown presbyter John identified the Gospel's author as a disciple of Peter, but he did not say where Peter and the disciple became acquainted—Antioch, Rome, or anywhere else. That attribution is not suspect in itself; the author may well have been a disciple of Peter. But other second-century traditions identify him with the Mark whom Paul calls a fellow prisoner (Philemon 24), and then also with John Mark of the Acts of the Apostles, the Mark mentioned in two pseudo-Pauline epistles, Colossians (4:10) and 2 Timothy (4:11), as well as the Mark called Peter's "son" in the pseudo-Petrine epistle 1 Peter (5:13). Nor did the tradition factory did stop there—he also became identified with Mark, the first Bishop of Alexandria.

No one today believes that all of these descriptions fit the author of this Gospel. Clearly, there was at least one Mark who was prominent in the earliest communities. Indeed, there was probably more than one Mark—the Roman name Marcus was quite common. There is no inherent reason why the evangelist could not have been a disciple of Peter or even someone associated with Peter and Paul, but neither is there any concrete historical evidence for such an association. Some scholars have raised the question of whether, in fact, the author was a woman, based on some of the evidence internal to the Gospel.[3] Again, while there is no inherent reason why this could not be the case, there is simply no way to identify who was the evangelist. Scholars continue to refer to this unknown evangelist as "Mark" out of respect for the tradition and for sheer convenience. Even if it could be proved that someone named Mark wrote the Gospel, it would not help very much without knowing more about the person. As it stands, what is known of "Mark" comes entirely from the Gospel itself.

Meeting the Need for New Holy Books

One of the key strategies in creating a new form of organization for the Jesus movement, not centered in Jerusalem nor as strongly rooted in Jewish practice, was the writing of new holy books to be read in

---

3. E.g., Mary Ann Tolbert, "Mark," in *The Women's Bible Commentary*, ed. Carol A. Newsom and Sharon H. Ringe (Louisville: Westminster John Knox, 1992), 263–74.

the weekly gatherings. Paul's letters already had been used this way, and the practice was familiar from the weekly synagogue services, which many members of the *ecclesia* still attended. The need for such writings became more acute as the first generation of believers, who knew Jesus himself, began to die out and were no longer available to tell their stories of his words and deeds. Some of these writings developed into a new kind of book, a genre combining elements of biography and theology. The new genre was called a *gospel*, meaning the good news of God's victory in the world (see Isa. 52:7; cf. 40:9).

Among these new books, which later were gathered into the collection called the "New Testament," scholars have identified the Gospel according to Mark as the earliest example of the narrative gospel genre. This identification is largely based on a comparison of the three "Synoptic" Gospels of Mark, Matthew, and Luke, which have quite a lot of material in common. Of the various explanations for this sharing of material, the most plausible is that Mark's Gospel was written first, and the other two evangelists borrowed their basic narrative structure (and indeed many passages verbatim) from Mark.

The Gospel according to Mark

Who wrote the book that is now called the Gospel according to Mark? When was it written, and where? The traditional view, first attested about two generations later by Bishop Papias of Hierapolis, holds that Mark dates from the 60s in Rome, and that it derives from the reminiscences of Peter as transmitted to John Mark.[4] Most contemporary scholars accept this dating (although not necessarily the attribution), with the caveat that the book would have to have been composed toward the end of that decade. Because of the apparent references to events of the Jewish War (e.g., Mark 13:7-23), including the destruction of the Jerusalem Temple (Mark 13:1-2), most would date the Gospel right about 70 CE.

Wilhelm Wrede's insistence that Mark is a dogmatic work challenged the prevailing notion that the Gospel was a straightforward

---

4. Eusebius, *Ecclesiastical History* 3.39.15–16.

history of Jesus' life and work.[5] Due in part to the rise of the redaction-critical approach to the New Testament (studying the editorial changes in a text), scholars came to appreciate the creative contribution of the author of Mark—as evangelist (storyteller) and theologian—in making explicit one understanding of Jesus Christ that was implicit in the earliest preaching about him.

Key Themes of Mark: God's *Basileia* Inaugurated by the Secret Messiah

One way to identify these distinctive contributions is to compare this Gospel with the others in the New Testament. There are recurrent themes, organizational patterns, and significant turning points that distinguish Mark from the other canonical Gospels. Two significant counterpoints in this Gospel are: (1) the proclamation that God's *basileia* ("reign" or "empire") has come near in Jesus, and (2) the assertion that both the *basileia* and Jesus are hidden realities marked by "mystery."

Wrede identified a recurring pattern in the Gospel of Mark where Jesus performs a miracle and then commands his audience not to tell anyone about it. This literary device, which Wrede dubbed the "messianic secret," seems to reflect a controversy in the evangelist's day over the identity and role of Jesus as the Christ. This earliest evangelist apparently believed that many of his contemporaries misunderstood Jesus' true identity. If Jesus really was the Messiah of Israel, why did no army (heavenly or otherwise) come to support and defend him at his arrest? How could Jesus really be the Messiah of Israel if in fact the empire of God did not appear to have come, for the Holy Land was still occupied by the empire of Rome? Against his detractors, the Gospel of Mark claims that Jesus was not a charlatan; rather, Jesus repudiated military force as the means of bringing about God's *basileia*. The evangelist emphasizes that Jesus' identity was revealed only in and through his death, not in his earlier healing miracles or other works of power.

---

5. Wilhelm Wrede, *Das Messiasgeheimnis in den Evangelien* (Göttingen: Vandenhoeck & Ruprecht, 1901). Wrede was the first to demonstrate that a Gospel author had theological reasons for depicting Jesus the way he does, rather than simply repeating traditions.

Key Markan Titles: Son of God and Son of Man

"Son of God" as a title for Jesus in the Gospel of Mark does not refer to biological sonship (as if God were embodied) nor to an ontological reality (i.e., divinity), but rather to a relational one. To Mark's audience this claim meant either that Jesus is the loyal agent of God acting on his behalf in the human world, like King David and Cyrus of Persia before him (a Jewish view), or that he is a semi-divine wonder-worker like Hercules (a Hellenistic view). The evangelist expends a fair amount of energy arguing for the former interpretation over the latter. In either case, it is anachronistic to read later creedal affirmations into this stage of the tradition.

Consequently, the term "Son of Man," as used in Mark, is not an opposite of the term "Son of God," but rather a closely related if not quite synonymous concept. Jesus as "Son of Man" (literally, "son of humanity") exemplifies what it means to be a *human* being in the fullest sense of the word: a person living in close contact with God, attending and being obedient to the divine will. Of course, this also is precisely what Jesus' disciples should be like, in spite of their present adversity.

Disagreements within the Markan Community

The three predictions of the passion in Mark play a key role in the arrangement of the Gospel account. The counter-point of Peter's three-fold denial highlights Mark's view that the truth of Jesus' identity is revealed only in his suffering. In some mysterious way, Jesus' suffering is a matter of divine necessity. Combined with the Markan emphasis on the servanthood of Jesus—even the same Jesus who has power over nature and against evil—these themes point to a conflict within the evangelist's own community concerning the understanding of Jesus as the Christ and, as a result, the understanding of what discipleship entails.

The miracle stories in Mark serve to relate the two views, the theology of glory and the mysterious theology of suffering. The apparently glorious miracles lead to Jesus' passion, while the apparently ignominious passion leads to Jesus' miraculous Resurrection unto glory. The intense apocalyptic imagery in Mark, especially in chapter 13, reinforces this intimate connection. While Mark's story appears to end in silence and failure (16:8), the simple fact of the audience's existence counters this impression and provides the unwritten sequel to the Resurrection proclamation (16:6). Thus the dialectic between the theology of glory and the mysterious theology of suffering provides the terminus as well as the beginning of the work.

Mark's Messiah and the Jewish War of Independence

In the context of the Jewish-Roman War, Mark's emphasis on the "suffering messiah" takes on a slightly different cast. The Jews who were involved in the revolt viewed it as God's holy war to oust the infidels and restore the Holy Land to God's chosen people. This war represented the final death throes of the present evil age, and Israel's victory would usher in the new age of God's reign of justice and peace. A restored Israel would then be ruled by a divinely-anointed king (that is, a Messiah) who was attentive to God's will, as David had been of old. Simon bar Giora and John of Gischala, two of the Jewish generals, were both celebrated by their respective troops as this Messiah. To the Jews who were fighting, these generals were what a *real* Messiah would be like, leading the fight to restore land and nation.

The fierce nationalism and messianic fervor of the Jews who were engaged in the revolt against Rome led some of them to view as suspect those Jews among them who did not support the war effort. Responses to such attitudes ranged from shunning to coercion and even assassination. Wherever Mark's community was located, they must have been feeling some of these effects.

Living as they did with one foot still in Judaism and one foot on the way toward a new religion centered on Jesus, Mark's community was in turmoil. Jesus had proclaimed, "This generation will not pass away" before the Son of Man would return on the clouds of heaven to gather God's elect to himself (Mark 13:28, 30). Like many Jews, Mark's community expected that this glorious coming of God's Chosen would be preceded by war, famine, and other portents. The "little apocalypse" of Mark 13 essentially catalogues the kinds of events that were anticipated before God's definitive act of salvation. All the disciples had to do was to look around to see that precisely such portents were taking place in their very midst. Were these the signs of his coming that Jesus had foretold? It is easy to see how some might have thought so. If they were the signs of Jesus' imminent return, then the logical choice for Jesus' followers would be to support this war and speed the day of his coming. Such a strategy would have the added advantage of allowing them to avoid persecution by their zealous neighbors. Glory and victory would belong to those who were faithful to the end.

Mark agreed that being faithful to the end is the call of every disciple, but he believed that faithfulness consisted in waiting expectantly for God to act rather than fighting the battle (Mark 13:7–13). This could not be God's war because it was not Jesus who was being exalted but messianic imposters (13:5–6, 21–22). Jesus was the true Messiah, and yet he ended up being crucified rather than glorified. Thus Mark urged those who could flee the war to do so (13:14), and recognized that those who did not join in the war effort would be persecuted by zealous Jews (13:9, 11–12). Jesus would not abandon his own, for his Spirit would be with them in their time of trial (13:11). The key to being a disciple was to emulate Jesus, the suffering Messiah, and submit to the suffering that was inevitable rather than fighting back and inflicting suffering on others. Fighting back would mean fighting against God, for all of these things must take place; they were part of the mysterious divine plan (13:7b).

This notion of fate or predestination also comes through Mark's formulaic expressions that Jesus *had to do* certain actions in order to fulfill the scriptures, and that God *prevented* some of Jesus' contemporaries from recognizing his true identity. It is probably no coincidence that the actions that were foreordained for Jesus to do were things that brought him suffering and rejection. And the disciple is not greater than the master.

Mark's community was living at a time when their non-Christ-believing Jewish contemporaries extolled the military power of their alternate "messiahs." This was God's holy war, and the Jewish generals were divinely appointed leaders of the nation, implementing God's justice on earth by overthrowing the Gentile powers in the land. There certainly were times when the Jewish forces had victories in battle, and it was no small feat to continue this revolt for so many years when they were fighting against the most powerful army on earth. If one believed that God's glory was to be manifested by victory in battle and re-establishing the Jewish nation, independent from Gentile control, there was more than enough evidence from current events to reinforce such a view.

Not only this, but also many of Mark's Christ-believing contemporaries emphasized the power and the glory of the risen Christ. For Jesus to be the Messiah, he had to be victorious. Looking at Jesus' death was not going to provide much evidence in favor of this claim, but the Resurrection certainly could be used in such a way. The fact of Jesus' death was an embarrassment that had to be overcome in talking to potential converts, but the Resurrection required no apology. It could be proclaimed as God's sign of approval of Jesus and his message, and as a foretaste of Jesus' glorious return to judge the world. Not only was the Resurrection of Jesus a watershed event of the past, it continued to have powerful affects in the communities of those who followed Jesus: there were miracles, tongues, prophecies, and other signs of the glory and power of Christ active among his people. Such a "glory theology" had great appeal, and could easily be used to support a militant attitude toward the war.

In contrast to this interpretation of the gospel, Mark emphasizes a message that cannot conceivably be used to support a pro-war agenda: the suffering and ignominious death of the human Jesus. Being a true disciple of Jesus the Christ does not mean glory but suffering; it means imitating Jesus even to the point of death (e.g., 8:34; 9:35; 10:39–40, 43–45). Suffering is, paradoxically, the present reward for faithfulness to Jesus as well as the guarantee of future glory at his coming. Any legal demands or ethical principles are strictly subordinated to this demand for faithfulness to the call of Jesus.

Was the Markan Community a Sect?

The complex of these three themes—fate (or predestination), Spirit endowment in a time of persecution, and the necessity of staying faithful to Jesus to the end—has led some to suggest that Mark's community was becoming a sect. This theory is supported by the fact that the primary model for community organization in Mark is the non-patriarchal family—that is, one without a "father,"—where not household ties but rather relationship to Jesus (i.e., discipleship) marks one as a family member. Moreover, it would not be surprising if Mark's community were wary of outsiders, given the kind of threat they seem to have faced. However, there is no evidence that they were becoming closed in upon themselves. Mark tells stories of Jesus healing both Jews and Gentiles, and the two feeding miracles show the boundless ability of Jesus to provide food for all people (Jews in chapter 6; Gentiles in chapter 8). Thus it would be stretching the evidence to claim that Mark's community was sectarian. Besides, it would be difficult to see how the gospel could be preached to all the nations (13:10) if Mark's community was not to be involved in spreading it.

In fact, the Gospel of Mark evinces a very positive attitude toward mission, including "all nations" (i.e., as in 13:10, even Gentiles) as objects. The antagonism of chief priests, elders, and scribes toward Jesus in Mark probably reflects a conflict between Mark's community and contemporary Jewish authorities. This may suggest a location in Palestine or some other region with a relatively large Jewish population, for example, one of the larger cities in Syria. The emphasis on Galilee as the place to await Jesus' *Parousia* or glorious return (14:28; 16:7) bolsters the notion that this Gospel originated near there, perhaps in the Syrian church, sometime during the Jewish

Some of the historical data suggest that Mark's Gospel was written in Syria. However, Mark 12:42 tells of a widow who donates two small coins (*lepta*), which the evangelist says equal a *quadrans*. Why would Mark explain the value of coins that were common in the Eastern Mediterranean, unless for the sake of readers in the West?

War against Rome (66–73 CE). Some scholars have argued that the emphasis upon a Gentile mission suggests a more thoroughly Gentile environment, and Ephesus or Rome typically are suggested as examples. However, there are even regions within first-century Palestine that have an inordinately strong Gentile "flavor"—parts of the Galilee, the Decapolis, and newer Roman cities like Caesarea Philippi. The question of where this Gospel originated remains undecided but, since there is a strong consensus that the first Romano-Jewish War was its historical context, the Gospel had to have been written in a region where the War was a real and pressing concern.

Writings in the Pauline Tradition: Colossians and Ephesians

Once the revolt had been suppressed, other Jesus-movement writings came to the fore. All of these seem to be from Asia Minor and are theological letters, modeled after the letters of Paul. In fact, it seems that Paul's writings were becoming important enough and his name influential enough that it was a useful device to attribute one's letters to Paul rather than write them under one's own name. This seems to be the case with Colossians and Ephesians. These two letters probably date to the mid- to late-seventies (or perhaps slightly later for Ephesians). Because of differences in style, use of language, and odd remarks concerning historical events, many scholars believe they are pseudonymous letters attributed to Paul but not actually written by him. The contents of both letters suggest that they were composed by a later Paulinist who viewed the Pauline tradition—or at least some interpretations of it—as problematic, and who wanted to reinforce and revise it to meet contemporary challenges.

The two letters have some interesting differences from the Gospel of Mark. The "gospel of glory" which Mark combats finds at least limited acceptance in Colossians and Ephesians (e.g., Eph. 1:17–23; Col. 1:11–14, 26–28; 3:1–4), rather than the strident rejection it receives in the Gospel. The letters speak of sufferings in a very general way, but mostly those sufferings are attributed to Paul rather than the recipients of the letters (e.g., Eph. 3:1; 4:1; Col. 1:24), and the authors nowhere encourage the readers to seek or endure suffering for Christ's sake. The struggle in these letters is against spiritual powers rather than human ones (Eph. 6:12; Col 2:8). This fits well with the situation in Asia Minor in this decade, where the Judean War had little or no impact and the most threatening problems were taxes, a "false philosophy" that encouraged too much asceticism (Col 2:20–23; cf. Mark, who encourages taking up one's cross to follow Jesus), overly independent wives, and uppity slaves (e.g., Eph. 5:22–33; 6:5–8; Col. 3:18–25). The fact that these two letters speak of both Christ-believing slaves and Christian masters suggests that the members of these communities are, on average, of a higher social class and economic level than those known from the previous two decades. Even the attractions of the "false philosophy" reinforce this impression, for it would not have been an issue unless a number of the believers in the audience had leisure time to devote to such intellectual concerns.

"Mark" of the Gospel and "Paul" of Ephesians and Colossians both attempted to help their communities face a future without those who knew Jesus. Mark did it by putting the words and deeds of Jesus into a written narrative that he created: a "gospel," an account of the good news of Jesus Christ. This permanent account meant that the community of believers no longer had to depend exclusively upon a living tradition that could be broken if those transmitting it died before training others to continue their work. This provided the Christ-believers with a new form of authority but not one that immediately replaced the familiar one, oral tradition. The importance of oral tradition continued well into the second century, as will become apparent in subsequent chapters.

The authors of Ephesians and Colossians took a different tack. They, too, created a written authority, not just by their own writings but also by elevating the status of the Apostle Paul. In Colossians, Paul is the teacher whose epistles are passed around to different churches and read publicly, presumably during liturgy (4:15–16), while Ephesians seems to be an introduction to a collection of Pauline epistles. The charismatic Paul was being institutionalized into a written authority. To some this debases Paul's message, but, realistically, how else could that message be maintained after his death? This is what had happened to the messages of the biblical prophets and was beginning to happen to Jesus' message as well. The charisma of the first age cannot be maintained indefinitely; some institutionalization is always necessary.

Colossians and "False Philosophers"

The letter addressed to Colossae presumes a community trying to live in faithfulness to the Pauline gospel, but troubled by teachers who spread a false "philosophy." This false teaching concerns the elemental spirits of the universe, and includes a set of cultic regulations that, if followed, will appease those spirits and (presumably) release the devotee from their power. Against this false *gnosis* (secret, heavenly knowledge), the author of Colossians affirms the universal lordship of Christ and the completeness of the divine message he revealed. In expressing some of the elements of this divine message, the author claims that the fullness (*plērōma*) of divinity is made known in Christ, and the liberation of the believer from cosmic powers is due solely to the activity of Christ vanquishing those powers, both divine and human.

The hymn in Colossians 1:15–20 depicts Christ as revealer and mediator between God and humanity, but does not mention the incarnation as the mode of this revelation or mediation. The creation of the church by Christ (1:18) is an act of redemption, and the eschatological process of revelation unto redemption is carried out by Christ, the crucified savior (1:19), through the preaching and life of the church he founded.

There are striking similarities between Colossians and Ephesians. Most commentators consider both works pseudonymous, although they preserve Pauline traditions. Ephesians is very general in stance and is concerned with the nature of the *ecclesia* as a whole. In composition and theology, it is one step further removed from Paul than is Colossians, upon which it frequently appears to be literarily dependent.

The Household Codes "Correct" Community Life

The term *household codes* refers to a particular format of ethical instruction, such as that found in Colossians and Ephesians. The format entails cataloging the various social roles into which a person might fit—husband, wife, parent, child, master, and slave—and describing the sort of conduct that is appropriate to a person in each category. The use of such codes in these two letters represents a later development and definition of ethical teaching versus that of the authentic writings of Paul. In addition to the catalogue of virtues and vices, which probably were used in the instruction of baptismal candidates, the household codes were likely to have been adopted as a way of encouraging the communal holiness and unity of the believing community. No doubt the authors of these two letters viewed the adoption of the household codes—along with the extended family metaphor for the *ecclesia*—as a natural development from Paul's teaching and example.

Such codes were commonplace in the popular philosophy of the Greco-Roman world (Gentile and Jewish), and the authors of Colossians and Ephesians borrow these popular traditions and baptize them. The particular guidelines in the codes presuppose the Greco-Roman patriarchal social structure and repeat common attitudes from ca. 80 CE—for example, that slaves should serve their (aristocratic) masters with a good will and cooperative spirit, and wives should be submissive and obedient to their husbands. These two letters present this hierarchical mode of human relationships as divinely ordained, and reflective of divine order itself where God is the "head" of Christ and Christ is the head of the *ecclesia*. A similar hierarchy is encouraged for the *ecclesia*, and the audience is exhorted to welcome the traditions that are handed on to them by their human leaders because they derive from God.

The inclusion of household codes in these two letters provides useful clues to the general demographic composition of the believing communities in Asia Minor. In Paul's own letters, there are references to slaves who are members of the *ecclesia*, but only one case where Paul addresses a slaveholder (Philemon). Paul calls himself a "slave (*doulos*) of Christ Jesus" (Rom. 1:1; cf. Gal. 1:10), thereby identifying with the least powerful members of the community. Baptized persons are no longer slaves to other human beings, according to Paul, for they have been claimed by God as bondservants of Christ (e.g., 1 Cor. 7:22; Gal. 3:28; cf. Col. 3:11). The author of the household codes mandates how slaves, women, and children are to behave, but cajoles the more powerful parties in the relationship—the masters, husbands, and fathers. This suggests, first of all, that some of the members of the *ecclesia* are indeed masters, husbands, and fathers of an aristocratic household. Secondly, the rhetorical differences in the author's modes of address to the subordinate versus superior parties seems to illustrate that the author's sympathies lie with the wealthy, aristocratic heads of household. Less than a generation earlier, there

In this third-century Roman carving, the differing sizes of the members of the household reflect their relative importance: the *paterfamilias* is disproportionately large. The household codes in later New Testament writings assume that the existing social hierarchy is divinely ordained.

would not have been enough aristocratic members of the *ecclesia* for Paul to spend much time talking to them. Clearly, by the time the household codes for Colossians and Ephesians were penned, circumstances had changed such that a critical mass of aristocratic men had started to join the communities of Christ-believers.

Reflecting on the Nature of the Ecclesia

Ephesians is a theological essay within a letter framework. In this document, some of the themes from Paul's letters and Colossians are reworked. The nature of the *ecclesia*, salvation history and its future perspective, and the unity of one Spirit and a variety of gifts—all these themes are explained in a series of long and complex sentences. The mere fact that the author had the leisure time to engage in theological and philosophical reflection implies an educated and likely upper-class individual, perhaps one with specific training as a scribe. So far had the movement come from the initial disciples of Jesus!

The author of Ephesians views the *ecclesia* as a structured, universal institution, founded on the (now dead) apostles (Eph. 2:20). As God's new creation, the body of Christ, the *ecclesia* continues to develop and grow toward its eschatological goal, the fullness of God in Christ. The new age is already dawning, and birth pangs are being felt. God provides believers with the armor to fight against the powers of evil; the audience is given a guarantee that God alone will be victorious.

Ephesians indicates that there is a disagreement among believers as to theological principles. The author responds to this situation by stressing the organic unity of the body of Christ, symbolized by the sacraments of baptism, Eucharist, and particularly by the sacramentally understood marital union of believers. Even this last point suggests a shift toward more affluent members of the *ecclesia*, since slaves could not marry and the type of marital relationship envisaged is contextualized in an aristocratic "household."

Alternative Views Engaging the Pauline Traditions: James

James, written ca. 80 CE, appears to be an "open letter" to believers who regarded themselves as the new Israel, and who lived outside of Palestine. The pseudonymous text is concerned with the daily conduct and experiences of disciples in the world. The author uses the Jesus tradition to recontextualize commonplace Jewish and Greek ethical teachings, presenting them as a sort of anthology, organized primarily by word association. This letter indicates sensitivity concerning a trend to favor wealthier members of the community, more in conformity with common Greco-Roman cultural mores than what the author considers to be appropriate to the *ecclesia*. This suggests that the growing number of aristocratic members, who quite naturally would be prone to bring with them the common social practices of their times, are causing others to be concerned that those practices do not fit with the gospel message and practice of Jesus.

James 2:14–26, on the question of faith and works, presupposes the first-generation debate on Paul's view—but the Pauline position is caricatured and presented in slogan form. The author of James affirms that the law of freedom is the law of the *ecclesia* (1:25; 2:12), and does so in ways not dissimilar to the Pauline approach (e.g., Rom. 8). Thus the attack in James is aimed at a parody of Pauline thought—or an extreme post-Pauline view—rather than at the authentic Paul. Are there some (wealthy?) believers who claim that "faith" is a personal, private phenomenon that needn't impact one's behavior?

The theological principle underlying the collection of maxims in James is the imitation of God. Although human beings are "double-minded" (1:8; 4:8; cf. 3:8–12), their ideal state is one of integrity and single-mindedness (1:4; 3:2). God is truly One, without change or duplicity, and every person should be single-minded as God is One.

One of the primary applications of this principle is to the contrast between rich and poor. The author is concerned about the potential for social schism due to having a wealthy patron for a believing community. A second concern is to turn a situation of communal correction of a sinner to a positive end, redeeming rather than exiling the errant party. Thus the author demonstrates the practical significance of this theological view.

Summary

The seventies were a time of consolidation and post-war recovery, both for the surviving traditionalist Jews (whose identity rapidly was morphing into Rabbinic Judaism) and the members of the Jesus movement. In the land of Israel itself, the decade began in turmoil because of the conquest of Jerusalem; destruction of the Temple; ongoing guerilla warfare with Rome and siege of Masada; and then finally the capture, execution, enslavement, and deportation of tens of thousands of Jews, carried to Rome in triumph and sold on the slave market. In Asia Minor, however, times were relatively peaceful, allowing for the extension of the reach of the gospel message.

Unlike in the earliest days, when most members of the Jesus movement tended to be lower-class individuals, including a critical mass of slaves to pagan masters, extant writings from the seventies begin to indicate an increasing number of aristocratic members of the communities, including slaveholders. Wealth disparities create a source of concern for some writers of this period, particularly when the wealthy are given preferential treatment at ecclesial gatherings and the poor are put last. This type of prejudicial behavior will continue to pose a concern for the evangelists and other writers of the next decade.

Questions for Review

1. What is "the delay of the *Parousia*" and what sort of problems did it pose for the followers of Jesus in this period?
2. Explain what is known (or not known) about the author of the Gospel according to Mark.
3. What do scholars mean by the "Messianic secret"?
4. Describe the meaning of the phrases "Son of God" and "Son of Man" in the Gospel of Mark.
5. How is Mark's understanding of the "Messiah" related to events of the Jewish War?
6. What evidence suggests that the letters to the Colossians and Ephesians are pseudonymous?
7. Describe the "philosophy" that the letter to the Colossians condemns as false.
8. How does Paul's teaching on faith and works compare to that of the letter of James?

Questions for Discussion

1. Many scholars would argue that Mark presents the story of Jesus specifically for the purpose of instructing the first-century audience about what it truly means to be a follower of Jesus. Does this seem to be a plausible interpretation of Mark's purpose? Why or why not?

2. The oldest and best surviving manuscripts of Mark's Gospel
    end at 16:8; women followers of Jesus found his tomb empty,
    and a "man" in a white robe announced to them that Jesus had
    risen from the dead—but "they said nothing to anyone, for they
    were afraid." Some scholars argue that this ending is too abrupt
    and odd to have been intentional; Mark's original ending must
    have been lost. Others argue that this ending fits Mark's Gospel
    perfectly. Who do you think is right, and why?

3. The "household codes" of Colossians and Ephesians assert that
    there is a form of ethical behavior appropriate to every station
    in life—husbands, wives, children, slaves—and that people need
    to know their place and accept it dutifully. In this regard, do
    you think the authors of these letters are being faithful to the
    teachings of Jesus and/or Paul?

CHAPTER 8

Coming to Terms with Life in the Roman Empire
(81–90 CE)

The tumultuous events of the seventies had led many of the followers of Jesus to believe that the *Parousia* ("second coming") of Christ was at hand. However, ten years passed after the destruction of Jerusalem and there was still no sign of an impending restoration. Roman emperors had come and gone, and the eruption of Mount Vesuvius destroyed the two Italian cities of Pompeii and Herculaneum, but there had been no fire and brimstone from heaven to destroy the empire as a whole, nor was there any evidence that Rome would fade away on her own. Indeed, the new emperor, Flavius Domitian, was a powerful man with a firm hold on the empire and no intention of relinquishing that power to anyone, human or divine.

The Roman Regime: Protests and Punishments

The decade of the 80s opened with a three-month-long festival celebrating the opening of the great Flavian Amphitheater erected by Titus[1] in honor of his father, Vespasian. Now known as the "Coliseum" because of the neighboring "Colossus" statue of Nero, this new Roman amphitheater was built by Jewish slave-laborers

---

1. Flavius Titus, Emperor between 79–81, had vanquished the Jews in their first revolt against Rome. Titus succeeded as supreme general of the Roman forces when Vespasian was acclaimed emperor and returned to Rome.

who had been captured in the First Jewish-Roman War. The construction and inaugural festival were funded by massive quantities of gold and silver looted from the Jews, including the treasures wrested from the Jerusalem Temple. (Rumor claimed that fifty tons of gold had been taken!) Finally complete by 82 CE, the edifice could seat 70,000 people. By that time, Domitian had succeeded his brother as emperor, and he celebrated both his accession and the honor to the "divine Caesars" with over a hundred days of games in which about 5,000 wild animals—and unknown numbers of Christ-believers—were slain.

Even if they did not live in the City of Rome, Jesus' disciples could not miss the imperial celebration of the victory and vanquishing of the Jews. As with other Jews, Christ-believers in the eighties had to face the fact that God's Holy City and Temple had been destroyed, many of their companions had been killed for the faith, and God had done nothing to prevent these things—nor even to punish the offenders. The blasphemous emperor proclaimed himself "*Dominus et Deus*" (Lord and God), redirected the Jewish "Temple tax" to the shrine of Jupiter Capitolinus, and even encouraged provincial cities to build temples for his worship, yet the heavens were silent in the face of all of this. It began to seem as if Jesus was in no hurry at all to make his glorious return, when he would rescue his faithful and establish God's kingdom on earth.

© Zev Radovan / biblelandpictures.com

This coin shows Domitian on the obverse; the reverse shows his infant son, identified as *divus* (divine) and surrounded by seven stars (cf. Rev. 1:16). The Apocalypse, probably written in Domitian's reign, condemns as Satanic the emperor's claim to divine status.

These harsh facts meant the disciples of Jesus had to develop a new approach to life in the Roman Empire. Many came to believe that they must have been mistaken about the Lord returning soon. Certainly, God must have a good reason for delaying Jesus' return. What could that be? It must mean that believers still had some important task(s) to perform to set the stage for the *Parousia*. What were Jesus' followers to do in the time remaining? What role were they to play in ushering in the kingdom of God that Jesus had proclaimed? Some influential believers turned their attention to working out answers to questions like these. The Gospels according to Matthew, Luke, and John illustrate three of these responses. Some distinctive views of each of these evangelists appear when parallel passages are compared.

Important Documents for Understanding This Period

The exact dates of none of the Gospels are known, nor have any original copies survived. Scholars use the evidence of such things as the dates of existing manuscripts and quotations by early church writers to infer dates for each Gospel. The consensus view holds that the Gospel according to Matthew[2] and the Gospel according to Luke come from sometime in the eighties, with Matthew probably the earlier of the two. The Gospel according to John seems to have been written in three distinct stages, with the last of the three dating from early in the nineties. Hence, this chapter will discuss the Gospels of Matthew and Luke, among other writings of the period, but John will be discussed in the next chapter. Since the Acts of the Apostles is a sequel to the Gospel of Luke and is thought to have been completed very close to the time of the Gospel itself, Acts will be discussed in this chapter in conjunction with Luke.

---

2. As is standard in works on the New Testament, the authors of the Gospels will be identified by their traditional designations—Matthew, Mark, Luke, and John—for convenience sake, even though the actual works are anonymous and their authors unknown.

Developing Ecclesial Structures: The Gospel according to Matthew

The Gospel according to Matthew comes first in the New Testament canon, but this does not mean that it was the first Gospel to be written. As was noted earlier, most scholars believe that the Gospel according to Mark was the first of the four New Testament Gospels to be completed, and that the authors of Matthew and Luke both used Mark as the basic framework for their own works. Matthew could have been placed first in the canon for a number of reasons: it is the longest of the four canonical Gospels, and often collected works were compiled according to descending size; it has many links with "the Law and the Prophets" (the Jewish Bible), which hitherto had been the only Bible used by Jesus' followers; it includes much regarding ecclesial structures and offices, so it might have served as a sort of ecclesiastical "handbook"; and it was widely used in church lectionaries.[3]

One of the ways in which the Gospel of Matthew responds to the issues raised by the delay of Jesus' *Parousia* is to develop an organizational structure for the Christ-believing community. It speaks of scribes in a way that suggest that this traditional Jewish office was carried over into the new organization that Matthew calls the *ecclesia*. This Gospel includes a scene that depicts Jesus giving Peter the nickname "Rock" (Cephas), the foundation on which "my *ecclesia*" will be built (Matt. 16:18). Jesus then gives Peter (presumably as representative of that *ecclesia*) the authority to "bind and loose," that is, to judge whether a person's sins will be forgiven or not. Since this authority traditionally belonged to the Temple priests, such a delegation sets the leaders of the Matthean community in opposition to Jewish leaders like those who were reorganizing in Jamnia (Yavneh), and sets the community itself apart from the nascent rabbinic Jewish movement. The evangelist does not claim credit for these developments, but instead portrays all of them as Jesus' ideas.

Roman officials in the 80s were nervous about whether the followers of Jesus were the kind of zealous troublemakers they recently

---

3. A lectionary is a special type of biblical text that divides the various books into smaller sections ("lections") that are to be read in the worship services on particular days of the year.

208 THE JESUS MOVEMENT

defeated in the first Romano-Jewish War. After all, their leader was crucified as a revolutionary. Jesus' disciples called him "Messiah," the same title the Jewish rebels gave their leaders. They called him "Lord" when Domitian Caesar was lord of this empire, and there was only room for one. If the emperor was willing to exile a member of his own family who showed sympathy for the Christ-believers, then there would be no reason to expect tolerance for Jesus' followers as a whole.[4]

Comparison with the earlier Gospel of Mark shows that the message of the Gospel of Matthew was adapted to respond to such difficulties in the present historical circumstances. It tells the story of Jesus' death in such a way as to eliminate any Roman antagonism toward Jesus. According to this Gospel, the Roman governor tried to prevent it; Jesus was framed through the political machinations of the Jewish leaders. Jesus' execution was clearly a mistake, for he was innocent of the trumped-up charges against him. Still, in some sense it "had to happen," for Jesus' death fulfilled Old Testament prophecy (e.g., Matt. 27:24, 31, 54).

This presentation of the story probably would not have satisfied imperial officials and eliminated their every suspicion of the disciples of Jesus as antisocial or antagonistic toward the Roman regime. To accomplish that goal, Matthew would have had to relinquish any claim to Jesus being the Messiah, which clearly was out of the question. The Jewish leaders at Jamnia may have been able to state unequivocally that they did not believe in or expect a messiah. Still, Matthew's way of telling the Jesus-story might suffice to calm the nerves of potential converts who were worried about putting themselves on the wrong side of the law by joining the Jesus movement.

Not only his death, but Jesus' life also completed the Law and the Prophets. In both the formal structure and content of this Gospel, the evangelist presents Jesus as a new lawgiver greater than Moses. Even the structure of Matthew helps to make this point: the evangelist designed the Gospel so that it presents five "books" of revelation from Jesus, with the birth story and the passion/Resurrection account forming the narrative *inclusio* (i.e., literary "bookends").

In the immediate aftermath of the First Romano-Jewish War, Antioch in Syria became a hot spot of Jewish-Gentile struggle.

---

4. E.g., see the next chapter for the case of Flavia Domitilla, one of Domitian's relatives, whom he punished with exile.

Josephus reports that one of the city leaders named Antiochus, ironically a man of Jewish parentage, roused the Gentile townsfolk against the Jewish inhabitants. Antiochus accused his own father, "who was governor of the Jews of Antioch,"[5] of conspiring with some other Jews to burn down the city. With the help of the Roman garrison, Antiochus perpetrated a systematic persecution aimed to extinguish Jewish religious practices. Jews were forced to sacrifice to pagan deities and work on the Sabbath. Seeing the events in Antioch, Josephus says that other nearby cities followed suit. "So the Jews were under great disorder and terror, in the uncertain expectations of what would be the upshot of these accusations against them."[6] Finally the imperial legate, Cneius Collegas persuaded the people to halt the persecution, having proven that the charges against the Jews were groundless.

In such a politically precarious climate as the 80s, followers of Jesus had to be extremely careful about what they preached and how they acted. A misstep on the part of one member of the community could lead to reprisals against the entire group. Matthew responded to this problem by making discipline within the community a central theme in this Gospel. In the Matthean *ecclesia*, there were gradations of rank for believers (18:10–14). Present church leaders were not apostles—missionaries who evangelize non-believers—but scribes and teachers who devote themselves to studying and understanding the Law, the Prophets, and the Gospel they had received. Consolidation is more important than mission. It was time to lay low and regroup those who already believe, fortifying them against the temptation to succumb to the political pressures to relapse to non-messianic Judaism—admittedly a much safer religious choice than being disciples of the Christ.

One major area of concern for Matthew was the relationship of this community to Judaism. On this subject, the whole spectrum of opinions has been maintained by scholars—which in itself shows the range of evidence in this Gospel. Matthew's Gospel uses the poetic technique of Hebrew parallelism to intensify the impact of important ideas (e.g., 21:5, 41, 43). It demonstrates that Jesus' life is the fulfillment of Old Testament prophecy. The Gospel sometimes

---

5. Josephus, *Jewish War* 7.3.3.

6. Ibid., 7.3.4.

seems to repudiate Judaism (27:25), but elsewhere it upholds Jewish leaders as teachers of the truth (23:2–3) and affirms the continuing validity of "the Law and the Prophets" (5:17–20). The evangelist rejects the hypocrisy of some Jewish leaders (ch. 23), but not their teaching. The story of Peter paying the Temple tax (17:24–27) shows that the Matthean community still supports the notion that the Jerusalem Temple is the center of Judaism and is owed support by Jesus' followers.[7] Moreover, the threefold pattern of each of the five sections of Matthew's Gospel (narratives and debate; discourse of Jesus; editorial conclusion) shows that the author wants to persuade the audience that Jesus' interpretation and expansion of the Torah is the most valid alternative.

Matthew's Gospel seems to have been written somewhat before the final break of the followers of Jesus from Judaism. The Gospel provides a critique of the Pharisaic form of Jewish practice, but not of the underlying theory of spiritualized worship and ethical practice based in synagogue communities. Matthew records some hostility of Jews toward his community, but even the reports of chastisement by the synagogues (e.g., 10:17) show that the members of the Matthean community still were identified as Jews. Still, it is critical for one to decide what kind of Jew to be: one who follows the rabbis or one who follows Jesus. Recognizing that many are rejecting the gospel, Matthew has Jesus predict that Israel will reject Jesus (and his disciples) and that then the fruits of God's reign will be given to a new nation, presumably now represented by the Matthean community (21:42–43). The choice for or against Jesus is a decision of ultimate importance; there can be no compromise with Pharisaic Judaism (28:15).

Matthew's Gospel uses apocalyptic imagery and allusions to impress upon the audience the significance of this point, to heighten the impact of the narrative, to enhance the power of Jesus' miracles, and to reinforce group solidarity in the current struggles with Pharisaism. The emphasis on apocalyptic symbols implies that the evangelist views the "end" as near at hand. Thus he urges the community to be vigilant, to endure until Christ's return, and to live out the gospel that has been entrusted to them.

---

7. It's not altogether clear what this could mean in an era when the Temple no longer existed. Minimally, one would think this reflects a desire to remain metaphorically "centered" in the land of promise and worship of the God of Israel.

The Qumran community may have been analogous to Matthew's, for their literature shows how an apocalyptic worldview serves to reinforce group boundaries and strengthen a group's sense of mission and purpose. The Qumran *Temple Scroll* proposes the final law, the Torah for the *eschaton*,[8] similar to the way scholars have viewed Matthew as presenting a new Torah revealed by Jesus. The Qumran community also used a distinctive form of Scriptural interpretation called *pesher*, which is inspired by an apocalyptic viewpoint. Matthew includes a very similar type of scriptural exegesis. In addition, the evangelist honors the role of the "scribe" (13:52), implying that he considered himself to be one.

Hence, the Matthean community stood within Jewish-Christianity, and the evangelist set himself the task of interpretation and exegesis of the Jewish scriptures, commenting upon their ultimate meaning in light of Christ and in relation to the community of Jesus' followers. Matthew's community was estranged from and in conflict with Pharisaic (now proto-rabbinic) Judaism. As a result, the evangelist sought to preserve the essence of the true Israel in a sectarian vision and discipline centered on Christ the teacher.

Matthew's Gospel is concerned less with converting the outsider than reinforcing the faith of those who already believe—especially in light of the "competition" from the growing rabbinic Jewish movement. Hence he emphasizes the fulfillment of scriptural prophecy in the words and deeds of Jesus. This Gospel has revised the parable material from his sources to support a "secrecy theory" different from that of Mark. For Mark, Jesus is the "secret" Messiah, fated to be victorious through death; for Matthew, Jesus unlocks "the secrets" of his teachings for the disciples, while they remain unintelligible to those who are outside the sect.

The theme of the secrecy of Jesus' teaching, and especially of the parables, does not imply that Matthew's Gospel has no interest in evangelistic mission. However, the historical mission of Jesus was directed toward Israel, and Israel should continue to be the focus of evangelism (10:5–6), though some scraps may fall to a few outsiders (15:21–31). The few indications of a Gentile mission during Jesus' public ministry reflect more a defensive or defiant stance on

---

8. *Eschaton* means "final" age in the sense of the time when God's plan for the creation has come to perfection.

Matthew's part than an intentional stratagem. (The "Great Commission" in Matthew 28:18–20 depicts a shift in strategy in the post-Resurrection period.) For Matthew's Gospel, there is a Gentile mission in the sense that there is a mission to incorporate Gentiles into the true Israel; the notion of a Gentile church *distinct from Judaism* is inconceivable.

Antioch in Syria is the traditional provenance for this Gospel, and there is much evidence to support this identification. To accept this locus would also have the effect of locating the primary influence of Simon Peter at Syrian Antioch, in contrast to the power of James the Great in Jerusalem. Luke's comment (Acts 11:26) that it was in Antioch that the disciples were first called "Christians" adds some interest to this theory of Matthean provenance.[9] Evidence of the early use of the Gospel of Matthew at Antioch (e.g., Ignatius of Antioch, *Letter to Smyrna* 1:1, dated ca. 100) further supports the theory, as does the use of this Gospel in the *Didache* or *Teaching of the Twelve Apostles*, another Syrian document dating from the mid-first to early-second centuries CE.

In Matthew, Christ and the *ecclesia* are inescapably linked; the picture of Christ is set in the framework of discipleship in the community of believers. Jesus as Messiah is the great teacher of the law for the last days, in expectation of which the true Israel lives. Christ brings salvation not to individuals, but to the community of the true Israel that follows this law. Moreover, the exalted Christ brings judgment upon those who do not follow this law—now through the mediation of church officials and, on the last day, in person. Thus the transcendent authority of Jesus and of his teaching is mediated in and to the world by Jesus' followers, who know the experience of "Emmanuel, God with us."

For Matthew's Gospel, Jesus is the goal of God's saving history, from Abraham through David to the present time. Jesus, the new Moses, reveals the truth of the God of Israel before the entire world, and brings Gentiles to worship Israel's God (ch. 4). Finally,

---

9. For example, was the Matthean *ecclesia* organized in such a way that they were easily differentiated from the wider Jewish population? The positive valuation for the role of scribal interpreters of the Jesus tradition suggests there even may have been a formal Matthean "school" connected with this community, which certainly would make the group more evident to outsiders.

Jesus deserves worship and reverence because he is "the son of the living God" (16:16). This heightens the guilt of the Jewish officials who caused Jesus' arrest and crucifixion: they did not recognize the Holy One of God. And they, like Judas, will be repaid for what they have done.

The moral issues raised by the passion narrative show that the tension between mercy and justice is at the heart of Matthew's message.[10] The evangelist tends to hedge the commands of Jesus with legalistic safeguards (or, occasionally, loopholes—see 5:32; 19:9) to ensure that the law is fulfilled.

Matthew's Gospel stresses the continuing validity of the law as it was interpreted by Jesus (5:17-20). While the law will be superseded when "all is accomplished," the last days are still in the future. Therefore, the law is still in force and must continue to be interpreted by those scribes trained for the kingdom of heaven. And "righteousness" (fidelity to the law) is the mark of the faithful Christ-believer.

In retelling the miracle stories, the Gospel of Matthew emphasizes four points that are significant to Jesus' coming:

1. Jesus' deeds (especially acts of healing) fulfill Old Testament prophecy.
2. Jesus is the victorious Servant of God, exalted and triumphant.
3. Jesus the Lord continues to directly help his *ecclesia*.
4. Jesus gives the disciples a share in his authority.

Likewise, the evangelist designs his interpretation of the parables to respond to the particular needs and concerns of this community. This is especially clear in the examples that relate to the apocalyptic expectations of his community. Thus he repeatedly emphasizes the themes of the universal dominion of God in Christ (especially expressed by Matthew's phrase "the kingdom of heaven"), the vindication of the righteous and punishment of the wicked, and the need for human response to God's invitation to the kingdom.

The key to understanding the matrix of ideas in the Gospel of Matthew is the sectarian identity of this community. Their increasing

---

10. E.g., the insistence upon Jesus' innocence raises the question of divine justice: How could God let a faithful servant be put to death in such a torturous way? How could those who conspired against Jesus get away with this injustice?

In this image from a Coptic church in Egypt (second to eighth century), Saint Peter holds an oversized key, representing the keys to the kingdom of heaven (see Matt. 16:19). Matthew's Gospel testifies to the tendency among Christ-believers in Antioch to regard Peter as the central figure among the Twelve.

rejection by their Jewish neighbors led them to reciprocate with a threat of absolute rejection by God, while those who receive the "little ones" of God hospitably are promised their reward.

The Matthean community—those who are trained in discipleship for the kingdom—is the *ecclesia* Jesus has founded as the true successor to Israel. The fact that Matthew's is the only Gospel in the New Testament canon that uses the word *ecclesia* (church) illustrates the special concern of Matthew for group identity, authority, and structure. The *ecclesia*—including Peter as the first disciple—is given the "keys" to unlock the kingdom of heaven to those who seek entry. Those who may fear that expulsion from the synagogues will cost them the kingdom are thereby reassured that the gates lie wide open to them if they only persevere in faithfulness to Jesus and his law to the end.

Challenges on the Roman Frontier

Meanwhile, all was not calm on the fringes of the Empire. In the winter of 85, the Dacians—led by King Decebalus ("Brave Heart")—crossed the frozen Danube south into Moesia, destroying farms and forts. They killed Moesia's provincial governor, Oppius Sabinus, and forced the outnumbered Roman troops to take defensive positions. Roman reinforcements arrived under General Cornelius Fuscus, accompanied by the Roman Emperor Domitian, who wasted his time in decadent living rather than helping with the campaign. Fuscus invaded Dacia but was killed and his Fifth "Alaudae" Legion soundly defeated. This defeat inspired a revolt against Rome by Pannonia, north of Dalmatia. To say the least, such a setback would not make the Romans more receptive to the Christ-believers' claims of Jesus being the Messiah who would usher in the final age of God's kingdom.

Christ-Believers in the Milieu of the Roman Empire: Luke-Acts

The Gospel according to Luke and the Acts of the Apostles form a two-volume work composed by the same author, a third-generation believer (Luke 1:3) who is dealing with the increasingly precarious position of the *ecclesia* over against the Roman Empire. Facing the facts of history and the lack of divine intervention in establishing a visible kingdom, the author of Luke-Acts decided that the apocalyptic urgency of the earliest disciples—which they heard in the message of Jesus himself—must have been unfounded. In contrast to Mark, the sense of urgency and impending fulfillment of Jesus' eschatological promise of the kingdom is considerably softened in Luke-Acts. This, combined with the very structure of the work as a two-volume piece, suggests that the author was setting out to explain the delay of the *Parousia* rather than to proclaim its imminence. The existence of Acts makes the story of Jesus part of past history, and shifts the spotlight from him to the community of his followers. The promise of fulfillment is retained, but it is spiritualized.

Acts implies that Luke's community felt they had "arrived," had crossed the frontier that separated a Palestinian Jewish sect from the influence and power of the Imperial City, Rome. Luke's spiritualized interpretation of the early Christian proclamation of the imminent reign of God left room for a history of salvation that included the Roman world as its providential setting.

In comparison to the author of Mark, Luke is quite an educated writer, with a high literary style. Luke's writings demonstrate a familiarity with both classical and later Greek literature, as well as the stories and ideas of the Jewish scriptures. Luke seems to have known Mark as well as a source available to Matthew (Q), and to have used these traditions and an independent source in composing his Gospel. As to the source for Acts, there is no scholarly consensus. Luke uses Greek and Jewish traditions, as well as the traditions he has received about Jesus and the earliest followers, to create a unique composition with a renewed message for his own generation.

Acts 1:8 gives the most succinct statement of Luke's program in the book: the Spirit-empowerment of Jesus' followers to be his witnesses "to the ends of the earth." Thus Luke sees Jesus' mission as universal, extending beyond the people of Israel to include every nation. Casting the first several chapters of Acts in Jerusalem shows the connection not only between Luke's two volumes, but also between the Lukan community and the earliest (Jewish) Christ-believers.

Luke uses a variety of literary devices popular in the ancient world. This, combined with his explicit theological program, warns against reading Luke-Acts as if it were history in the modern sense. Luke's history, like other ancient histories, is aimed to gain the sympathy of readers for a particular cause and to persuade them to a particular response (for Luke, discipleship.)

Thus Luke writes a schematized history of salvation that ties in with key events in the history of the Roman world. This history comprises three stages:

1. The time of Israel, of the Old Testament (the Law and Prophets)
2. The center point of time, the time of Jesus' ministry
3. The time between Jesus' ministry and the *Parousia*, the age of the Spirit and the *ecclesia*

The continuity of prophecy and succession of prophets provides the connection of one stage to the next (Old Testament prophets and John the Baptist; Jesus Christ; Jesus-Way prophets/apostles).

Since the preaching in Luke-Acts is addressed to both Jews and Romans, it may be that Luke intended his work for quite a wide audience, including not only Christ-believers but perhaps also the non-Christian world at large. His convictions regarding the universal relevance of Jesus and his message are clear.

Luke seems to portray a strongly deterministic view. All political situations serve God's purposes. The passion and death of Jesus, as carried out by worldly authorities, are necessary to fulfill God's will expressed in Old Testament prophecy. Those who carry out this divine plan are either exonerated or forgiven, because the responsibility for their actions lies ultimately with God.

Luke-Acts depicts a significant amount of conflict between Jesus and the Jewish authorities, and then between those authorities and the disciples. Luke's account of Jesus' arrest, trial, and crucifixion clearly depicts the Jewish authorities as the antagonists, while Pilate, representative of Roman authority, declares Jesus innocent. Yet Luke also depicts some ordinary Jews as sympathetic to Jesus. This portrayal suggests that the Lukan community experienced significant conflict with some Jewish officials, and smarted from the rejection of the gospel by the more militant Judaism of their time.

Luke argues that these Jews' rejection of the gospel fulfilled God's plan and proved Jesus to be the culmination of a long line of prophets rejected by their people. Thus the Jesus-Way has continuity with Israel through Jesus himself, but not only through him. The conversion story told in Acts 2:5–42 illustrates that many other Jews, especially Diaspora Jews, did accept Jesus as the Christ. Moreover, the significance of the Twelve and the Seventy-Two in Luke-Acts is their representation of the twelve tribes and of "greater Israel" (the Dispersion) receiving Jesus as Christ and witnessing to this faith.

Luke portrays the Roman authorities quite favorably, and shows great concern for Roman law and order. He frequently depicts officials protecting Paul against his enemies, implying that reasonable Romans have nothing to fear from the Jesus movement.

As a result of these and other features of Luke-Acts, some scholars have suggested that the author's primary aim is to produce an apology for the Jesus movement. The incident at Thessalonica (related in Acts 17:1–9) is a clear example of the Lukan apologetic that the political charges against Christ-believers are unsubstantiated;

the disciples, like Jesus, are innocent victims of Jewish troublemakers. Given incidents at cities like Antioch, such a polemic would be likely to gain a receptive audience.

While the theme of the innocence of Jesus and his followers is of importance for Luke, it is not the sole reason for the work. Nor is it likely that the primary objective of Luke-Acts was to persuade the imperial administration. The teachings and actions of Jesus himself may have made Roman officials quite uncomfortable, since they ultimately do have revolutionary consequences. Rather, lesser Roman officials, citizens, and other influential persons were more likely the intended audience of Luke-Acts.

Two issues are of particular importance in Luke-Acts:

1. The continuity of the traditions of Israel in the history of salvation, in the context of a prophetic critique and wider frame of reference
2. A positive attitude toward the social structures and good government represented by the Roman Empire

Thus, while Luke-Acts may not be an apology for the Jesus movement to Rome, the text is quite consistent with an apology for the virtues of the Roman Empire to the Christ-believers.

Luke depicts Jesus as a prophet, the fulfillment of the prophetic scriptures and the prototype of the prophetic ministry in which the early *ecclesia* was engaged. Luke views Jesus' persecution and death as a sign confirming his prophetic identity. A comparison with his portrayal of the arrest and death of Stephen (Acts 6:8–8:4) further illustrates this fact. Luke's portrayal of Jesus as the expected messianic prophet served to make the significance of Jesus intelligible to Greeks and Romans, while at the same time maintaining the Jewish roots of Jesus.

Luke depicts Jesus as indifferent to political rulers, since all power and authority belong to God. Jesus does resist some Jewish structures, but Luke has softened the story of the "cleansing" of the Temple to suppress most of the cleansing activity (Luke 19:45–48). It is Jesus' prophetic teaching that elicits conflict; Jesus does not incite insurrection.

Luke's understanding of Old Testament prophecy focuses on Jesus as its fulfillment, and on the idea of the Jubilee year as having been fulfilled in Jesus (Luke 4:21). This vision does not affect the immediate future except in the insistence upon ethical practice within the believing community.

The *orans* posture (in which a person holds both arms outstretched with hands raised to the heavens) was a customary practice in communal prayer. A common motif in early Christian art, this example comes from a Roman catacomb. Luke emphasizes the prayer life of Jesus in the Gospels, with parallels in the prayer life of Jesus' followers in the Acts of the Apostles. In this, as in many respects, Luke depicts the early Christ-believers as continuing the works of Jesus.

Jesus' parables are used by Luke to illustrate ethical behavior as Jesus understood it. The parables of the Sower and of the Good Samaritan are two examples of how Jesus' original stories are reapplied for Luke's own community.

Luke presents Jesus as exemplar to the believing community. For example, Jesus is often mentioned as praying, and in his prayer Jesus receives the inspiration of the Holy Spirit for his prophetic ministry (cf. Acts 2:4)). Jesus' inaugural experiences of baptism and temptation provide another significant example of this Lukan tendency.

Overall, the portrayal of Jesus' words and deeds as chiefly matters of personal ethics makes the Gospel of Luke much "safer" for Roman consumption than would have been the case in Jesus' own context, where personal and communal ethics were virtually inextricable. Whereas a focus on the salvation of Israel (as exhibited by the message of Jesus) had the potential to encourage movements of social change and political challenge, a narrower focus on individual ethics would short-circuit such a move. The "good thief" could enter the kingdom because he admitted the justice of the Roman sentence condemning his behavior (Luke 23:40–43). Although the Romans executed the innocent Jesus, Luke insisted that they could not be held accountable for this action. To bring home this claim, Luke depicts Jesus hanging on the cross and yet interceding for them with God, begging their forgiveness because they were ignorant of what they were doing (23:34).[11]

The birth stories in Luke's Gospel carry forward this subtly pro-Roman apologetic while at the same time expressing the theological purpose of his work. They provide a bridge between the Old Testament and Jesus just as the opening chapters of Acts provide a bridge between Jesus and the infant church.

Three key theological emphases characterize the birth narratives:

1. The action of the Spirit is prophetic and creative.
2. Past prophecy is fulfilled in the present new age of Christ and the community of disciples.
3. The titles of Jesus (Savior, Messiah, and Lord) show that Christ is the center of God's historical process of salvation from the days of the people of Israel to the life of the *ecclesia* in the Roman Empire.

The group for whom Luke writes, being historically removed from Jesus himself, looks back to the events of Jesus' life as a sequence of past history that has a definitive religious meaning in the present. Luke's community has continuity with God's salvation

---

11. Note, however, that textual critics have questioned the authenticity of this verse or whether it was a later addition to Luke's Gospel. See, e.g., Jacobus H. Petzer, "Eclecticism and the Text of the New Testament," in *Text and Interpretation: New Approaches in the Study of the New Testament*, ed. Patrick J. Hartin and Jacobus H. Petzer (Leiden: Brill, 1991), 47–62, at 54–60.

for Israel—especially the legacy of Diaspora Judaism—and recognizes the value of the political structures of the Roman Empire. The *ecclesia* was closely attached to Paul (though Luke did not necessarily agree with Paul or understand him very well), and takes the theme of the new covenant inaugurated by Christ to mean a new age in salvation history being worked out in the life and ministry of the believing community.

The imitation of Christ is the central ethic of this community, a fact illustrated both by the content of Luke-Acts and by the formal parallels between the portrayal of Jesus in this Gospel and the portrayal of the disciples in Acts. The concern for the poor and lowly is another key ethical ingredient, as well as being another form of imitation of Christ. However, this concern flows not out of identification with those who are downtrodden, but rather from an enlightened "middle-class" position. While Luke wants the disciples to imitate Christ, he also wants the community not to confront society but rather to serve as leaven within the existing (Roman) social system. Thus positive accommodation to the Roman Empire is a significant value for the Lukan community.

Summary

The decade after the defeat of the Jews in their revolutionary war against Rome was marked by increasing sensitivity on the part of the disciples of Jesus to the complexities and challenges of life in the Roman Empire. Some, like the Matthean community in Antioch, viewed Rome as potentially hostile toward the *ecclesia*. The response was to make somewhat of a shift inward, organizing the community of believers to fend for themselves and govern themselves in such a way as to attract as little attention from outsiders as possible. Others, like the author of Luke-Acts, took a more positive view of Rome, even portraying Roman officials as protective of the Jesus movement against trumped-up charges and unruly mobs. The birth of the Messiah came at a propitious moment in history marked by the *Pax Romana*, good roads, and a virtually universal language. This propitious moment was planned by God but, in many ways, was made possible by the Roman Empire, which provided the infrastructure to allow the rapid spread of the gospel of

Jesus the Christ from Jerusalem to "the ends of the earth"—or, at least, to its center in the imperial capital, Rome.

Questions for Review

1. Why do most scholars believe that Matthew's Gospel was written after Mark's?
2. Given that Mark was probably written first, why has Matthew traditionally been placed first in collections of the Gospels?
3. What are some features of Matthew's Gospel that show a strong connection to the Jewish roots of the Jesus movement?
4. How does Luke's understanding of the delay of the *Parousia* relate to his decision to join his Gospel to a second volume, the Acts of the Apostles?
5. Identify the three periods of history assumed by Luke in his Gospel and the Acts of the Apostles.
6. Describe the ethics of the Gospel of Luke.

Questions for Discussion

1. Matthew is concerned to reinforce the identity of his community of Jesus-followers in a context of increasing rejection by their fellow Jews; explain how Matthew does this, and the affects of his approach upon subsequent generations of Christians.
2. Compare the ways that Matthew and Luke deal with the problem of the delay of the *Parousia*. Do you see the two approaches as compatible? What are the advantages and disadvantages of each approach?
3. What can be inferred about the communities for whom the Gospels of Matthew and Luke were written? How were these communities similar? How were they different?

CHAPTER 9

Christ-Believers' Responses to Roman Pressures to Conform

(91–100 CE)

In this decade, the Jesus movement began to interact more and more with the Roman Empire and with its culture. The interactions were not always positive. New Testament books such as the Gospel according to John, the Johannine Epistles (1–3 John), and the Apocalypse of John (or Revelation) illustrate the range of Christ-believers' responses to the empire and to the constant socio-economic and political pressures to conform to the mores of Greco-Roman culture. Roman historians such as Suetonius and Dio Cassius tell about major actors on the imperial stage, including the Emperor Domitian himself, while the church historian Eusebius of Caesarea provides an angle on the events from the viewpoint of the followers of Jesus.

Domitian Degenerates

The decade opened with Domitian as emperor. At the beginning of his reign (in 81), he had worked to be a good example for the people, supporting the traditional religion and punishing those who violated traditional mores. He had three Vestal virgins executed for failing to keep their vows; the chief Vestal was buried alive. He promoted festivals, restored public buildings such as the capitol (which had been destroyed by a second fire), and saw to the building of new ones. He paid much attention to the army, raising the soldiers' pay and campaigning in person against the barbarian tribes who threatened the empire's frontiers. He was careful with money and put the state on a firm financial footing.[1]

This does not mean that Domitian "let bygones be bygones." He stringently imposed the *fiscus Judaicus*—the two-denarius poll tax paid by all Jews aged three to sixty—including requiring payment of any back taxes from people who had not been included on the rolls for this tax in previous years. Suetonius says that "those were prosecuted who without publicly acknowledging that faith yet lived as Jews, as well as those who concealed their [Jewish ethnic] origin and did not pay the tribute levied upon their people."[2] Thus Gentiles who kept the Sabbath or had adopted other Jewish customs were now included in the levy, as were those of Jewish ethnic origin who had denounced their ancestral religion. The disciples of Jesus would be included in the former group, while some of their keenest enemies would be included in the latter.

Gradually Domitian became more lax and cruel. He was an autocrat, and an arrogant one at that. He demanded to be called "Lord" and "God," in speech as well as written documents.[3] Unlike previous emperors, who had supported the building of temples in honor of their "divine" predecessors, Domitian encouraged provincial cities to build temples in his own honor. Those that did received tax breaks.

Anti-Jewish (and, hence, anti-Jesus-Way) sentiment was on the rise during this period, whether on the part of Latin authors, the Roman governing class, or Roman nationalists in the Greek cities. The Province of Asia, which was the center of growth for the Jesus movement at the time, experienced crop failures, drought, and a serious famine in the early 90s.[4] Matters were made worse by the opportunism of wealthy Romans who, instead of selling their stores

---

1. Suetonius, *Lives of the Caesars: Titus Flavius Domitianus* 3–9.

2. Ibid., 12.2b.

3. Dio Cassius, *Roman History* 67.4.7.

4. For example, Barbara Levick (*The Government of the Roman Empire: A Sourcebook* [Totowa, NJ: Barnes & Noble Books, 1985], 111–12), quotes an edict of Lucius Antistius Rusticus, praetorian legate of Domitian, in response to a famine in the colony of Antioch caused by "persistently cold winter weather"; Rusticus prohibits the storage of any excess grain and sets a ceiling on its sale price.

of grain, kept it back and waited for prices to rise.[5] All but the wealthiest individuals suffered from these conditions and, as is not uncommon, many looked for a scapegoat to blame for the situation. The famine and attending price increases for basic goods gave rise to "boycotts and trade sanctions directed against the Christians in the towns (Rev. 13:16–17). These were accompanied by the banishment of some of the leading Christians to penal settlements in the Aegean Islands, and the execution of others, such as Antipas (Rev. 2:13)."[6] These were the actions of local groups and officials however, not of the emperor.

Domitian never worked well with the Roman Senate, and the other aristocrats resented him. He foiled a conspiracy in 87 and put down a revolt in 89. He feared assassination and once complained that no one believed an emperor to be in danger until he had been assassinated. He struck out at those around him, until even those closest to him—including his wife—formed a successful conspiracy in the year 96.[7] Domitian was murdered in September of that year.

Did Domitian Persecute Christ-Believers?

Christian tradition has portrayed Domitian as a persecutor, mostly based upon an account by a pagan historian named Dio Cassius (ca. 164–ca. 230). Dio wrote, "And the same year [95] Domitian slew, along with many others, Flavius Clemens the consul, although he was a cousin and had to wife Flavia Domitilla, who was also a relative of the emperor's. The charge brought against them both was that of atheism, a charge on which many others who drifted into Jewish ways were condemned. Some of these were put to death, and the rest were at least deprived of their property. Domitilla was merely banished to Pandateria [a prison island]."[8]

---

5. Revelation 6:6 reflects this reality when the Seer inveighs against the exorbitant prices for staple commodities while the cost of luxury items remains stable.

6. W. H. C. Frend, *Martyrdom and Persecution in the Early Church: A Study of a Conflict from the Maccabees to Donatus* (London: Basil Blackwell, 1965; Grand Rapids: Baker, 1981), 212.

7. Dio Cassius, *Roman History* 67.14–17.

8. Ibid., 67.14.1–3a.

Emperor Domitian

This account makes no explicit mention of Christ-believers but Dio Cassius loathed the Jesus movement and practically made it a point not to mention them. The reference to those who "strayed off into the Jewish religion" may refer to members of the Jesus movement since there is evidence that pagan Romans did not yet distinguish the two. In 49 Claudius expelled the Jews from Rome because of trouble stirred up by "Chrestus," as noted in chapter 3, and in Acts 18:12–17, Luke portrays the Roman official Gallio telling the Jews of Corinth that their dispute with the Apostle Paul was "a matter of questions about words and names and your own law" (v. 15). Dio mentions that the victims were accused of "atheism"; this might seem to eliminate Christ-believers, but they were often accused of atheism by the Romans, not because they did not worship a deity but because they refused to worship the gods of Rome.[9]

Eusebius states unequivocally that the high-ranking Roman matron, Flavia Domitilla, was a Christ-believer who was sent into exile (along with many others) "because of her confession of Christ."[10] However, he gets some details wrong, calling her the *niece*, not the *wife* of Flavius Clemens, and he identifies the prison island as Pontia, not Pandateria.

Dio Cassius reports Domitian plotting and carrying out a series of executions, with the implication that virtually all were based on trumped-up charges.[11] All of these appear to have been politically or economically motivated moves, however. Eusebius is the main source

---

9. See chapter 6, especially pp. 163–65.

10. Eusebius, *Ecclesiastical History* 3.18.4.

11. Dio Cassius, *Roman History* 67.11–13.

for the tradition that Domitian persecuted Christ-believers, and he cites a North African writer named Tertullian (ca. 160–ca. 220), who also referred to a persecution by that emperor. But there may have been another non-religious explanation for at least some of these arrests.[12] Domitian's father and brother had defeated the Jews in the Jewish War and had destroyed Jerusalem. The emperor may have feared that Jewish conspirators would assassinate him. Eusebius writes that Domitian gave orders for the execution of the descendants of David, the great Israelite king. Some relatives of Jesus were denounced to the emperor as Davidic. They were brought to the emperor, who questioned them and satisfied himself that they were poor and harmless. He then asked them about Christ and learned that his kingdom was not of this world and would come at the end of the age. Domitian scorned them as simpletons and let them return to their homes in Judea, where they became "leaders of the churches, both for their testimony and for their [kinship] relation to the Lord."[13] After meeting these men, Domitian concluded he had nothing to fear and canceled "the persecution of the church."[14]

This account has several problems. These men were denounced to the emperor because they were descendants of David, not because they were relatives of Jesus, and some Jews of this era still hoped for the coming of a true Davidic messiah-king. Belief in Messiah Jesus may never have entered into the picture. This "non-Christian" interpretation also fits well with Dio Cassius' statement that Domitian persecuted people for their interest in Judaism.

On the other hand, Jesus' Davidic ancestry was a prominent part of early Christian teaching, stressed especially in the infancy narratives of both Matthew and Luke. Furthermore, all the Synoptic Gospels preserve Jesus' claim that the Christ was greater than David (Matt. 22:41–46; Mark 12:35–37; Luke 20:41–44). Domitian may

---

12. Eusebius, *Ecclesiastical History* 3.20.1–6.

13. Ibid., 3.20.6; the "testimony" here refers to their witness to their faith in Jesus Christ. In the eyes of the other Christ-believers, surviving such an interrogation gained a witness the status of "confessor," one who remained firm in the faith under threat of mortal danger.

14. Ibid., 3.20.4.

have persecuted the disciples for what one might view (anachronistically) as more "political" than "religious" reasons: by giving Jesus a variety of royal and messianic titles, they highlighted that he was a descendant of the Israelite King David.

Eusebius claims that these descendants of David became leaders of Christ-believing communities after proving their faith as confessors. What adds credibility to this account is his point that they gained these offices because they were relatives of the Lord. Eusebius lived in Palestine and knew the believing communities there. The first known head of the Jerusalem *ecclesia* was James, the brother of the Lord, and Eusebius records that "Simeon the son of Clopas, . . . a cousin of the Savior," followed James in that office.[15] Eusebius does not say where these other relatives of Jesus held ecclesial offices, but the general idea of Jesus' relatives playing leadership roles fits with what little is known about the Christ-believing communities in that area.

So, did Domitian persecute? Yes. The evidence is not extensive, but it is there. His efforts seem to have been against those whom he felt threatened him personally. He did not persecute Christ-believers purely because of their "religious" beliefs, but because of their claims that Jesus was of Davidic ancestry and was even greater than King David. In such claims, Domitian saw a potential Jewish threat to his status as emperor and his claim to Roman control of the land of Israel. Thus Domitian's persecution had a very similar agenda to that of Vespasian after the capture of Jerusalem.[16] Perhaps Domitian is remembered for "persecution" (whereas Vespasian typically is not) because he engaged in this activity deliberately and steadfastly, in a time of relative peace, rather than as an act of reprisal against a conquered foe.

---

15. Ibid., 3.11; "Mary the wife of Clopas" is mentioned as having been present at Jesus' crucifixion (John 19:25).

16. Domitian was not innovating in this focus on blood relatives of Jesus and members of the Davidic family. Eusebius remarks that "Vespasian, after the capture of Jerusalem, ordered a search to be made for all who were of the family of David, that there might be left among the Jews no one of the royal family and, for this reason, a very great persecution was again inflicted on the Jews" (*Ecclesiastical History* 3.12).

Nerva's Succession and the Domitianic *Damnatio Memoriae*

As with his predecessor, Nero, the Roman Senate was unwilling to make allowances for Domitian's behavior; after his assassination, the Senate voted to damn Domitian's memory. They chose one of their own number, Nerva (30–98 CE), to be the new emperor. Similar to the way Nero's successors repudiated most of his works, Nerva rejected Domitian's. In particular, he made no attempt to harm the Christ-believers. In fact, he forbade all accusations of treason, including accusations about people's status as Jews or following the Jewish way of life. He relaxed the enforcement of the "Jewish tax," returning to the practice of Vespasian and Titus.

Since he ruled for only sixteen months, Nerva acheived little of lasting significance, but he did introduce one important change. Domitian had been popular with the army, and the soldiers pressured Nerva to execute Domitian's assassins. Having seen the power of the army, Nerva feared a civil war after his death, since he was childless and had no legally recognized successor. To forestall civil unrest, Nerva abolished the tradition of dynastic succession; instead he adopted as heir someone he thought would be an excellent ruler. That person was Trajan, a Spaniard, a successful soldier, and an experienced governor. The Senate accepted Nerva's choice and, when he died in 98, Trajan succeeded with no difficulty.

Trajan enjoyed much success, personally leading the army on two campaigns

This inscription from Thyatira (not far from contemporary Izmir, Turkey) has been subjected to *damnatio memoriae*; five lines from the top, a name (Domitian's?) has been erased.

in the Near East, campaigns that stretched the empire to new boundaries. He strengthened the economy, built up the infrastructure of roads and bridges, and presided over an extensive building campaign. He also had an important impact on Christianity, but that came after this decade.

Christian Writings from the 90s

Christ-believing writers in the decade of 91–100 produced the last of the four canonical Gospels (John), the three Johannine Epistles, the Apocalypse of John (Revelation), as well as the earliest datable extra-canonical book, Clement of Rome's *First Epistle to the Corinthians*.[17] Both the Apocalypse and *1 Clement* are dated by scholars to the last years of Domitian's reign (95–96). The Apocalypse reflects the realities of believing communities in Asia Minor, especially in the region surrounding the city of Ephesus. *First Clement*, on the other hand, provides valuable information about the Christ-believers in Rome, along with some information about the Corinthian community and the Jesus movement in general.

The Community of the Beloved Disciple: The Gospel according to John

Perhaps the most significant figure of the Gospel of John next to Jesus himself is the one identified simply as the "Beloved Disciple." As a result, the *ecclesia* that produced this Gospel has been dubbed the "community of the Beloved Disciple." Irenaeus of Lyons (ca. 175 CE) claimed that the Apostle John, son of Zebedee, wrote the Fourth Gospel.[18] But Irenaeus did not have first-hand information, and his attribution now is widely rejected. The

---

17. The title is misleading, since it implies that Clement wrote more than one epistle. Sometime around 130 CE, an anonymous author wrote a homily that later (by the fourth century) acquired the name *Second Epistle of Clement of Rome to the Corinthians*. No one today accepts it as an authentic letter from Clement. Still, because it is an important and well-known work, the title survives; thus, the original and only letter of Clement of Rome is known as his "first" epistle.

18. As a result of this long tradition, scholars continue to refer to this work as the Gospel according to John, although the author's identity is unknown.

scholarly consensus dates the final edition of the Gospel of John to around 90 CE and speaks of authorship by a Johannine "school" rather than an individual.[19] The Beloved Disciple (understood as John the apostle) is seen as the founder of the Johannine community and the "eyewitness" mentioned in the Fourth Gospel; but the Beloved Disciple is the figurehead behind the Gospel rather than the author of it. Occasional rough spots in an otherwise highly crafted work suggest more than one author or editor in a series of compositional and editorial stages.[20]

The Johannine Community

Probably originating in the city of Antioch, in Syria, the Gospel of John has several distinctive features that reflect information about the community that produced it:

1. A "high" Christology (i.e., one that views Christ as divine)
2. An argumentative approach to the Jews
3. A realized eschatology (the kingdom of God is viewed as already present)
4. A strong emphasis on the work of the Paraclete
5. A surprising lack of organizational structures and practices
6. A paucity of ethical teaching

John makes two shocking claims for Jesus that become the focus of the entire Johannine Christology: Christ pre-existed, and Christ is divine. The use of the term *Logos* (Word) to refer to Christ combines the two notions in a way that would be accessible both to educated Jews and Greeks, especially those familiar with Stoic philosophy. This fact alone suggests that the community had at least some members who were affluent enough to afford higher education. Combined with the evidence of multiple editors and the series of highly theological discourses, scholars have inferred that the community had a scribal school.

19. Raymond Brown (*The Gospel according to John*, 2 vols. [Garden City, NJ: Doubleday, 1970]) posited three redactions to the Gospel, the first dating ca. 70 CE and the final version, which is the one now found in the Bible, dating to around 90.

20. E.g., chapter 21 is viewed as an appendix, added in the last stage of composition of the Gospel.

John's Gospel also uses some unique titles for Jesus and some traditional titles in unique ways. For example, the title "Lamb of God" has traditional roots, but the explanatory note that this lamb "takes away the sin of the world" (John 1:29) is quite original to this Gospel. The title "Son of God" was used of Jesus in the Synoptic Gospels and of Israel's king in the coronation Psalms, but for John the title embraces more than these symbolic meanings of Messiah (Christ) and King of Israel. Jesus is indeed Messiah and King, but to call Jesus "Son of God" also describes a real divine relationship. "Son of Man" is not an opposite expression but rather portrays Jesus as the descending and ascending redeemer who joins heaven and earth, and who reveals his glory in being "raised up" in crucifixion and in exaltation. The title "Savior of the world" depicts Jesus' impact beyond the borders of Israel (e.g., John 4:42, in Samaria), while the term "Lord" refers to Jesus as one who brings eternal life and is worthy of worship. While all of these titles had clear theological significance, the titles Son of God, King, Savior, and Lord also had political significance. Claiming these titles for Jesus implied a rebuke of Roman imperial propaganda and posed a direct challenge to Emperor Domitian's attempts to assert his divine status.

The "I AM" sayings use this traditional theophanic formula to project the Logos' own self-communication. Thus Jesus is the "bread of life" who provides the spiritual nutrition for human survival as well as the eschatological messianic banquet (6:35). Jesus is also the light of the world (8:12); the good shepherd (10:11); the door of the sheep (10:7); the resurrection and the life (11:25); the way, the truth, and the life (14:6); and the vine who gives life to the branches (15:1). Although none of these pose a direct refutation of Judaism, this appropriation of images from the Hebrew Bible implies that God's act of salvation is fulfilled in Jesus and experienced in the Jesus movement, not Rabbinic Judaism.

The Fourth Gospel portrays everyone, including John the Baptist, in supporting roles to Jesus to make clear that Jesus is the one to revere. The striking de-emphasis on the role of the Baptist (in comparison to the Synoptic tradition) suggests a dispute between the Johannine community and a group of Baptist sectarians.

While the Gospel of John emphasizes the divinity of Christ, it also focuses on the flesh-and-blood reality of Jesus. This suggests a polemic against a contemporary sect, the gnostics. Especially the pointed omission of Simon of Cyrene helping to carry the cross of Jesus demonstrates the desire to avoid any doubt that Jesus himself was in fact crucified and killed. The Johannine emphasis on Jesus' human fatigue, thirst, and grief serves to ground the divine Christ in human life and history.

The Gospel of John presents a distinctive answer to the questions of how and why Jesus appeared among human beings. Jesus' early life is left in obscurity in the Fourth Gospel, with his first appearance recorded at his meeting with John the Baptist. The ascent of Jesus receives much clearer attention, and the events of Jesus' passion, death, ascension, and glorification become compressed into one ascending movement called the "hour." The reason for Jesus' coming was to bring to human beings the choice to come to him for fullness of life and light, or to reject him and retreat into darkness. Through his teaching, Jesus sought to attract people to a relationship with him of understanding, belief, and mutual love. This was all that God required, although the cosmos chose rather to reject than to embrace Jesus.

This Gospel posits a stark contrast between light and darkness, those who accept Jesus and those who reject him. Many scholars have viewed this aspect of the Gospel as evidence that the Johannine community was sectarian, cut off from the wider society. If Antioch was their location, a turn inward would have served as a protective mechanism to prevent members being denounced to the local authorities; recall from the previous chapter that these authorities at least occasionally moved against the Jewish community and, by extension, the Jesus movement.

The Fourth Gospel provides a series of interpretations of the crucifixion, each of which contributes to the overall interpretive matrix:

1. Jesus' death was his ascent to glory. This view runs through the main body of John's Gospel, and is confirmed by Jesus with his dying breath.
2. Jesus died for others.
3. Jesus' death for others was a cleansing activity.
4. Jesus' death for others was an example to his followers.
5. Jesus' death for others was a sacrifice for sin.

The first of these views is the most prominent in the Johannine Gospel, while the other four themes have supporting roles in the overall interpretive matrix. The series of emphases suggests that the Johannine community was engaged in a dispute with other Christ-believers who preached a "gospel of glory" focused more on the Resurrection than on the cross. (Compare Phil. 2:8 and Gal. 6:14, where Paul combats the same problem.) The Gospel of John makes Jesus' cross and glory inseparable.

Arguments with the Jews

The Gospel of John explores the theological question of the status of Jesus over against Judaism more profoundly than do the Synoptic Gospels. The miracle at the Cana wedding (2:1–11) shows that Jesus provides something vastly superior to the "old wine" of the Torah. The cleansing of the Temple (2:13–25) shows Jesus revolutionizing the primary cultic institution, and offering to replace the Temple with his body. The evangelist knows that Jewish festivals could no longer be observed because the Temple had been destroyed. John's Gospel shows that Jesus replaces the best that Judaism can offer in teaching and worship. But not everyone appreciated this fact about Jesus.

"The Jews" who opposed Jesus are linked with the cosmos that is opposed to God. The final result of John's schema is that the Jews who opposed Jesus are seen as moved by the powers of darkness.

Those who misunderstand Jesus (e.g., Nicodemus, 3:10; the synagogue congregation, 6:34, 42, 52) do so because they misunderstand the heavenly or spiritual dimension of his identity and of his offer of salvation. They refuse to acknowledge his true status, even though John the Baptist, Jesus' works, God the Father, Moses, and the Jewish scriptures all testify to Jesus (chapter 5). Denying the truth of Jesus' claim to be one with "the Father," the opposition party decides that Jesus is a blasphemer and determines to kill him (chapters 7–10). They also excommunicate his followers from the synagogue (chapter 9), and plan to suppress evidence of Jesus' true power by killing Lazarus (12:10–11).

John presents Jesus' "hour" as a necessary event, the divine provision for bringing about Jesus' return to the Father. While, at one level, the devil brings about Jesus' betrayal, unconsciously the devil brought about his own judgment. Judas and "the Jews" are the primary human agents involved in Jesus' death; the Romans receive little blame. Of course, this is not historically accurate. Instead, this way of telling the story reflects the antagonism between the Johannine community and nascent Rabbinic Judaism.

The Johannine community was originally composed of Jewish Christ-believers, but their relationship with Judaism had become unfriendly. Because they came to believe that the Messiah Jesus had fulfilled and surpassed the teachings, worship, festivals, and traditions of Judaism, the Johannine disciples were compelled to leave the synagogue. Thus the high Christology of John emerged in a conflict where the opponents denied any messianic status to Jesus. As a result of the controversy, the Johannine proponents of Jesus, previously on the fringe of Judaism, became a Christ-believing sect.

The Paraclete and Christ-Believers Living at the End of Time

The Fourth Gospel is characterized primarily by a realized rather than futuristic eschatology. The Johannine believers already have passed through judgment, have eternal life, and have witnessed the "return" of Jesus in the role of the Paraclete.

The Paraclete testifies to Jesus, glorifying him and judging the cosmos that condemned him. To Johannine believers, the Paraclete brings the joy and peace of the messianic age even now (John 16:7–15).

The Johannine Jesus gives no commands to evangelize, baptize, or commemorate him in the Eucharistic meal of bread and wine; instead, he charges the disciples to imitate him in the foot-washing (13:14). The Johannine disciples obviously know and practice baptism, and the foot-washing story explains its significance. The "I am the true vine" speech (chapter 15), which expounds the implications of Eucharistic fellowship, is set in the context of the Farewell Discourse, but the specifically Eucharistic teaching in the Gospel of John occurs not at the Last Supper (chapter 13), but in the "great feeding" story and "bread of life" discourse (chapter 6).

No less striking than the absence of an explicit account of the institution of baptism and communion is the Johannine avoidance of such official terms as "apostle." Instead, the evangelist prefers the term "disciple," and gives Jesus' disciples no other authority or status than that they "follow" him. This pointed reinterpretation of "apostleship" as "discipleship," a role without prestige or power, indicates a reaction against the way other Christ-believers were living. Similarly, the foot-washing story provides a Johannine prescription for upholding the central theme of the Johannine community: the fellowship, unity, and love of the followers of Jesus. The Fourth Gospel thus offers a pointed alternative to the hierarchical model presented in the Gospel according to Matthew, in which scribes hold special teaching authority and Peter holds "the keys to the kingdom." If both Gospels originated in Antioch, they provide evidence of a significant debate there between two different understandings of the message of Jesus and how it should be put into practice.

The Fourth Gospel, especially in the Farewell Discourse, promotes a twofold code of ethics: love "one another" as Christ has, and keep the commands of Jesus. The inward-turning restriction of the love command to "one another" implies a sectarian mentality,[21] though no disciplinary measures are set out for those who may fall short of this expectation.

In sum, the Johannine community originated from Judaism and engaged in a heated debate with it, apparently having been involuntarily excluded from synagogue participation. The community retained a deep consciousness of the Jewish scriptures, but with a transformed understanding in light of Christ. Their highly developed Christological views resulted from disputes not only with "the Jews," but also with the followers of John the Baptist, and "heretics" who believed Jesus was not really human. Derived from this Christology is a "low" theology of the church in which all believers are disciples (not apostles or scribes) and the hallmark of the believing community is foot-washing.

---

21. Compare the Synoptic Gospels' command to "love your neighbor" (Matt. 19:19; Mark 12:31; Luke 10:27) or even "love your enemy" (Matt. 5:44; Luke 6:27).

The Johannine Community Viewed from the Epistles: 1–3 John

The Johannine Epistles presume the same thought-world as the Fourth Gospel but show considerable differences in vocabulary and style. Thus the epistles originated from the same community but not the same author as the Gospel. The epistles probably are to be dated slightly later than the Gospel. The enemies attacked in the epistles are former members of the Johannine community who have broken fellowship due to a different Christology and are now viewed by the authors of the epistles as "antichrists" (1 John 2:18, 22; 4:3; 2 John 7).This means there was another Christ-believing community in the same vicinity as the community of the Beloved Disciple. First John focuses on the role of the Holy Spirit in affirming the reality of Christ's incarnation and the spiritual experience of Christ within and among Christians. Perhaps some of the Johannine community's opponents (the "gnostic" group?) made extravagant claims for Spirit-led power, which led to schism with the Johannine community.

The authority of the authors of the epistles is not based on some ecclesial office but rather the readers' respect, affection, and trust in their communion with the original, true teaching of Christ. The author of 1 John wields paternalistic authority over his readers, but claims no title or status justifying this. The author of 2 and 3 John claims to be the *presbyter* ("elder"; 2 John 1; 3 John 1), but the significance of this title is unclear. By 2 John, the community is tightening group boundaries; anyone who refuses the doctrine of Christ "does not have the Father" (1 John 2:23); Johannine Christians should shun such false believers.

One theory suggests that the original community that produced the Fourth Gospel was subsequently rent by schism, with the smaller part of the community (including, for example, the authors of 1 and 2 John) joining the broader *ecclesia* and bringing their Gospel with them. The larger part of the community—the people 1 John identifies as opponents—went on to develop an increasingly docetic and gnostic gospel. The "appendix" to the Fourth Gospel (chapter 21) was written at the time of the merger of the Johannine community with the broader *ecclesia*, and had a twofold purpose:

1. To persuade Petrine disciples to recognize the importance of the Johannine community's founder-figure, the Beloved Disciple, as one who, without needing instructions, remained an unfailing witness to Christ

2. To help Johannine believers to accept the claim of Petrine pre-eminence and his Christ-given role in shepherding the church

If this theory is correct, it shows that the development of a hierarchical form of *ecclesia* government and a more rigid discipline in the Johannine community was made during the time the epistles were written and under pressure from the schismatic group. Unprepared to deal with those who voluntarily violated the Eucharistic communion, the Johannine community struggled for a defense against the false teachers and, eventually, chose the same authoritarian strategy as was being adopted by the broader *ecclesia*.

The Johannine Gospel and Epistles show a community in evolution. Dangers on the horizon of the evangelist's view became concrete in the days of the Epistles, and brought with them schism and great suffering. From one united community came at least two antagonistic groups who shared many basic views, but whose differences concerning the human reality of Christ—especially his incarnation and death—and concerning the reality of sin and the need for ethical conduct finally led them to resort to mutual exclusion and excommunication. A remnant finally joined with the broader *ecclesia*. As a result, the heritage of the Johannine community, its loves and struggles, became available to all its spiritual heirs.

John the Seer and the Communities of Asia Minor: Revelation

The Revelation of John (or Apocalypse) is unique in the New Testament because it is a full-scale apocalypse, a revelation of an otherworldly or future truth through a narrative framework that recounts the disclosure of a transcendent reality, via a mediator, to a human recipient.

The seven letters at the beginning of the Apocalypse (chapters 2–3) locate its recipients in Asia Minor and provide information about the situation of the communities addressed by the Apocalypse. The Apocalypse depicts a group with a strong sense of mission. Within this group, "witness" is both a title of great honor and an action that is to characterize every believer's life, leading the disciple, in imitation of Christ, from suffering to glory. John the Seer presents the situation as a battle with the cosmic forces of evil, yet the war is won already by Christ.

John the Seer is a prophetic leader of the Christ-believing communities of Asia, apparently one among other prophets in those communities (e.g., see Rev. 2:6, 15, 20). This model of leadership varies from the hierarchical model that was operative in other places,[22] but fits the charismatic model found in Pauline communities such as those in Galatia and Corinth. That John writes this "Apocalypse of Jesus Christ" under his own name rather than under a pseudonym (as do other post-Pauline writers) illustrates that "prophecy and prophetic leadership were still highly respected in the churches of Asia Minor at the turn of the first century CE."[23] John knew that his own authority as a prophet still commanded respect in the communities of Asia. Nor is there any sign that the acceptance and influence of John's prophetic authority is threatened by a rising episcopacy. The only competition in sight is a rival prophetic circle.

These believers are under severe stress caused by several factors:

1. Social contempt and ostracism
2. The threat of social and economic sanctions against those who do not conform to the requirements of the imperial cult
3. Conflicts with opponents within the communities

The Apocalypse of John emphasizes the roles of prophets and martyrs in the leadership of the Christ-believing community, both now and after the victory of the gospel. Prophecy and martyrdom are both charismatic gifts, which God bestows upon people according

---

22. E.g., see the discussions of the Gospel according to Matthew (pages 206–14) and *1 Clement* (pages 241–48).

23. Elisabeth Schüssler Fiorenza, *The Book of Revelation: Justice and Judgment* (Minneapolis: Fortress, 1985), 151; cf. Adela Yarbro Collins, *Crisis and Catharsis: The Power of the Apocalypse* (Philadelphia: Westminster, 1984), 49–50.

to his good pleasure. The call of Christ and the gift of the Spirit—irrespective of one's social class, sex, or ethnic origin—make the believer a prophet or a martyr. John rejects other prophets whom he views as teaching accommodation to Greco-Roman culture; this, for John, is the height of apostasy.[24] The Christ-believing community is called to live a counter-cultural lifestyle largely separate from the Greco-Roman environment. John's prophecy calls the members of his audience to a counter-cultural lifestyle in preparation for martyrdom.

The key to the Apocalypse is its message of non-compliance with the Roman socio-cultural and economic system, which is viewed as being in direct conflict with the faith.[25] The Roman authorities appear to have agreed with John's estimation of the severity of the conflict, for John was writing from exile "because of the word of God and the testimony of Jesus" (Rev. 1:9). The Roman response to John's stance spoke clearly of their opposition to John's prophetic and apocalyptic understanding of the gospel.

> John's banishment made evident once again the precarious legal position of Christians, especially those who combined an anti-Roman political perspective with hope for the future and with prophecy. It obviously must have been a traumatic experience for John himself. It is likely that it was at least unsettling for his allies and followers.[26]

The seven letters that open the Apocalypse show that the members of John's churches responded to this Roman pressure to conform in basically two ways: either they allied themselves with John and rejected the Roman state and culture, or they modified their

---

24. While John never explicitly validates the notion that the prophetic gift may rest upon a woman, it is significant that neither does he at any point explicitly validate the idea that this prophetic gift may rest upon any other man. At the point in the Apocalypse where discussion of a female prophet does arise, John uses scathing rhetoric to repudiate her prophecy. Yet this tactic differs in no way from his approach toward rival male prophets. And John places his main focus not upon the mediator of the prophecy, but its content. The rival prophets are false because their prophecy is false, not because they are female or male. Their prophecy calls for the sort of cultural accommodation that will help the Christian community avoid martyrdom.

25. Yarbro Collins, *Crisis and Catharsis*, 106–7.

26. Ibid., 104.

beliefs and practice to assimilate to Greco-Roman culture.[27] The prophetic and apocalyptic radicalism of John's community grew out of its socio-cultural situation, especially Roman pressure for Christ-believers to assimilate. This insight contributes not only to an understanding of Revelation, but also to our knowledge of the variety of believers' responses to these late first-century cultural, economic, and socio-political pressures to assimilate to Roman culture.

As a response to these stressful forces, the Seer emphasizes seven theological ideas:

1. The transcendent power of God as creator, and of Christ as redeemer
2. The relationship of the believer through Christ to God in the Spirit
3. The interaction of worship and witness for the church in the world
4. The transitory nature of this age (even in its religious dimension)
5. The element of self-sacrifice inherent in witness to Christ
6. The political implications of living this witness
7. The power of a vision of hope, even in a context of suffering

For the Christ-believers in the communities of Asia, the Revelation of John offered a message of hope aimed to help them stay faithful in the face of pervasive social and political pressures.

Clement and the Communities of Rome and Corinth: *I Clement*

Clement is known only from this epistle, and even that does not actually provide his name. He wrote the epistle in the name of the Roman community; About 170 Bishop Dionysius of Corinth wrote to the Romans and mentioned the letter "which was earlier sent to us through Clement."[28] Irenaeus of Lyons (*fl.* ca. 170–180) also

---

27. For a good discussion of the seven letters, see Colin J. Hemer, *The Letters to the Seven Churches of Asia in Their Local Setting,* Journal for the Study of the New Testament Supplement Series 11 (Sheffield, UK: JSOT Press, 1986).

28. Eusebius, *Ecclesiastical History* 4.23.

identifies Clement as the author of the letter. Who was this Clement? The early *ecclesia* favored identifying him as the "fellow worker" whom Paul mentions in Philippians 4:3. While possible, this identification cannot be proven; Clement was a common name. Roman tradition identifies Clement as the third successor of Peter as bishop of Rome, presiding over that community from approximately 91–100 CE. Clement certainly was not the bishop (as his letter shows), but he may have served as a leader of the community.

Was he in any way connected with Flavius Clemens, Domitian's cousin and victim of his wrath? One possibility is that this Clement was a freedman of Flavius Clemens; it was not uncommon for a freedman to adopt the name of his former master. Association with such a prominent figure as Flavius Clemens probably would have enhanced Clement's status in the Roman *ecclesia*. But there is no direct evidence linking him with Flavius Clemens; nor, as discussed earlier, is it entirely certain that this cousin of the emperor was a Christ-believer. The possible connection of Clement with the Flavian family remains conjectural.

Most of what is known about Clement derives from an analysis of his letter. He wrote in Greek, the language used by all New Testament authors. This suggests that the Roman community was composed mainly of foreigners, but the persons mentioned as delegates who took Clement's letter to Corinth (*1 Clement* 65.1) all have Latin names: Claudius Ephebus, Valerius Vito, and Fortunatus.

Some scholars think the author was Jewish because one-fourth of the letter consists of quotations from the Jewish Bible, but Clement always cites the Greek version, the Septuagint, and shows no knowledge of Hebrew. The Jewish element in the Roman community would have been strong, going back to the time of Priscilla and Aquila during the reign of the Emperor Claudius (Acts 18:1–2), and most of the missionaries in Rome would have been Jews, who acquainted their Gentile converts with the Jewish scriptures. By the time Clement wrote this letter, the Roman community was almost a half-century old; there had been plenty of time for Gentile converts to become knowledgeable readers of the Old Testament. Thus it is not impossible that Clement was Jewish, but neither is there strong evidence that he was. Clement writes during a time of persecution (7.1) but refers to such predecessors in martyrdom as the "pillars" of the church, Peter and Paul (5.1–6), and "a great multitude of the elect" (6:1), including "women, the Danaids and Dircae . . . [who] suffered terrible and unspeakable torments" (6.2).[29] While a bit cryptic, Clement's reference to Dirce (pronounced Dirki) and the Danaids implies that these women martyrs were forced to re-enact mythological scenes as part of the murderous "entertainments" in the amphitheater.[30] Clement remarks that "jealousy hath estranged wives from their husbands and changed the saying of our father Adam, 'This now is bone of my bones and flesh of my flesh' " (6.3). He may be implying that these women had been denounced by their own husbands. Since these earlier martyrs were killed during the persecution under Emperor Nero, the contemporary persecution to which Clement referred must have occurred during the reign of Domitian.

Clement wrote to Corinth in an attempt to heal the strife that was dividing the community. (One familiar with Paul's letters to Corinth will find such factionalism a familiar theme.) Clement had

---

29. Unless otherwise noted, the English translation of *1 Clement* cited throughout is that of Alexander Roberts and James Donaldson, eds., *The Apostolic Fathers with Justin Martyr and Irenaeus: Clement of Rome, Mathetes, Polycarp, Ignatius, Barnabas, Papias, Justin Martyr, Irenaeus*, revised and chronologically arranged, with brief prefaces and occasional notes by A. Cleveland Coxe, Ante-Nicene Fathers 1 (1885; repr. Peabody, MA: Hendrickson, 1994); online at *Christian Classics Ethereal Library*, Grand Rapids, http://www.ccel.org/ccel/schaff/anf01.html.

30. According to the Greek myth, Dirce was executed by being tied to the horns of a bull and then tossed and dragged around until dead. This would be one form of execution for a woman sentenced "*ad bestias*" (condemned to be killed by wild beasts). A full-scale sculpture of this scene was discovered in the Baths of Caracalla in the sixteenth century.

In the most common version of the myth of the Danaids, the fifty daughters of Danaus were pledged to marry the fifty sons of their father's twin brother Aegyptus, but Danaus decided he did not want his daughters to follow through with these marriages. Instead, he made them promise to kill their husbands on their wedding nights, which all but one of them did. (Hypermnestra spared her husband Lynceaus because he respected her desire to remain a virgin.) The sole surviving brother, Lynceaus, avenged the deaths of his brothers by killing Danaus. The daughters were condemned to spend eternity in Tartarus carrying water in a vessel full of holes.

George Park Fisher (*The Beginnings of Christianity: With a View of the State of the Roman World at the Birth of Christ* [New York: Charles Scribner's Sons, 1889], 530–32) discusses various possible scenarios that would fit Clement's description. He suggests that "those who were exhibited as Danaids may have been slain by one who personated Lynceaus, or they may have been forced to undergo different forms of torture which were described in the fables of Tartarus, until death put an end to their agony" (532).

heard that certain members of the community had removed some of their leaders without cause, for they had been fulfilling their ministerial duties and living "blamelessly" (44.5; Greek 44.6). Accusing them of jealousy (14.1), Clement reprimanded the community for following one or two troublemakers in unseating their elders (47.6). Citing examples of great figures of Israel's past, of members of the *ecclesia*, and even a few selfless pagans (55–56), Clement invites the seditionists to re-submit themselves to the authority of the unseated elders and "receive correction so as to repent, bending the knees of your heart" (57.1).

What was at the root of this dissention in the Corinthian *ecclesia*? Perhaps Clement was mistaken about the situation and the behavior of the unseated elders deserved such an action against them. Or perhaps the Corinthians simply had not abandoned the fractious ways of the preceding generation. Then again, Paul's letters to Corinth refer to a competition over spiritual gifts in the community, so perhaps the "seditionists" were charismatic leaders who felt impelled by the Spirit to force the others out of office. Whatever happened, the outcome of this reprimand from the Roman community is not known; the Corinthian *ecclesia* slips into historical obscurity soon after Clement's letter.

While *1 Clement* offers important information about the Corinthian community, it also gives a great deal of information about Christ-believers in Rome. Scholars put much emphasis on Clement's choice to write in the name of the entire community rather than in his own name, and most believe that the Roman *ecclesia* of this time was led by a group of elders or *presbyters* rather than a single governing bishop (usually called a monarchical bishop). Significantly, Clement speaks of leaders having been appointed by the apostles, who also provided that "other approved men should succeed them in their ministry . . . with the consent of the whole Church" (44.2; Greek 44.3). This implies that Rome viewed their ministerial offices as marked by an "apostolic" succession. Clement appears to use the terms "elder" (*presbyter*) and "bishop" interchangeably, which has led some scholars to speak of "presbyter-bishops" at this stage of development in the Roman *ecclesia*.[31]

---

31. Raymond E. Brown and John P. Meier, *Antioch and Rome*, New Testament Cradles of Catholic Christianity (New York: Paulist Press, 1983), 168–80.

In fact, there is no evidence of a monarchical bishop at Rome before the late second century. This view is reinforced by the tone of the letter, which is fraternal, not judicial. Clement hopes to win back the Corinthians by reminding them of the harm that division has caused in other communities. He expects them to change, not because he is ordering them to do so, but because he expects them to recognize and do the right thing.

Although it is not exactly clear what these presbyter-bishops did, they apparently had strong liturgical obligations (see, e.g., 40–41). The community also had obligations of hospitality that the presbyter-bishops would have monitored. Clement also gives evidence of the growing acceptance of the books that would form the New Testament. He knows the Synoptic Gospels (Matthew, Mark, and Luke) as well as several letters (Romans, 1 Corinthians, Galatians, Philippians, Ephesians, Hebrews, and 1 Peter)—although, somewhat surprisingly, not 2 Corinthians. He also quotes as scripture several passages not found in modern Bibles, such as Moses saying, "I am but as the smoke from a pot" (17.3), not known from any Jewish or Christian sources, and an unattributed remark, "Cleave to the holy, for those that cleave to them shall [themselves] be made holy" (46.2), which sounds Pauline but is found in no extant Pauline work. There is currently no way to determine the sources of these remarks, but they prove that, in a society dependent upon oral tradition, the array of available sources was far wider than what has survived in writing.

For the long-term history of the church, the real importance of this letter is the evidence it provides of the growing acceptance of the Roman way of life and of Roman authority. As noted in the previous chapter, Luke abandoned the eschatological idea and wrote a sequel to his Gospel (Acts) to show the ongoing victory of the gospel in the context of the Roman Empire. Like Luke, Clement makes no mention of the impending end of the age. He is concerned about the Corinthians' behavior because the communities need stability in order to survive and function in the world. Clement expects Christ-believers to be obedient to governmental authorities (60–61), just as he expects them to be obedient to ecclesiastical authorities and biblical teachings. Such sobriety and traditionalism characterized much of Roman life and would figure significantly in the later history of the Roman *ecclesia*.

However, living in the Roman world involved more than mere conformity. In chapter 20 Clement speaks of the harmony of the world: "The heavens, revolving under His government, are subject to Him in peace. Day and night run the course appointed by Him, in no wise hindering each other. The sun and moon, with the companies of the stars, roll on in harmony according to His command, within their prescribed limits, and without any deviation." These remarks reflect the view of the Stoic philosophers, who believed that the gods had established the daily harmony of the cosmos, a notion that would be easy for Jesus' disciples to assimilate. To impress upon his readers the importance of order, Clement invokes the image of the Roman army: "All are not prefects, nor commanders of a thousand, nor of a hundred, nor of fifty, nor the like, but each one in his own rank performs the things commanded by the king and the generals" (37.3). Remarkably, he wrote those admiring words at a time of persecution.

The most noteworthy example of Clement's adoption of Roman culture comes in a discussion of the resurrection of the dead (24–25). He uses as an example of resurrection "a certain bird which is called a phoenix. This is the only one of its kind, and lives five hundred years. And when the time of its dissolution draws near that it must die, it builds itself a nest of frankincense, and myrrh, and other spices, into which, when the time is fulfilled, it enters and dies. But as the flesh decays a certain kind of worm is produced, which, being nourished by the juices of the dead bird, brings forth feathers (25:2–3)." Thus a new phoenix comes into being. Although hardly a convincing proof of the resurrection, Clement's use of the story of the phoenix demonstrates how comfortable he felt using examples from pagan traditions. Not everyone agreed with this acceptance of pagan culture, as John the Seer, the mysterious author of the book of Revelation, demonstrates.

Like all important historical sources, Clement's letters raise some questions that scholars cannot answer. For example, he speaks (ch. 5) of the Apostle Paul's having reached the limits of the West, which implies that Paul's desire to go to Spain (Rom. 15:23–24) was actually realized. Almost no modern scholars believe this to be the case. Perhaps Clement simply assumed that, since Paul mentioned this desire, he must have achieved it. Furthermore, Clement does not specifically mention Spain.

In this first-century sign from a *taverna* in the ruins of Pompeii, a caption identifies the large bird in the center as a phoenix. In his epistle, Clement of Rome draws an analogy between the rebirth of the mythical phoenix and the Resurrection of Christ.

In that same chapter, Clement speaks of the deaths of Peter and Paul as having been caused by jealousy and rivalry. Such words seem to eliminate pagans as the villains of the piece. Does Clement mean the Jews of Rome? Possibly, but Luke (Acts 28:17–28) says that the Roman Jews came to Paul's residence and debated with him "from morning until evening"; some agreed with Paul, and those who did not left peaceably. If Luke is accurate here, then that leaves only other Christ-believers as the jealous rivals. It is clear from his epistles that Paul had rivals within the Jesus movement, people about whom he spoke very bitterly: "I wish those who unsettle you would castrate themselves!" (Gal. 5:12). Acts implies that "false believers" denounced Paul in Jerusalem (Acts 21:27ff.). It is not clear, however, whether Peter was involved in such rivalries; he appears not to have stirred up people the way Paul did. Clement is not explicit on this point, but it is possible that other Christ-believers denounced the other great apostle during Nero's persecution.

Summary

Social and political pressures upon the Christ-believers grew in the 90s for a multiplicity of reasons: Domitian's jealousy for the divine titles he claimed for himself, concerns about potential competitors for the throne from among the descendants of the Israelite King David, and intensified enforcement of the *fiscus Judaicus* put social and economic pressure on the disciples of Jesus. Enforcement of "emperor worship" through the ceremonial offering of incense in honor of the living emperor, and provision of tax incentives to cities that would erect temples in honor of Emperor Domitian as a living God, posed a direct challenge to the faith commitments of the Christ-believers. The responses of the latter ranged from withdrawal to direct confrontation with the imperial authorities. Authenticity of belief and level of commitment to life in communion with other believers became key issues in the various communities, and constitute key elements of the theological discourse in the Johannine Gospel and Epistles as well as the Apocalypse and *1 Clement*. Such issues would continue to pose challenges to Christ-believers in the coming decades, as the roll of martyrs continued to grow in time with increasing pressures to conform the gospel to the mores and customs of the surrounding Roman world.

Questions for Review

1. Describe the evidence that Domitian persecuted "Christians," and explain his apparent motives for doing so.
2. Summarize Eusebius' description of Domitian's search for and questioning of the surviving descendants of David. Why is this account considered plausible?
3. Who was the author of *1 Clement*? What problem does the Epistle address, and how does the author seek to resolve that problem?

4. Describe the role of "presbyter-bishops" in the Christ-believing communities of this period.

5. What are some of the examples Clement invokes to demonstrate the value of order within the community?

6. List some of the major concerns of the Revelation of John.

7. What are some of the differences in viewpoint (e.g., regarding Jesus or ecclesial authority) between the Gospel of John and the other canonical Gospels?

8. What was the point of contention between the author of the Johannine Epistles and the rival Christian group condemned in those epistles?

Questions for Discussion

1. Christ-believers in this period seem to have held a range of attitudes toward the Roman Empire, from the *Epistle of Clement* at one extreme to the Revelation of John at the other. Describe this range of attitudes. Which position seems most in keeping with the teachings of Jesus?

2. It seems that in this period there were some disciples of high social status, possibly even members of the emperor's family; what effect do you think it had upon the Jesus movement to have members of such high rank? What effect do you think it had upon the empire to have persons of high rank who were Christ-believers?

3. The Gospel of John takes a distinctive approach to the identity of Jesus and the significance of his death and Resurrection. If the broader church had not accepted John's Gospel, do you think Christianity would look very different today?

CHAPTER 10

Peace and Prosperity
(101–110 CE)

By modern gauges of time, this decade marked the opening of a new century, but the familiar BC–AD or BCE–CE calendar did not come into existence until the sixth century CE. Most citizens of the Roman Empire would have used the Roman calendar, also called the Julian calendar because it dates back to Julius Caesar (100–44 BCE); this calendar would indicate which month and day it was. In terms of years, however, most dates in Roman records were based on who held the office of Consul at the time. In addition, residents of various provinces—for example, the Judeans and Egyptians—also had their own local calendars.

The decade was relatively quiet. As a former soldier, the Emperor Trajan (53–117 CE) had the support of the Roman army, which was becoming a more important factor in maintaining the throne and, therefore, stability in the empire. Although he was of Italian descent, his non-patrician origins in Hispania Baetica (modern Andalusia) gave hope to ambitious provincials who saw that the full extent of the cursus honorum, the route to high public office, was no longer restricted to Italy.

Second Thessalonians and the *Cursus Honorum*

The letter known as 2 Thessalonians is attributed to Paul of Tarsus, although the accuracy of this authorship claim has been challenged by many scholars since at least the nineteenth century. Much of this challenge derives from evidence internal to the letter.[1] Often 2 Thessalonians is classified as a "deuteropauline" letter, that is, a letter written by a second-generation Christ-believer from one of the communities founded by Paul. If the letter derives from Paul himself, it would have to be dated to the early 50s, in relatively close proximity to Paul's first letter, now known as 1 Thessalonians. If, as most scholars believe, it was composed by a later Paulinist, then the dating of this letter is difficult to determine. One proposed date has been the mid-nineties, about the time that John the Seer wrote the Apocalypse, because both works speak of an "anti-Christ" figure (e.g., 2 Thess. 2:3–4; Rev. 13) and continue to anticipate the glorious *Parousia* of Christ (e.g., 2 Thess. 2:8; Rev. 1:7), in opposition to other Christ-believers who have relinquished this claim (see, e.g., 2 Thess. 2:1–4; Rev. 19–20).[2] If the letter is pseudonymous, then a date right around 100 CE is likely.

One of the more problematic sections of 2 Thessalonians involves a discussion of a group of "unruly" members of the community.[3] The author's penalty for these disorderly disciples is excommunication (2 Thess. 3:10, 14–15), which suggests that their behavior has caused scandal to the other members of the *ecclesia*. The chief offense of these "unruly" believers is that they do not "work." Although the letter provides no evidence to identify the unruly non-workers, commentators often have envisioned them as poorer members of the community who have quit their jobs and are living off the charity of wealthy members of the *ecclesia*.[4] Perhaps this inference derives

1. See Helmut Koester, *Introduction to the New Testament* (Philadelphia: Fortress; Berlin and New York: Walter De Gruyter, 1982), 2:281.

2. The two most common strategies for setting aside the belief in the *Parousia*— that is, the concrete, future coming of Christ in glory and judgment—was to spiritualize this "coming" and equate it with the spiritual presence of Christ in the community (e.g., John 14–16 on the Paraclete; Col. 2:11–12; 3:1–3), or to dismiss it as meaningless because of the length of time that had passed since its original proclamation (e.g., the opponents mentioned in 2 Pet. 3).

3. 2 Thess. 3:6–12. The Greek term here is the plural form of *ataktos*, which is used by Xenophon to refer to an undisciplined soldier whose conduct is disorderly.

4. For a more extensive discussion of this passage, see Sheila E. McGinn and Megan T. Wilson-Reitz, "Welfare Wastrels or Swanky Socialites: 2 Thess 3:6–15 and the Problem of the *Ataktoi*," in *By Bread Alone: Approaching the Bible Through a Hermeneutic of Hunger*, ed. Sheila E. McGinn et al. (Minneapolis: Fortress, anticipated 2014; tentative title).

from the fact that the term for "work" here refers to manual labor,[5] and the interpreters have not expected wealthy people to work with their hands.

The other key term in this section of the letter typically is translated as "busybody," which raises the question of whether there is a connection between minding other people's affairs and the avoidance of manual labor. One circumstance where these two factors would coexist are in the case of clients of a wealthy patron, who are expected to "mind the affairs" of their patron, waiting upon the person for hours at a time, accompanying him (rarely her) to the forum, baths, Senate, or other place of "business." The client would accomplish absolutely nothing other than giving honor to the patron, whose prestige would increase in proportion to the number of clients he had in tow.

Why would someone spend so much time and energy waiting on the pleasure of a wealthy patron? This was the only way to "get ahead" in Roman society. In modern times, people might advance their careers by education, by what they know. "Networking" is of secondary importance; it allows other people to see what one knows and that one is qualified to do the work one sets out to do. In the ancient world, on the other hand, those connections were all-important. Having the right patron made the difference between getting ahead or not. To follow the *cursus honorum*, an ambitious man needed to gain the attention and support of a well-connected patron who could open the right doors to the types of offices that would increase the client's social status and financial situation. The example of Trajan showed that even a non-patrician provincial could advance to the pinnacle of imperial power. It would not be surprising if other ambitious provincials, in Thessalonica or elsewhere, set their sights to climb the ladder of success.

If such a choice were being made by a non-believer, whose only hope lay in transient worldly success, the author of 2 Thessalonians would likely have understood the decision. The problem, from the author's point of view, is that the hope of the Christ-believer has a

---

5. The Greek term here is *ergazomai*, which refers primarily to manual labor (*ergon*, as in farmers who "work" the land, ranchers who engage in animal husbandry, or blacksmiths who "work" a bellows); secondarily to building, and thirdly to engaging in trade. Scholars, philosophers, politicians, and others who engage in "the life of the mind" do not "work" in the sense meant by this term.

dramatically different character than this type of worldly choice. Jesus was executed by the Romans, and the power structures of Rome belong to the "present evil age" that is doomed to pass, giving way to the reign of God. Climbing the Roman ladder of success could only carry the believer away from Christ and the divine *imperium*. A return to manual labor would mean relinquishing any attempt to gain honor and achieve success in the same Roman *imperium* that had slain the Lord Jesus. Trajan's elevation may have posed a serious temptation to those who still harbored a desire for worldly success, but the author of 2 Thessalonians upheld Jesus' injunction against divided loyalties: one cannot "serve [both] God and wealth" (Matt. 6:24).

Trajanus Optimus: The Most Excellent Trajan

Roman historians' reports of Trajan's reign are universally positive. The people of Rome in particular greeted Trajan's accession with a sigh of relief after their recent experience with the bloody and tyrannical Emperor Domitian. Trajan continued Nerva's policy of freeing those who had been unjustly imprisoned by Domitian and returning private property he had confiscated. This favorable treatment of the patrician families and even-handed administration of justice[6] endeared Trajan to the Roman Senate, who awarded him the title "*Optimus*" (Most Excellent").[7] Even after being awarded other titles due to military conquest, Dio Cassius asserts that Trajan "took much greater pride in the title of *Optimus* than in all the rest, inasmuch as it referred rather to his character than to his arms."[8]

Still, Trajan's military prowess underlay much of his popularity, both with the populace and the army. He led the greatest military expansion in Roman history, securing and extending the imperial borders into Armenia, Parthia, Dacia (in the northern Balkans), Mesopotamia, Arabia, and elsewhere. By the end of Trajan's reign, the Roman Empire covered the widest geographical area it ever had or would achieve, whether before his time or afterwards. Trajan himself

---

6. E.g., see Dio Cassius, *Roman History* 68.5.3 on Trajan's lenient treatment of conspirators.

7. Ibid., 68.23.1.

8. Ibid., 68.23.2.

took the field in these military expeditions, marching with the rank-and-file of the Roman Army.[9] The suppression of the border wars with Parthia and Dacia created a sense of security within the empire, the like of which had not been experienced in decades, perhaps since the time of Augustus himself. The defeat of King Decebalus ("Brave Heart") of Dacia, to whom Domitian had capitulated in what many Romans viewed as a shameful peace agreement, restored the pride and confidence of the Army and citizenry alike.

Ancient historians—and many modern ones as well—tend to glorify war, focusing on the victors without dwelling on the harsh realities of rape, pillage, and enslavement of the conquered peoples, which were engrained in the fabric of ancient warfare.[10] Thus one must recognize the inherent bias of the Roman historians in their treatment of Trajan's campaigns. Still, some conquerors were known for their brutality and indiscriminate slaughter,[11] whereas others were noted for their clemency. Trajan fell into this latter category.[12]

We have no way of knowing how many people were killed and enslaved in these wars of expansion, nor how the conquests affected the social, political, and economic life of the subjugated peoples. With the conquest of Dacia, the empire acquired gold and silver mines. In addition, Trajan would have acquired substantial sums of money from the war booty and sales of enslaved captives—funds that were used to finance these costly wars. The wars and the mines were profitable enough to allow Trajan to engage in extensive public works, in Rome and elsewhere. As is the case with all imperial economies, most of the wealth and other benefits of this expansion flowed to the imperial center.

For Christ-believers who, perhaps even more than some of the newly conquered peoples, lived at the fringes of Roman society, the

---

9. Ibid., 68.23.1.

10. The one exception among ancient historians was Flavius Josephus, whose account of the Jewish War includes death tolls and numbers of those enslaved. (See, e.g., see *Jewish War* 6.9.2–4.) Of course, while Josephus was writing this history for his Roman patron, he himself was a Jewish war captive and so had a personal affinity with the Jews whose defeat he was recounting.

11. See, e.g., Josephus' account of the conquest of Jerusalem (*Jewish War* 5.11.1, 4; 6.9.2–4).

12. Dio Cassius, *Roman History* 68.18.3.

wars and public building projects would have served as constant reminders of the power of the empire. Even though Trajan had not moved against them, he clearly was not one to brook opposition from those allied with other kingdoms, divine or otherwise. It was not long since Domitian had exiled, imprisoned, and executed some of their number. In the early period of Trajan's reign, there is no record of persecution of Christ-believers, although there is evidence of imperial action against the Jesus movement in the following decade.[13] Keeping a low profile and trying to blend in with Roman society would be a safer strategy for the community of believers than the kind of confrontational stance encouraged in ecclesial writings such as the Apocalypse.[14]

Trajan proved to be a good administrator, working to improve the imperial economy, including the *alimenta*, a "welfare program" for the Italian poor, especially fatherless and abandoned children. The new harbor at Ostia provided a steady influx of grain from North Africa to feed the poor of Rome. In true imperial style, Trajan held triumphs and sponsored festivals with free food and extravagant games involving, on one occasion, ten thousand gladiators.

The Plight of the Poor

All these efforts could not change the fact that the vast majority of those who lived under Roman rule were chronically poor, underemployed or unemployed, and had little or no hope of rising above this level. While Trajan's many building projects provided temporary employment to able-bodied laborers, it did not improve the long-term condition of the lower ("plebian") classes. Sporadic series of games fed hungry people for a time, but it didn't provide them with the means to ensure that they would be able to feed themselves once the games were ended.

The gospel message of a radically different kingdom of God, which the meek would inherit, found a ready audience among the poor and disenfranchised of the Roman Empire. The regular communal meals and compassion shown for their "brothers and sisters"

---

13. Pliny, *Letters* 10.96–97. See the next chapter for discussion of this subject.

14. See the previous chapter for a fuller treatment of this topic.

in the Christ-believing community provided the mutual support and sustenance to keep alive the hope of fullness of life in a truly divine empire ruled by the self-giving Savior who "filled the hungry with good things" (Luke 1:53).

Other Ecclesial Writings of the Period

The members of the Jesus movement continued to follow his example in their daily lives and, as part of their process of mutual support, they reflected together on the significance of his life and message. Some of those reflections gave rise to letters and other types of writings to support and educate each other in the faith. Much (though not all) of that literature is anonymous or pseudonymous. Two examples from this period will be discussed here: a doctrinal text from Syria called the *Didache,* and selected writings from a leading figure from Asia Minor, Papias of Hieropolis.

The Didache

The Teaching of the Twelve Apostles or *Didache*, a late first- or early second-century CE text from Syria,[15] includes one of the earliest "church orders" or descriptions of ministries and relationships in the community of Christ-believers. The ministerial structure outlined in the *Didache* demonstrates that the Syrian *ecclesia* does not yet have a "monarchical episcopate," that is, a hierarchy in which one *episkopos* or "bishop" presides over the entire community and all its other ministers. Even the idea of such a structure is alien to the Syrian community. Rather, according to *Didache* 11.7, prophets still have unchallenged authority in the Christ-believing community. They preside over Eucharistic services, and their status is compared to that of the Jewish high priest.[16] The *Didache* provides

---

15. For a useful collection of essays on the *Didache*, see Willy Rordorf, *Liturgie Foi et Vie des Premiers Chrétiens,* Théologie Historique 75 (Paris: Beauchesne, 1986), 139–223.

16. *Didache* 10.7. The Eucharistic service involved prayer and praise of God, blessing of at least the basic elements of a meal (bread and wine), and a communal banquet. It probably also included proclamation of the gospel and prophetic interpretation of the Jewish scriptures or "Old Testament."

for the community to nominate overseers (*episkopoi*, pl.) and deacons to preside at Eucharist if no prophet is present, which suggests that itinerant prophets are becoming less common, but are
not extinct.[17] Indeed, the *Didache* also provides that, if a wandering
prophet chooses to settle in one place, then that prophet should be
supported by the local *ecclesia*. Whenever a prophet is present at
the Eucharistic celebration, the prophet—rather than one of the
local overseers or deacons—presides over the worship and communal banquet.

In addition to this discussion of the roles of community leaders
and rules for the Eucharistic meal, the *Didache* includes a section
of moral teaching for believers. This section follows a traditional
Jewish model called the Two Ways doctrine. One manner of living constitutes the path to fullness of life; the other path leads to
death and alienation. Given that the *Didache* derives from the *ecclesia* in Syria and also exhibits this Jewish model for ethical teaching,
it is plausible that the Christ-believing community in Syria still
retained close ties to the synagogue at the time the *Didache* was
being written. In conjunction with the Gospel according to Matthew,
the *Didache* provides a small window into the close but conflicted
relations between the Jesus movement and developing Rabbinic
Judaism in the city of Antioch-on-the-Orontes around the turn of
the second century.[18]

---

17. *Didache* 15.1. There also appears to be a problem with charlatans, because rules
are developed for discerning false prophets (11:3-6). Interestingly, the rules provide for
discerning false *prophets* (11:8-12), not false *prophecy*; testing of ecstatic utterances is
expressly forbidden (11:7).

18. The community in Antioch of Syria provides a very interesting case of
long-lasting and close relationships between "church" and "synagogue." The
fourth-century prelate, John Chrysostom (354–407), who was a native of Antioch,
inveighs against members of his congregation who continue to frequent the synagogue
and celebrate Jewish festivals, claiming that he sought "to cure those who are sick with
the Judaizing disease. . . . For if they hear no word from me today, they will then
join the Jews in their fasts; once they have committed this sin it will be useless for
me to apply the remedy" (John Chrysostom, *Homilies* 1.5). Many have objected to
Chrysostom's anti-Judaism, as well they might. For purposes of this discussion, however, his remarks demonstrate that, 300 years after the start of the Jesus movement, at
least some Christ-believers in Antioch still practiced as Jews—and saw no inherent
faith conflict in doing so.

Papias of Hierapolis

Papias (ca. 60–135 CE) served as bishop in the town of Hierapolis in western Asia Minor (modern Turkey). At about the turn of the century, Papias composed some works that, unfortunately, do not survive intact. However, fragments of Papias' writings survive in the form of quotes found in the writings of other early Christ-believers, especially Eusebius of Caesarea. Papias witnesses to both the diversity within the Jesus movement in this period and to the gradual process of unification of these diverse strands.

Papias believed in a concrete, material, divine kingdom. He reported a saying attributed to Jesus that described the kingdom of God as a place of bountiful harvests and harmonious relationships between the various aspects of God's creation:

> The days will come in which vines shall grow, having each ten thousand branches, and in each branch ten thousand twigs, and in each true twig ten thousand shoots, and in every one of the shoots ten thousand clusters, and on every one of the clusters ten thousand grapes, and every grape when pressed will give five-and-twenty metretes of wine.[19] And when any one of the saints shall lay hold of a cluster, another shall cry out, "I am a better cluster, take me; bless the Lord through me." In like manner, [He said] that a grain of wheat would produce ten thousand ears, and that every ear would have ten thousand grains, and every grain would yield ten pounds of clear, pure, fine flour; and that apples, and seeds, and grass would produce in similar proportions; and that all animals, feeding then only on the productions of the earth, would become peaceable and harmonious, and be in perfect subjection to man. . . . Now these things are credible to believers. And Judas the traitor, . . . not believing, and asking, "How shall such growths be accomplished by the Lord?" the Lord said, "They shall see who shall come to them." These, then, are the times mentioned by the

---

19. An ancient Greek liquid measure, one *metretes* was equivalent to about nine gallons or forty liters.

prophet Isaiah: "And the wolf shall lie down with the lamb," etc. (Isa. 11:6 ff.).[20]

Wheat would grow in the same abundance as well as "the rest of the fruits and seeds" while "the animals, using these foods which are received from the earth, [will] become peaceful and in harmony with one another, being subject to men in complete submission."[21] Clearly, Papias had in mind the restoration of the Garden of Eden, an earthly paradise rather than a purely heavenly, spiritual one. He also accepted the view presented in the Apocalypse of John that, after the second coming and the resurrection of the dead, the just would reign with Christ for a thousand years over a divine kingdom on earth.[22] These views became less popular as the second century progressed. As church leaders became more Romanized and more educated in Greco-Roman philosophy, they began to be embarrassed by Papias' expectation of a concrete kingdom of God on earth. Rejection of such an expectation also made the disciples' message more palatable in a Roman world that was becoming progressively more suspicious of and hostile to any message about a kingdom other than that of the "divine" Caesar. In spite of the risk it entailed, Papias held to this older tradition.

His traditionalism stands behind another famous remark of his: "For I did not imagine that things out of books would help me as much as utterance of a living and abiding voice."[23] Papias makes no bones about it; he prefers oral tradition to written works. Contemporary readers in a literate culture tend to assume that oral traditions are inferior to written texts and, therefore, that written works

---

20. Papias, *Fragments* 4; English translation taken from Alexander Roberts and James Donaldson, eds., *The Apostolic Fathers with Justin Martyr and Irenaeus: Clement of Rome, Mathetes, Polycarp, Ignatius, Barnabas, Papias, Justin Martyr, Irenaeus*, revised and chronologically arranged, with brief prefaces and occasional notes by A. Cleveland Coxe; Ante-Nicene Fathers 1 (1885; repr. Peabody, MA: Hendrickson, 1994); online at *Christian Classics Ethereal Library*, Grand Rapids, http://www.ccel.org/ccel/schaff/anf01.vii.ii.iv.html.

21. Ibid.

22. This belief is called *chiliasm*.

23. Eusebius, *Ecclesiastical History* 3.39. Is this also an offside rebuke of Christ-believers who have studied Greek philosophy and other works of pagan writers?

The *Gospel of Thomas*, shown here, is essentially a collection of sayings of Jesus, as was the "sayings source" Q. Papias claims that the disciple Matthew wrote down the *logia* (sayings) of the Lord. Later Christians assumed Papias meant the canonical Gospel of Matthew, but he may have meant a sayings collection like *Thomas*.

naturally would supplant oral traditions as people adopted the use of such texts to preserve the words and deeds of Jesus. On the contrary, oral tradition had carried believers through the difficult early decades, and Papias was hardly alone in preferring this proven, reliable way of preserving the Jesus-traditions rather than new-fangled writings. On the other hand, his remark in support of oral tradition implies that the use of written traditions was catching on; that slowly but surely the disciples were turning to written sources to learn about Jesus.

Given his comments, it is ironic that Papias provides a very early witness to some of those written sources. Eusebius cites him as having claimed that the Gospel of Mark comprised Mark's interpretation of the recollections of Peter—although Papias also scores a point for oral tradition by insisting that Peter "used to adapt his teaching to the occasion without making a systematic arrangement of the Lord's sayings."[24] This makes Papias the first witness to Markan authorship of the Second Gospel. He is also the first witness for Matthew's composition of the First Gospel. In the same passage he says, "Matthew compiled the sayings [of Jesus] in the Hebrew language, and everyone translated them as well as he could."[25] This

---

24. Ibid.
25. Ibid.

passage convinced generations of biblical exegetes that Matthew had written his Gospel in Aramaic, the everyday language of the Jewish people, and later he or someone else translated it into Greek. However, literary evidence demonstrates that the Gospel of Matthew originally was composed in Greek, not Aramaic. So what is one to make of Papias' statement?

Perhaps he simply is mistaken and has preserved an erroneous tradition. On the other hand, an intriguing possibility appears when he says that Matthew wrote down the "sayings" of Jesus, not the sayings and the deeds. *The Gospel of Thomas*, just a bit later than Papias, contains only sayings of Jesus, and, as noted in chapter three, Q appears to have been a sayings source as well. Since Papias was not referring explicitly to the canonical Gospel of Matthew, he may have known a collection of sayings, no longer extant, attributed to Matthew and preserved in Jesus' native tongue. If such a collection existed—and there is no way of knowing with certainty—it is not possible to draw any conclusions about it except to observe, once again, how many ways the early communities preserved accounts of Jesus.

In stating his preference for oral traditions, Papias provides a small window into how Christ-believers worked at the turn of the first century. When he wanted to have authentic teaching, Papias inquired as to what Andrew, Peter, Thomas, James, or John had been teaching, as well as what "Aristion and the presbyter John, disciples of the Lord, were *still* teaching."[26] He saw himself organically linked to the age of Jesus. He felt a closeness that later generations could never share.

Eusebius also mentions that Papias was in contact with the four prophetic daughters of Philip (Acts 21:8–9) and knew about the later career of Justus Barsabas, the unsuccessful candidate to replace Judas in the Twelve (Acts 1:23–26). While there is no source to corroborate these traditions, neither is there any evidence to refute them. Eusebius asserts that later in life Papias became a companion of Polycarp

---

26. Ibid., emphasis added. Nothing else is known about Aristion. Although later generations interpreted Papias' "presbyter John" to be John of the Twelve, Papias does not say that and such an identification is highly unlikely, especially since John was a very common name. In the New Testament alone there are four men named John: John the Baptist, John of the Twelve, John Mark, and John the Seer of the Apocalypse.

© Kean Collection / Getty Images

Eusebius of Caesarea

of Smyrna (ca.70–156 CE), a bishop who helped point the way to a new type of ecclesial structure that was more hierarchical than Papias would have liked.

Papias can best be understood as a transitional figure, an open-minded person who cherished the past but did not condemn the future—a believer who envisioned a material kingdom of Christ but who lived long enough to see people turn to a spiritual one; a teacher who preferred oral tradition to written works but who passed on traditions about the Gospel writers; a leader who knew the prophetic daughters of Philip but also was a companion of an important second-century bishop. It is unfortunate that so little is known about this obscure and sometimes maligned figure.

Summary

The first decade of the second century was relatively quiet in terms of the relationship between the Jesus movement and Roman imperial authorities. Perhaps because of the rather placid relations, more aristocrats began to be attracted to the movement. Some of the writings from this period illustrate tensions that were arising within certain communities of disciples due to this demographic shift. Naturally enough, some converts brought into the *ecclesia* common patterns of social interaction from the wider culture, not recognizing how much these patterns of behavior diverged from the gospel message. Documents like 2 Thessalonians provide a window into the situation—including the remedy proposed by the second-generation Pauline author. The *Didache* and the writings of Papias convey the continuing significance of oral tradition and provide information about developments in leadership structures, including the ongoing debate over the value of prophetic leadership versus institutional, hierarchical offices. None of these debates were resolved by the end of this period. In fact, the issues increased in significance as the communities of disciples continued to grow and develop. As the next decade illustrates, continuing pressures from the wider society forced significant changes in the self-understanding and practices of the *ecclesia* and gave rise to a clearly delineated, emergent new religion that is now called Christianity.

Questions for Review

1. What was life like for Christ-believers in the earlier years of the reign of the Emperor Trajan?
2. Who was Papias? What does he say about the *Parousia*?
3. What does Papias say about the writing of the Gospels?
4. What is the *Didache*? Where was it produced?
5. What information does the *Didache* supply about developments in ecclesial leadership during the late first and early second centuries?

Questions for Discussion

1. Papias reasserts a literal understanding of the coming kingdom of God; what does this suggest about the Jesus movement in this period?
2. Although there appear to have been several collections of sayings of Jesus circulating among the early communities, only the sayings of Jesus that were embedded in a narrative of Jesus' life and death (in the Gospels of Matthew, Mark, Luke, and John) were eventually accepted as canonical. Why do you think the "sayings of Jesus" collections died out?
3. The *Didache* emphasizes the role of the prophet more than institutional leadership, and Papias emphasizes the living voice of tradition rather than a stable, unchanging written text. Why

do you think both of these views were eventually superseded? Do you think that was a good development for the evolving church? What values were the *Didache* and Papias trying to protect by emphasizing the living (oral) tradition and prophetic voice? How would you evaluate the relative importance of those values compared with the ones that are represented by an institutional leadership structure and set of written canonical texts?

CHAPTER 11

Martyrdom and Monarchy
(111–120 CE)

The figure of Ignatius of Antioch, bishop and martyr, embodies the ongoing struggle the Jesus movement had to face as the second century unfolded. As the gospel began to claim the attention and allegiance of more educated aristocratic men, the Jesus movement experienced not only external but also internal pressures to conform to the structures and mores of the wider Greco-Roman society. At least in theory, the more the *ecclesia* looked like other Greco-Roman organizations, the easier it would be to escape the notice of the authorities—and potential martyrdom at their hands. Many Christ-believers resisted this strategy of assimilation to the wider culture, viewing it as a betrayal of the fundamental challenge of Jesus' life and message. This "identity-crisis" left a twofold legacy, on the one hand marked by testimony and martyrdom and on the other hand by a set of ecclesial strictures and structures that modeled the wider culture's emphasis on monarchy and titles.

Four sets of documents provide particular insight into the internal developments in the Jesus movement during this decade and its shifting relationship with the empire: a set of correspondence between Emperor Trajan and one of his provincial governors; the correspondence between Ignatius of Antioch and a number of communities of Christ-believers on the route from Antioch to Rome; the Pastoral Epistles, a group of writings representing a third-generation Pauline tradition; and the growing tradition of popular legends about exemplary and even heroic Christ-believers. The first, second, and fourth sets of sources provide information about imperial persecution of Christ-believers and forms of resistance to that persecution; the third set of documents provides an inside view of one of those responses, the move toward a more hierarchical structure for the *ecclesia*.[1]

Trajan, Pliny the Younger, and the Christ-Believers

Right about 110 CE, the Emperor Trajan appointed a new governor to the Roman province of Bithynia in northwestern Asia Minor (modern Turkey): Gaius Plinius Caecilius Secundus, more frequently (and more easily) called Pliny the Younger.[2] Two of the many letters that Pliny wrote while he was governor are particularly important for the history of the early church. One clarifies a question of how strenuously to apply one of Trajan's mandates,[3] and another provides information about the Christ-believers in his province.[4] Since Pliny died no later than 113, these two letters are more reliably dated than any other documents from this period. The two Roman historians, Tacitus (ca. 56–ca. 120), who wrote of Nero's persecution of the Christians, and Suetonius (ca. 70–ca. 130), who wrote about "*Chrestus*" stirring up the Roman Jews, were contemporaries of Pliny. Pliny's witness is especially valuable because it constitutes a "primary source," one that derives from direct and personal contact with the Christ-believers rather than a second-hand report.

The first set of Pliny's letters under consideration are primarily concerned not with disciples of Jesus, but rather with a volunteer fire

---

1. Technically this "hierarchy" comprises a patriarchal structure, that is, one in which the "father" rules while other males (e.g., sons, male slaves) and all females take subordinate and submissive positions. Patriarchy also includes an understanding of women and slaves as "chattels," human property, with limited (if any) inherent rights and no standing as a "person" under the law.

2. He is called Pliny "the Younger" to distinguish him from his uncle, Pliny "the Elder," who died of asphyxiation from the poisonous gases while trying to rescue survivors of the eruption of Mount Vesuvius in 79 CE.

3. Pliny, *Epistles* 10.33.

4. Ibid., 10.96.

department! Pliny wrote to Trajan about a massive fire in Nicomedia (modern İzmit, Turkey), an ancient city that lay east of Byzantium (now Istanbul) and due south of Nicaea. The governor requested the emperor's permission to establish a fire-fighter's guild to handle similar emergencies that might arise in the future.[5] Pliny explained that the group would be limited in size (150 firefighters) and would not be permitted to congregate for purposes other than fire-fighting, so they should present no threat to the state.[6] In spite of Pliny's careful assurances, Trajan refused to grant permission.[7] He warned that such societies, whatever their ostensible purpose and however closely regulated, frequently became factious and disturbed the peace.[8] The emperor offered some alternatives for dealing with the fire problem, but absolutely rejected the idea of forming a society for that purpose.[9]

It may seem paranoid of Trajan to think a firefighters' guild might turn into a political faction and cause social upheaval, even granting his claim that this sort of thing had happened in the past. Of greater importance is the fact that Pliny felt obligated to ask the Emperor's permission to establish such an association. This set of letters indicates how seriously Trajan's mandate against associations was to be taken. If even firefighters cannot meet, one might infer that the communities of disciples—who pledged to live in imitation of Jesus, a messianic figure who had been executed for subversion—would be viewed as posing a much more serious threat to social stability.

Not long afterwards, probably around 112, Pliny wrote to Trajan for explicit advice on how to deal with the Christ-believers. Both the information Pliny gives and the emperor's reply are valuable for understanding the situation of the disciples in Asia Minor in this early part of the second century.[10]

---

5. Ibid., 10.33.

6. Ibid.

7. Ibid., 10.34.

8. Ibid.

9. Ibid.

10. Ibid., 10.96–97; the full text of Pliny's letter and Trajan's reply can be found online at *http://www9.georgetown.edu/faculty/jod/texts/pliny.html.*

© Scala / Art Resource, NY

Pliny the Younger

Pliny starts out by admitting that he had never been present at the questioning of Christians, and was unclear about what such questioning should entail or what kinds of punishment should be employed.[11] The phrasing of Pliny's inquiry suggests that criminal proceedings against Christ-believers were routine, something with which the emperor would be familiar even if Pliny were not. Since the emperor was at Rome and Pliny had lived there most of his life, perhaps investigations of this kind had occurred in the capital. No large-scale persecutions are known after that of Domitian, but apparently individual cases still were prosecuted. Furthermore, Pliny assumes that some sort of punishment necessarily would result from the examination.

He asks the emperor a number of questions dealing with specific types of cases. Should he make a distinction between children and adults accused of being Christ-believers? What of those who repented after their arrest, or those who had been believers in the past but, even before their arrest, had returned to paganism?

Pliny then goes on to the most crucial set of questions. Is the Christian name itself culpable, even if there is no other crime connected with it? Apparently some officials did not equate being a Christian with being a criminal while others did. Should he punish only crimes that are connected with the name "Christian," or should punishment be imposed on account of the name itself? Interestingly, Pliny assumes that Christ-believers routinely committed crimes, the nature of which would be known to the emperor. He does not specify what these crimes were, but later Roman and ecclesial sources both

---

11. Ibid., 10.96.

mention the Christ-believers' refusal to worship the state gods as well as charges of incest and cannibalism.[12]

Pliny provides the earliest extant account of how the Romans tried the Christ-believers. He says,

> I interrogated [the accused] whether they were Christians; if they confessed it I repeated the question twice again, adding the threat of capital punishment; if they still persevered, I ordered them to be executed. For whatever the nature of their creed might be, I could at least feel no doubt that contumacy and inflexible obstinacy deserved chastisement.[13]

In other words, Pliny executed Christ-believers simply because (a) they were "Christians" and (b) they refused to recant when they were given second and third chances. Those who were Roman citizens, on the other hand, he remanded to the emperor for sentencing.

Pliny's harshness provoked some unwanted consequences. He began to receive an influx of anonymous denunciations, including a "placard" (*libellus*) with a whole list of names. Pliny took those denunciations seriously and had the accused arrested. He told the accused of the charges and gave them the chance to recant. If they denied the accusations, he had them invoke the gods and do reverence to the image of the emperor, "which I had ordered to be brought for that purpose, together with those of the Gods." He also had them "curse Christ," because he had learned that real Christians could not be compelled to do so. If they did all this, Pliny thought it appropriate to let them go.[14]

Pliny's approach is very Roman—straightforward and no-nonsense. The accused are asked to venerate the gods and the emperor's image

---

12. The charge of "incest" likely derives from the common practice of the believers calling each other "sister" and "brother" (even those married to each other), combined with the common assumption that, because their ceremonies often occurred at night, they involved sexually promiscuous behavior. The charge of cannibalism, on the other hand, almost certainly comes from a misunderstanding of Eucharistic terminology, when believers spoke of eating the "body" and drinking the "blood" of Christ. See the discussion on pages 163–65, above.

13. Pliny, *Letters* 10.96. Translations of Pliny's letters in this chapter are from the Loeb Classical Library, ed. E. Capps, T. E. Page, and W. H. D. Rouse, trans. William Melmoth, rev. W. M. L. Hutchinson (London: William Heinemann; New York: G. P. Putnam's Sons, 1927).

14. Ibid.

and to curse Christ. If they do all that, they are released. If they refuse, they are convicted as Christians and must face the penalty.

Some of those who performed the required rites told Pliny that they had been disciples but had given it up three years earlier. It is not clear what event three years previous might have prompted some Christ-believers to abandon their faith. Others claimed to have abandoned the movement up to twenty-five years before. Is this an echo of Domitian's persecution, when some believers apostasized? Yet these ex-disciples retained enough of a sense of loyalty that they did not denounce their former co-religionists as criminals. On the contrary, they affirmed that the Christ-believers' practice was

> to meet together before it was light, and [antiphonally] to sing a hymn to Christ, as to a god . . . ; and to oblige themselves by a sacrament [or oath], not to do anything that was ill: but that they would commit no theft, or pilfering, or adultery; that they would not break their promises, or deny what was deposited with them, when it was required back again; after which it was their custom to depart, and to meet again at a common but innocent meal, which they had left off upon that edict which I published at your command, and wherein I had forbidden any such conventicles.[15]

The remark about the "innocent meal" answers the charge of cannibalism, while the list of crimes that they pledged not to commit may refer to the Ten Commandments. Pliny accepted the apostates' claims that they were no longer Christ-believers but, curiously, he did not accept their characterization of the movement. He apparently was not persuaded of the innocence of the movement itself, in spite of what they told him about their faith and practices.

The last remark, about the disciples having "left off" their communal meals as a result of an imperial edict, must refer to Trajan's mandate against associations. Pliny mentions this mandate both here and in *Epistles* 10.33, but nothing more is known about it.

Another enormously important reference is the remark that the Bithynian disciples venerated Christ "as a god" in their liturgies. This accords with the divine image of Christ found in the Gospel of John,

---

15. Ibid.

which probably was written in Asia Minor. This pagan account of the disciples' liturgical practice has considerable importance, demonstrating that the Johannine understanding of Christ—or something very like it—was radiating beyond John's community and deepening the faith of other believers.

After talking to the former believers, who claimed that the common meals had stopped after Trajan's prohibition, Pliny decided he needed to use torture to discover more. He had two *ministrae* (deaconesses) interrogated but still "could discover nothing more than depraved and excessive superstition."[16] He does not describe the nature of this "superstition," only that it confirmed his negative views about the Christ-believers. Because the denunciations were increasing, and the courts could barely handle the load, Pliny decided to adjourn the proceedings and consult the emperor.[17] Pliny notes that the Christian "superstition" had attracted individuals from across the entire social spectrum: aristocrats and lower class, men and women, young and old, city folk and villagers. He was overwhelmed by the sheer numbers of persons who were "infected."

Pliny's persecution had temporary benefits to the Romans. The pagan temples won back some of their adherents, the popularity of sacred festivals revived, and "there [was] a general demand for sacrificial animals, which for some time past [had] met with but few purchasers."[18] Even though the Jesus movement was spreading widely, Pliny took these signs as indicating that his prosecutions ultimately would "stop its spread and root it out." He was, of course, dead wrong.

Pliny's comments here reveal another aspect of the impact of the Jesus movement on Roman culture. The Christ-believers would not purchase animals for sacrifice nor would they purchase meat from animals that had been sacrificed. This meant that local landowners were producing more livestock than people wanted, and that in turn meant that prices went down, threatening their livelihood. Since the landowners were of the aristocratic class, they would have had the governor's ear. In addition, there would have been a decrease in tax revenue that Pliny could not have failed to notice. No matter how

---

16. Ibid.

17. Ibid.

18. Ibid. Clearly the Christ-believers in Bithynia had been observing the injunction "to abstain from what has been sacrificed to idols" (Acts 15:29).

unintentional, the rise of the Jesus movement would have economic effects. Its increasing popularity threatened the livelihood of the pagans in Bithynia.[19]

The spread of the Christ movement also had social effects. Like most public institutions in small cities or towns, temples were social centers where old friends saw one another and where they venerated the traditional deities of their ancestors. The Jesus movement changed all that. Many pagans practiced syncretism, venerating many gods from different traditions. For example, the third-century Roman Emperor Elagabalus (218–222) venerated the Unconquered Sun but also had statues of Abraham and Jesus in his private chapel. However, the Christ-believers, like Jews, accepted only one God. This meant that they could not attend the events at pagan temples, which cut them off from their fellow-citizens, friends, and sometimes even family members, if only one or two converted and the others did not.[20]

© www.holylandphotos.org

In his letter to Trajan, Pliny complains that attendance at the pagan temples of Bithynia (like the one shown here) had dropped because so many of the inhabitants of that province had converted to the Christ-movement. As a result, demand for sacrificial animals had also declined.

---

19. Cf. the situation in Ephesus, where the silversmiths rioted against Paul because, their leader said, "We get our wealth from this business" (Acts 19:25).

20. Decades later, the famous North African Christian martyr Perpetua (d. 203) was vilified by a Roman judge for letting her religion divide her family.

Trajan wrote a brief reply to Pliny.[21] The emperor generally approved of how he had handled the situation. Still, Trajan was concerned about the problem of informers, so he told Pliny not to seek out Christ-believers. Trajan corrected him, however, about using accusations published anonymously. Such denunciations "without the accuser's name subscribed must not be admitted in evidence against anyone, as it is introducing a very dangerous precedent, and by no means agreeable to the spirit of the age."[22] Unfortunately, such advice came too late for many of the Christ-believers in Bithynia.

Imperial Expansion

The Emperor Trajan's concern to establish peace in the Near East and to expand the Roman Empire brought him to Antioch-on-the-Orontes in 114 CE. The Parthian Empire, successor to the old Persian Empire (which included modern Iran and Iraq), had become a major rival of Rome and had begun to impose its will on Armenia, a buffer state between the two empires. Trajan had little difficulty incorporating Armenia into his empire. Buoyed with confidence, he invaded Parthia and succeeded in going down the Tigris River into central Mesopotamia, capturing the Parthian capital in 116 and thereby expanding the Roman Empire to its greatest geographical extent. However, while Trajan was occupied with his war of expansion, Diaspora[23] Jews had revolted in Egypt, Cyprus, and Cyrene. Trajan thought it best to halt his campaign and suppress

---

21. Pliny, *Epistles* 10.97 (often called "Trajan's Rescript"); available online at *http://www9.georgetown.edu/faculty/jod/texts/pliny.html*.

22. Ibid.

23. *Diaspora* means "dispersion"; it refers to the Jewish population "dispersed" throughout the world rather than living in the land of Israel. The phenomenon began with the Babylonian Exile 587–532 BCE), but included many Jews who fled to Alexandria in Egypt and other parts of North Africa. When Cyrus of Persia conquered the Babylonian Empire and brought the Jews' time of exile to an end, many returned to their ancestral homeland but others remained in Babylon. The conquest of Jerusalem in 70 CE and the destruction of the Second Temple caused another wave of Jewish emigration. By the end of the first century, of an estimated five to seven million Jews living within the Roman Empire, well over half of them lived outside the land of Israel.

the uprising. He was returning to Italy when he died unexpectedly in August of 117.

The Diaspora Revolt(s) of 114–117 CE

There likely were many causes of the revolt of Jews from various regions of the Diaspora. Trajan tightened the collection of tariffs on the trade route that ran through Mesopotamia to India, thereby cutting the profits of traders and merchants. His war of expansion required fully half of the Roman Army, drawing resources and manpower from the imperial frontiers. In addition, these conquests extended the boundaries of the empire so far that it became virtually impossible to maintain its borders. Trajan himself was already in his sixties, which may have led foreign rulers and client kings alike to view him (and his armies) as vulnerable. Perhaps a comet really did appear and revive Messianic hopes.[24] Whatever the factors that inspired them, a number of Jewish revolts erupted in regions throughout the Diaspora as Trajan was trying to complete his conquest in the East.

The uprisings do not seem to have been systematically coordinated but rather to have resulted from a sort of "domino effect." The action began in Cyrene (in modern Lybia), and then spread to other regions, including Cyprus, Egypt (both Thebes and Alexandria), and Mesopotamia (Seleucia, Ctesiphon, and Nisibis). Knowledge of an uprising in one region seems to have helped inspire revolution in another.

The Roman historian Dio Cassius and the churchman Eusebius of Caesarea both present reports of the events. Dio's account reveals his strong anti-Jewish inclinations, whereas that of Eusebius is more cursory and slightly less prejudiced. Both take the part of the Romans, presenting the insurgencies as unjustified sedition "incited by some terrible and factious spirit."[25] Since Eusebius seems to have based his account on that of Dio, and since Dio's report of the events was written closer to the actual time when they took place, basic

---

24. The Roman poet Juvenal may hint at such an event when he bemoans the unseemly behavior of uppity women: "She's the first to locate a comet that threatens the kings of Parthia and Armenia" (*Satires* 6.407).

25. Eusebius, *Ecclesiastical History* 4.2.

historical method suggests that Dio's version should provide more reliable historical details. However, allowance must be made for Dio's clear anti-Jewish polemic.[26]

Apparently the revolt originated in Cyrene when Andreas Lukuas proclaimed himself Messiah and King of the Jews. Those who rallied to his standard began demolishing pagan temples and attacking worshipers there, "destroying both the Romans and the Greeks."[27] Dio goes on to charge the revolutionaries with cannibalism and other atrocities:

> They would eat the flesh of their victims, make belts for themselves of their entrails, anoint themselves with their blood and wear their skins for clothing; many they sawed in two, from the head downwards; others they gave to wild beasts, and still others they forced to fight as gladiators.[28]

The first series of charges is patently false; such actions are expressly forbidden in the Torah and abhorrent in Jewish culture. The charges are aimed to inspire outrage in the readers, to what particular end is not clear. The next charge, that Andreas' army "sawed [their enemies] in two," while not absolutely impossible, seems an exaggeration; literally cutting someone in half from head to toe would be not only grotesque but time-consuming and thus would be impractical in battle. The last two charges may have some merit—and also might shed light on this one. Condemnation *ad bestias* and forced gladiatorial combat were both common Roman forms of execution. Apparently Dio has conflated battle tactics with modes of capital punishment. He portrays the Jews as inflicting upon their prisoners the precise types of execution that the Romans inflicted upon their own prisoners— including those who had been captured in the First Jewish War. If the charge of hewing their enemies in two has any basis in fact, it is better understood as another form of torturous capital punishment.

---

26. Similarly, the account in the *Seven Books of History against the Pagans* by the later church historian Paulus Orosius (ca. 375–420) is not independent. One fragment from Appian of Alexandria (ca. 95–165) speaks of his narrow "escape from the Jews during the war in Egypt," saved by a series of omens from crows (Appian, *Roman History* 24), but this story contributes little to the overall picture of the revolt.

27. Dio Cassius, *Roman History* 68.32.1.

28. Ibid., 68.32.1–2.

Some of the survivors apparently fled Cyrene for Alexandria, where they avenged themselves on the Jews in that city, who then rose up against the Greeks and Romans there. Andreas followed and engaged in strategic warfare, gaining control of Thebes and Alexandria, and in the process disrupting the grain supply, which was the only resource that stood between the hungry masses of Rome and utter starvation. This last posed the most serious strategic threat, for grain riots in Rome would strike at the very heart of the Empire.

Meanwhile, another revolt broke out on the island of Cyprus, where another claimant named Artemion proclaimed himself Messiah and King of the Jews. Artemion led the Jews on a rampage in which Dio claims 240,000 people perished.[29] While this figure must be exaggerated—it would be equivalent to 15 percent of the Cypriote population at the time—the rebellion must have inspired tremendous fear because the Roman reprisals were severe. Once the Romans regained control of the island, Trajan expelled the entire Jewish population. No Jews were allowed to live on Cyprus for the next thousand years.

Rebellion spread to Mesopotamia, and Trajan responded by expelling the Jews from that region as well. He commissioned his best cavalry commander Lucius Quietus for the task, and Lucius "slew a great multitude" of Jews in a fit of ethnic cleansing.[30] (Trajan rewarded Lucius' success by making him governor of Judea.) Trajan sent Quintus Marcius Turbo to crush the rebellion in Egypt. This goal finally was achieved in the summer of 117. So many people died in the war that North Africa had to be repopulated. Trajan used war booty confiscated from the Jews to pay for the reconstruction of pagan temples that had been destroyed in the uprisings.

Ignatius of Antioch, Bishop and Martyr

Ignatius, bishop of Antioch in Syria during the reign of Trajan, revived the genre of the pastoral letter, using it to address his concerns for the disciples in Asia Minor. The letters of Ignatius serve as

---

29. Ibid., 68.32.2–3.

30. Eusebius, *Ecclesiastical History* 4.2.5. Because of the great slaughter of Jews caused by Quietus, sometimes Jewish literature refers to the entire Diaspora revolt as the "War of Kittos."

a bridge between the relatively placid period for Christ-believers in the first half of Trajan's reign and the somewhat more troubled times in the second half of his principate. Ignatius was the earliest extant writer to identify himself explicitly as a bishop. His writings provide information both about himself and about the direction he wanted the second-century *ecclesia* to go.

The date of Ignatius' birth is uncertain. Eusebius says that he succeeded Euodius as bishop of Antioch but provides no date. Ignatius was sent to Rome to be martyred during the reign of Trajan (98–117), and scholars usually date his trip from Antioch to Rome in about 115. On the way, Ignatius wrote seven letters. From Smyrna he wrote four letters to the churches of Ephesus, Magnesia, Tralles, and Rome; from Troas he wrote letters to the churches of Philadelphia and Smyrna as well as a personal letter to Polycarp, bishop of Smyrna. Three of the churches, Ephesus, Philadelphia, and Smyrna, previously had received letters from John the Seer, author of Revelation. Clearly, these were important communities, although neither John's nor Ignatius' letters provide much information about them.

Composed after his arrest and during his journey to Rome for trial, Ignatius' seven letters address matters of doctrine and ecclesial leadership; they also include reflections upon his impending death *ad bestias*.[31] Ignatius' arrest and consignment to the spectacles in Rome was probably intended to intimidate the Christian community into conforming or at least maintaining a lower profile.[32] As previously noted, this was not the first time that opponents in Antioch took action against the disciples of Jesus.

Unfortunately it is not clear what or who precipitated the action against Ignatius, but at least some of the circumstances may be guessed. As mentioned above, Trajan himself was in Antioch at about this time to prosecute the war in the East. While he was there, a terrible earthquake hit the region, and Dio's account seems to point to the city of Antioch as the epicenter.[33] He speaks of aftershocks that continued for several days after the initial quake, and describes

31. William R. Schoedel, *Ignatius of Antioch: A Commentary on the Letters of Ignatius of Antioch*, ed. Helmut Koester, Hermeneia: A Critical and Historical Commentary on the Bible (Philadelphia: Fortress, 1985), 11.

32. Schoedel, *Ignatius of Antioch*, 11; citing Ignatius, *Ephesians* 10.

33. Dio Cassius, *Roman History* 68.24.1–25.4.

Trajan's own miraculous escape: "Some being, of greater than human stature, had come to him and led him forth" through a window.[34] Did the pagan population of the city blame the Christ-believers for the calamity? It would not be the first time that the disciples were made scapegoats (cf. the Great Fire of Rome), and it would not be surprising if their leader were arrested for having instigated the troubles.

Another possibility is that the *ecclesia* in Antioch continued to meet together for their communal meals, and this became a problem when Trajan came to town. Pliny's letters show that the prohibition of meetings applied in Bithynia, yet there is no evidence of an empire-wide prohibition.[35] Did the meetings become a problem once the emperor arrived in town? Or did someone denounce Ignatius personally to the authorities when Trajan was there, knowing that the emperor's policies would require them to take action against the *ecclesia*'s leader? The situation that prompted Ignatius' arrest cannot be known with certainty, but any of a number of possibilities would explain why Ignatius was remanded for trial in Rome.

Ignatius calls himself "a prisoner for the Name,"[36] a designation similar to the one Luke gave to the disciples who "were considered worthy to suffer dishonor for the sake of the Name" (Acts 5:41). This was one of many ways in which Ignatius saw himself standing in the apostolic tradition.

Curiously, as the prison caravan made stops along the way, Ignatius routinely met with local ecclesial leaders; he even names some of them. Why were these leaders not afraid to meet with Ignatius in front of his Roman guards? Moreover, why were they themselves not arrested? Was Ignatius charged with more than simply being a Christ-believer? Three times he refers to peace being restored to the community in Antioch.[37] Did religious disputes spill out into the streets, so that he was convicted of fomenting riots?[38] Or did

---

34. Ibid., 68.25.5.

35. In fact, associations are known from the neighboring regions of Phrygia, Lydia, and Asia Minor. See Ilias N. Arnaoutoglou, "Roman Law and *Collegia* in Asia Minor," *Revue Internationale des Droits de l'Antiquité* 49 (2002): 27–44; especially 35–37.

36. Ignatius, *Ephesians* 1.

37. Ignatius, *Philadelphians* 10; *Smyrneans* 11; *Polycarp* 11.

38. Recall the troubles in Rome supposedly instigated by "*Chrestos*" in 49 CE.

the visitors avoid arrest because there was no uniform Roman policy against Christ-believers—that is, did the Roman authorities in Antioch persecute while those in Asia Minor did not? If Ignatius' arrest was prompted by Trajan's presence in the city, that would explain why his visitors did not risk arrest when coming to meet with him on the long road to Rome.

However uncertain the cause of Ignatius' arrest, there is no doubt how valuable he is for understanding the history of the development of the Jesus movement, both practically and theologically, and particularly in its structure. Ignatius envisions a local community governed by a bishop, apparently selected by the community. But he also urges the recipients of his letters to send congratulatory embassies to his unnamed replacement.[39] Did these ambassadors gather in Antioch simply to congratulate the new bishop, or is this evidence of some regional endorsement as a way of strengthening the office? At the very least, this gathering would be a visible symbol of the unity shared by the Christ-believing communities in the region, and ultimately of the unity of the universal *ecclesia*.

Ignatius' reflections on what he views as his opportunity to gain the martyr's crown provide a rare, first-hand view of the attraction for and power of the martyr in the second century CE.[40] In addition, his remarks on ministries and his understanding of prophecy provide insight into the intra-ecclesial dynamics of one of the most significant communities in this early period.

The Monarchical Episcopate

Ignatius provides the first thorough-going argument for a monarchical episcopate,[41] a bishop who serves as *permanent* president of the council of elders (*presbyters*), ordained to office after being chosen from among those elders. According to Ignatius' model of ecclesial

---

39. Ignatius, *Philadelphians* 10.

40. The effect is heightened by Ignatius' use of a popular style of rhetoric known as "Asianism." See Othmar Perler, "Das vierte Makkabäerbuch, Ignatius von Antiochien und die ältesten Märtyrerberichte," *Rivista di archeologia cristiana* 25 (1949): 47–72; cited in Schoedel, *Ignatius of Antioch*, 8 n. 44.

41. The term *monarchical bishop* should not be misinterpreted to mean an unrestrained, dictatorial rule.

order, deacons are assistants to the bishop, caring for distribution of alms, taking communion to the sick, and so forth.[42]

Ignatius sees the bishop as the servant of the community and as a symbol of unity, and he speaks repeatedly of the importance of submission of community members to the bishop so that this unity will not be harmed. God is "the bishop of us all" and the bishop is "in the place of God."[43] As the Lord "never acted independently" of the Father, "so you yourselves must never act independently of your bishop and clergy."[44] Disciples should look to the bishop "as though he were Jesus Christ."[45] No valid Eucharistic liturgy occurs without the bishop or his representative being present.[46] The teaching of the bishop offers a safeguard against false teaching.[47] Yet a careful reading of his epistles shows that most of the time he refers to the bishop with his clergy. He assumes that the bishop will not act without them and that they will work together harmoniously. Obviously, the bishops and members of the clergy would have disagreed on some issues, but Ignatius does not mention that because he wants to stress their unity. This, in turn, both symbolizes and reinforces the unity of the members of local church with the bishop.

To legitimate his church order, Ignatius employs a cosmological argument rather than a doctrine of "apostolic succession." He describes the relationships among God, Christ, and the apostles in a descending hierarchy, and argues for the same hierarchical relationship among the bishop, deacons, and presbyters of a community.[48] This model offers the first thorough-going attempt to distinguish between "clerical" and "lay" members of the Christ-believing

---

42. In Ignatius' writings, the only women who appear to have an office in the churches are "widows." In *Smyrnaeans* 13.1, Ignatius greets "the virgins called widows," showing that for him this is also an ideal state, and one which can be chosen by young women as well as old. This is the only occurrence where Ignatius explicitly deals with the ecclesial roles available to female members of the communities. However, based upon the cosmological rationale for Ignatius' church order, it follows that no woman could be included in the clerical offices of bishop, presbyter, or deacon.

43. Ignatius, *Ephesians* 3.6.

44. Ibid., 3.7.

45. Ignatius, *Trallians* 2.

46. Ignatius, *Philadelphians* 4.

47. Ignatius, *Trallians* 6–7.

48. See Ignatius, *Magnesians* 6.1 and *Trallians* 3.1.

community; in Ignatius' thinking, non-clerics apparently occupy the bottom of the divinely-established hierarchy, below the clerics, who interpret for them "the orders of the Lord and the apostles."[49]

Ignatius argues for the primacy of a single bishop in any given location using rhetoric that suggests such a monarchy has cosmological, theological, and moral significance. His principle of "one God, one bishop, one *ecclesia*" links the monarchical episcopacy with the unity of God and the order of creation. Hence, Ignatius views the hierarchical leadership structure itself as a defense of monotheism and of the divine will. Linking the monarchical episcopate with the unity of the community implies that any who oppose this ecclesial order are both immoral and heretical.[50]

No other ecclesial writing of this era offers such a prominent role for a sole bishop. The Pastoral Epistles and *1 Clement* speak of bishops always in the plural, and the latter does not distinguish clearly between bishops and presbyters. The focus on a monarchical bishop may not have been unique to Ignatius, but it certainly was not yet the norm.[51] Perhaps there was a situation in Antioch that thrust the bishop into the forefront of the community and required such a concentration of leadership. If so, the nature of the situation is not entirely clear, but divisions within the community are likely to have been part of the problem.

---

49. Ignatius, *Magnesians* 13; cf. *Ephesians* 2:2–4:2.

50. While Ignatius argues in enthymemes, as is appropriate in this style of discourse, one could expand the basic enthymeme to form a completed syllogism such as the following:

a. God wills that the church give witness to the one true God by virtue of its unity and orthodoxy (cf. *Ephesians* 3–4; 20; *Philadelphians* 4).

b. This unity and orthodoxy of the church is ensured by submission to the one bishop (e.g., *Magnesians* 6–7; *Trallians* 2–3; *Philadelphians* 3; *Smyrnaeans* 8–9).

c. All who oppose the monarchical episcopate thereby oppose the unity and orthodoxy of the church (cf. *Trallians* 7; *Philadelphians* 8).

d. Such opponents are immoral, because in arrogance they disobey the will of God (*Ephesians* 5; cf. *Magnesians* 3; epistolary prescript to *Philadelphians*).

e. They also are heretical, whether intentionally or not, because they deny the one true God by violating the unity of God's one church and giving way to Satan's powers (*Ephesians* 16; cf. *Philadelphians* 3, 6).

51. See Elisabeth Schüssler Fiorenza, *The Book of Revelation: Justice and Judgment* (Minneapolis: Fortress, 1998), 142–44; Schoedel, *Ignatius of Antioch*, 22.

Strife in Antioch

Ignatius presents a picture of a local church split into factions. On the right stood the "Judaizers" who insisted that Christ-believers should continue to follow at least some of the traditional Jewish practices and regulations. Ignatius warned, "If we are still living in the practice of Judaism . . . we have failed to receive the gift of grace."[52] This is remarkable evidence of the continuing appeal of the messianic-Jewish option for Christ-believers. The original disciples of Jesus have been dead for half a century, and Christ-believers in a largely Gentile city are still replaying the "circumcision" debate of the 40s and 50s. Against these Messianic-Jewish believers, Ignatius invokes "our saintly and renowned Paul of blessed memory," who had struggled against their spiritual ancestors.[53]

Of far greater concern to Ignatius were those "who assert that [Jesus'] sufferings were not genuine."[54] Ignatius asserts that "[Jesus'] passion was no unreal illusion, as some skeptics aver who are all unreality themselves."[55] Ignatius insists that Jesus "was the son of Mary; he was truly and actually born and ate and drank."[56] Who were these skeptic believers? Scholars refer to them as Docetists, from the Greek verb *dokeo*, "to seem," because they believed that Jesus did not really have a body but only *seemed* to have one. What people saw was a phantom; Jesus was not actually human.

By the end of the first century, as more and more non-Jews converted to the Jesus movement, Christ-believers gradually came to the faith-insight that Jesus was divine.[57] The God of the Hebrew Bible acted routinely in human affairs, demonstrating that the created material world is good (Gen. 1). The Hebrew Bible never depicts God taking human form, but the idea that God might take a human body is compatible with the belief that God acts in the material world.

---

52. Ignatius, *Magnesians* 8.

53. Ignatius, *Ephesians* 12.

54. Ignatius, *Trallians* 10.

55. Ignatius, *Smyrneans* 2.

56. Ignatius, *Trallians* 9.

57. This view appears already in the Gospel of John; Pliny also says it was held by the Bithynian Christ-believers.

Many Greek-educated converts viewed God as purely spiritual. The prospect of the Son of God taking on human flesh, to say nothing of being executed as a common criminal, was incomprehensible or even repulsive. The essence of the human person is the soul, not the body. Socrates called the body "the prison of the soul."[58] A spiritual savior made sense; one who took on human physicality did not. Yet the Gospels spoke of Jesus' birth; of his taking part in ordinary human activities like eating, drinking, and undergoing human emotions (for example, weeping upon hearing of Lazarus' death); and of his suffering, death, and Resurrection. How could all this be explained?

Docetists believed that Jesus took on a phantom body. Some cited Paul's description of the risen Christ as having a spiritual body (1 Cor. 15:35–49) to support the belief that Jesus never had a physical one. Docetists were sincere believers, Gentile converts who were trying to reconcile their new faith with their prior philosophical views. To them, Docetism had much to recommend it. It preserved the divine nature of Jesus while explaining how the disciples could have seen his "body."

However, the Hebrew Bible was the Bible of Jesus; Ignatius and other critics realized that they could not ignore this fact. The physical world was good, and Jesus had come to save that world. Thus Docetism undercut the reality of the redemption. If Jesus did not have an actual body, then he did not really become a human being and did not redeem the human race by his actual suffering, dying, and rising.

The Docetists represented a strong group at Antioch. Ignatius saw the bishop as a point of unity in a community torn by schism. For him the bishop represented both spiritual and practical unity, a man symbolizing the authority of the Father or of Jesus Christ, but also one responsible for the daily functioning of a local church. Such a view placed on the bishop the burden of appearing as a symbol of spiritual union while also managing the details of daily church life. Ignatius' vision set the stage for future developments in church structures.

Did other leaders and communities share this view? Ignatius hoped that the churches to which he wrote would be receptive to his

---

58. Plato, *Phaedo* 81e.

arguments, but there is no way to know how his audiences responded. He likely made his argument so fervently because he knew that others had reservations about a monarchical episcopate.

What about communities outside Asia? No one can say for sure how they viewed monarchical bishops. There is evidence that the hierarchical structure caught on rapidly in the Romanized cities; by the middle of the second century, most had bishops as leaders. In his letter to the Romans, Ignatius does not use the word bishop. This may support the view that Rome had a communal leadership, but this case should not be pressed. Ignatius did not know the Roman community well and may thus have written in general terms. Furthermore, Ignatius' salutation speaks of "the church holding the chief place in the territories of the district of Rome,"[59] suggesting that the Roman church exercised some leadership function among churches in the urban region. While this is not the primacy known to later generations, it would require some sort of organization, probably more effectively headed by bishops. (Roman tradition cites Alexander I as bishop when Ignatius was writing).

Martyrdom

Inadvertently Ignatius also provides some information about the influence of the Roman community. He wants to die as a martyr but fears that the Roman believers will try to save him. "What you are bent on doing will certainly present no difficulties for yourselves, but for me it is going to be very hard to get to God unless you spare me your intervention."[60] In the 90s, as mentioned earlier, some evidence suggests that the Emperor Domitian's relative, Flavia Domitilla, was a Christ-believer. That may be debatable, but it probably reflects a historical reality, that some Roman believers had financial resources and occupied positions of influence; Ignatius had good reason to fear that they could thwart his desire for martyrdom.

Ignatius introduced into the Jesus movement a spirituality of martyrdom. He describes his anticipated death in liturgical and Eucharistic terms: "Please leave me to be a meal for the beasts [in the

---

59. Ignatius, *Romans*, epistolary opening.

60. Ignatius, *Romans* 1.

Ignatius of Antioch wrote a series of letters while en route to Rome to be executed *ad bestias* in the Coliseum, a fate he eagerly embraced. His letters testify to the development of a spirituality of martyrdom within the early Christ-believing community.

arena], for it is they who can provide my way to God. I am his wheat, ground fine by the lions' teeth to be made purest bread."[61] He also describes his martyrdom in terms of rebirth and re-creation, familiar baptismal imagery. "The pangs of birth are upon me; have patience with me my brothers, and do not shut me out of life, do not wish me to be stillborn. Here is one who only longs to be God's; do not make a present of him to the world again or delude him with things of earth. Suffer me to attain the light."[62]

Bishops or Prophets?

For Ignatius, the argument in favor of obedience to the monarchical bishop goes hand-in-hand with an argument against the independent authority of prophets. Indeed, Ignatius gives the first sign of the "annexation" of prophecy to the bishop *ex officio*.[63] The epistolary

---

61. Ibid., 4.

62. Ibid., 6.

63. That is, solely by virtue of his office as bishop. Ignatius also encourages Polycarp to seek revelations (Ignatius, *Polycarp* 2.2).

prescript in each of these seven letters claims for Ignatius the title *The-ophorus* ("God-inspired"), much like Paul claimed for himself the title "apostle." In each letter, the "God-inspired" bishop of Antioch goes on to urge obedience to and unity with the bishop, presbyters, and deacons of the church.[64] In *Philadelphians* 5.2, Ignatius claims that the Hebrew prophets were in the unity of Jesus Christ,[65] implying that they supported the church order he is encouraging. Later, in *Philadelphians* 7, he claims that his command to "pay heed to the bishop, the presbytery, and the deacons" is itself divinely-inspired prophecy; likewise, it is the Spirit who urges, "Do nothing apart from the bishop."

While arguing on the one hand that the bishop is the true prophet and that the reverence and authority once granted to the prophet should now be granted to the monarchical bishop, Ignatius argues on the other hand that even the bishop's silence is more significant and revelatory than is prophetic speech or "chatter."[66] Revelations should not be demanded of the bishop, for it is his silence rather than oracles that shows that he is circumspect, not under the sway of unruly passions but faithful to the Word who came forth in silence. Ignatius claims that he could relate more of his own heavenly revelations, but he keeps silent to prevent being overtaken by pride and harming those who are spiritually less mature than himself.[67] One might expect Ignatius' opponents to demand that he demonstrate that the monarchical bishop really has the prophetic gift as he claims. Ignatius sidesteps this objection by redefining the nature of prophecy. If opponents view the bishop as prophesying less than the prophet, this is because they misunderstand the nature of true prophecy.

Ignatius' Anti-Prophetic Polemic

Ignatius of Antioch's letters show that he wants the bishop to enjoy a monarchical type of authority that has not been the case hitherto. As was seen in the *Didache* and Papias, this viewpoint was by no means universally accepted among the Christ-believers in Asia Minor in the early second century. In fact, the discrepancy between his view

---

64. Ignatius urges Polycarp to demand such adherence (e.g., *Polycarp* 2.1; 3.1).

65. Cf. Ignatius, *Magnesians* 8–9.

66. Ignatius, *Ephesians* 6.1; 15.1–2; *Philadelphians*, 1.2.

67. Ignatius, *Trallians* 4.1; 5.1–2.

and that of the *Didache* suggests that this monarchical leadership model was not even the norm in his own community in Antioch, although this cannot be known for certain. What is clear, however, is that Ignatius of Antioch does not express the mainstream opinion among Christ-believers in second-century Asia Minor. Rather, his is an outsider's view.

> Ignatius . . . went beyond local [Asia Minor] expectations in drawing the lines between those whom he considered authentic Christians and those he did not. . . . He sensed an independence of mind in his opponents that threatened the unity [among believers] that he regarded as essential to the success of his own martyrdom. Consequently *he insists on the authority of bishops in what appears to be unprecedented ways* (cf. *Mag.* 4). The presumed threat to his own leadership in Antioch could only have increased his sensitivity to the disruptive possibilities of theological novelties and *loose forms of organization.*[68]

The "loose form of organization" of the churches in Asia Minor that rivals Ignatius' hierarchical model of church order is one that values prophets and prophecy. Ignatius' letters combine an anti-prophetic polemic with an attempt to assimilate prophetic power and authority to a patriarchal mono-episcopacy. This strategy fits well with his basic attitude toward the empire and its patriarchal form of social organization. For Ignatius,

> Christians are to cause no offense to pagans and to offer no grounds for criticism of the church (see *Tr.* 8:2). Ignatius, in short, is prepared to come to terms with the world. The relative openness of his attitude is further suggested by the extent to which elements of popular culture have penetrated his thought. . . . Here we note in particular that Ignatius' conception of the Christian community seems to owe something to models provided by the Hellenistic club and the Hellenistic city.[69]

---

68. Schoedel, *Ignatius of Antioch*, 12; emphasis added.

69. Ibid., 14.

Ignatius was ready and willing to assimilate the ecclesial social organization to the predominant patriarchal culture of the Roman Empire; indeed, he seems to have seen no reason to avoid this. Events in the next decade would encourage further developments in this direction.

Even so, Ignatius the bishop did not go unchallenged by Christ-believers in Asia Minor.[70] Among them, prophets and prophecy held the primary authority in Ignatius' own day; in fact, at least in some parts of this region, they continued to do so for decades afterward. Ironically, Ignatius himself, after his death, was revered by disciples in Asia Minor not for his hierarchical status as bishop but for his status as a martyr—a role which falls well outside the categories of rank and hierarchy.

The Legacy of Ignatius

Several additional significant points appear in Ignatius' writings. He speaks of "Christianity," providing the earliest known instance of that word.[71] Significantly, his city of Antioch was the place where, Luke reported, the followers of Jesus were first called "Christians" (Acts 11:26), so apparently the name had become acceptable to Jesus' followers over the course of the first century. This term has more than linguistic significance. Ignatius has begun to think of a spiritual reality beyond a collection of local communities. He mentions it in a comparison with Judaism, and he may be using the term to distinguish the Jesus movement from its parent faith. After Ignatius, the term became increasingly common.

He also provides the first witness to the notion of Christian marriage. He tells his friend Polycarp "when men and women marry, it is desirable to have the bishop's consent to the union so that the wedding may be a tribute to the Lord."[72] He does not require the bishop's consent, but this is implied by the fact that he speaks of the marital union immediately after he speaks of disunity in the community. The marriage will reflect the unity the *ecclesia* should have.

---

70. Ignatius, *Philadelphians* 7.

71. Ignatius, *Magnesians* 10.

72. Ignatius, *Polycarp* 5.

The Gospel of John tells of Jesus' attendance at a Jewish wedding at Cana where he performed the first of his signs, and Paul spoke of the importance of observing the marriage bond, but Ignatius is the first to link marriage explicitly with the lifestyle of the believers.

In sum, the life and letters of Ignatius of Antioch provide a unique window on the struggles and hopes of a third-generation leader in the Jesus movement who lived at a key moment in its maturation. Ignatius the bishop argued for a new model of the *ecclesia*, in which a sole bishop supplanted the authority of the spirit-led prophets and presided over a hierarchy of elders and deacons. Yet, ironically, Ignatius the martyr became a model of Spirit-inspired leadership, rallying other believers as he made the long journey to the Eternal City, where he would enter the lists of those whose death *ad bestias* provided "the seed of the church."[73]

The Pastoral Epistles

The three Pastoral Epistles—1 Timothy, 2 Timothy, and Titus—contain instructions and exhortations about church leadership, organization, and administration, about Christian discipline, and about the qualifications and remuneration of church leaders. The audience is also encouraged to confess the faith fearlessly, and to hold the line against false doctrine.

While Titus and Timothy, the purported recipients of the Pastorals, were co-workers of Paul, the historical situations addressed by the Pastorals have not been fitted into a Pauline chronology derived from the seven-letter corpus and Acts. One must postulate Paul's release from prison at Rome, a mission to Spain, and further travels in the eastern Mediterranean. Add to this the fact that the vocabulary and style of the Pastoral Epistles are markedly different from Paul's, and that the "letters" are closer to the literary genre of the "mandate," and most scholars conclude that the Pastorals derive from a pseudonymous author after Paul's death, who saw himself preserving the Pauline legacy.

The Pastorals show an adoption of popular Hellenistic philosophy and ethics, an attitude of active accommodation toward

---

73. Tertullian, *Apology* 50.

Greco-Roman society—for example, in the notion of the church as "the household of God" (1 Tim. 3:15)—and a rarifying of the Christian proclamation as a "deposit" (*parathēkē*) of faith (2 Tim. 1:14). The author of the Pastorals seeks to defend his interpretation of the Pauline tradition against opponents who are described in a vague and stereotypic way, and with whom he refuses to debate. The author responds to the conflict by bolstering the ecclesiastical hierarchy, tightening church discipline, and restating the demand for obedience to the "deposit" of faith as interpreted by the author.

The Use of Pseudonymity

It is generally accepted that the Pastoral Epistles were written by a third-generation disciple in the Pauline tradition. The argument for pseudonymity focuses on four central points: vocabulary and style, theology, situation, and historical details supplied by the author. The personal notes included in the Pastorals have never been fitted into a chronology of Paul's life. Thus one cannot use these data to reconstruct the life of Paul; rather, they are a literary device of the pseudonymous writer (the "Pastor") to lend greater plausibility to the compositions. Pseudonymous letters actually exhibit what has been called "double-pseudonymity" because neither the named author nor the named recipients of pseudonymous letters can be the actual author or intended recipients. For such a device to function, the Pastorals must have some personal notes such as these, both to add plausibility to the claim of Pauline authorship and to bolster the authority of the church leader who uses this letter—received now from "Timothy" or "Titus"—to check the behavior of dissident members of his community. Remarks that show the intimacy of Paul with his co-workers tend to bolster the authority of the "co-workers" who have taken over the reins of church leadership since the days thus enshrined in the Pastorals.

Date

There is no conclusive evidence to date the Pastorals before the mid-second century. Some regard Polycarp's *Philippians* as evidence of him quoting the Pastorals, but this cannot be demonstrated.

Marcion did not include the Pastorals in his canon, nor are they found in P⁴⁶, the earliest surviving manuscript of a collection of Paul's letters. The evidence for Pauline attribution is even later.[74] The church order found in the Pastoral Epistles has close affinities with those of the second-century "Apostolic Fathers," including Ignatius of Antioch.[75] All these facts argue for a second-century date for the letters.[76]

The Pastoral Epistles react against the legend traditions popular in second-century Asia Minor.[77] Such legends as *The Acts of Paul and Thecla* emphasize the spiritual endowments, leadership, and missionary activities of Christian women, all of which the Pastorals aim to restrict or perhaps even eliminate.

Ministry and Church Order

In the Pastorals, the primary model under which ministry is understood to arise is that of ordination. "Timothy" is reminded that his "gift" was given him "through prophecy with the laying on of hands by the council of elders" (1 Tim. 4:14). A different tradition—that "Paul" laid hands on him—appears in 2 Timothy 1:6. These reports raise more questions than they answer.

a. Is prophecy required for ordination?
b. Whose "prophetic gift" was given—that of the community, the elders, or Timothy?
c. Who has the power to ordain?

---

74. "The earliest evidence for the existence of the Pastorals within the body of Pauline letters is all from the second half of the second century (the Muratorian Canon, A.D. 175–200, and the late second century writers Irenaeus, Tertullian, and Clement of Alexandria). This relatively late attribution of the Pastorals to Paul is clearly at variance with both Marcion [*fl.* 150, Rome] and P46 [ca. 200], neither of which support Pauline authorship." Arland J. Hultgren, "I–II Timothy and Titus," in Arland J. Hultgren and Roger Aus, *I–II Timothy, Titus, II Thessalonians*, Augsburg Commentary on the New Testament (Minneapolis: Augsburg, 1984), 11–189, at 18.

75. Ibid., 15.

76. Helmut Koester has argued for a date ca. 125; see Helmut Koester, *Introduction to the New Testament* (Minneapolis: Fortress, 1982), 2:305.

77. See Dennis Ronald MacDonald, *The Legend and the Apostle: The Battle for Paul in Story and Canon* (Philadelphia: Westminster John Knox, 1983).

Interestingly, like Ignatius of Antioch, the Pastor projects a hierarchical model of ministry transmitted through ordination by the ecclesial authorities (Paul, the elders). Yet, as Ignatius promoted the office of bishop by connecting "prophecy" with it, the author of the Pastorals apparently still felt the need to validate this ministerial ordination by connecting it with the charismatic gift of prophecy. Hierarchy may be on the rise, but prophecy has not yet faded entirely out of the picture of ecclesial authority.

In the Pastorals, the duties, qualifications, and remuneration of church officials are detailed. Here are some significant changes of past practices.[78] For example, while the worthy (male) presbyter-presidents are to receive double pay (1 Tim. 5:17–18), the "widows" are to be severely restricted. The number of widows on the rolls is to be drastically reduced, and many are to be taken off the payroll altogether (1 Tim. 5:3–16). Those who remain on the rolls are to become subject to stringent controls. They are no longer allowed to do catechesis in the home; they are prohibited altogether from catechizing men, and from speaking during services (where the group is, presumably, mixed).

The Pastorals give evidence of a continuing development of the gender role definitions outlined in the "household codes" in Colossians and Ephesians. To the schema outlined in these deuteropauline letters is added the heightened theological justification that "Eve sinned first"; thus, while men should pray aloud in the ecclesial gatherings (1 Tim. 2:8), women (as the daughters of Eve) must be silenced and controlled by their husbands (1 Tim. 2:9–15).[79]

The Pastor's model for ecclesial organization is neither incidental to nor antagonistic toward such a patriarchalizing trend in the family.[80] On the contrary, the Pastor chooses the patriarchal household for his description of the community of disciples ("the household of God"), and actively engages in reforms of community relationships that will bring them into line with the patriarchal social

---

78. For further discussion of these issues, see Ibid., 54–77.

79. For an extended discussion of the background to 1 Tim. 2:13–15, and an interpretation that sets it in the context of Hellenistic Judaism, see Anthony Tyrrell Hanson, *Studies in the Pastoral Epistles* (London: SPCK, 1968), 65–77.

80. In contrast, for example, to Paul's views in Galatians.

system.[81] Central among these is the consolidation of power in a few, hierarchically organized, male leaders.

Thus the *episkopos* (overseer) becomes the *paterfamilias* of the church, in conjunction with the *presbyteroi*—the male (and female?) heads of households (1 Tim. 3:1–7; Titus 1:7–9). This presbyter-president or *episkopos* "tends the flock." Among other things, this involves overseeing the administration of congregational resources, taking care of dependent members of the community, preserving right doctrine, and correcting those who err (1 Tim. 5:17–20; Titus 1:5–6; cf. 1 Pet. 5:1–4). There are also other members of the ecclesiastical patriarchal household who have designated roles and statuses: *diakonoi* (ministers, 1 Tim. 3:8–13), *presbyteroi* (elder men, 1 Tim. 5:1; Titus 2:2), *presbyterai* (elder women, 1 Tim. 5:2; Titus 2:3–5), and *chērai* (widows, 1 Tim. 5:3–16). All of the groups fall under the leadership of the *presbyter*-president, the *paterfamilias*, who is to brook no challenge to his authority or to the established status differences (Titus 2:15).

The *episkopos* is charged with the enforcement and rationalization of other social status divisions, which are now recognized as normative within the believing community as well as outside it. He is encouraged to teach the submission of subjects to rulers (1 Tim. 2:1–4; Titus 3:1; cf. 1 Pet. 2:13–17), of slaves to masters (1 Tim. 6:1–2; Titus 2:9–10; cf. 1 Pet. 2:18–25), and of wives to husbands (Tit. 2:3–5; cf. 1 Pet. 3:1–8). He is to help minimize the impact of inequitable distribution of wealth by exhorting the rich to be generous and not haughty (1 Tim. 6:17–19).

Anti-Sophist Schema of the Pastorals

In his attack on his opponents, the author of the Pastorals does not argue substantive matters, nor even describe the opponents; he attacks the opponents in diatribe style by using the common *topoi* that a popular philosopher would use against an adversary.[82] These

---

81. On this subject, see the extended discussion of David C. Verner in *The Household of God: The Social World of the Pastoral Epistles*, SBL Dissertation Series 71 (Chico, CA: Scholars Press, 1983).

82. Robert J. Karris, "The Background and Significance of the Polemic of the Pastoral Epistles," *Journal of Biblical Literature* 92 (1973): 549–50.

common *topoi* comprise an argument from *ethos*, that is, an argument concerning the ethical (or, in this case, unethical) character of the opponents. The author of the Pastorals uses the traditional schema for arguing against sophists, originated by Plato, which provides a sixfold attack on the character of the opponents: (1) they are greedy, (2) they are deceivers (and are themselves deceived), (3) they do not practice what they preach, (4) they engage in verbal disputes and quibbles, (5) they are characterized by the entire catalogue of vices, (6) they are successful among women.[83]

The last charge in the schema—of success among women—is leveled less frequently than the others.[84] While one cannot guarantee any basis in fact for the first five of the charges against sophists, the relative infrequency of use of the last charge suggests that, when it is used, then one may credit it with relatively more historical validity than the rest. In the case of the Pastorals, this seems particularly true of 2 Timothy 3:6—especially in light of the author's redaction of the *topos* in 2 Timothy 3:7 and the general emphasis on restricting the roles of women in the life of the community (1 Tim. 2:11–15; 5:13; Titus 2:5).[85]

The polemic of philosophers against sophists was designed and used specifically to attack and dissociate oneself and one's audience from a rival teacher.[86] The analogy with the use of this schema by Philo, Dio Chrysostom, Tatian, Athenagoras, and Clement of Alexandria

> suggests that the author views his teaching as genuine wisdom, philosophy, truth, and that he views the teaching of his opponents as false wisdom, as sophistry. . . . Moreover, it is the author's desire to show that *he alone has the right* to and actually does impart the truth, that *he and his disciples alone have the power* to teach correctly. Furthermore, by using this schema, the author wants to cause aversion for

---

83. Karris, "Background," 551–54.

84. Although Karris ("Background," 554) points out that Lucian includes it in his attack on wandering Cynics (*Fugitivi* 18–19).

85. Karris, "Background," 560.

86. Ibid., 555, 563.

his opponents in the minds of his readers and to establish a strong alternative to their view of the Pauline tradition. *This strong alternative can be seen in the office of the bishop and in the sound teaching which the bishop is commissioned to impart.* The sound teaching is not esoteric, but rooted in Paul's understanding of grace (1 Tim 1:14; 2 Tim 1:9–10; Tit 2:11–14; 3:4–7) and in the *Haustafel* [household code], one of the most enduring and signal heritages of the Greco-Roman world.[87]

In sum, the general trend in the community organization envisioned by the Pastor is aimed toward neutralizing the authority of the patrons (many of whom were women who had supported the communities in the early days of the Jesus movement) and undercutting the authority of prophets (local and mendicant), with the subsequent consolidation and vesting of this power in the hierarchically organized *episkopoi*, elders, and deacons of the local *ecclesia*. In his discussion of the Christ-believers' way of life, the author "espouses the aristocratic social values associated with leadership circles in the municipalities of the Hellenistic-Roman world."[88] In doing so, he shows that assimilation to the predominant aristocratic and patriarchal culture is central to his understanding of the place of the Christ-believing community (and message) in his socio-political situation.

The Acts of Paul and Thecla

The apocryphal acts, especially the Thecla traditions, offer contravening positions on community order and the Christ-believers lifestyle to those argued in the letters of Ignatius and in the Pastoral Epistles. They give evidence to the existence of alternative developments in the early Christian tradition, which later were suppressed in favor of the patriarchal household model of the *ecclesia*.[89]

---

87. Ibid., 563–64, emphasis added.

88. Verner, *The Household of God*, 183.

89. For extended discussion of these issues, see MacDonald, *The Legend and the Apostle*.

Community Order

In this tradition, ordination is not mentioned; rather, leaders are set aside by charismatic gift. Bishops, presbyters, and deacons are nowhere mentioned. Instead, prophetic authority is paramount. Charismatic teachers and prophets, female and male, are chosen by the Spirit. Their preaching ministry is supported by free-will offerings. These same prophetic teachers are also sacramental ministers when the need arises (e.g., Thecla baptizing).[90]

Christian Lifestyle

This tradition allows for no variations on the Christian lifestyle. All Christians are called to a life of strict asceticism, culminating in martyrdom. The status divisions of the dominant (Greco-Roman) society are to be repudiated via voluntary poverty and rejection of patriarchal authority. The societal gender roles are also repudiated via the "virginal life" of the disciple; inherent in this is the repudiation of patriarchal marriage.

Summary

The second decade of the second century involved landmark changes in the relationship between the Jesus movement and the Roman Empire as well as internal developments within the *ecclesia* to make its structure look more and more like the wider Greco-Roman society. Changing demographics meant that a critical mass of aristocratic men was joining the communities of disciples, which provided both the human resources and the incentive to change the internal structures of the *ecclesia*. In addition, external pressures from the authorities, including localized acts of persecution, provided increasing incentive for the communities to conform to the external structures of Roman society, with aristocratic men as leaders and spokesmen to outsiders. This cultural assimilationist trajectory adopted patriarchal and hierarchical forms of organization and emphasized the distinctions between community leaders and other members. Irenaeus and the author of

---

90. For example, the women Theonoe, Stratonica, Eubulla, Artemilla, Nympha, and Philia are all represented as such ministers in the *Acts of Paul and Thecla*.

the Pastoral Epistles represent this trend toward cultural assimilation of ecclesial structures to the culture at large.

Not every community of Christ-believers was willing to make this type of compromise. A counter-cultural, prophecy-based, strand of the tradition continued to flourish, especially in the smaller towns and villages. This charismatic trajectory was egalitarian in vision, not patriarchal in structure, and tended toward an ascetic lifestyle that rejected the wider culture as contrary to the gospel. Martyrdom was to be expected—though not sought—because a lifestyle faithful to the life and message of Jesus, who was killed by the Roman state, was bound inevitably to lead to the same end. Legend traditions like *the Acts of Paul and Thecla* represent this continuing egalitarian and charismatic tradition.

In the egalitarian trajectory of the Jesus movement, community leadership continued to be open to women and men, as well as persons of various social classes, dependent only upon the community's recognition of the divine distribution of charismatic gifts. In the patriarchal trajectory, women and lower-class men began to be excluded from leadership roles in the *ecclesia*, and charismatic manifestations such as prophecy—which, by definition, cannot be controlled by the hierarchical leadership—begin to be discounted, suppressed, or (as in the letters of Ignatius) co-opted by the hierarchical officers.

The reign of the Emperor Trajan saw the increasing dominance of the patriarchal, cultural assimilationist trajectory of the Jesus movement. For some Christ-believers, the ambivalent imperial policy encouraged keeping a very low profile through moderation of their practices and rhetoric to assimilate to the broader culture. Remarkably, several documents that have survived from second-century Asia Minor do not support the theological and practical trend to suppress the egalitarian trajectory of the Jesus tradition. These documents show that the conflict between patriarchal accommodation and the charismatic, egalitarian vision of the Christ-believing community was by no means ended by Ignatius or the Pastoral Epistles.

Over the next several decades, a protracted debate ensued between adherents of the egalitarian interpretation of the Jesus tradition and those who promoted the hierarchical, patriarchal view. More popular in the important cities, the latter view eventually was victorious and became the "orthodox" model for the Christ-movement.

Groups later denoted as "heretical" (e.g., Gnosticism, Montanism) tended to support the more charismatic model of the *ecclesia*, but the Romanized city communities won over most of the Jesus movement to the hierarchical model ubiquitous in the wider Roman culture. This strategic change in ecclesial models allowed the communities of Christ-believers to blend in with other "associations" in Greco-Roman society, which made them less prone to suspicion and persecution by unsympathetic outsiders.

Questions for Review

1. Who was Pliny the Younger, and why is he important?
2. In Pliny's letter, what crimes are Christians accused of committing?
3. Who was Ignatius, and why is he important?
4. Describe the role of the bishop, as depicted in the letters of Ignatius.
5. Who were the Docetists and what did they believe?
6. Why would Docetism have been appealing to at least some Gentile believers?
7. What organizational and ministerial changes did the author of the Pastoral Epistles want to make in the *ecclesia* of the early second century? What socio-cultural and political forces prompted this move?
8. What do the legend traditions contribute to an understanding of leadership roles in this period of the history of the *ecclesia*? In particular, what information do they supply about women's roles in this period?

Questions for Discussion

1. Pliny offers a brief description of what took place at the Christ-believers worship services in his time. How does his description compare to Christian worship services today?

2. Do you agree with Ignatius that a docetic understanding of the nature of Jesus is incompatible with the Gospels and the teachings of Paul? Explain why or why not.

3. What do you think of Ignatius' and the Pastoral Epistles' emphasis on hierarchical (patriarchal) authority structures for the *ecclesia*? Given the socio-cultural and political forces of the time, do you think this was a good move?

Conclusion

This volume was designed to provide a narrative history of the Jesus movement's first hundred years as it arose in and interacted with the wider world of the Roman Empire, presenting the findings of contemporary historical scholarship in a format accessible to non-specialist readers. Taking a chronological approach to this formative period of 20–120 CE allows one to focus on the wider context of both canonical and non-canonical books and the communities that produced them. Doctrinal issues addressed in the writings of this period illuminate the various ways these communities were developing and the challenges they were facing.

Beginning with background on the world into which Jesus was born, the story moved to the life and ministry of Jesus himself and then, decade-by-decade, discussed political, social, and economic developments within the Jesus movement. The narrative explored the relationships between these various external influences and the structural changes and theological choices made by the early Jesus-communities over time.

Discussion of the women disciples of Jesus and women's roles in the later Jesus movement has been integrated into the overall story. As a result, in some places the historical narrative offered here differs from other expositions that have ignored the women altogether or have taken an "add women and stir" approach. Women's roles changed dramatically over this period, but the standard "history" anachronistically assumes that the strictures on women's behavior imposed by later church fathers already were operative from the outset of the Jesus movement. This survey, however, has shown that women disciples were active from the start but, beginning around the turn of the first century, various social and political developments prompted some ecclesiastical leaders (notably the author of the Pastoral Epistles) to attempt to limit or even eliminate women's leadership roles in the burgeoning communities of Jesus' disciples, promoting instead aristocratic men as leaders and figureheads for the *ecclesia*, especially in the Romanized cities.

History versus Anachronism

The introduction to this volume made a series of claims contradicting many popular preconceptions about the movement anachronistically called early Christianity[1]—claims which, it is hoped, have been substantiated in the course of this book. To reiterate briefly, neither Jesus nor any of his early disciples (including Peter, Paul, and other well-known leaders of that first generation) were Christians. The early followers of Jesus did not self-identify as Christians and were indistinguishable from Jews until at least the 60s. In some places (like Antioch in Syria), they continued to identify with and participate in Jewish synagogues for decades and even centuries. Neither Jesus nor Paul aimed to start a new religion or "found the church" as an entity separate from Judaism. They called people to serve communities of disciples, but did not "ordain" anyone to the kinds of priestly ministries that some Christian communities have today. The Jesus movement of this period situated itself among the people of Israel, and understood itself as a "Way" to honor the claims and commands of the God of Israel, including the prophetic vision of welcoming Gentiles to this path of faithfulness to God.

Jesus himself began as a disciple of John the Baptist, only gradually recognizing his own unique calling from God. His words and deeds led to his being hailed by some of his peers as God's "Messiah." He was neither the first nor the last first-century Jewish man to be thus acclaimed—and killed because of it. Jesus' miracle-working was not unique for the time, nor did the miracles "prove" divine status.

Important figures of the Jesus movement included the Twelve, a distinct group among the disciples of Jesus, as well as hundreds of disciples, including many women. Some of these disciples became missionaries, taking the gospel message to peoples and places beyond Jesus' immediate circle and, eventually, throughout the Diaspora. The Jesus-communities founded by such "apostles," including Paul of Tarsus, had women missionaries, teachers, preachers, prophets,

---

1. See pages 21–23.

deacons, patrons, and apostles. This was not an insignificant or sporadic phenomenon. Rather, in the first century, women served as leaders in various capacities in communities of disciples across a wide geographic area, from the Holy Land to Asia Minor, from Macedonia to Rome. By the end of the period under discussion, a social backlash began to curtail such activities by women leaders of the *ecclesia*, but the backlash was prompted by the significance of women's leadership and their success as ministers of the gospel.

Contexts of the Movement

The early Jesus movement sprang from an increasingly apocalyptic Second Temple Judaism subject to Rome. To most citizens of the empire at that time, Jesus' faction would have appeared as a mere blip on the radar of current events. It would have astounded the Roman populace that surrounded this upstart religion to know that this little group would "go global" over the next two millennia. It is one of the great mysteries of history that a small, marginal group of disciples in first-century Galilee created perhaps the most successful faith movement of all time. Because Christianity is a historical religion that continues to grow and develop today, students, Christians and non-Christians alike, need to understand the dynamics of its nascent period. Knowing the central features of the birth and early development of the Jesus movement provides a baseline for appreciating contemporary Christianity in its many and various forms. Recognizing the significance of the Jewish, Greek, and Roman influences on early Christ-believers provides the starting point for the journey toward the center of historical Christianity.

Jesus and his followers lived and died in the age of empires. Greece and its mighty city-states had fallen not many centuries before. The Greek way of life, Hellenism, had been subsumed by Rome, that great borrower of culture. Rome itself had, in the person of Caesar Augustus, forsaken republic for empire. Jesus was born into a society ruled closely by functionaries at many levels, each of whose ultimate loyalty was to Caesar. This produced a certain level of anxiety among the masses, but it also ensured political stability. Local officials could be usurious and cruel, but they were not free to act with impunity. Rome was a legal state and, while this may only have comforted Roman citizens, especially the elite, it allowed reasonable safety for business and associations. Jesus and company benefitted directly and indirectly from this state of affairs. Christ-believers moved entirely within the ambit of a world power that facilitated travel, everyday commerce, and literacy, all of which abetted their movement.

Of course, first-century Rome did not find the Jesus movement, or the many movements like it, particularly amenable. Jesus and his earliest followers belonged to a people with a long history of quiet yet active disdain for their conquerors. Jewish factions seen through Roman eyes always presented the potential for trouble. Indeed, Rome would consider Jesus' followers nothing but trouble for centuries to come. Jesus was hailed as the Jewish Messiah, King of the Jews. Perhaps some of his earliest followers even understood him to be divine. Whatever the case, they lived in a time when it was not unusual to speak of an incarnate deity; Jesus was not unique, he was competition. Local and imperial leaders knew what political upstarts could mean—and religion and politics widely overlapped in the first century. Furthermore, they knew just how to handle such upstarts. Crucifixion was only one of the means.

To do justice to the history of the Jesus movement, one must understand its beginnings within the larger ancient Mediterranean context of Rome. It was not isolated from the heavily Hellenistic culture of Rome, nor from local customs throughout the empire. To be sure, the nascent *ecclesia* shaped the wider culture in which it moved, but it also was shaped by that very time and culture. Jesus himself was an insignificant figure on the world stage, a marginal figure within an already marginal ethnic-religious group, the Jews. It therefore should not be surprising that little is known about his life. One finds a much fuller picture of him than of most figures of his era, but the extant sources present not mere "history" but rather a blend of history, theology, and doctrinal ideology. They were developed by local groups of his followers, "churches" related by basic beliefs and practices. Precious little is known even of these communities of Jesus' disciples. What is certain, however, is that nascent "Christianity" was not a monolith but a mosaic.[2] Identifying the

---

2. One is not remiss in speaking of early Christiani*ties.*

features of these various strands of the movement poses a significant challenge for historians. The sources, biblical and extra-biblical, tend to be less concerned with historical exactitude than moral example and spiritual encouragement.

Trajectories of Early "Christianity"

Because the Jesus-Way was from birth a historical movement focused on theology and faith, it is understandable that its texts were composed and read for both historical and spiritual purposes. Jesus was both a historical figure and the risen Christ of faith, the Savior-God of Christianity. In the first generations after his crucifixion, Jesus' followers seized upon his identity as Messiah, Savior of the World, more than the "historical Jesus" from first-century Nazareth. In the Jesus movement's literature between roughly 50 and 100 CE, Jesus' divine mission and significance for the faith community loom larger than any biographical concerns. Not until the 80s and 90s (Matthew and Luke) does an interest in Jesus' prior identity arise in that corpus, hence the two infancy narratives. No longer a semi-isolated movement in the Jewish homeland, by the middle of the first century, the Jesus movement was known and active all around the Mediterranean world, due to the arduous missionary efforts of believers like Paul.

Having thus expanded, communities of Jesus-followers in different locations were developing distinct personalities. From Paul's letters, one can infer that the *ecclesia* in Jerusalem was generally poor and that the *ecclesia* in Corinth displayed the "worldly" traits of an urban elite struggling with an egalitarian religion. Hot topics within these congregations waxed and waned. Believers in diverse locales would become concerned with the *eschaton*, social-class boundaries, gender roles, sexual morality, and their relation to the state. Perhaps the most significant challenge for ecclesial leaders was how to respond to these issues in a way that was edifying to the entire community rather than merely a few at the expense of the many. The surviving literature from the Christ-believers of this period attests to ecclesial growing pains and a maturation process.

Part of this ecclesial growth had to do with the tension and cooperation between the early Jesus-communities and the outside world. There was far more tension than cooperation. Nero engaged in a vitriolic yet short-lived persecution of Jesus' followers in the 60s. He justified this persecution by claiming that Christ-believers set the fire that had ravaged Rome, but this and all future attacks on Christians would include charges of cannibalism, sexual deviance, and atheism—staples of group fulmination in antiquity. By the end of that decade, Rome had gone through numerous emperors and many of the Jesus movement's heroes were no more (James, Peter, Paul). Following Jesus in the last decades of the first century would not have made life any easier. At the same time, the Jesus movement was very much part of the Roman Empire. As a small but growing religious association present in many corners of the empire, the Jesus-Way could not have escaped the radar of political leaders. As an offshoot of Judaism, the Jesus movement looked suspicious to Romans after the Jewish revolt of 67–73. But Christ-believers spanned the social spectrum, and for the most part they probably lived quietly and minded their own affairs (1 Thess. 4:11; cf. 1 Tim. 2:2).

In the 70s, following the destruction of Jerusalem and the subsequent loss of the Jerusalem *ecclesia*, formerly the epicenter of the Jesus movement, the believing communities changed dramatically. Ephesus, Antioch, and Rome became the Christ-believers' leading cities as the empire relaxed once again into peaceful stability. With eyewitnesses of Jesus all but extinct, a desire to preserve the oral tradition for later generations led an anonymous writer to pen the first Gospel: Mark. The 70s also saw the composition of the pseudo-Pauline letters to Colossae and Ephesus, which dealt with matters of faith, family, and "worldly" philosophy. Theologies evolved along different lines in different communities, and distinct groups appeared. Prominent among these camps were a Pauline "faith" school and a "James" school reacting against the idea that faith need not impact everyday behavior. The "faith and works" debate was in full swing. As the Jesus movement grew in numbers, attracting both the wealthy and the impoverished, intra-ecclesial relationships became increasingly problematic.

Soon a nagging suspicion began to take hold in the believing communities that Jesus' return (the *Parousia*) would not occur anytime soon. The Roman Empire, with its emperor worship and "false gods," still stood, and Jesus' followers were forced to come to terms with Roman reality. Different communities did this in different ways.

The Gospel of Matthew looked to "the Law and the Prophets" to better understand who Jesus was and how he fulfilled the messianic promises to Israel; the Old Testament was the Jesus movement's "Bible" after all. The author of Matthew, relying on Mark's basic outline, used traditional Jewish modes of interpretation (like *midrash* and *pesher*) to convey the significance of Jesus' life and teaching, including the gathering of the *ecclesia* (Matt. 16:18) to continue his legacy. The evangelist also defined the Jesus-Way as legitimate Judaism over against Pharisaic Judaism. All of divine revelation through Israel's prophets, all of God's promises to their ancestors Abraham, Moses, and David, indeed all of salvation history found fulfillment in Messiah Jesus. Shortly after this, the Gospel of Luke defended Christianity to the Roman world and the Roman world to Christianity. The Jesus-followers, increasingly Gentile, were presented as a legitimate religion within a legitimate state, setting a good example for everyone. Subsequently, in the Acts of the Apostles, the same author would stress the Holy Spirit's role and presence within the early Christ-believing communities as they changed the world for the better.

In the last decade of the first century, the Jesus-Way followers' ties to Judaism came back to bite them once again. Heavy taxes were imposed on all quasi-Jewish sects, and Domitian's self-deification had weighty consequences for "rebellious" monotheists, especially those who emphasized Jesus' (royal) Davidic lineage. Not for the first time, believers were forced to wonder how God could allow his chosen people to suffer at the hands of evil worldly powers. The example of Israel, cited by Paul's writings and the Gospel of Matthew, was one way they explained this phenomenon. In their late first-century writings, the faithful began to provide cosmic (and divine) explanations of Jesus' identity. John's Gospel and epistles came from a community characterized by a high Christology, realized eschatology, and a surprising lack of ethical emphasis relative to other ecclesial writings then extant. One only needed to enter into the salvific reality of Jesus' death, which liberated the believer from a world of sin, to enter into fellowship with the Father through the Spirit sent by the Son (Jesus). No one living in such fellowship could do works of darkness.

A more blatantly apocalyptic writing was the Apocalypse of John. This narrative presents a stratified universe (underworld, earth, heaven) where supernatural forces determine world events. Neither the first nor last apocalypse written, the Apocalypse of John continues a tradition of explaining evil, suffering, and injustice in terms of extraterrestrial forces of darkness at war with God and God's forces of light. Uniquely, this apocalypse is framed as a vision for the seven "churches" of Asia Minor. The author uses this powerful literary genre to combat what he sees as syncretism with Rome within these ecclesial communities in the ambit of Ephesus. Loyalty to Messiah Jesus and to God's kingdom must be demonstrated through passive resistance to the forces of evil in the world of the Roman Empire.

The extra-canonical *1 Clement*, a letter from a community leader in Rome to the *ecclesia* at Corinth, likewise stresses ecclesial order and unity as well as personal piety. Like the contemporaneous literature from the Johannine community, this letter demands radical faith and unswerving commitment to the Lord. As Rome and the Jesus movement perdured as contiguous realities with irreconcilable worldviews, believers became increasingly uneasy about the *ecclesia* and its ties to the world. They adapted earlier literary forms and adopted creative literary means by which an otherworldly reality might be emphasized and an otherworldly way of living encouraged.

The tension between the gospel message of righteous living and the Roman ethos of honor and social mobility continued to grow over the first decades of the second century. Converts to the faith did not recognize at first the significance of the conflict between the two. Christ-believers lived in relative freedom within the empire. The vast majority of the population still lived in poverty, and many believers were concerned and active in remedying this hardship, but others were not. Within the *ecclesia* itself, leadership was variegated, and discussion proliferated concerning the nature of ecclesial leadership and qualifications of leaders. Cultural pressures lead some of the more vocal believers to push for a more hierarchical leadership structure in place of the traditional prophetic model. This shift would have effects for centuries and even millennia to come.

The second century also saw some persecution of Christians. Pliny the Younger's letter to Trajan shows that punishment of Christ-believers was practiced to some extent in the empire. Ignatius of Antioch gives the most famous example of martyrdom, which would become immensely prestigious in ensuing centuries. Some of this persecution arose because officials were beginning to realize the difference between the Jesus movement and traditional Judaism. Persecution could also come from the opposite cause: many outsiders still saw Christ-believers as somehow related to Judaism. The Diaspora revolts of 115–117 CE could not have helped believers' relations with the Roman authorities. Such potential conflict posed a conundrum for a religion that was winning more and more converts from the upper classes; it was tempting to become more "Roman."

This temptation to compromise with Roman values led some communities of believers to advocate a stricter lifestyle of abstention from "worldly" affairs. Works like *The Acts of Paul and Thecla* encouraged Christ-believers, male and female, to dedicate themselves exclusively to God as wandering evangelists. The egalitarian ideal of the legend traditions clashed with the patriarchal structures of the wider society. The Pastoral Epistles, written in Paul's name, take the opposing view, promoting a patriarchal household structure as part of "orthodox" living. The author mandates this authority structure for both *ecclesia* and household. Because of the way it harmonized with the power structures of the wider Roman world, this patriarchal ecclesial model eventually would become the dominant, "orthodox" model of churches throughout the Roman Empire. The former egalitarian and charismatic ecclesial model continued to attract many supporters, especially among disciples who valued a strict ascetical lifestyle. As the patriarchal model of *ecclesia* became dominant, communities who maintained the earlier charismatic model began to be considered "heretical." Thus Gnostic and Montanist Christianities experienced marginalization along with the ascetic and monastic communities.

Final Thoughts

This work leaves off in the age of the Second Sophistic, an age of respect for classical philosophy and complex rhetoric. This was the world in which the Christ-believers would have to find their way. Already by the end of the first century, some Jesus-followers found accommodation to Roman life appealing, and the cultural ethos of the second century would prove particularly attractive to many aristocratic believers. Conversely, other followers of the Way did not appreciate the philosophies of "this age" and attempted to avoid entirely the Hellenistic influences of Rome. Some of these disciples retreated to the desert; some created their own sects; others (later known as "apologists") spoke out against the pagan philosophers and rhetors of their times. But Christianity was here to stay. The Roman Empire, despite its later attacks upon the movement, both physical and ideological, could not squelch the growing church. Christianity was part of Rome, and Rome was part of Christianity. What had begun as a small group of Jewish peasants following an unlikely Jewish carpenter had mutated into another (semi-) legitimate Roman association within a complex social web of cultural diversity. Second-century Christianity certainly remained very Jewish, but it was by and large Hellenistic and Roman as well. In regard to the gradual transformation of the Jesus movement into what we now call "Christianity," Heraclitus' famous saying was justified: "Πάντα χωρεῖ καὶ οὐδὲν μένει" and "δὶς ἐς τὸν αὐτὸν ποταμὸν οὐκ ἂν ἐμβαίης."[3]

---

3. "Everything changes and nothing remains the same" and "you cannot step into the same river twice" (Heraclitus, as quoted in Plato, *Cratylus* 402a).

Appendix 1

Paul and His Theology

Next to Jesus of Nazareth, Paul of Tarsus is the most hotly debated person from early Christianity. Paul has been characterized as everything from the "founder of Christianity" to the Hellenizing perverter of the message of Jesus; Jewish reformer to anti-Semitic apostate; misogynist patriarch to liberationist visionary; prophetic abolitionist to autocratic guardian of traditional social roles. The range of evaluations is mind-boggling.

This appendix focuses on significant aspects of Paul's background, his missionary career, his writings, and key teachings, including his distinctive understanding of the *Parousia*, the crucifixion and Resurrection of Christ, and the unity of all those who by faith are "in Christ" (and how that truth bears upon the "circumcision question"). It addresses such questions as: Who was Paul? What was his Jewish background? What kind of education did he have? What was his relationship to the Roman imperial power structure? What did his "conversion" involve? What was the nature of his relationship with other key disciples of Jesus, especially Peter and James? Finally, what was his assessment of the Jewish law in light of his conviction that Jesus was the promised Messiah and eschatological prophet? These are not the only issues currently debated, but they certainly are fundamental to understanding this influential figure in the first-century Jesus movement.

The two sources for answering these questions are Paul's own letters and, with certain reservations, the Acts of the Apostles. Where the letters and Acts disagree, the former will receive the precedence appropriate to a primary source versus a secondary one. For the most part, the reader will find this reconstruction of Paul's life and thought to harmonize fairly well with the traditional, consensus view—but not quite.

Who Was Paul?

Paul was a Jew of the Diaspora, born in Asia Minor. A descendant of the tribe of Benjamin, Paul was educated as an interpreter and a strict observer of the Torah as understood by the Pharisaic tradition. Even after his call to be a missionary for Messiah Jesus, Paul viewed his previous lifestyle as "blameless" under the law (Phil. 3:6). He characterized his shift from being a zealous Pharisee to a missionary for Jesus as a continuation of God's action in his life via a commission from God to preach Christ to the Gentiles (Gal. 1:15–16). The notion that this was a "conversion" experience—meaning a rejection of his Jewish faith—derives not from Paul but from the vivid presentations in Acts, a secondary source that should not be given precedence over the letters. As noted earlier, Paul's call experience occurred sometime in the mid-30s. In Galatians 1:17, he says that immediately afterward he went into "Arabia," although he does not specify what cities or towns he visited in the process. Then he returned to Damascus.

In general this agrees with the Acts account, which reports Paul preaching in Damascus after his baptism by Ananias, although Luke omits the journey to Arabia. However, he does mention a dramatic escape from the Damascene King Aretas (Acts 9:23–25; cf. 2 Cor. 11:32–33), where Paul is let down over the city wall in a basket. Paul mentions a trip to Jerusalem in the late 30s to consult with Peter and James, and then says he spent fourteen more years in missionary activity before he returned to the Holy City.

Paul spent most of the 40s on journeys to found churches in key cities along the main Roman roads through Asia and along the Mediterranean trade routes to key ports in Asia (e.g., Ephesus), Greece (e.g., Corinth), and Macedonia (e.g., Philippi). After founding a community of believers and ensuring that local leaders could continue the work of teaching and preaching in that town, Paul would move on to another city, keeping in personal contact with the fledgling churches through letters and messengers.

Paul's letters suggest a highly emotional and energetic person, a man of fierce action and words. Paul was a man of many contrasts, but his zeal was one point of continuity between his previous life and his life after the commissioning experience. For Paul, the Resurrection of Jesus was the watershed event that showed that the final age was drawing near. Jesus' glorious coming (*Parousia*) would usher in God's direct rule over the earth and its peoples. Paul was convinced that the *Parousia* would happen in his own lifetime. However, the gospel must be preached to all nations before the Lord would return, hence the urgency of Paul's message and the intensity and breadth of his missionary activity. He compared himself to a runner in a footrace, pressing on "toward the goal" (Phil. 3:13–14) to receive the imperishable crown of salvation (1 Cor. 9:25).

The Letters of Paul

Paul's letters are occasional writings, that is, documents addressed to specific, real-life situations. This means that knowing the backgrounds of both writer and audience, and the circumstances that gave rise to each letter, is essential to accurately understanding them.

Of the many communities founded by Paul and his companions, only four can be positively associated with Paul's surviving letters: Thessalonica, Galatia, Philippi, and Corinth. The letter to Philemon is addressed to a house-church possibly in Asia Minor, perhaps in the area of Laodicea and Colossae, but no specific town is mentioned. The letter to Rome, Paul's last, was addressed to a church he had never visited, and Paul does not mention who was its founder, if he even knew. Paul is known to have written more than these seven letters, and it seems certain that these seven contain fragments of other letters that have not survived intact; perhaps the ones that were preserved were seen as containing teachings important to a wider audience than their initial addressees.

While the letters are occasional writings and therefore cannot be expected to delineate the entire content of Paul's message, one can certainly garner key themes and issues for Paul and his churches from them. Looking at the letters in their order of composition also shows that at least some of Paul's ideas developed over time as Paul's initial formulations were tested and adapted to new situations.

The chronology of Paul's letters is somewhat debated, but most scholars agree that the first of these was 1 Thessalonians (ca. 48) and the last was Romans (ca. 58). Galatians was probably written around 53, and the four "imprisonment letters" (1 Corinthians, 2 Corinthians, Philippians, and Philemon) were composed over the course of the next three years (54–56). At least one of these, 2 Corinthians, is likely to be a composite of what originally were shorter letters (e.g., 2 Cor. 8–9). In addition, there is at least one letter that Paul wrote that is now lost; scholars believe that a fragment remains in 2 Corinthians 6:14–7:1. Six other letters in the New Testament bear Paul's name, but they generally are viewed as coming from some of Paul's successors in the churches he founded.

The seven undisputed letters from Paul give an inside view of what kinds of concerns arose in some of the early church communities that he founded in Asia Minor, Macedonia, and Greece. Certainly there were other questions raised by these early converts, and of course there would have been many things handed down through oral tradition (teaching, preaching, prophecy), but there is no way of knowing what those might have been. While the letters of Paul cannot give the entire picture of Pauline Christianity—even less of Christianity in general—they are the best surviving evidence for reconstructing this influential strand of the Jesus movement.

Key Themes in Paul's Theology

Several themes recur in those seven letters written over the decade of 48–58 CE. Chief among these are the death and Resurrection of Christ as the watershed event that marks the final age of God's creative activity in the world, defeating injustice and death and reconciling human beings with their Creator.

The Imminent *Parousia* of Christ

From the start, Paul's teaching was marked by an existential tension: God's final plan for the world was "already" present and active among Christians, who were incorporated into Christ's death through baptism, but "not yet" fully actualized. This tension would be resolved only at the *Parousia* of Christ, which Paul and his followers eagerly awaited. This expectation of an imminent culmination to the divine plan is seen most clearly in the first of Paul's surviving letters, the one to Thessalonica, written in the late 40s (ca. 48) and before the conference in Jerusalem (ca. 50) with James, Peter, and John (Gal. 2; Acts 15). Paul's preaching of the immediacy of Christ's

Parousia seems to have led at least some of his converts in Thessalonica to believe that Jesus' disciples no longer would suffer death, for the Lord would return very soon (cf. 1 Thess. 4:17).

A problem then arose when some members of the Thessalonian community died at the hands of local opponents of the fledgling *ecclesia* (1 Thess. 2:14). Their survivors seem to have been confused about whether the dead were now lost to God—or whether the *Parousia* had come and bypassed the living. Paul was probably in Corinth when he heard about this issue and penned his response. Paul's comforting message is that neither group had lost out; the *Parousia* was on the horizon but still in the future. Indeed, the surviving Thessalonians would see it in their own lifetime and, through sharing in Jesus' Resurrection, so would the faithful dead (1 Thess. 4:13–18). Significantly, Paul does not relinquish his belief in an imminent *Parousia*; he simply adapts or clarifies his teaching by spelling out the traditional Pharisaic belief in the resurrection of the just at the coming of the Messiah—whom Paul now recognizes to be Jesus.

"Christ Crucified" and Raised from the Dead

While the hallmark of Christian preaching was the proclamation of "Jesus the Messiah," Paul's distinctive way of putting it is "Christ crucified" and raised from the dead (1 Cor 1:23). He never says specifically why he initially rejected the gospel and opposed the followers of Jesus, but it is logical to infer that the reason is related to this later proclamation. Paul's entire symbolic matrix revolves around the cross, which he views as God's mysterious confutation of human wisdom (1 Cor. 1:18–25). Paul admits that "Christ crucified" was a stumbling block[1] to Jews, and it is likely that, initially, it had been a stumbling block to Paul himself. The crucifixion is such a commonplace for later readers that it is difficult for them to grasp why this would have posed a problem for Paul and his contemporaries. But the Messiah was supposed to be successful and victorious, not killed at the hands of Israel's enemies. The recognition that God chose to allow the Messiah to be killed and then justified him by raising him

---

1. Literally, a "scandal," from the Greek *skandalon*.

from the dead had an earth-shattering effect upon Paul, the significance of which he developed throughout his remaining letters.

Circumcision versus the Unity of Life "in Christ"

The letter to the churches of Galatia is probably Paul's second, written (from Corinth?) about 52 or 53 while Paul was on his third missionary journey. Here an angry Paul charges his converts with betraying the gospel because they have begun to accept some Torah regulations as binding upon Gentile Christians (Gal. 3:1–5). Paul seems to think that his version of the gospel was being controverted by other missionaries coming from the church in Jerusalem, who have been dogging his footsteps so they can "complete" the gospel that Paul was teaching. Their program, as Paul imagines it, could be summed up thus: "Paul taught you the faith; now we will teach you the practice."

The fundamental difference between Paul and his opponents is how they answer what is often called the "circumcision question"—whether Gentile converts must first become Jews in order to become disciples of the Messiah Jesus. Remarkably for a former Pharisee, Paul's answer is a resounding "No." One of the most famous passages from all of the Pauline correspondence is the "baptismal formula" (Gal. 3:26–29) repeated at the culmination of Paul's argument for why the laws of the Torah are no longer binding upon those who follow "the faith of Christ" (Gal. 2:16). Those who are "in Christ" live in the eschatological reality (the "already") where all human divisions have ceased and God has restored the unity of the human race intended from the beginning of creation.

Conclusion

Paul is not the "founder of Christianity" in the sense of a lone ranger who blazed the trail for a new religion distinct from Judaism. (In fact, he likely would be incredibly dismayed to hear people claim this of him!) He certainly was not alone among the early missionaries for the faith of Jesus Christ, and likely was much less influential in his own time than he became in later years because of the survival of the *corpus* of his letters, which is a unique phenomenon at this early stage. More importantly, however, Paul never wanted Christ-believers to separate from Judaism. Ideally, for Paul, all Jews would recognize the truth and ultimate significance of God's work of eschatological redemption in Jesus the Christ (cf. Rom. 11:25–29) and become Christ-believers. Meanwhile, those Gentiles who became Christ-believers were incorporated into the chosen people by virtue of their faith and the baptismal rite that marked their "adoption" by God and incorporation into the "body" of the Living Christ.

Much of the energy in Paul's letters—and, if they are any indication of his preaching, the energy of his apostolic ministry—was expended on this question of the relationship between Jewish identity and the messianic movement that arose around Jesus. To Paul, the saving act of God in Christ Jesus marked the fulfillment of Judaism and of God's promises to the people of Israel. This relationship did not involve replacing or "superseding" Judaism but rather fulfilling the eschatological expectations of Isaiah 60–62, which envisioned the worship of the (one true) God of Israel being spread to the ends of the earth. This would result in the incorporation of the Gentiles into the chosen people. Paul viewed this eschatological reality as taking place in his own time through the transforming death and Resurrection of Messiah Jesus. Paul took seriously the vision of Isaiah 62:10–12 and spent his life responding to its challenge.

> Go through, go through the gates, prepare the way for the people; build up, build up the highway, clear it of stones, lift up an ensign over the peoples. The LORD has proclaimed to the end of the earth: Say to daughter Zion, "See, your salvation comes; his reward is with him, and his recompense before him." They shall be called, "The Holy People, The Redeemed of the LORD"; and you shall be called, "Sought Out, A City Not Forsaken."

The restoration and fulfillment of the promise to Israel *of necessity* involved the Gentiles coming to faith so that they too could be called "The Holy People, The Redeemed of the LORD" (Isa. 62:12). Paul's message to the Gentiles, the "gospel" of Jesus Christ, certainly had features that were new to Judaism, but it rested on the centuries-old prophetic proclamation: "Behold your Savior comes, his reward with him, and his work before him!"[2] For Paul, Jesus the Christ indeed was coming, his work of reconciling the world to God accomplished and his reward—of fullness of life through his Resurrection and conquest of death—held in a hand outstretched to all those willing to respond to his invitation.

---

2. Literally, "his work before his face." This translation derives from the Septuagint version (LXX) of Isaiah, which is likely to be the text Paul pondered. Whenever he quotes the First Testament, Paul invariably cites the LXX.

Appendix 2

The *Logion-Quelle*

An important development that likely took place in the 50s was the creation of the "Logion Source" or "Sayings Source"—"*Quelle*" in German, usually abbreviated Q—which comprised a Greek collection of sayings of Jesus that has not survived.

Christians for centuries had assumed that the so-called Gospel according to Matthew was the earliest Gospel and that its author was indeed Matthew, one of the Twelve (Matt. 9:9). Parallel passages in Mark and Luke then could be explained, at least in part, by the other two evangelists copying material from Matthew's Gospel. In the nineteenth century, German New Testament scholars demonstrated instead that Mark's Gospel was written first, and that Matthew and Luke both had Mark in front of them when they wrote their Gospels.

The close links among the three Gospels in chronology, structure, content, and even perspective earned them the name *Synoptic*, that is, "seeing together." These similarities had been known since the second century, and generations of scholars had tried to explain it, especially in the places where the evangelists differed in their presentations. The new hypothesis of Markan priority solved many of the old problems but also created some new ones.

When scholars compared the Synoptic Gospels, they soon isolated material common to all three, such as Jesus' calming the storm at sea (Matt. 8:23–27 // Mark 4:35–41 // Luke 8:22–25). They also discovered material unique to each of the three—actually very little for Mark but quite a bit for Matthew and Luke. For example, only Luke's Gospel tells the parable of the Good Samaritan (10:29–37) and only Matthew's tells the parable of the Laborers in the Vineyard (20:1–16). Since Matthew and Luke had not gotten their unique material from Mark's text as it now stands, scholars labeled the unique material *M* for Matthew and *L* for Luke. They thus had two groups of material in the Gospel of Matthew and two groups of material in the Gospel of Luke: elements taken from Mark, and elements unique to the later two evangelists. But their investigations turned up a third group of elements, material common to both Matthew and Luke yet not found in Mark—for example, the Lord's Prayer (Matt. 6:9–15 // Luke 11:2–4) and the command to love one's enemies (Matt. 5:43–48 // Luke 6:27–36).

Clearly Matthew and Luke had access to a common source other than Mark. Since German scholars pioneered this research, this source was called Q from the German word *Quelle* or "source." Further investigation of Q revealed something else. Although the Q material includes a few narrative passages, such as the healing of the centurion's servant (Matt. 8:5–13 // Luke 7:1–10), most of it consists of sayings of Jesus. Many scholars use the phrase "Sayings Source" to describe it. No text of Q survives. Possibly it had never been written down but was always an oral collection, although a purely oral collection is unlikely given the number of close verbal parallels between the two Gospels.

When was Q composed? Obviously it predates Matthew and Luke, which scholars date to the 80s. Most scholars think that Mark's Gospel, written about the year 70, also gives a clue. Mark includes many sayings of Jesus, but these fit into his overall narrative of Jesus' public career. Since Matthew, Luke, and John followed Mark's example and also wrote of his public career, clearly Mark set the pattern for the future evangelists. To phrase it differently, once the narrative form became accepted, it would have been difficult for a simple collection of sayings to become popular—although it was not impossible, as the survival of the apocryphal *Gospel of Thomas* proves. It is therefore more likely that Q had been composed before Mark wrote his Gospel, that is, sometime in the 50s or early 60s. Since Mark wrote his narrative Gospel to meet the perceived needs of his community, the desire for a narrative format may have been growing in the 60s. Although Q can fit into either the 50s or 60s, the earlier decade appears more probable. By then the work of missionaries like Paul had spread the gospel into heavily Greek-speaking areas, and a collection of Jesus' sayings in Greek would have been desirable for the catechesis of these communities.

Scholars cannot determine where Q was composed. Since Q is known only from Matthew's and Luke's Gospels, and since those were probably written in the environs of Antioch in Syria, Q could well have originated in that area, but this is merely a learned speculation.

Although Q is a scholarly creation that does not exist in any manuscript form, the New Testament does offer two examples of sayings of Jesus being quoted apart from a narrative setting. In 1 Thessalonians 4:15, Paul claims, "For this we declare to you by the word of the Lord, that we who are alive, who are left until the coming of the Lord, will by no means precede those who have died." In Acts 20:35, Luke has Paul directly quote a saying of Jesus: "It is more blessed to give than to receive." Neither saying appears anywhere in the Gospels nor is either one placed in the context of a narrative of Jesus' public career. A number of purported sayings of Jesus, not found in the Gospels, occur in the writings of early church fathers. The scholarly term for such sayings is *agrapha*, meaning "things not written (i.e., in the Gospels)." Some of these, recorded by Papias of Hierapolis, were discussed in chapter 10. Clearly, sayings of Jesus, in written or oral form, circulated widely in the early Christian communities. The Sayings Source "Q" may have constituted the first attempt to collect these sayings of Jesus into an easily retained (and memorized?) list, which could be used by early Jesus-movement scribes and teachers in their work of education and faith formation.

Appendix 3

Glossary

AD Abbreviation of *anno Domini,* "the year of the Lord"; refers to the period of history after the birth of the Messiah (for Christians, Jesus Christ).

Agapētos Greek word meaning "beloved." In a Jewish context, bestowing this title on a son endows him with the rights of the firstborn. In the Synoptic Gospels, the scenes of the baptism of Jesus include a voice from heaven declaring him "my beloved Son" (see Mark 1:11 and parallels).

ANE Abbreviation for the ancient Near East.

Apocalypse Unveiling; a synonym for revelation.

Apostle An emissary or ambassador; one who is sent out to represent someone else.

Baptism A one-time water rite that marks the initiation of persons into the Christian community.

Basileia tou Theou Greek for the "kingdom of God."

BCE Abbreviation for before the Common Era (= period before Christ).

Bible The books; library. A collection of books viewed as normative by Jews and Christians.

Bishop An overseer (Greek, *episkopos*); during the first century CE, this word began to denote specific Christians who were leaders of their particular community.

Ca. Abbreviation for "circa," meaning "at about that time."

Call story A story that recounts an event where a human being experiences a theophany—i.e., is visited by God or one or more of God's messengers—and given a particular task to carry out; this "visitation" can be depicted either as an audition, a dream or vision, or as an appearance of God in the form of a material being (e.g., a burning bush, fiery pillar, or human being).

Canon The list of biblical books; a set of writings that provide one's "rule of life."

Catechesis Teaching someone a religious tradition; faith formation.

CE Abbreviation for Common Era; refers to the same period of time that Christians call AD.

Christ See Messiah.

Christian Follower of Christ.

Christology Study of Christ.

Circumcision (Hebrew, *bris*) the removal of the foreskin of the penis. In Genesis 17, God tells Abraham that he and his male descendants should be circumcised so that God will have a physical sign of their belonging to the covenant and being heirs to God's promises to Abraham.

Collegium A type of group organization that involves rotating leadership and inclusion of each member in decision-making.

Commandments Ordinances; rules for life. Rabbinic tradition recognizes 613 commandments in the Torah.

Conflict story A narrative depicting a verbal and/or physical struggle between two parties.

Covenant n., A treaty, contract or agreement between two parties. v., To establish a covenant relationship.

Creation The doctrine that the things that exist form a coherent universe that is the result of divine choice and initiative. Genesis 1–3 contains two stories or "creation myths" depicting how the universe came to be and how God is related to that created world, especially human beings.

Curse The invocation of divine retribution upon someone, especially as a reprisal for violating a covenant witnessed by that deity.

Deacon Servant, waiter (Greek, *diakonos*); toward the end of the first century CE, this word comes to denote a specific group of people within the Christian community who are in charge of celebrating the Lord's Supper, the agape feast.

Deuteropauline Coming from a "second Paul;" refers to those writings in the New Testament that claim to be from Paul but are believed by scholars to come from one or more of Paul's "students."

Diakonos See *Deacon.*

Election The doctrine that a person or people is specially chosen by God for a specific role or task in the world.

Epiphany Greek word meaning "appearance" or coming; the deuteropauline letters use this term to denote the coming of Christ in glory to judge the world.

Episkopos See *Bishop*.

Epistle A letter of pastoral guidance.

Eschatology Study of the "last things," the end of the world as it currently exists and the establishment of a new era of peace and justice under divine rule.

Eschaton The last things, i.e., the things pertaining to the coming of God's kingdom and/or the end of the world as it currently exists.

Essene One of the four sects of first-century CE Judaism, this was a group of radical purists who led monastic lives in the desert near the Dead Sea and awaited God's salvation through two messiahs: a kingly (and warrior) messiah of David's line and a priestly messiah descended from Aaron.

Eucharist Literally, "thanksgiving"; a term used in early Christian literature to refer to the communal agape meal or "love feast."

Evangelist One who proclaims the good news. Also, author of a Gospel.

Exegesis The process of discerning the meaning of a text for its original, historical audience. See also *Literal meaning*.

Exile Being forcibly evicted from one's homeland. The ancient Israelites (technically, the Judeans, since it was the southern kingdom) were sent into exile in Babylon when King Nebuchadnezzar of Babylonia conquered the Kingdom of Judah, destroyed Solomon's Temple, and took possession of the city of Jerusalem in 587 BCE.

Exodus A coming forth; the story told in the second book of the Bible. In particular, the act of God, through the leadership of Moses, liberating the Israelites from slavery in Egypt (ca. 1250 BCE) and drawing them forth into the promised land.

Fundamentalism A focus on the "fundamental" beliefs of Christianity, including the verbal inspiration and infallibility of the scriptures.

Futuristic eschatology A view of the "last things" as not yet accomplished.

Genealogy An ordered list of someone's ancestors; a family tree (e.g., Matt. 1).

Gnōsis Knowledge of divine mysteries revealed only to a chosen few, called the "elect."

Gnosticism Late first-century CE religious movement characterized by the belief that one is saved through illumination, i.e. being initiated into secret knowledge (*gnōsis*) known only to members of the sect.

Gospel Good news; especially, the good news of salvation through Jesus Christ who died and whom God has raised from the dead. Also, a literary work that uses narrative to proclaim the significance of Jesus.

HB Abbreviation for the Hebrew Bible; the Jewish Bible; sometimes the Christian "Old Testament," even though some of its books were written in Greek.

Hellenist A promoter of the Greek language, culture, and ways of thought.

House-church A community of Jesus' followers who meet in a private home, usually one belonging to one of the members of the community; the householder serves as patron to the group (see *Patron*).

Household code A list of roles in the patriarchal household (e.g., *paterfamilias*, wife/matron, children, slaves) and what behavioral codes apply to each of these roles; in some of the later NT writings that view the church as "the household of God" (e.g., 1 Peter, 1–2 Timothy, Titus), the roles include the offices of bishop, deacon, presbyter, and widow.

Hymn A song addressed to a deity, usually in poetic form.

Inerrancy A view of the Bible that claims it is without error, especially in regard to faith and morals.

Inspiration "God-breathed"; the doctrine that the Bible represents God's Word expressed in human language.

Interpretation The process of discerning how the original meaning of a text can be appropriated for a contemporary audience.

Jesus Name meaning "Yahweh saves." Also, Jesus of Nazareth, born ca. 4 BCE, who was a wandering preacher in first-century CE

Palestine, executed by the Romans for subversion ca. 30 CE. His followers claimed that God raised him from the dead, proving that he was the long-awaited Messiah.

Jewish-Roman War (first) An armed rebellion against Roman occupation of Israel, involving different Jewish groups acting sometimes in concert and sometimes opposing each other. The hostilities began in 67 CE, led partly by disaffected priests and partly by nationalistic zealots who followed Jewish militants. Each group had a leader whom they viewed as God's messiah (e.g., John of Gischala and Simon bar Giora), but they did not agree with the other groups as to the identity of the messiah. The Roman army, first under Vespasian and then under Titus, eventually put down the insurrection, sacking Jerusalem in 70 CE and taking Masada, the last stronghold, in 73.

Kērygma Greek for "proclamation"; refers to the central elements of the Christian faith: Christ died according to the scriptures to deliver people out of the present evil age; he was buried; God raised him up on the third day according to the scriptures; he is exalted at the right hand of God; he will come again as Judge and Savior of the world. A "shorthand" version of this is "Christ has died; Christ is risen; Christ will come again."

Kingdom of God In Jesus' teaching, the universal rule of the one, true God, who rules with justice.

Kosher That which is required by Torah to maintain ritual purity before the God of Israel. The laws of kosher reflect the order of creation, where God differentiated the birds of the air, the animals of the sea, and those of the land, and differentiated humans from them all (e.g., Lev. 11; cf. Exod. 22:19; 34:26b).

L Abbreviation for a hypothetical (oral or written) source used by the third evangelist, "Luke."

Libertinism Literally, belief in freedom of ethical practice; in regard to the NT Pauline corpus, it is the belief (expressed, e.g., by some Corinthians) that "all things are lawful" to those who are in Christ, that is, that individual conscience (apart from social impact) need be the only guide for ethical behavior; also known as antinomianism.

Literal meaning In common parlance, the "face value" meaning of the text for a contemporary audience. In biblical studies, the meaning the biblical text had for its original, historical audience; the understanding a contemporary reader can gain from the text by using lexical aids and information on the history and culture of the author(s).

Literalism An approach to the Bible that insists that everything it includes must be taken as historical fact and at face value; historicism.

Literary criticism The study of an author's style, vocabulary, etc.

Liturgy Literally, the "work of the people"; in Christian tradition, this term refers to the regular (weekly?) gatherings for prayer and a common meal, which soon took on a common pattern or structure.

M Abbreviation for a hypothetical (oral or written) source used by the evangelist known as Matthew.

Messiah Anointed one (Greek *Christos*); one anointed or set apart by God for a special task (e.g., king of Israel, prophet).

Metaphor From "*metapherō*," to carry across; an implied comparison of two dissimilar realities stated in terms of equivalency (e.g., God is "King," Jesus is God's "Son," Jesus is the "Lamb" of God).

Midrash A type of interpretation where one Biblical passage is used to uncover the meaning of another, or where two passages that pose an apparent contradiction to one another are harmonized by means of a third passage that resolves the contradiction.

Miracle An event that occurs in the natural world but that is contrary to the conventional understanding of what is "normal," and hence is attributed to divine intervention (e.g., cure of serious illness without the use of medicines, raising someone from the dead).

NT Abbreviation for the New Testament.

Oracle A message from a deity, often transmitted through a human voice; also the person who is the medium of this divine message.

Ordination Consecration of a priest or other religious functionary.

Parable A story that challenges the preconceptions of the audience and, thus, invites them to adopt a totally different view of the world (and God); Mark says Jesus used parables so people would not understand his teachings.

Parousia Greek word meaning "coming, appearance"; usually refers to the coming of a king or emperor with great power and glory. Paul uses it to refer to the coming of Christ in glory to judge the world.

Patriarch Oldest male who is head of a family or clan.

Patriarchy Father-rule; a hierarchical form of group organization that recognizes the group's patriarch as the unquestioned (and, to some extent, unrestrained) leader.

Patron In the Greco-Roman period, a person who financially supports a group (or individual) and advocates for them, usually providing the economic resources for group activities such as shared meals, and often providing meeting space in the patron's villa; as financial backer, the patron has a direct interest in the group's public activities and has the leverage to shape group organization and policies.

Pentateuch The first five books of the Bible; Torah.

Pericope A set of verses that form one coherent unit or thought.

Pesher A type of commentary where a Biblical passage (even in a historical book) is viewed as a prophecy that has been fulfilled in some specific events, usually of the present or very recent past.

Pharisee One of the four sects of first-century CE Judaism, this was a lay movement to revive religious practice and study of the Torah, especially in rural areas, by organizing synagogues. This group believed in angels, in the resurrection of the dead, and in interpreting the Torah in light of the present circumstances.

Presbyter Old man, elder. In Christian usage, it eventually becomes an ordained office of "elder" or, in the high-church traditions, a "priest."

Prophecy The word of God for a particular people at a particular time and place; in the Hebrew Bible, not to be confused with prediction of the future, although some NT texts tend to use it in this way.

Prophet One who "speaks forth" the word of God.

Proverb A pithy saying; a statement of common wisdom.

Providence Term referring to the religious affirmation of God's on-going activity to sustain and develop the universe God created.

Psalm A poetic hymn addressed to God.

Pseudonymous Having a false name; refers to those writings in the NT in which the author claimed to be Paul (or Peter, James, or Jude) but really was someone else.

Q Abbreviation for *Quelle*, the German word for "source"; Q is a hypothetical sayings source shared by Matthew and Luke. Many scholars have attempted to reconstruct this source, often viewed as a literary collection similar to what is found in the *Gospel of Thomas*, and dated to between 50–150 CE.

Rabbi A "teacher"; refers in particular to a person who studies and who helps others to know the Torah. This came to be the common title for a leader among the Jews in the period after the destruction of the Second Temple, on account of which the form of Judaism that develops during this period is called Rabbinic Judaism.

Realized eschatology The belief that the "final things" are a present reality for the elect of God.

Redaction history The study of the history of the editing of a text and how different literary stages of the text were used.

Redactor Editor.

Reign of God See *Kingdom of God.*

Resurrection In Christian tradition, God's justification of Jesus by raising him from the dead to new life in the body; God's public declaration that Jesus was innocent of the charges brought against him and that his testimony about God was true. By extension, the restoration of embodied human life at the final judgment to the righteous dead.

Revelation Unveiling; the doctrine that God makes the divine self known to human beings. For Christians, this comes especially through Christ. Also, the last book of the NT, also called the Apocalypse.

Rhetoric The art of persuasion.

Righteousness Living in conformity with the will and law of God.

Ritual consecration A ceremony where someone or something is set aside and dedicated to divine service (e.g., anointing of a priest).

Romano-Jewish War See *Jewish-Roman War*.

Rubrics "Stage directions" for what should be done during a religious ceremony.

Sabbath See *Shabbat*.

Sacrifice The ritual slaughter of a living creature, animal, or human, and roasting of it on an open fire as an offering to a particular deity. Typically, the offering is then shared out and eaten by those who participated in the ritual. At other times, the sacrifice is totally incinerated in the fire, in which case it is called a "holocaust."

Sadducee One of the four sects of first-century CE Judaism, this was a group of priests who promoted the Jerusalem Temple cult, believed in Torah alone, did not believe in angels or the resurrection of the dead, and tolerated the control of Rome over Palestine.

Sanhedrin In Greek, *synedrion*; the Jewish court, based in Jerusalem; a judicial body composed of 71 members, 70 of whom were priests and scribes (Sadducees and Pharisees), with the high priest presiding. Their jurisdiction was over Jews, primarily those in Jerusalem, and was limited to matters involving alleged infringement of the Jewish law (the Torah) and taxes. During the time of Roman occupation of the Land of Israel, the jurisdiction of the Sanhedrin was limited by Rome and the decisions of the court seem to have required the approval of the Roman governor, at least in matters involving the death penalty. Occasionally, during a vacancy of the Roman procuratorship, the Sanhedrin seems to have imposed the death penalty without Roman consent or review.

Scriptures "Writings"; for Jews and Christians, the writings that comprise the Bible.

Seer A visionary; one who conveys a divine message in visual imagery.

Shabbat Hebrew for the seventh day of the week (the Sabbath), the day of rest (according to Gen. 2:1–4a) when God completed the creation. Sabbath observance involves the human imitation of God by likewise avoiding work and spending time in re-creation.

Sōtēria Greek term meaning "health" or "wholeness"; derivatively, "salvation."

Soteriology The study or discussion of "*sōtēria*."

Synagogue A gathering of Jews (including at least ten men) for prayer.

Synopsis A summary (not to be confused with synoptic).

Synoptic Having a similar view (not to be confused with synopsis). The Gospels according to Matthew, Mark, and Luke are known as the Synoptic Gospels.

Temple The center of Jewish life and worship from the time when it was built by Solomon (ca. 950 BCE), the son and heir of the great King David. Deuteronomy teaches that there must be only one place of sacrificial worship in Israel, and that is the Temple in Jerusalem. Destroyed first by the Babylonians in 587/586 BCE, it was rebuilt under Cyrus of Persia after he freed the Israelites from exile ca. 538 BCE. The Second Temple was expanded under Herod the Great (in the first century BCE), but then destroyed by the Roman General Titus when Jerusalem was sacked in 70 CE. The Jews were dispersed from the city and the Temple has never been rebuilt.

Textual criticism The process of determining the most reliable reading for a text from the study of many manuscripts.

Theocracy Rule by God or, in an extended sense, by divine law and/or God's (human) agents.

Theophany An appearance of God or divine messengers to a human or group of humans, typically in material form or when the recipients are in a dreamlike state.

Torah Hebrew for "teaching, instruction," the proper noun refers to the first five books of the Bible (Genesis, Exodus, Leviticus, Numbers, Deuteronomy), which comprise the central teachings of Judaism; also called the Pentateuch.

Two Ways doctrine A traditional Jewish approach to moral teaching that highlights the two ways open to human beings, the way of life (faithfulness to God, especially through observance of the Torah; following the inclination to do what is good and just) or the way of death (disobedience to God and the

Torah; following the inclination to do evil). *The Didache*, one of the early Christian writings from the first or second century CE, includes a section of moral teaching that utilizes the Two Ways doctrine.

Vision A Divine message expressed in pictorial form.

Widow An unmarried woman (or one no longer married) who engaged in teaching, preaching, and hospitality ministries in early Christian (esp. Pauline) churches.

Word of God An expression referring to God's self-revelation; for Christians, in the Incarnation of Christ; in the words and deeds of Jesus and the disciples; in the oracles of the Hebrew prophets; in divine acts in history, etc. Also, a short-hand expression for the scriptures that are understood as a vehicle for that "word" to be made manifest in the present.

Yahweh The unspeakable Divine Name; proper name for the God of Israel, which probably means "I am the one who will be there [for you]."

Yeshua Aramaic name meaning "Yahweh is my salvation"; transliterated "Joshua" or "Jesus" in English.

Yetzer ha-ra Hebrew for the human inclination to do injustice, evil; one of the "two ways" discussed in traditional Jewish moral teaching.

Yetzer ha-tov Hebrew for the human inclination to do justice, goodness, "the right thing"; one of the "two ways" discussed in traditional Jewish moral teaching.

Zealot One of the four sects of first-century CE Judaism, this was a group of radicals who wanted to use force to oust the Romans and re-establish an independent theocratic Jewish state in Palestine.

Zion Mountain on which the city of Jerusalem was built; also, the city of Jerusalem itself.

Zionism Political movement supporting the modern State of Israel, based on the assertion that the Levant region is the Promised Land that God gave to the ancient Israelites; thus it ought now to belong to the Jewish people by divine right.

Appendix 4

Important People
in the Second Testament Era

Andronicus A Jewish man who converted before Paul and then became an "outstanding apostle" associated with the Christ-believing community in Rome (Rom. 16:7, SEM); he seems to have been married to another apostle of Rome named Junia, and the two apparently were imprisoned with Paul for a time.

Apollos An Egyptian Jew and native of Alexandria, he was converted by Prisca and Aquila, who then took him to their home in Corinth, where he preached for some time. Apollos was known for his eloquence and forceful rhetoric (Acts 18:24–28).

Aretas IV King of Damascus who had Paul arrested for inciting to riot; Paul escaped his imprisonment by being let down over the city wall in a basket (2 Cor. 11:33–34; Acts 9:23–24).

Augustus (Octavian) The first Emperor of Rome, from 27 BCE to 14 CE; he brought peace after decades of civil war. Jesus was born during his reign.

Balaam A prophet of Ba'al (Num. 22–24) who was asked to curse the Israelites, but was only able to bless them because the Lord gave him the words of prophecy. The Apocalypse uses this name to characterize some of the "false" prophets who oppose the message of John the Seer, instead teaching Jesus' followers to "eat food sacrificed to idols and practice fornication" (Rev. 2:14).

Barabbas Name meaning "son of the father"; in the Gospel stories of Jesus' trial, an outlaw by this name is said to have been freed instead of Jesus (Matt. 27:21). Other sources give the name as "Jesus bar Abbas."

Barnabas An emissary (*apostolos*) from the *ecclesia* in Jerusalem to Antioch (Acts 11:22–26), he then retrieved Paul from Tarsus and spent some time with him at Antioch. Later, he and Paul were sent from the *ecclesia* in Antioch as missionaries to Cyprus,

Perga, Antioch in Pisidia, Iconium, Lystra, and Derbe (Acts 13–14). He also was one of the Antiochene emissaries to the Council of Jerusalem.

The Beloved Disciple A literary figure in the Fourth Gospel, the Beloved Disciple represents the ideal follower of Jesus. The appellation is attested four times in the Gospel of John (19:26–27; 20:2; 21:7, 20), along with numerous references to "the other" (unnamed) disciple (18:15–16; 20:2–4, 8; 21:23). Ecclesiastical tradition identifies the Beloved Disciple as Jesus' disciple John, son of Zebedee, and attributes to him authorship of the Fourth Gospel (21:24), although most modern scholars consider this unlikely.

Cassius Dio Son of a Roman family in Nicaea in Bithynia, Lucius (or Claudius) Cassius Dio Cocceianus (ca. 155–235 CE) is most noted for his extensive *Roman History* (composed in Greek) covering the approximately 1400-year period from the age of the legendary Aeneas (ca. 1200 BCE), Trojan refugee and ancestor of Rome, through Dio's own lifetime, culminating with the reign of Marcus Aurelius Severus Alexander Augustus (emperor from 222–235 CE). Researched and written during a period of over two decades, many of the eighty books of Dio's history survive, at least in fragmentary form, thus providing scholars with a detailed perspective on Roman history. Books 37–54 and 56–60, which cover the period 65–12 BCE and 9–54 CE are nearly complete and provide much of the extant evidence for understanding the Roman world in the time of Jesus and his earliest disciples.

Claudius Emperor of Rome from 41–54 CE; in the late 40's, he issued an edict expelling Jewish leaders from Rome because of riots in the name of one "Chrestus." This edict was rescinded when Nero took the purple.

Constantine the Great Flavius Valerius Constantinus (b. ca. 280 CE) was Emperor of Rome from 306–337 CE; in 313 he issued an edict that legalized Christianity in the Roman Empire. In 325 he made Christianity the official religion of the empire and outlawed other forms of religion.

Cornelius A centurion in Acts 10 who becomes the model Gentile believer. His acceptance by Simon Peter signifies God's acceptance of Gentiles as well as Jews among the followers of Jesus.

Epaenetus The first Asian convert to the Jesus movement (Rom. 16:5)

Euodia A woman who was one of the leaders of the *ecclesia* at Philippi (Phil. 4:2–3)

Eusebius of Caesarea A Palestinian Christian by birth, Eusebius (ca. 260–339 CE) survived the persecution of Diocletian to become the "first church historian" in the post-apostolic period. Eusebius became bishop of the church in Caesarea Maritima about 314 CE and played an important role at the Council of Nicaea (325 CE). An apologist for the Christian faith and biblical scholar, he is most noted for his extensive *Ecclesiastical History* (which preserves important texts and traditions from the apostolic period onwards) and his panegyric materials on Constantine the Great.

Flavius Domitian Emperor of Rome from 81–96 CE; a major persecution of Christ-believers broke out under him. The book of Revelation was written during his reign.

Gaius Caligula Emperor of Rome from 37–41 CE; he was a lunatic who tried to set up a statue of himself (to be worshiped as a god) in the Temple in Jerusalem but was assassinated before this order could be carried out.

Gamaliel II A leader of Rabbinic Judaism following Johanan ben Zakkai; he organized the reform of the synagogue service ca. 91 CE that included a curse on the followers of "the Nazarene," which separated Christ-believers from other Jews.

Herod Agrippa A successor to Herod the Great; he is noted in the New Testament for hearing Paul preach after his detention by Porcius Festus (Acts 25:13–26:32). Luke portrays Paul's message as so convincing that King Agrippa is nearly converted (26:28).

Herod Antipas A successor to Herod the Great, he is noted in the NT for his incestuous marriage to the divorced wife of his living brother, and for the beheading of John the Baptist.

Herod the Great Appointed by Rome as King of the Jews, he ruled Palestine from 37–4 BCE; he was a megalomaniac hated by nearly all of his subjects, and is famous for ordering the murder of one child in each family so people would mourn his death.

Ignatius of Antioch Born ca. 50 CE and martyred ca. 107 CE, ecclesiastical tradition claims that Ignatius was the third bishop of the *ecclesia* of Antioch in Syria (if one includes Simon Peter in the list). Like his friend Polycarp, Ignatius is reported to have been a disciple of John and to have received the gospel from his lips. Ignatius wrote seven letters to various Christ-believing communities while he was on his way to Rome, in chains, to be executed in the amphitheater. The letters emphasize ecclesial unity around the local bishop; his theology sometimes is characterized as promoting a "monarchical episcopate." Ignatius also appealed to Christ-believers to be faithful in the face of persecution, and to welcome the martyr's crown as the seal of true faith in Christ.

James ben Zebedee Son of Zebedee and one of Jesus' first disciples, a distinct group known as the Twelve.

James bar Joseph Also known as James the Just, James the Righteous, and James of Jerusalem, he is identified in the New Testament as "brother of the Lord" (Gal. 1:19). He was not one of Jesus' original disciples but became a believer later, after the Resurrection. He became the leader of the Jerusalem *ecclesia*, possibly as early as the late 30s.

Jesus of Nazareth Born ca. 4 BCE, he was a wandering preacher and healer in first-century CE Palestine executed by the Romans on a charge of subversion (ca. 30 CE). His followers claimed that God raised him from the dead to prove that he was the long-awaited (Jewish) Messiah.

Jezebel Wife of Ahab (1 Kings 16:31), King of Israel (Samaria); she and her husband were devotees of Ba'al rather than Yahweh, God of Israel, and executed many of the prophets of Yahweh (1 Kings 17–18), also threatening Elijah with the sword. The Apocalypse uses this name to characterize one of the "false" prophets who oppose the message of John the Seer by "teaching and beguiling my servants to practice fornication and to eat food sacrificed to idols" (Rev. 2:20).

Johanan ben Zakkai Regarded as the founder of Rabbinic Judaism in the aftermath of the First Jewish War against Rome (67–73 CE); he was instrumental in the re-organization of Judaism in

Jamnia (Jabneh or Yavneh) after the Roman destruction of the Second Temple and expulsion of Jews from Jerusalem.

John ben Zebedee One of the original disciples of Jesus (Mark 1:19), he later became a leader of the Jerusalem *ecclesia*; the fourth canonical Gospel (completed ca. 90 CE) takes its name from him.

John the Baptist A prophet contemporaneous with Jesus, he preached the imminent coming of the reign of God. Tradition has it that he and Jesus were cousins (Luke 1), and that John was born a few months before Jesus (i.e., ca. 6–5 BCE). Jesus became one of his followers (at least for a time), submitting to baptism by John in the Jordan River, probably about 27 CE (Matt. 3:13–17). Herod Antipas had him imprisoned and then beheaded (Mark 6:14–29) about a year later.

John of Ephesus (a.k.a. "John the Seer") The Seer of the Book of Revelation (Rev. 1:9); he was a prophet and visionary who had led the Christ-believing communities of Asia until he was exiled on the island of Patmos "because of . . . the testimony of Jesus," i.e., because he had been preaching the gospel of Messiah Jesus.

Joseph ben Matityahu (Titus Flavius Josephus) Born in Jerusalem in 37 CE, shortly after the death of Jesus, Josephus served as general of one of the Jewish armies during the First Jewish War against Roman occupation of the Holy Land. Josephus was captured relatively early in the war (67 CE) by Vespasian, who held him hostage and used him as an interpreter. After Vespasian became emperor, he emancipated Josephus, who honored his patron by taking the Flavian family name. Soon thereafter he defected to the Roman side and served as a Roman spy for the rest of the war. Titus Flavius Josephus wrote two extensive historical works, the *Antiquities of the Jews,* which recounts the history of the 3833 years from "the Creation" to the period of the Procurator Gessius Florus (whom he blames for precipitating the revolt), and the *Jewish War,* which covers the period from the onset of the revolt through the capture of Masada and the suppression of dissidents in the Diaspora (especially Alexandria and Cyrene). His writings were aimed for a Roman audience and therefore are skewed somewhat in favor of the Romans.

Nevertheless, they remain the best non-canonical sources for much of the New Testament period.

Judas Iscariot One of Jesus' original disciples; the Gospels report that Judas betrayed Jesus to the Jewish authorities and helped them plan Jesus' arrest.

Julia A Christ-believer who apparently led a house-church with four other disciples in Rome (Rom. 16:15).

Junia A Jewish woman who converted before Paul and then became an "outstanding apostle" associated with the *ecclesia* of Rome (Rom. 16:7, SEM); she seems to have been married to another Roman apostle named Andronicus, and the two apparently were imprisoned with Paul for a time.

The Lamb In the Apocalypse, the Seer's favorite word for Jesus—humble, pure, meek, slaughtered by God's adversary (Rev. 5). Revelation reveals the "Lion" side of the Lamb as well, coming in justice and divine judgment, but without relinquishing the suffering side of the Lamb, which links the Lamb with the oppressed followers of Jesus Messiah.

Lazarus A poor man, in the Gospel of Luke, who lived as a beggar outside a rich man's estate (Luke 16:19–31). In the Fourth Gospel, this is the name of the brother of Mary and Martha of Bethany, who died and then was raised by Jesus after being in the tomb four days (John 11).

Luke Name given to the author of the Third Gospel and the book of Acts (dated ca. 85 CE, possibly from Ephesus); traditionally thought to be a Gentile convert who was a physician and companion of Paul on one of his missionary journeys.

Lydia A householder and seller of purple cloth in Thyatira; she was a "worshiper of God" (Acts 16:14) whom Paul converted. She hosted a house-church at Philippi (16:40).

Mark Name given to the author of the earliest Gospel (dated ca. 70 CE). The Pastoral Epistles mention a Mark among the companions of Paul (2 Tim. 4:11). Mark was not one of Jesus' original disciples.

Martha and Mary of Bethany According to John 11, sisters of Lazarus. Luke 10:38–42 says that Mary sat at the feet of Jesus, learning the gospel directly from him. In John 12:1–8, she prophetically anointed Jesus beforehand for his burial.

Mary of Magdala A woman from whom Jesus is said to have cast out seven demons; she became one of Jesus' intimate disciples (Luke 8:2). She is reported to have been a witness to the crucifixion, and all four canonical Gospels claim that she was (alone, according to John 20:1–8) the first witness to the Resurrection and that she brought the message to Simon Peter and some of the other disciples, who did not believe her. Medieval Christians called her "*apostola apostolorum*," "apostle of [the] apostles"; grammatically, this form means either "apostle to the [other] apostles" or "supreme among the apostles."

Mary of Nazareth The mother of Jesus, depicted by Mark as an outsider to Jesus' circle of disciples (Mark 3:21, 31–32), but in John's Gospel and Acts as prominent among his disciples (John 19:25–27; Acts 1:14).

Mary of Rome A Jewish Christ-believer and a leader of the *ecclesia* in Rome (Rom. 16:6).

Matthew A tax collector who gave up his profession and became a disciple of Jesus (Matt. 9:9–13); tradition attributes the First Gospel (written ca. 80 CE, probably in Syria) to Matthew, but most scholars believe this to be erroneous.

Nero Emperor of Rome from 54–68 CE; a major persecution of Christ-believers took place under him. Peter and Paul were killed during his reign.

Nerva Emperor of Rome from 96–98 CE.

Nicolaitans The Apocalypse uses this name to characterize some of the "false" prophets who oppose the message of John the Seer (2:6, 15); otherwise, it is unknown.

Onesimus A slave converted by Paul during his imprisonment in Ephesus; Paul wrote the biblical Epistle to Philemon, his master, to plead for Onesimus' freedom.

Papias Born in Smyrna ca. 60 CE, he later became bishop of Hierapolis, near Colossae in the Lycus River Valley. He valued oral tradition above written accounts. In the process of discussing oral traditions, he provides information on the authors and writing of the canonical Gospels. He died ca. 130 CE.

The Pastor A figure postulated as pseudonymous author of the Pastoral Epistles (1–2 Timothy and Titus).

Paul of Tarsus Also known as Saul, a Pharisaic Jew who persecuted Christ-believers; he had a vision of the risen Christ and became a fervent missionary and preacher of the gospel (Gal. 1:11–24). While he preached to both Jews and non-Jews, he called himself "apostle to the Gentiles." Paul was arrested in Jerusalem and taken to Rome in chains, where he was executed ca. 62 CE.

Philemon An aristocratic, slave-holding Christ-believer from Asia Minor (perhaps near Colossae) who hosted a house-church; the only surviving "personal" letter of Paul was addressed to him.

Philip From the town of Bethsaida, he became one of the Twelve close disciples of Jesus (Matt 10:3//Mark 3:18//Luke 6:14; John 1:45). He likely should be distinguished from Philip "the evangelist" mentioned in Acts (6:2–5; 8:4–40; 21:8).

Phoebe of Cenchrea A wealthy woman who was president of the *ecclesia* near Corinth and who, according to Romans 16:1–2, gave monetary support to many Christ-believing missionaries, including Paul.

Pliny the Younger Gaius Plinius Caecilius Secundus (61–ca. 112 CE) was the Roman Governor of Bithynia during the reign of the Emperor Trajan. He wrote numerous letters, most famously one concerning the proper trial of Christians.

Polycarp of Smyrna Bishop of the *ecclesia* in Smyrna (modern-day Izmir, Turkey); he lived ca. 70–155 CE. Eusebius claims he was a pupil of the Apostle John. His letter to the *ecclesia* at Philippi discourages materialism and offers advice concerning how to handle financial dishonesty of community members. Polycarp rejected the gnostic teachings of Marcion.

Pompey The Roman general who subdued Palestine in 63 BCE, beginning the period of Roman rule there.

Pontius Pilate Appointed by Rome to be procurator of Judea from 26–36 CE; the Gospels record that, under him, Jesus was tried and convicted of subversion.

Prisca Also known as Priscilla; she was an evangelist and missionary with whom Paul worked at Corinth. She and her husband,

Aquila, were "leather workers" like Paul, and made their primary home in Rome (Acts 18:1–3).

Silas A companion of Paul and Barnabas in Acts; he was an early Christian leader (15:22) and prophet (15:32) who suffered and served with Paul (15:40; 16:19; 17:10) and Timothy (17:14–15; 18:5).

Simon Peter Formerly a fisherman, he became one of Jesus' first disciples (Mark 1:16–17). He is famous for denying any association with Jesus during his passion (Mark 14:66–72), but later being rehabilitated and becoming a leader of the Jesus movement. Galatians refers to him as a "pillar" of the Jerusalem *ecclesia* (Gal. 2:9). Medieval Christians claimed he was the first pope.

Stephen A follower of Jesus who came from Greek-speaking, Diaspora Judaism, he is remembered in Acts 7 as the first Christ-believer to be martyred. According to that account, he was stoned to death (ca. 33 CE) for preaching that the Jerusalem Temple was no longer necessary now that Jesus the Messiah had come.

Suetonius Gaius Suetonius Tranquillus (c. 69–125) was a Roman historian who wrote during the early imperial period. Of particular importance is his *De Vita Caesarum*, biographies of twelve successive Roman rulers from Julius Caesar to Flavius Domitian. He is an important source for reconstructing the early Christian era.

Syntyche A woman who was one of the leaders of the *ecclesia* at Philippi (Phil. 4:2–3)

Tacitus A Roman orator, senator, and historian, Publius Cornelius Tacitus (ca. 56–120 CE) wrote two major works—the *Annals* and the *Histories*—that span the history of the Roman Empire from the death of Augustus (in 14 CE) to the years of the First Jewish–Roman War in 70 CE.

Thecla According to an early legend (see *Acts of Paul and Thecla*), she was a wealthy Roman woman converted by Paul of Tarsus. As a result, she renounced her engagement, cut her hair short, and became a charismatic preacher and wandering missionary like Paul; she was revered by the early *ecclesia* as a female apostle and miracle-worker.

Thomas "the Twin" One of Jesus' early disciples, the Fourth Gospel says he doubted the veracity of the other disciples' reports of Jesus' Resurrection and post-Resurrection appearances (John 20:24–29). Two extra-canonical gospels are named after him.

Tiberius Caesar Emperor of Rome from 14–37 CE; Jesus was executed during his reign.

Timothy A Jewish Christ-believer who was one of the missionary companions of Paul of Tarsus (Acts 16:1–3). Two of the pseudonymous Pastoral Epistles purport to be addressed to him.

Titus A Gentile Christ-believer who was one of the missionary companions of Paul of Tarsus (2 Cor. 7:13–15). One of the pseudonymous Pastoral Epistles purports to be addressed to him.

Titus Flavius Emperor of Rome 79–81 CE; he succeeded his father, Vespasian, as general of the Roman forces in Palestine and concluded the war with the Jews (begun in 67), first by sacking Jerusalem in 70 and finally by taking the fortress Masada in 73 CE.

Trajan Emperor of Rome from 98–117 CE after a successful military career and service as consul (91), he was known for his public works, state loans to landowners, and welfare for poor Italian children. A revolt of Diaspora Jews occurred during the final years (114–117) of his reign. His reply to a letter from Pliny the Younger provides important information about the Roman policy of interrogation and persecution of Christians at that time.

Tryphaena A Christ-believing woman who, with her sister, Tryphosa, served as a minister to the Roman *ecclesia* (Rom. 16:12).

Tryphosa A Christ-believing woman who, with her sister, Tryphaena, served as a minister to the Roman *ecclesia* (Rom. 16:12).

Vespasian General of the Roman forces combatting the Jewish insurgents in Palestine (67–69 CE); he was acclaimed emperor at the death of Vitellius in 69 CE. Vespasian's son, Titus, succeeded him as general and then as emperor at Vespasian's death in 79.

Zacchaeus According to Luke 19:1–10, a short, rich tax-collector who climbed a tree to see Jesus; when Jesus called him, Zacchaeus immediately was converted and pledged to repay fourfold all those he had cheated.

Select Bibliography

Primary Source Materials

Ancient Texts and Authors

Anon. *Acts of Paul.*

    Acts of Paul and Thecla.

    Didache (*The Teaching of the Twelve Apostles*).

    Infancy Gospel of Thomas.

    Protoevangelion of James.

    Second Epistle of Clement of Rome to the Corinthians.

Appian of Alexandria. *Roman History.*

Clement of Rome. *1 Clement.*

Dio Cassius. *Roman History.*

Eusebius of Caesarea. *Ecclesiastical History.*

Ignatius of Antioch. *Letters.*

John Chrysostom. *Homilies.*

Josephus, Flavius. *The Antiquities of the Jews, The Jewish War.*

Juvenal. *Satires.*

Lucian of Samosata. *Fugitivi.*

Orosius, Paulus. *Seven Books of History against the Pagans.*

Papias of Hierapolis. *Fragments.*

Philo Judaeus. *On the Special Laws.*

Plato. *Phaedo.*

Pliny the Younger. *Epistles.*

Quintilian. *Declamations.*

Gaius Suetonius Tranquillus. *The Lives of the Twelve Caesars.*

Cornelius Tacitus. *Annals.*

Talmudic Sources: M. *Nazir;* T. *Sukkah; Bereshith; Genesis Rabbah.*

Tertullian. *Apology.*

Valerius Maximus. *Memorable Doings and Sayings.*

Collections and Series

Bible Works 9 [BW9] (software with a variety of versions of the HB and NT in addition to many other useful tools)

Corpus Christianorum Ecclesiorum Latinorum [CCEL] (critical editions of the primary texts) *www.ccel.org/node/70.*

Early Church Fathers: Ante-Nicene Fathers [ANF]. 10 Vols. Edited by Alexander Roberts and James Donaldson. Revised and chronologically arranged, with brief prefaces and occasional notes by A. Cleveland Coxe. Buffalo and New York: Christian Literature Company; London: T. & T. Clark, 1885–1897; repr. Peabody, MA: Hendrickson, 1994. Online at *Christian Classics Ethereal Library www.ccel.org/fathers.html.*

Cited in this volume:

Ignatius of Antioch. *Letters. www.ccel.org/ccel/schaff/anf01.v.v.html.*

Papias of Hierapolis, Fragments 4. *www.ccel.org/ccel/schaff/anf01.vii. ii.iv.html.*

The Apostolic Fathers with Justin Martyr and Irenaeus: Clement of Rome, Mathetes, Polycarp, Ignatius, Barnabas, Papias, Justin Martyr, Irenaeus. www.ccel.org/ccel/schaff/anf01.html.

Early Church Fathers: Nicene and Post–Nicene Fathers, Series 1 [*NPNF1*]. 14 vols. Edited by Philip Schaff. Buffalo: Christian Literature Company, 1886–1890.

Early Church Fathers: Nicene and Post–Nicene Fathers, Series 2 [*NPNF2*]. 14 Vols. Edited by Philip Schaff and Henry Wace. Peabody, MA: Hendrickson, 1994.

Loeb Classical Library [LCL]. 520 vols. Edited by T. E. Page, W. H. D. Rouse, Edward Capps, George Goold, and Jeffrey Henderson. London: William Heinemann; New York: G. P. Putnam's Sons, 1912–1989; Cambridge, MA and London: Harvard University Press, 1989–2012.

Cited in this volume:

Pliny. *Epistles.* Edited by E. Capps, T. E. Page, and W. H. D. Rouse. Translated by William Melmoth. Revised by W. M. L. Hutchinson. Loeb Classical Library, vols. L055 and L059. London: William Heinemann; New York: G. P. Putnam's Sons, 1927.

Nestle–Aland, *Novum Testamentum Graece,* 27th ed. [NA27] Stuttgart: Deutsche Bibelgesellschaft, 1994.

Basic Research Tools

Aland, Kurt. *Synopsis of the Four Gospels.* English ed. New York: American Bible Society, 2010.

Bauer, Walter, W. F. Arndt, F. W. Gingrich, and F. W. Danker. *Greek–English Lexicon of the New Testament and Other Early Christian Literature* [BAGD]. 3d ed. Chicago and London: University of Chicago Press, 2000.

Brown, Raymond, Joseph Fitzmyer, and Roland Murphy, eds. *The New Jerome Biblical Commentary* [*NJBC*]. Englewood Cliffs, NJ: Prentice–Hall, 1990.

Sakenfied, Katherine Doob, et al., eds. *The New Interpreter's Dictionary of the Bible* [*IDB*]. 5 vols. Nashville: Abingdon, 2006–2009.

Theological Dictionary of the New Testament [*TDNT*]. Edited by G. Kittel and G. Friedrich. Translated by G. W. Bromiley. Grand Rapids: Eerdmans, 1964–1976.

Thesaurus Linguae Graecae [*TLG*]; *http://www.tlg.uci.edu/.*

Thesaurus Linguae Latinae [*TLL*]; *http://www.thesaurus.badw.de/english/.*

Important Journals, Periodicals, and Series

AGJU	Arbeiten zur Geschichte des antiken Judentums und des Urchristentums
AnBib	Analecta Biblica
ANRW	*Aufstieg und Niedergang der römischen Welt*
ATANT	Abhandlungen zur Theologie des Alten und Neuen Testaments
BA	*Biblical Archaeologist*
BAR	*Biblical Archaeology Review*
BASOR	*Bulletin of the American Schools of Oriental Research*
BerOl	Berit Olam
Bib	*Biblica*
BibInt	*Biblical Interpretation*
BibOr	Biblica et Orientalia. Rome: Biblical Institute Press.
BJRL	*Bulletin of the John Rylands Library*
BR	*Biblical Research*
BRev	*Bible Review*

BSac	*Bibliotheca Sacra*
BTB	*Biblical Theology Bulletin*
BZ	*Biblische Zeitschrift*
BZNW	Beihefte e zur Zeitschrift für die neutestamentliche Wissenschaft
CBQ	*Catholic Biblical Quarterly*
CBW	*Conversations with the Biblical World: Proceedings of the Eastern Great Lakes Biblical Society and the Midwest Region Society of Biblical Literature;* formerly *Proceedings: Eastern Great Lakes Biblical Society and Midwest Region Society of Biblical Literature*
CH	*Church History*
CurBS	*Currents in Research: Biblical Studies*
DJD	Discoveries in the Judean Desert
Elenchus	*Elenchus bibliographicus biblicus*
EPRO	Etudes préliminaires aux religions orientales dans l'empire romain
FCB	Feminist Companion to the Bible
HNT	Handbuch zum Neuen Testament
HTR	*Harvard Theological Review*
ICS	*Illinois Classical Studies*
JAAR	*Journal of the American Academy of Religion*
JBL	*Journal of Biblical Literature*
JECS	*Journal of Early Christian Studies*
JJS	*Journal of Jewish Studies*
JR	*Journal of Religion*
JSHRZ	*Jüdische Schriften aus hellenistisch–römischer Zeit*
JSNT	*Journal for the Study of the New Testament*
JSNTSup	Journal for the Study of the New Testament: Supplement Series
JSPSup	Journal for the Study of the Pseudepigrapha: Supplement Series
Neot	*Neotestamentica*
NovT	*Novum Testamentum*
NovTSup	Novum Testamentum Supplements

NTA	*New Testament Abstracts*
NTS	*New Testament Studies*
OTA	*Old Testament Abstracts*
RB	*Revue Biblique*
RelSRev	*Religious Studies Review*
RevQ	*Revue de Qumran*
SBLEJL	Society of Biblical Literature Early Judaism and Its Literature
SBLSP	Society of Biblical Literature Seminar Papers
SecCent	*Second Century*
SemeiaSt	Semeia Studies
SJLA	Studies in Judaism in Late Antiquity
TBT	*The Bible Today*
VC	*Vigiliae christianae*
ZAC	*Zeitschrift für Antikes Christentum*
ZAW	*Zeitschrift für die alttestamentliche Wissenschaft*
ZKG	*Zeitschrift für Kirchengeschichte*
ZKT	*Zeitschrift für katholische Theologie*
ZNW	*Zeitschrift für die neutestamentliche Wissenschaft und die Kunde der älteren Kirche*
ZTK	*Zeitschrift für Theologie und Kirche*

Commentary Series

AB	Anchor Bible: New Testament
BBC	Blackwell Bible Commentaries
BNTC	Black's New Testament Commentaries
CBQMS	Catholic Biblical Quarterly Monograph Series
Herm	Hermeneia
IB	Interpreter's Bible
ICCNT	International Critical Commentary on the Greek New Testament
Int	Interpretation Series
NAC	New American Commentary
NICNT	New International Commentary on the New Testament

NIGTC	New International Greek Testament Commentary
NTMess	New Testament Message Series
OTL	Old Testament Library Series
SP	Sacra Pagina
WBC	Word Biblical Commentary

Dictionaries and Reference Works

Aune, David E., ed. *The Blackwell Companion to the New Testament*. Malden, MA: Wiley-Blackwell, 2010.

Buckland, William Warwick. *The Roman Law of Slavery: The Condition of the Slave in Private Law from Augustus to Justinian*. Cambridge Library Classics. Cambridge: Cambridge University Press, 1908. Repr. 2010.

Chilton, Bruce, Howard Clark Kee, Amy-Jill Levine, Eric M. Meyers, John Rogerson, and Anthony J. Saldarini, eds. *The Cambridge Companion to the Bible*. Part 2, *Jewish Responses to Greek and Roman Cultures, 322 BCE to 200 CE*. 2nd ed. Cambridge: Cambridge University Press, 2007.

Evans, Craig A., and Stanley E. Porter, eds. *Dictionary of New Testament Background: A Compendium of Contemporary Biblical Scholarship*. IVP Bible Dictionary Series. Downers Grove, IL: IVP Academic, 2000.

Freedman, David Noel, ed. *The Anchor Bible Dictionary*. 6 vols. New York: Doubleday, 1992.

Futrell, Alison. *A Sourcebook on the Roman Games*. London: Blackwell, 2006.

Green, Joel B., Scot McKnight, and I. Howard Marshall, eds. *Dictionary of Jesus and the Gospels: A Compendium of Contemporary Biblical Scholarship*. IVP Bible Dictionary Series. Downers Grove, IL: IVP Academic, 1992.

Hawthorne, Gerald F., Ralph P. Martin, and Daniel G. Reid, eds. *Dictionary of Paul and His Letters: A Compendium of Contemporary Biblical Scholarship*. IVP Bible Dictionary Series. Downers Grove, IL: IVP Academic, 1993.

Kittel, Gerhard, Gerhard Friedrich, and Geoffrey W. Bromiley, eds. *Theological Dictionary of the New Testament: Abridged in One Volume*. Grand Rapids: Eerdmans, 1985.

Kroeger, Catherine Clark, and Mary J. Evans, eds. *The IVP Women's Bible Commentary*. Downers Grove, IL: InterVarsity, 2002.

"Legion." In *Ancient Origins*. Tempe, AZ: Piranha Interactive; London, UK: Maris Multimedia, 1997.

Levick, Barbara. *The Government of the Roman Empire: A Sourcebook.* 2nd ed. Routledge Sourcebooks for the Ancient World. New York: Routledge, 2000.

Levine, Amy-Jill, ed. *Feminist Companion to the New Testament and Early Christian Literature.* 14 vols. Sheffield, UK: Sheffield University Press. New York and London: Continuum; Cleveland, OH: Pilgrim Press, 2001–.

Martin, Ralph P., and Peter H. Davids, eds. *Dictionary of the Later New Testament and Its Developments: A Compendium of Contemporary Biblical Scholarship.* IVP Bible Dictionary Series. Downers Grove, IL: IVP Academic, 1997.

Miller, Patricia Cox, ed. *Women in Early Christianity: Translations from Greek Texts.* Washington, DC: The Catholic University of America Press, 2005.

Murray, Peter, and Linda Murray. *The Oxford Companion to Christian Art and Architecture.* Oxford and New York: Oxford University Press, 1996.

Pilch, John J., and Bruce J. Malina. *Handbook of Biblical Social Values.* Grand Rapids: Baker Academic, 2009.

Reed, Jonathan L. *The HarperCollins Visual Guide to the New Testament: What Archaeology Reveals about the First Christians.* New York: HarperOne, 2007.

Schüssler Fiorenza, Elisabeth, ed. *Searching the Scriptures: A Feminist–Ecumenical Commentary and Translation.* 2 vols. New York: Crossroads, 1993–1995.

Stevenson, J., and W. H.C. Frend. *A New Eusebius: Documents Illustrating the History of the Church to AD 337.* Rev. ed. Grand Rapids: Baker Academic, 2013.

Introductory Surveys and Topical Studies

Aageson, James W. *Paul, the Pastoral Epistles, and the Early Church.* Peabody, MA: Hendrickson, 2008.

Arnaoutoglou, Ilias N. "Roman Law and *collegia* in Asia Minor." *Revue Internationale des Droits de l'Antiquité* 49 (2002): 27–44.

Bilezikian, Gilbert G. *The Liberated Gospel: A Comparison of the Gospel of Mark and Greek Tragedy.* Grand Rapids: Baker, 1977.

Borg, Marcus J. *Evolution of the Word: The New Testament in the Order the Books Were Written.* New York: HarperOne, 2013.

Bradley, Keith. *Slavery and Society at Rome.* Cambridge : Cambridge University Press, 1994.

Brooke, George J. *Dead Sea Scrolls and the New Testament.* Minneapolis: Fortress, 2004.

Broshi, Magen. "The Role of the Temple in the Herodian Economy." *isites. harvard.edu/fs/docs/icb.topic1202633.files/Lesson%208 /8c%20Broshi.pdf.*

Brown, Raymond E. *The Gospel according to John.* 2 vols. Garden City, NJ: Doubleday, 1970.

Brown, Raymond E. *An Introduction to the New Testament.* New York: Doubleday, 1997.

Brown, Raymond E., and John P. Meier. *Antioch and Rome: New Testament Cradles of Catholic Christianity.* New York: Paulist, 1983.

Burge, Gary M., Lynn H. Cohick, and Gene L. Green. *The New Testament in Antiquity: A Survey of the New Testament within Its Cultural Context.* Grand Rapids: Zondervan, 2009.

Clark, Elizabeth A. *Women in the Early Church: Message of the Fathers of the Church.* Wilmington, DE: Michael Glazier, 1983.

Corley, Kathleen. *Private Women, Public Meals: Social Conflict in the Synoptic Tradition.* Peabody, MA: Hendrickson, 1993.

Corley, Kathleen. *Women and the Historical Jesus: Feminist Myths of Christian Origins.* Salem, OR: Polebridge, 2002.

Crossan, John Dominic. *The Birth of Christianity: Discovering What Happened in the Years Immediately after the Execution of Jesus.* New York: HarperOne, 1999.

Crossan, John Dominic. *The Cross That Spoke: The Origins of the Passion Narrative.* San Francisco: Harper & Row, 1988.

Crossan, John Dominic. *The Historical Jesus: The Life of a Mediterranean Jewish Peasant.* New York and San Francisco: HarperOne, 1993.

Crossan, John Dominic, and Jonathan L. Reed. *Excavating Jesus: Beneath the Stones, Behind the Texts.* New York: Harper Collins, 2001.

Crossan, John Dominic, and Jonathan L. Reed. *In Search of Paul: How Jesus' Apostle Opposed Rome's Empire with God's Kingdom.* New York: Harper Collins, 2003.

Davies, Stephen L. *The New Testament: An Analytical Approach.* 2nd ed. Santa Clara, CA: Polebridge, 2011.

DeSilva, David A. *An Introduction to the New Testament: Contexts, Methods and Ministry Formation.* Downers Grove, IL: IVP, 2004.

Dickson, John P. *Mission-Commitment in Ancient Judaism and in the Pauline Communities: The Shape, Extent and Background of Early Christian Mission.* Wissenschaftliche Untersuchungen Zum Neuen Testament 2, 159. Tübingen: Mohr-Seibeck, 2003.

Donfried, Karl P., and Peter Richardson, eds. *Judaism and Christianity in First-Century Rome.* Grand Rapids: Eerdmans, 1998.

Dunn, James D. G. *Unity and Diversity in the New Testament: An Inquiry into the Character of Earliest Christianity.* Rev. ed. London: SCM, 2005.

Eisen, Ute E. *Women Officeholders in Early Christianity: Epigraphical and Literary Studies.* Linda Maloney, trans. Collegeville: Liturgical Press, 2000.

Evans, Craig A. "Mark's Incipit and the Priene Calendar Inscription: From Jewish Gospel to Greco-Roman Gospel." *craigaevans.com/ Priene%20 art.pdf.*

Ferguson, Everett. *Backgrounds of Early Christianity.* Grand Rapids: Eerdmans, 2003.

Finley, Moses I. *Ancient Slavery and Modern Ideology.* Exp. ed. Edited by Brent D. Shaw. Princeton, NJ: Markus Wiener, 1998.

Fisher, George Park. *The Beginnings of Christianity: With a View of the State of the Roman World at the Birth of Christ.* New York: Charles Scribner's Sons, 1889.

Frend, W. H. C. *Martyrdom and Persecution in the Early Church: A Study of a Conflict from the Maccabees to Donatus.* London: Basil Blackwell, 1965; Grand Rapids: Baker, 1981.

Frend, W. H. C. *The Rise of Christianity.* Philadelphia: Fortress, 1984.

Funk, Robert W. *The Five Gospels: What Did Jesus Really Say? The Search for the Authentic Words of Jesus.* New York: HarperOne, 1996.

Gager, John. *Kingdom and Community: The Social World of Early Christianity.* Englewood Cliffs, NJ: Prentice-Hall, 1975.

Garnsey, Peter. *Ideas of Slavery from Aristotle to Augustine.* New York: Cambridge University Press, 1996.

Geertz, Clifford. *The Interpretation of Cultures.* New York: Basic Books, 1973.

Glancy, Jennifer A. *Slavery in Early Christianity.* 2nd ed. Minneapolis: Fortress Press, 2006.

Gryson, Roger. *The Ministry of Women in the Early Church.* Collegeville: Liturgical Press, 1976, 1980.

Hanson, Anthony Tyrrell. *Studies in the Pastoral Epistles.* London: SPCK, 1968.

Hemer, Colin J. *The Letters to the Seven Churches of Asia in Their Local Setting.* Journal for the Study of the New Testament Supplement Series 11. Sheffield, UK: JSOT Press, 1986.

Herzog, William R., II. *Prophet and Teacher: An Introduction to the Historical Jesus.* Louisville: Westminster John Knox, 2005.

Hezser, Catherine. *Jewish Slavery in Antiquity.* Oxford: Oxford University Press, 2006.

Horsley, Richard. *Galilee: History, Politics, People.* Valley Forge, PA: Trinity Press International, 1995.

Hultgren, Arland J. "I–II Timothy and Titus." In *I–II Timothy, Titus, II Thessalonians,* Augsburg Commentary on the New Testament, edited by Arland J. Hultgren and Roger Aus, 11–189. Minneapolis: Augsburg, 1984.

Hultgren, Arland J. *The Rise of Normative Christianity.* Minneapolis: Fortress, 1994.

Jones, A. H. M. "Slavery in the Ancient World." *The Economic History Review* 9, no. 2 (1956): 185–99.

Joshel, Sandra R., and Sheila Murnaghan, eds. *Women and Slaves in Greco-Roman Culture: Differential Equations.* London and New York: Routledge, 1998.

Karris, Robert J. "The Background and Significance of the Polemic of the Pastoral Epistles." *Journal of Biblical Literature* 92 (1973): 549–50.

Koester, Helmut. *Introduction to the New Testament.* 2 vols. 2nd ed. Philadelphia: Fortress; Berlin and New York: Walter de Gruyter, 1982.

Kraemer, Ross Shephard. *Unreliable Witnesses: Religion, Gender, and History in the Greco-Roman Mediterranean.* Oxford: Oxford University Press, 2011.

Lampe, Peter. *From Paul to Valentinus: Christians at Rome in the First Two Centuries.* Edited by Marshall D. Johnson. Translated by Michael Steinhauser. Minneapolis: Fortress, 2003.

Lane Fox, Robin. *The Classical World: An Epic History from Homer to Hadrian.* London: Allen Lane, 2005.

Lane Fox, Robin. *Pagans and Christians in the Mediterranean World from the Second Century AD to the Conversion of Constantine.* Rev. ed. New York and London: Penguin, 2006.

LaPorte, Jean. *The Role of Women in Early Christianity.* New York: Edwin Mellon, 1982.

Levick, Barbara. *Government of the Roman Empire. A Sourcebook.* London and New York: Routledge, 2000.

Levick, Barbara. "Women, Power, and Philosophy at Rome and Beyond." In *Philosophy and Power in the Græco-Roman World*, edited by Gillian Clark and Tessa Rajak, 133-56. New York: Oxford University Press, 2002.

Levine, Amy-Jill. *The Misunderstood Jew: The Church and the Scandal of the Jewish Jesus*. New York and San Francisco: HarperCollins, 2006.

Levine, Amy-Jill, ed. *"Women Like This": New Perspectives on Jewish Women in the Greco-Roman World*. Early Judaism and Its Literature 1. Atlanta: Scholars Press/Society of Biblical Literature, 1991. American Council of Learned Societies, ACLS History E-Book Project, 2006.

Levine, Amy-Jill, Dale C. Allison, Jr., and John Dominic Crossan, eds. *The Historical Jesus in Context*. Princeton Readings in Religion. Princeton, NJ: Princeton University Press, 2006.

Levine, Lee I. *The Ancient Synagogue: The First Thousand Years*. New Haven, CT: Yale University Press, 2000.

Levinskaya, Irina. *The Book of Acts in Its Diaspora Setting*. The Book of Acts in Its First-Century Setting 5. Edited by Bruce W. Winter. Grand Rapids: Eerdmans, 1993.

Longenecker, Bruce W., and Kelly D. Liebengood. *Engaging Economics: New Testament Scenarios and Early Christian Reception*. Grand Rapids: Eerdmans, 2009.

MacDonald, Dennis R. *The Homeric Epics and the Gospel of Mark*. New Haven: Yale University Press, 2000.

MacDonald, Dennis R. *The Legend and the Apostle: The Battle for Paul in Story and Canon*. Philadelphia: Westminster John Knox, 1983.

Madigan, Kevin J., and Carolyn Osiek, eds. and trans. *Ordained Women in the Early Church: A Documentary History*. Baltimore: Johns Hopkins University Press, 2005.

Malina, Bruce J. *The New Testament World: Insights from Cultural Anthropology*. 3rd ed. Louisville: Westminster John Knox, 2001.

Martimort, Aimé Georges. *Deaconesses: An Historical Study*. San Francisco: Ignatius Press, 1986.

Matera, Frank J. *New Testament Theology: Exploring Diversity and Unity*. Louisville: Westminster John Knox, 2007.

McGinn, Sheila E. "'*Exousia echein epi tês kephalês*': 1 Cor 11:10 and the Ecclesial Authority of Women," *Listening/Journal of Religion and Culture* 31, no. 2 (1996): 91–104.

McGinn, Sheila E., and Megan T. Wilson-Reitz. "Welfare Wastrels or Swanky Socialites: 2 Thess 3:6–15 and the Problem of the *Ataktoi.*" *Conversations with the Biblical World: Proceedings of the Eastern Great Lakes Biblical Society and Midwest Region Society of Biblical Literature* XXXII (2012). [delayed; in press]

McGinn-Moorer, Sheila E. "The New Prophecy of Asia Minor and the Rise of Ecclesiastical Patriarchy in Second-Century Pauline Traditions." PhD diss. Northwestern University, 1989.

McKnight, Scot, Joseph B. Modica, and Andy Crouch. *Jesus Is Lord, Caesar Is Not: Evaluating Empire in New Testament Studies.* Downers Grove, IL: IVP Academic, 2013.

McRay, John. *Archaeology and the New Testament.* Grand Rapids: Baker Academic, 2008.

Meeks, Wayne A. *The First Urban Christians: The Social World of the Apostle Paul.* 2nd ed. New Haven, CT: Yale University Press, 2003.

Niang, Aliou Cissé, and Carolyn Osiek, eds. *Text, Image, and Christians in the Græco-Roman World: A Festschrift in Honor of David Lee Balch.* Eugene, OR: Pickwick, 2011.

Oakman, Douglas. *Jesus and the Economic Questions of His Day.* Lewiston, NY: Edwin Mellen, 1986.

Osiek, Carolyn. *What Are They Saying about the Social Setting of the New Testament?* Mahwah, NJ: Paulist, 1992.

Osiek, Carolyn, and David L. Balch. *Families in the New Testament World: Households and House Churches.* Westminster John Knox Press, 1997.

Osiek, Carolyn, and Margaret Y. MacDonald, with Janet H. Tulloch. *A Woman's Place: House Churches in Earliest Christianity.* Minneapolis: Fortress, 2005.

Pearson, Birger A. "Earliest Christianity in Egypt: Some Observations." In *The Roots of Egyptian Christianity,* edited by Birger A. Pearson and James E. Goehring, 132–59. Studies in Antiquity and Christianity. Philadelphia: Fortress, 1986.

Perler, Othmar. "Das vierte Makkabäerbuch, Ignatius von Antiochien und die ältesten Märtyrerberichte." *Rivista di archeologia cristiana* 25 (1949): 47–72.

Pervo, Richard I. *Profit with Delight: The Literary Genre of the Acts of the Apostles.* Philadelphia: Fortress, 1987.

Petzer, Jacobus H. "Eclecticism and the Text of the New Testament." In *Text and Interpretation: New Approaches in the Study of the New Testament,* edited by Patrick J. Hartin and Jacobus H. Petzer, 47–62 . Leiden: Brill, 1991.

Pomeroy, Sarah B. *Goddesses, Whores, Wives, and Slaves: Women in Classical Antiquity.* New York: Schocken, 1975.

Robbins, Vernon K. *Who Do People Say I Am? Rewriting Gospel in Emerging Christianity.* Grand Rapids: Eerdmans, 2013.

Robinson, James McConkey, and Helmut Koester. *Trajectories through Early Christianity.* Philadelphia: Fortress, 1971. Repr. ed. Eugene, OR: Wipf & Stock, 2006.

Roetzel, Calvin J. *The World That Shaped the New Testament.* Rev. ed. Louisville: Westminster John Knox, 2002.

Rordorf, Willy. *Liturgie Foi et Vie des Premiers Chrétiens.* Théologie Historique 75. Paris: Beauchesne, 1986.

Rostovtzev, Mikhail. *The Social and Economic History of the Roman Empire.* Rev. ed. Oxford: Clarendon, 1963.

Saller, Richard P. "Symbols of Gender and Status Hierarchies in the Roman Household." In *Women and Slaves in Greco-Roman Culture,* edited by Sandra R. Joshel and Sheila Murnaghan, 85–91. New York and London: Routledge, 1998.

Schoedel, William R. *Ignatius of Antioch: A Commentary on the Letters of Ignatius of Antioch.* Edited by Helmut Koester. Hermeneia: A Critical and Historical Commentary on the Bible. Philadelphia: Fortress, 1985.

Schottroff, Luise. *Lydia's Impatient Sisters: A Feminist Social History of Early Christianity.* Louisville: Westminster John Knox, 1996.

Schüssler Fiorenza, Elisabeth. *The Book of Revelation: Justice and Judgment.* Rev. ed. Minneapolis: Fortress, 1998.

Schüssler Fiorenza, Elisabeth. *In Memory of Her: A Feminist Theological Reconstruction of Christian Origins.* 2nd ed. New York and London: Crossroad/SCM, 1994.

Seltman, Charles. *Women in Antiquity.* Westport, CN: Hyperion, 1981.

Spence, Stephen. *The Parting of the Ways: The Roman Church as a Case Study.* Interdisciplinary Studies in Ancient Culture and Religion 5. Leuven: Peeters, 2004.

Stagg, Evelyn, and Frank Stagg. *Women in the World of Jesus.* Philadelphia: Westminster, 1978.

Standaert, Benoît. *Évangile selon Marc: Composition et Genre Littéraire.* Brugge: Zevenkerken, 1998.

Stegemann, Wolfgang, Bruce J. Malina, and Gerd Theissen. *The Social Setting of Jesus and the Gospels.* Minneapolis: Fortress, 2002.

Strett, R. Alan. *Subversive Meals: An Analysis of the Lord's Supper under Roman Domination during the First Century.* Eugene, OR: Pickwick, 2013.

Tabor, James D. *Paul and Jesus: How the Apostle Transformed Christianity.* New York and London: Simon & Schuster, 2012.

Tolbert, Mary Ann. "Mark." In *The Women's Bible Commentary,* edited by Carol A. Newsom and Sharon H. Ringe, 263–74. Louisville: Westminster John Knox, 1992.

Tolbert, Mary Ann. *Sowing the Gospel: Mark's World in Literary-Historical Perspective.* Minneapolis: Fortress, 1989.

Verner, David C. *The Household of God: The Social World of the Pastoral Epistles.* SBL Dissertation Series 71. Missoula, MT: Scholars Press/Society of Biblical Literature, 1983.

Veyne, Paul. "Homosexuality in Ancient Rome." In *Western Sexuality: Practice and Precept in Past and Present,* edited by Philippe Aries and Andre Bejin, 26–35. Oxford: Blackwell, 1985. First published as *Sexualities Occidentales.* Paris: Editions du Seuil/Communications, 1982.

Vines, Michael E. *The Problem of Markan Genre: The Gospel of Mark and the Jewish Novel.* Boston: Brill, 2002.

White, L. Michael. *From Jesus to Christianity: How Four Generations of Visionaries & Storytellers Created the New Testament and Christian Faith.* New York and San Francisco: HarperCollins, 2004.

Wiefel, Wolfgang. "The Jewish Community in Ancient Rome and the Origins of Roman Christianity." In *The Romans Debate: Revised and Expanded Edition,* edited by Karl P. Donfried, 85–101. Peabody, MA: Hendrickson, 2005.

Wilken, Robert Louis. *The Christians As the Romans Saw Them.* 2nd ed. New Haven: Yale University Press, 2003.

Witherington, Ben, III. *New Testament History: A Narrative Account.* Grand Rapids: Baker Academic, 2003.

Wrede, Wilhelm. *Das Messiasgeheimnis in den Evangelien.* Göttingen: Vandenhoeck & Ruprecht, 1901.

Yarbro Collins, Adela. *Crisis and Catharsis: The Power of the Apocalypse.* Philadelphia: Westminster, 1984.

Online Resources

"Abbreviations in Theology and Biblical Studies." *ecumenism.net/docu/ abbrev.htm.*

"An Annotated Bibliography of Reference Works and Commentaries on the Greek New Testament." Compiled by Jon Weatherly. *www.letsread greek.com/resources/annotated bibliography.pdf.*

Bible Lands Museum Jerusalem Virtual Tour. blmj.org/en/Virtual_Tour.php.

Christian Classics Ethereal Library. www.ccel.org.

Διοτίμα: Materials for the Study of Women and Gender in the Ancient World. Compiled by Ross Scaife. *www.stoa.org/diotima/.*

Duke Papyrus Archive. *library.duke.edu/rubenstein/scriptorium/papyrus/texts/ homepage.html.*

E.N.T.E.R.—Electronic New Testament Educational Resources. Felix Just. *catholic-resources.org/Bible.*

Flavius Josephus Home Page. Compiled and edited by G. J. Goldberg. *www. josephus.org/.*

Internet Ancient History Sourcebook: Rome. Edited by Paul Halsall. *www. fordham.edu/Halsall/.*

Internet Classics Archive. *Massachusetts Institute of Technology. classics.mit.edu.*

Lacus Curtius: Into the Roman World. Compiled and edited by William P. Thayer. *penelope.uchicago.edu/Thayer/E/Roman/home.html.*

New Testament Gateway. Comp. Mark Goodacre. *www.ntgateway.com.*

Online Medieval and Classical Library. Compiled by Douglas B. Killings and Roy Tennant. Edited by Roy Tennant. *www.omacl.org.*

Orion Center for the Study of the Dead Sea Scrolls and Associated Literature. Orion Center, Hebrew University, Jerusalem. orion.mscc.huji.ac.il.

Perseus Digital Library. Edited by Gregory R. Crane. Tufts University. *www. perseus.tufts.edu.*

Project Gutenberg Classical Antiquity Bookshelf. Founded and edited by Michael Hart. *www.gutenberg.org/wiki/Classical_Antiquity_(Bookshelf).*

Resources for Studies of the Bible and Early Christianity. Compiled by Sheila E. McGinn. *www.jcu.edu/bible.*

"Student Supplement for the SBL Handbook of Style (Revised)." Compiled by Melanie Greer Nogalski, James D. Nogalski, Sophia G. Steibel, and Danny M. West. Edited by Joel M. LeMon and Brennan W. Breed. Atlanta: Society of Biblical Literature, 2009. *www.sbl-site.org/assets/ pdfs/SBLHSrevised2_09.pdf.*

Unbound Bible. Biola University. *unbound.biola.edu/.*

Index

Footnotes are indicated with "n" followed by the note number and captions with "cap."